CAMBRIDGE

IN

# English
# Japanese-English

## Word to Word®
## Bilingual Dictionary

Compiled by:
C. Sesma, M.A.

Translated by:
Chiaki Hasegawa

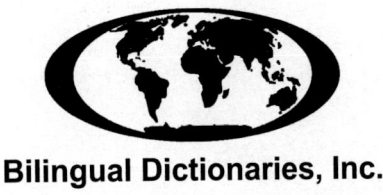

**Bilingual Dictionaries, Inc.**

**Japanese Word to Word® Bilingual Dictionary**
1st Edition © Copyright 2011

Published in the United States by:

**Bilingual Dictionaries, Inc.**
PO Box 1154
Murrieta, CA 92562
T: (951) 461-6893 • F: (951) 461-3092
www.BilingualDictionaries.com

ISBN13: 978-0-933146-42-6
ISBN: 0-933146-42-6

# Preface

Bilingual Dictionaries, Inc. is committed to providing schools, libraries and educators with a great selection of bilingual materials for students. Along with bilingual dictionaries we also provide ESL materials, children's bilingual stories and children's bilingual picture dictionaries.

Sesma's Japanese Word to Word® Bilingual Dictionary was created specifically with students in mind to be used for reference and testing. This dictionary contains approximately 19,500 entries targeting common words used in the English language.

# List of Irregular Verbs

**present - past - past participle**

arise - arose - arisen
awake - awoke - awoken, awaked
be - was - been
bear - bore - borne
beat - beat - beaten
become - became - become
begin - began - begun
behold - beheld - beheld
bend - bent - bent
beseech - besought - besought
bet - bet - betted
bid - bade (bid) - bidden (bid)
bind - bound - bound
bite - bit - bitten
bleed - bled - bled
blow - blew - blown
break - broke - broken
breed - bred - bred
bring - brought - brought
build - built - built
burn - burnt - burnt *
burst - burst - burst
buy - bought - bought
cast - cast - cast
catch - caught - caught
choose - chose - chosen
cling - clung - clung
come - came - come
cost - cost - cost
creep - crept - crept
cut - cut - cut
deal - dealt - dealt

dig - dug - dug
do - did - done
draw - drew - drawn
dream - dreamt - dreamed
drink - drank - drunk
drive - drove - driven
dwell - dwelt - dwelt
eat - ate - eaten
fall - fell - fallen
feed - fed - fed
feel - felt - felt
fight - fought - fought
find - found - found
flee - fled - fled
fling - flung - flung
fly - flew - flown
forebear - forbore - forborne
forbid - forbade - forbidden
forecast - forecast - forecast
forget - forgot - forgotten
forgive - forgave - forgiven
forego - forewent - foregone
foresee - foresaw - foreseen
foretell - foretold - foretold
forget - forgot - forgotten
forsake - forsook - forsaken
freeze - froze - frozen
get - got - gotten
give - gave - given
go - went - gone
grind - ground - ground
grow - grew - grown
hang - hung * - hung *
have - had - had

| | |
|---|---|
| **hear** - heard - heard | **ring** - rang - rung |
| **hide** - hid - hidden | **rise** - rose - risen |
| **hit** - hit - hit | **run** - ran - run |
| **hold** - held - held | **saw** - sawed - sawn |
| **hurt** - hurt - hurt | **say** - said - said |
| **hit** - hit - hit | **see** - saw - seen |
| **hold** - held - held | **seek** - sought - sought |
| **keep** - kept - kept | **sell** - sold - sold |
| **kneel** - knelt * - knelt * | **send** - sent - sent |
| **know** - knew - known | **set** - set - set |
| **lay** - laid - laid | **sew** - sewed - sewn |
| **lead** - led - led | **shake** - shook - shaken |
| **lean** - leant * - leant * | **shear** - sheared - shorn |
| **leap** - lept * - lept * | **shed** - shed - shed |
| **learn** - learnt * - learnt * | **shine** - shone - shone |
| **leave** - left - left | **shoot** - shot - shot |
| **lend** - lent - lent | **show** - showed - shown |
| **let** - let - let | **shrink** - shrank - shrunk |
| **lie** - lay - lain | **shut** - shut - shut |
| **light** - lit * - lit * | **sing** - sang - sung |
| **lose** - lost - lost | **sink** - sank - sunk |
| **make** - made - made | **sit** - sat - sat |
| **mean** - meant - meant | **slay** - slew - slain |
| **meet** - met - met | **sleep** - sleep - slept |
| **mistake** - mistook - mistaken | **slide** - slid - slid |
| **must** - had to - had to | **sling** - slung - slung |
| **pay** - paid - paid | **smell** - smelt * - smelt * |
| **plead** - pleaded - pled | **sow** - sowed - sown * |
| **prove** - proved - proven | **speak** - spoke - spoken |
| **put** - put - put | **speed** - sped * - sped * |
| **quit** - quit * - quit * | **spell** - spelt * - spelt * |
| **read** - read - read | **spend** - spent - spent |
| **rid** - rid - rid | **spill** - spilt * - spilt * |
| **ride** - rode - ridden | **spin** - spun - spun |

spit - spat - spat
split - split - split
spread - spread - spread
spring - sprang - sprung
stand - stood - stood
steal - stole - stolen
stick - stuck - stuck
sting - stung - stung
stink - stank - stunk
stride - strode - stridden
strike - struck - struck (stricken)
strive - strove - striven
swear - swore - sworn
sweep - swept - swept
swell - swelled - swollen *
swim - swam - swum
take - took - taken
teach - taught - taught
tear - tore - torn

tell - told - told
think - thought - thought
throw - threw - thrown
thrust - thrust - thrust
tread - trod - trodden
wake - woke - woken
wear - wore - worn
weave - wove * - woven *
wed - wed * - wed *
weep - wept - wept
win - won - won
wind - wound - wound
wring - wrung - wrung
write - wrote - written

**Those tenses with an * also have regular forms.**

# English-Japanese

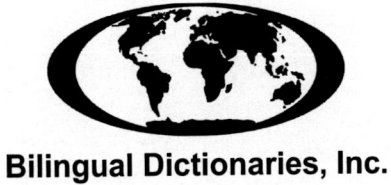

**Bilingual Dictionaries, Inc.**

# Abbreviations

**a** - article
**n** - noun
**e** - exclamation
**pro** - pronoun
**adj** - adjective
**adv** - adverb
**v** - verb
**iv** - irregular verb
**pre** - preposition
**c** - conjunction

# A

a *a* ある〜
abandon *v* 遺棄する
abandonment *n* 放棄
abbey *n* 大修道院
abbot *n* 修道院長
abbreviate *v* 短くする
abbreviation *n* 短縮
abdicate *v* 辞任する
abdication *n* 放棄、退位
abdomen *n* 腹、腹部
abduct *v* 誘拐する
abduction *n* 誘拐、拉致
aberration *n* 逸脱、脱線
abhor *v* 憎悪する
abide by *v* 〜に従う
ability *n* 能力
ablaze *adj* 輝いている
able *adj* することができる
abnormal *adj* 異常な
abnormality *n* 異常性
aboard *adv* 乗って
abolish *v* 無効にする
abort *v* 中止、中断
abortion *n* 妊娠中絶
abound *v* 豊富である
about *pre* 〜について
about *adv* およそ
above *pre* 〜の上に
abreast *adv* 平行して

abridge *v* 短縮する
abroad *adv* 海外に
abrogate *v* 廃止する
abruptly *adv* 不意に
absence *n* 不足、欠席
absent *adj* 不在の
absolute *adj* 絶対的なもの
absolution *n* 免除
absolve *v* 無罪を言い渡す
absorb *v* 吸収する
absorbent *adj* 吸収力のある
abstain *v* 控える、慎む
abstinence *n* 自制、節制
abstract *adj* 抽象的なもの
absurd *adj* ばかげた
abundance *n* 豊富
abundant *adj* 豊富な
abuse *v* 悪用する
abuse *n* 悪用、虐待
abusive *adj* 口汚い
abysmal *adj* 底知れぬ
abyss *n* 地の底
academic *adj* 学問的な
academy *n* 学会、協会
accelerate *v* 加速する
accelerator *n* 加速するもの
accent *n* 強勢
accept *v* 受諾する
acceptable *adj* 受諾できる
acceptance *n* 受諾すること
access *n* 接近
accessible *adj* 接近可能な

accident *n* 偶然
accidental *adj* 偶然の
acclaim *v* 称賛する
acclimatize *v* 慣れる
accommodate *v* 適応する
accompany *v* 同行する
accomplice *n* 共犯（者）
accomplish *v* 達成する
accomplishment *n* 達成
accord *n* 調和
according to *pre* 〜によれば
account *n* 口座
account for *v* 占める
accountable *adj* 責任がある
accountant *n* 会計士
accumulate *v* 蓄積する
accuracy *n* 正確さ
accurate *adj* 精密な
accusation *n* 告発、非難
accuse *v* 告発する
accustom *v* 慣らす
ace *n* 名手、名人
ache *n* 痛み
achieve *v* 達する
achievement *n* 達成、成果
acid *n* 酸
acidity *n* 酸性
acknowledge *v* 承諾する
acorn *n* ドングリ
acoustic *adj* 音響の
acquaint *v* 知らせる
acquaintance *n* 知人

acquire *v* 得る
acquisition *n* 取得
acquit *v* 釈放する
acquittal *n* 無罪放免
acre *n* エーカー
acrobat *n* 曲芸師
across *pre* 横切って
act *v* 行動する
action *n* 行動
activate *v* 活発にする
activation *n* 活性化
active *adj* 活発な
activity *n* 活動
actor *n* 俳優
actress *n* 女優
actual *adj* 実際の
actually *adv* 実際は
acute *adj* 鋭い、強烈な
adamant *adj* 固い、頑固な
adapt *v* 適応する
adaptable *adj* 適応性のある
adaptation *n* 適応
adapter *n* アダプター
add *v* 加える
addiction *n* 中毒
addictive *adj* 中毒性の
addition *n* 追加
additional *adj* 追加の
address *n* 住所
address *v* (問題）を扱う
addressee *n* 受け取り人
adequate *adj* 適正な

adhere ᵥ 付着する

adhesive ₐ₄ⱼ 粘着性のもの

adjacent ₐ₄ⱼ 近くの

adjective ₙ 形容詞

adjoin ᵥ 〜に隣接する

adjoining ₐ₄ⱼ 隣の

adjourn ᵥ 一時休止する

adjust ᵥ 順応する

adjustable ₐ₄ⱼ 順応できる

adjustment ₙ 調節

administer ᵥ 管理する

admirable ₐ₄ⱼ 立派な

admiral ₙ 提督

admiration ₙ 称賛

admire ᵥ 称賛する

admirer ₙ 称賛者

admissible ₐ₄ⱼ 許容できる

admission ₙ 入ること

admit ᵥ 認める

admittance ₙ 入場

admonish ᵥ 勧告する

admonition ₙ 勧告、忠告

adolescence ₙ 青年期

adolescent ₙ 青年期の人

adopt ᵥ 採用する

adoption ₙ 採用する

adoptive ₐ₄ⱼ 養子縁組をした

adorable ₐ₄ⱼ 愛らしい

adoration ₙ 崇拝、敬愛

adore ᵥ 崇拝する

adorn ᵥ 装飾する

adrift ₐ₄ᵥ 漂流している

adulation ₙ お世辞

adult ₙ 大人

adulterate ᵥ 混ぜ物をした

adultery ₙ 不倫、不貞

advance ᵥ 前へ進む

advance ₙ 前進、進歩

advantage ₙ 有利、利点

Advent ₙ 出現、到来

adventure ₙ 冒険

adverb ₙ 副詞

adversary ₙ 敵、対抗者

adverse ₐ₄ⱼ 反対する

adversity ₙ 逆境、不運

advertise ᵥ 宣伝する

advertising ₙ 宣伝

advice ₙ 助言を求める

advisable ₐ₄ⱼ 賢明な

advise ᵥ 助言する

adviser ₙ 助言者

advocate ᵥ 主張する

aeroplane ₙ 航空

aesthetic ₐ₄ⱼ 美学の

afar ₐ₄ᵥ 遠くに

affable ₐ₄ⱼ 愛想のよい

affair ₙ 事柄、件

affect ᵥ 作用する

affection ₙ 愛情

affectionate ₐ₄ⱼ 優しい

affiliate ᵥ 提携する

affiliation ₙ 提携、加入

affinity ₙ 強い好み

affirm ᵥ 棄却する

**affirmative** *adj* 断定的な

**affix** *v* 加える

**afflict** *v* 悩ます

**affliction** *n* 苦痛

**affluence** *n* 豊富、豊かさ

**affluent** *adj* 豊富な

**affordable** *adj* 手ごろな価格の

**affront** *v* 侮辱する

**affront** *n* 侮辱する

**afloat** *adv* 船上に

**afraid** *adj* 恐れて

**afresh** *adv* 新たに、再び

**after** *pre* 後で

**afternoon** *n* 午後

**afterwards** *adv* その後

**again** *adv* 再び

**against** *pre* 不賛成で

**age** *n* 年齢

**agency** *n* 代理店

**agenda** *n* 議題

**agent** *n* 代理人

**agglomerate** *v* 塊にする

**aggravate** *v* 悪化させる

**aggravation** *n* 悪化

**aggregate** *v* 集合体

**aggression** *n* 武力侵略

**aggressive** *adj* 積極的な

**aggressor** *n* 攻撃者

**aghast** *adj* あきれかえって

**agile** *adj* 素早い

**agitator** *n* 扇動者

**agnostic** *n* 不可知論者

**agonize** *v* 苦闘する

**agonizing** *adj* 苦痛の

**agony** *n* 苦痛、苦悩

**agree** *v* 同意する

**agreeable** *adj* 喜んで同意する

**agreement** *n* 同意、合意

**agricultural** *adj* 農業の

**agriculture** *n* 農業の

**ahead** *pre* 前方に

**aid** *n* 援助、救助

**aid** *v* 手伝う、助ける

**aide** *n* 助手

**ailing** *adj* 病んでいる

**ailment** *n* (慢性的な) 病気

**aim** *v* 狙い、目標

**aimless** *adj* 目的のない

**air** *n* 空気

**air** *v* 放送される

**aircraft** *n* 航空機

**airfare** *n* 航空運賃

**airfield** *n* 飛行場

**airline** *n* 航空会社

**airliner** *n* 定期旅客機

**airmail** *n* 航空便

**airplane** *n* 飛行機

**airport** *n* 空港

**airspace** *n* 空域、領空

**airstrip** *n* 滑走路

**airtight** *adj* すきのない

**aisle** *n* 通路

**ajar** *adj* 少し開いて

**akin** *adj* 血族の、同族の

alarm *n* 警報

alarm clock *n* 目覚まし時計

alarming *adj* 人を驚かせる

alert *n* 警戒態勢

alert *v* 警戒した

algebra *n* 代数学

alien *n* 外国人、異星人

alight *adv* 降りる

align *v* 整列する

alignment *n* 整列

alike *adj* 似ている

alive *adj* 生存して

all *adj* 全ての

allegation *n* 申し立て

allege *v* 断言する

allegiance *n* 忠誠、忠実

allegory *n* 寓喩、寓意

allergic *adj* アレルギー症の

allergy *n* アレルギー

alleviate *v* 軽減する

alley *n* 裏通り、路地

alliance *n* 同盟、連合

allied *adj* 同盟している

alligator *n* アメリカワニ

allocate *v* 割り当てる

allot *v* 割り振る

allotment *n* 割り当て

allow *v* 考慮に入れる

allowance *n* 許容、値引き

alloy *n* 合金

allure *n* 魅力

alluring *adj* 魅力的な

allusion *n* ほのめかし

ally *n* 同盟国、同盟者

ally *v* 同盟する

almanac *n* 暦、年鑑

almighty *adj* 全能の

almond *n* アーモンド

almost *adv* 大体

alms *n* 施し物

alone *adj* 独りで

along *pre* 沿って

alongside *pre* 平行して

aloof *adj* 高飛車な

aloud *adv* 声を出して

alphabet *n* 文字

already *adv* すでに

alright *adv* 大丈夫で

also *adv* 〜もまた

altar *n* 祭壇

alter *v* 変わる、変える

alteration *n* 変更、修正

altercation *n* 口論

alternate *v* 交互に行う

alternate *adj* 代わりの

alternative *n* 代替物

although *c* 〜ではあるが

altitude *n* 高さ

altogether *adj* 全く、完全に

aluminum *n* アルミニウム

always *adv* いつも

amass *v* 蓄積する

amateur *adj* アマチュア

amaze *v* あきれさせる

amazement n 驚き、仰天
amazing adj 驚くべき
ambassador n 大使
ambiguous adj あいまいな
ambition n 大望、抱負
ambitious adj 大望のある
ambivalent adj 両面感情の
ambulance n 救急車
ambush v 待ち伏せする
amenable adj 従順な
amend v 改心する
amendment n 改正、修正
amenities n 快適装備
American adj アメリカ人
amiable adj 愛想の良い
amicable adj 友好的な
amid pre 〜に囲まれて
ammonia n アンモニア
ammunition n 銃弾、弾薬
amnesia n 記憶喪失
amnesty v 大目に見る
among pre 〜の間に
amoral adj 道徳心がない
amorphous adj 非結晶質の
amortize v 分割返済する
amount n 量、総計
amount to v 合計〜になる
amphibious adj 水陸両生の
amphitheater n 円形競技場
ample adj 十分な
amplifier n 増幅器
amplify v 増幅する

amputate v 切断する
amputation n 切断術
amuse v 面白がせる
amusement n 楽しみ
amusing adj 面白い
an a 一つの
analogy n 類似、一致
analysis n 分析、解析
analyze v 分析する
anarchist n 無政府主義者
anarchy n 無政府状態
anatomy n 生態構造
ancestor n 先祖
ancestry n 祖先、家系
anchor n いかり
anchovy n アンチョビ
ancient adj 古代の
and c 〜と、そして
anecdote n 逸話、秘話
anemia n 貧血、無気力
anemic adj 貧血症の
anesthesia n 麻酔
anew adv あらためて
angel n 天使
angelic adj 天使のような
anger v 怒る
anger n 怒り
angina n アンギナ
angle n 角度
Anglican adj 英国教会の
angry adj 腹をたてて
anguish n 激しい苦痛

animal *n* 動物
animate *v* 生気を与える
animation *n* 動画、活気
animosity *n* 敵意、悪意
ankle *n* 足首
annex *n* 別館、離れ
annexation *n* 併合
annihilate *v* 滅ぼす
annihilation *n* 全滅、絶滅
anniversary *n* 記念日
annotate *v* 注釈をつける
annotation *n* 注釈をつける
announce *v* 知らせる
announcement *n* 告示
announcer *n* アナウンサー
annoy *v* 気にする
annoying *adj* うっとうしい
annual *adj* 年次、年報
annul *v* 無効にする
annulment *n* 取り消し
anoint *v* 塗る
anonymity *n* 匿名
anonymous *adj* 匿名の
another *adj* もう一つ
answer *v* 答える
answer *n* 答え
ant *n* アリ
antagonize *v* 敵に回す
antecedent *n* 前例、先例
antecedents *n* 素性、身元
antelope *n* アンテロープ
antenna *n* アンテナ

anthem *n* 国歌
antibiotic *n* 抗生物質
anticipate *v* 予想する
anticipation *n* 予想
antidote *n* 解毒剤
antipathy *n* 反感、嫌悪
antiquated *adj* 古風な
antiquity *n* 大昔、古さ
anvil *n* 金床
anxiety *n* 心配、不安
anxious *adj* 心配して
any *adj* どれでも
anybody *pro* 誰か、誰でも
anyhow *pro* とにかく
anyone *pro* 誰も、誰にも
anything *pro* 何でも
apart *adv* 離れて
apartment *n* アパート
apathy *n* 冷淡、無関心
ape *n* 類人猿
aperitif *n* 食前酒
apex *n* 頂点、先端
aphrodisiac *adj* 媚薬
apiece *adv* 個々に
apocalypse *n* 啓示書
apologize *v* 謝る
apology *n* わび、謝罪
apostle *n* 使徒
apostolic *adj* 使徒の
appall *v* ぞっとする
appalling *adj* 恐ろしい
apparel *n* 衣服

apparent *adj* 明らかな

apparently *adv* 明らかに

apparition *n* 幻影、亡霊

appeal *n* 懇願、魅力

appeal *v* 懇願する

appealing *adj* 魅力的な

appear *v* 見える

appearance *n* 出現、外見

appease *v* なだめる

appeasement *n* 緩和

appendicitis *n* 虫垂炎

appendix *n* 付録

appetite *n* 食欲

appetizer *n* 前菜

applaud *v* 拍手する

applause *n* 拍手、称賛

apple *n* りんご

appliance *n* 電化製品

applicable *adj* 適用できる

applicant *n* 応募者

application *n* 申し込み

apply *v* 当てはまる

apply for *v* 〜に申し込む

appoint *v* 任命する

appointment *n* 約束

appraisal *n* 評価、査定

appraise *v* 評価する

appreciate *v* 感謝する

appreciation *n* 感謝、上昇

apprehend *v* 捕まえる

apprehensive *adj* 聡明な

apprentice *n* 見習い

approach *v* 近づく

approach *n* 近づくこと

approachable *adj* 近づきやすい

approbation *n* 賛同、認可

appropriate *adj* 適切な

approval *n* 承認

approve *v* 承認する

approximate *adj* おおよその

apricot *n* アンズ

April *n* 四月

apron *n* エプロン

aptitude *n* 才能、適性

aquarium *n* 水族館

aquatic *adj* 水の

aqueduct *n* 水管

Arabic *adj* アラビアの

arable *adj* 耕作可能な

arbiter *n* 調停者

arbitrary *adj* 気ままな

arbitrate *v* 解決する

arbitration *n* 調停、仲裁

arc *n* 円弧

arch *n* アーチ

archaeology *n* 考古学

archaic *adj* 古風な

archbishop *n* 大司教

architect *n* 建築家

architecture *n* 建築

archive *n* 公文書

arctic *adj* 北極の

ardent *adj* 熱烈な

ardor *n* 情熱、熱意

arduous *adj* 困難な

area *n* 地域、区域

arena *n* 競技場

argue *v* 言い争う

argument *n* 議論、討論

arid *adj* 乾燥した

arise *iv* 起こる、生じる

aristocracy *n* 貴族政治

aristocrat *n* 貴族

arithmetic *n* 算数、計算

ark *n* ノアの箱舟

arm *n* 腕、武器

arm *v* 武装する

armaments *n* 軍需

armchair *n* ひじ掛けいす

armed *adj* 武装した

armistice *n* 休戦、停戦

armor *n* よろい

armpit *n* 脇の下

army *n* 軍隊、陸軍

aromatic *adj* 香りの良い

around *pro* 周りに

arouse *v* 目覚める

arrange *v* 手配する

arrangement *n* 手配する

array *n* 配列、配置

arrest *v* 逮捕される

arrest *n* 逮捕

arrival *n* 到着

arrive *v* 到着する

arrogance *n* 尊大、ごう慢

arrogant *adj* 尊大な

arrow *n* 矢、矢印

arsenal *n* 貯蔵武器

arsenic *n* ヒ素

arson *n* 放火、放火罪

arsonist *n* 放火犯

art *n* 芸術、美術

artery *n* 動脈

arthritis *n* 関節炎

article *n* 記事、論説

articulation *n* 明瞭な発音

artificial *adj* 人工的な

artillery *n* 大砲

artisan *n* 職人

artist *n* 芸術家

artistic *adj* 芸術的な

artwork *n* 手工芸品

as *c* 〜のように

as *adv* 〜のままで

ascend *v* 上がる、登る

ascendancy *n* 優勢

ascertain *v* 解明する

ascetic *adj* 禁欲的な

ash *n* 灰

ashamed *adj* 恥ずかしい

ashore *adv* 岸へ、浜へ

ashtray *n* 灰皿

aside *adv* わきへ

aside from *adv* 〜それて

ask *v* 尋ねる

asleep *adj* 就寝中の

asparagus *n* アスパラガス

aspect *n* 様子、外見

asphalt *n* アスファルト
asphyxiate *v* 窒息する
asphyxiation *n* 窒息
aspiration *n* 強い願望
aspire *v* 熱望する
aspirin *n* 解熱剤
assail *v* 攻撃する
assailant *n* 攻撃者
assassin *n* 暗殺者
assassinate *v* 暗殺する
assassination *n* 暗殺
assault *n* 肉体的暴力
assault *v* 襲撃する
assemble *v* 集まる
assembly *n* 集合、集会
assent *v* 同意する
assert *v* 断言する
assertion *n* 主張、表明
assess *v* 評価する
assessment *n* 評価、査定
asset *n* 有用な
assets *n* 資産
assign *v* 指名する
assignment *n* 割り当て
assimilate *v* 同化する
assimilation *n* 同化、吸収
assist *v* 支援する
assistance *n* 援助、支援
associate *v* 付き合う
association *n* つながり
assorted *adj* 盛り合わせの
assortment *n* 種類、品揃え

assume *v* 仮定する
assumption *n* 仮定
assurance *n* 確実さ
assure *v* 確実にする
asterisk *n* 星印
asteroid *n* 小惑星
asthma *n* ぜんそく
asthmatic *adj* ぜんそくの
astonish *v* 驚かす
astonishing *adj* 驚くべき
astound *v* 仰天させる
astounding *adj* 驚異的な
astray *v* 道に迷って
astrologer *n* 占星術師
astrology *n* 星占い
astronaut *n* 宇宙飛行士
astronomer *n* 天文学者
astronomic *adj* 天文学の
astronomy *n* 天文学
astute *adj* 明敏な
asunder *adv* バラバラの
asylum *n* 保護施設
at *pre* 〜に、〜で
atheism *n* 無神論
atheist *n* 無心論者
athlete *n* 運動選手
athletic *adj* 運動競技の
atmosphere *n* 雰囲気
atmospheric *adj* 大気の
atom *n* 原子、アトム
atomic *adj* 原子の
atone *v* 償う

atonement *n* 償い、補償

atrocious *adj* 残虐な

atrocity *n* 残虐行為

atrophy *v* 衰える

attach *v* 付着する

attached *adj* 付着した

attachment *n* 付着、連結

attack *n* 攻撃

attack *v* 攻撃する

attacker *n* 攻撃者

attain *v* 達する

attainable *adj* 遂げられる

attainment *n* 獲得、到達

attempt *v* 試みる、企てる

attempt *n* 試み、企て

attend *v* 出席する

attendance *n* 出席、参加

attendant *n* 案内係、付き人

attention *n* 注意、注目

attentive *adj* 用心深い

attenuate *v* 弱まる

attenuating *adj* 減衰する

attest *v* 証言する

attic *n* 屋根裏部屋

attitude *n* 態度

attorney *n* 法律家

attract *v* ひきつける

attraction *n* 魅力

attractive *adj* ひきつける

attribute *v* 起因とする

auction *n* 競売

auction *v* 競売にかける

auctioneer *n* 競売人

audacious *adj* 独創性に富む

audacity *n* 大胆、勇敢

audible *adj* 聞こえる

audience *n* 聴衆

audit *v* 会計検査

auditorium *n* 観衆席

augment *v* 増加する

August *n* 八月

aunt *n* 叔母

auspicious *adj* 幸先の良い

austere *adj* 切り詰めた

austerity *n* 厳格

authentic *adj* 本物の、真の

authenticate *v* 確証をたてる

authenticity *n* 真偽

author *n* 作者

authoritarian *adj* 権威主義の

authority *n* 権威主義の

authorization *n* 権限付与

authorize *v* 権限を与える

auto *n* 車、乗用車

autograph *n* 自署、サイン

automatic *adj* 自動

automobile *n* 自動車

autonomous *adj* 自主的な

autonomy *n* 自治

autopsy *n* 検視解剖

autumn *n* 秋

auxiliary *adj* 予備の

avail *v* 効力がある

available *adj* 利用できる

avalanche *n* 雪崩
avarice *n* 強欲、貪欲
avaricious *adj* 強欲な
avenge *v* 復讐をする
avenue *n* 大通り
average *n* 平均
averse *adj* 嫌って
aversion *n* 反感、嫌悪
avert *v* 避ける、防ぐ
aviation *n* 航空、飛行
aviator *n* 飛行士
avid *adj* 熱烈な
avoid *v* 避ける
avoidable *adj* 回避できる
avoidance *n* 回避
avowed *adj* 公言した
await *v* 待ち受ける
awake *iv* 目が覚める
awake *adj* 目が覚めて
awakening *n* 覚醒、目覚め
award *v* 授与する
award *n* 賞、賞品
aware *adj* 気がついて
awareness *n* 認識、自覚
away *adv* 遠くに
awe *n* 畏敬の念
awesome *adj* 畏敬すべき
awful *adj* 不愉快な
awkward *adj* 不器用な
awning *n* 日よけ
ax *n* おの、大なた
axiom *n* 原理、公理

axis *n* 軸
axle *n* 車軸

# B

babble *v* 無駄口をたたく
baby *n* 赤ちゃん
babysitter *n* ベビーシッター
bachelor *n* 独身者、学士号
back *n* 背中、背後
back *adv* 背後の、裏の
back *v* 後退する
back down *v* 引き下がる
back up *v* 後ろ向きに登る
backbone *n* 背骨
backdoor *n* 裏口、勝手口
backfire *v* 逆火をおこす
background *n* 背景
backing *n* 援助、後援
backlash *n* 反発、反動
backlog *n* バックログ
backpack *n* バックパック
backup *n* 後援、擁護
backward *adj* 逆の、後方へ
backwards *adv* 逆へ、後ろへ
backyard *n* 裏庭
bacon *n* ベーコン
bacteria *n* バクテリア

**bad** *adj* 悪い

**badge** *n* 記章、バッジ

**badly** *adv* 悪く、まずく

**baffle** *v* 迷わせる

**bag** *n* カバン

**baggage** *n* 手荷物

**baggy** *adj* だぶだぶの

**baguette** *n* バゲット

**bail** *n* 保釈、横木

**bail out** *v* 保釈する

**bailiff** *n* 延史

**bait** *n* 餌、誘惑

**bake** *v* オーブンで焼く

**baker** *n* パン職人

**bakery** *n* パン屋

**balance** *v* 平衡を保つ

**balance** *n* 差額

**balcony** *n* バルコニー

**bald** *adj* はげ頭の

**bale** *n* 俵、災い

**ball** *n* 玉、ボール

**balloon** *n* 気球

**ballot** *n* 票、投票

**ballroom** *n* 舞踏場

**balm** *n* 香油、慰め

**balmy** *adj* 芳香の

**bamboo** *n* 竹

**ban** *n* 禁止

**ban** *v* 禁止する

**banality** *n* 陳腐さ

**banana** *n* バナナ

**band** *n* 楽隊、バンド

**bandage** *n* 包帯、救急絆

**bandage** *v* 包帯をする

**bandit** *n* 強盗

**banish** *v* 追い出す

**banishment** *n* 国外追放

**bank** *n* 銀行

**bankrupt** *v* 破産させる

**bankrupt** *adj* 破産した

**bankruptcy** *n* 破産、倒産

**banner** *n* 国旗、軍旗

**banquet** *n* 宴会、祝宴

**baptism** *n* 洗礼

**baptize** *v* 洗礼を施す

**bar** *n* 柵、酒場

**bar** *v* かんぬきをする

**barbarian** *n* 野蛮人

**barbaric** *adj* 野蛮人の

**barbarism** *n* 野蛮、未開

**barbecue** *n* バーベキュー

**barber** *n* 理髪師

**bare** *adj* 裸の

**barefoot** *adj* はだしの

**barely** *adv* 辛うじて

**bargain** *n* 安売り、取引

**bargain** *v* 交渉で決める

**bargaining** *n* 交渉、取引

**barge** *n* はしけ、荷船

**bark** *v* ほえる

**bark** *n* ほえ声、叫び声

**barley** *n* 大麦

**barmaid** *n* バーのホステス

**barman** *n* バーテンダー

**B**

**barn** *n* 納屋、物置
**barometer** *n* 指標、気圧計
**barracks** *n* 兵舎、布袋
**barrage** *n* 集中砲火
**barrel** *n* たる
**barren** *adj* 不毛の
**barricade** *n* 障害物
**barrier** *n* 垣根、障壁
**barring** *pre* ～がなければ
**bartender** *n* バーテンダー
**barter** *v* 物々交換する
**base** *n* 土台、基礎
**base** *v* 基礎を形成する
**baseball** *n* 野球
**baseless** *adj* 基礎のない
**basement** *n* 地下室
**bashful** *adj* 臆病な
**basic** *adj* 基礎の
**basics** *n* 基本にかえる
**basin** *n* 洗面器
**basis** *n* 土台、基盤
**bask** *v* 日光浴をする
**basket** *n* かご
**bastard** *n* 非嫡子
**bat** *n* バット
**batch** *n* 一束、一団
**bath** *n* 浴槽、風呂
**bathe** *v* 水を浴びる
**bathrobe** *n* バスローブ
**bathroom** *n* 浴室
**bathtub** *n* 浴槽
**baton** *n* 警棒

**battalion** *n* 大隊、大群
**batter** *v* 連打する
**battery** *n* バッテリー
**battle** *n* 戦い、戦闘
**battle** *v* 戦う
**battleship** *n* 戦艦
**bay** *n* 湾、入り江
**bayonet** *n* 銃剣
**bazaar** *n* バザー
**be** *iv* ～の状態で
**be born** *v* ～で生まれた
**beach** *n* ビーチ、海辺
**beacon** *n* 水路標識
**beak** *n* くちばし
**beam** *n* はり、船腹
**bean** *n* 豆
**bear** *n* クマ
**bear** *iv* 耐える、支える
**bearable** *adj* 耐えられる
**beard** *n* あごひげ
**bearer** *n* 運搬人
**beast** *n* 獣性
**beat** *iv* たたく、殴る
**beat** *n* 脈拍
**beating** *n* 打つこと
**beautiful** *adj* 美しい
**beautify** *v* 美しくする
**beauty** *n* 美しさ
**beaver** *n* ビーバー
**because** *c* なぜならば
**because of** *pre* ～のために
**beckon** *v* 手招きする

become _iv_ ～になる
bed _n_ 寝場所
bedding _n_ 寝具類
bedroom _n_ 寝室
bedspread _n_ ベッド掛け
bee _n_ 花蜂
beef _n_ 牛肉
beef up _v_ 増強する
beehive _n_ ミツバチの巣箱
beer _n_ ビール
beet _n_ ビート
beetle _n_ カブトムシ
before _adv_ 前に、以前に
before _pre_ ～の前に
beforehand _adv_ 事前に
befriend _v_ 友人になる
beg _v_ 懇願する
beggar _n_ 物ごい
begin _iv_ 始まる
beginner _n_ 初心者
beginning _n_ 初め、開始
beguile _v_ だます、欺く
behalf (on) _adv_ 擁護する
behave _v_ 振舞う
behavior _n_ 態度、素行
behead _v_ 首を切る
behind _pre_ ～の後ろに
behold _iv_ 見守る
being _n_ 存在
belch _v_ 噴出する
belch _n_ 噴出
belfry _n_ 鐘楼

Belgian _adj_ ベルギーの
Belgium _n_ ベルギー
belief _n_ 信念
believable _adj_ 信じられる
believe _v_ 信じる
believer _n_ 信じる人
belittle _v_ ～を見くびる
bell _n_ 鐘、鈴
bell pepper _n_ パプリカ
belligerent _adj_ 好戦的な
belly _n_ 腹
belly button _n_ へそ
belong _v_ 属する
belongings _n_ 所持品
beloved _adj_ 最愛の
below _adv_ 下に、以下に
below _pre_ ～より下に
belt _n_ ベルト、帯
bench _n_ ベンチ
bend _iv_ 曲げる
bend down _v_ 下に曲げる
beneath _pre_ ～の真下に
benediction _n_ 祝福
benefactor _n_ 後援者、恩人
beneficial _adj_ 有益な
beneficiary _n_ 受益者
benefit _n_ 利益、手当
benefit _v_ 得をする
benevolence _n_ 慈善、博愛心
benevolent _adj_ 慈悲深い
benign _adj_ 良性の
bequeath _v_ 遺言で譲る

B

bereaved _adj_ 死別した
bereavement _n_ 死別
beret _n_ ベレー帽
berserk _adv_ 凶暴な
berth _n_ 寝台、停泊所
beseech _iv_ 嘆願する
beset _iv_ 〜を悩ませる
beside _pre_ 〜のそばに
besides _pre_ それに加えて
besiege _iv_ 〜を包囲する
best _adj_ 最も良い
best man _n_ 介添人
bestial _adj_ 野獣の
bestiality _n_ 残虐性
bestow _v_ 〜を授ける
bet _iv_ 賭ける
bet _n_ 賭け
betray _v_ 裏切る
betrayal _n_ 裏切り
better _adj_ より良い
between _pre_ (二つの) 間に
beverage _n_ 飲料
beware _v_ 注意する
bewilder _v_ 〜を当惑させる
bewitch _v_ 魅力的である
beyond _adv_ かなたに
bias _n_ 偏見、偏り
bible _n_ 聖書
biblical _adj_ 聖書の
bibliography _n_ 参考文献
bicycle _n_ 自転車
bid _n_ 入札

bid _iv_ 入札する
big _adj_ 大きい
bigamy _n_ 重婚
bigot _adj_ 思いあがった
bigotry _n_ 偏見、頑固
bike _n_ バイク
bile _n_ 胆汁
bilingual _adj_ 二言語使用者
bill _n_ 勘定書、請求書
billiards _n_ ビリヤード
billion _n_ 10億
billionaire _n_ 億万長者
bimonthly _adj_ ひと月おきの
bin _n_ ふた付容器
bind _iv_ 練る
binding _adj_ 拘束力のある
binoculars _n_ 双眼鏡
biography _n_ 伝記、経歴
biological _adj_ 生物学の
biology _n_ 生物学の
bird _n_ 鳥
birth _n_ 出生、誕生
birthday _n_ 誕生日
biscuit _n_ 小型の丸いパン
bishop _n_ 主教、司祭
bison _n_ 野牛
bit _n_ 少し、わずか
bite _iv_ かみつく
bite _n_ かむこと
bitter _adj_ 苦い
bitterly _adv_ 苦々しく
bitterness _n_ 苦味、苦痛

| | |
|---|---|
| **bizarre** *adj* 奇妙な | **blessing** *n* 神の惠み |
| **black** *adj* 黒い | **blind** *v* 失明させる |
| **blackberry** *n* ブラックベリー | **blind** *adj* 盲目の |
| **blackboard** *n* 黒板 | **blindfold** *n* 目隠し |
| **blackmail** *n* 脅迫、恐喝 | **blindly** *adv* 無分別に |
| **blackmail** *v* ～を脅かす | **blindness** *n* 失明 |
| **blackness** *n* 黒さ | **blink** *v* まばたき |
| **blackout** *n* 停電 | **bliss** *n* 至福 |
| **blacksmith** *n* 鍛冶屋 | **blissful** *adj* おめでたい |
| **bladder** *n* 膀胱 | **blister** *n* 水膨れ |
| **blade** *n* 刃、翼板 | **blizzard** *n* 猛吹雪 |
| **blame** *n* 非難、責め | **bloat** *v* 膨れる |
| **blame** *v* 非難する | **bloated** *adj* 膨れた |
| **bland** *adj* 穏やかな | **block** *n* 角材 |
| **blank** *adj* 空白、空欄 | **block** *v* 妨害する |
| **blanket** *n* 毛布 | **blockade** *v* 封鎖する |
| **blaspheme** *v* 冒とくする | **blockade** *n* 封鎖 |
| **blasphemy** *n* 神への冒とく | **blockage** *n* 妨害物 |
| **blast** *n* 爆風、突風 | **blond** *adj* 金髪の |
| **blaze** *v* 燃えさかる | **blood** *n* 血液 |
| **bleach** *v* 漂白する | **bloodthirsty** *adj* 血に飢えた |
| **bleach** *n* 漂白剤 | **bloody** *adj* 血の |
| **bleak** *adj* 寒々とした | **bloom** *v* 開花、花盛り |
| **bleed** *iv* 出血する | **blossom** *v* 開花する |
| **bleeding** *n* 出血 | **blot** *n* 汚れ、染み |
| **blemish** *n* 傷、汚点 | **blot** *v* 染みをつける |
| **blemish** *v* 傷つける | **blouse** *n* ブラウス |
| **blend** *n* 混合 | **blow** *n* 殴打、一撃 |
| **blend** *v* 混ざる | **blow** *iv* 風が吹く |
| **blender** *n* ミキサー | **blow out** *iv* 吹き消す |
| **bless** *v* 清める | **blow up** *iv* 膨らませる |
| **blessed** *adj* 神聖な、尊い | **blowout** *n* 破裂、噴出 |

**B**

**bludgeon** *v* こん棒で殴る
**blue** *adj* 青い
**blueprint** *n* 青写真
**bluff** *v* やせ我慢をする
**blunder** *n* 大失敗
**blunt** *adj* とがっていない
**bluntness** *n* 無愛想さ
**blur** *v* ぼやける
**blurred** *adj* ぼやけた
**blush** *v* 赤面する
**blush** *n* 赤面
**boar** *n* 雄ブタ
**board** *n* 板、台
**board** *v* 乗車、搭乗する
**boast** *v* 自慢する
**boat** *n* ボート、船
**bodily** *adj* 肉体的に
**body** *n* 体
**bog** *n* 沼地、湿地
**bog down** *v* 泥沼に落ち込む
**boil** *v* 沸騰する
**boil down to** *v* 煮詰まって
**boil over** *v* 煮こぼれる
**boiler** *n* ボイラー
**boisterous** *adj* 騒々しい
**bold** *adj* 大胆な
**boldness** *n* 大胆さ
**bolster** *v* 支える
**bolt** *n* ボルト
**bolt** *v* ボルトで留まる
**bomb** *n* 爆弾
**bomb** *v* 爆発する

**bombing** *n* 爆撃
**bombshell** *n* 砲弾
**bond** *n* 接着
**bondage** *n* 緊縛、束縛
**bone** *n* 骨
**bone marrow** *n* 骨髄
**bonfire** *n* たき火
**bonus** *n* 特別賞与
**book** *n* 本
**bookcase** *n* 書棚
**bookkeeper** *n* 簿記係
**bookkeeping** *n* 簿記
**booklet** *n* 小冊子
**bookseller** *n* 書籍販売人
**bookstore** *n* 本屋
**boom** *n* 急成長
**boom** *v* とどろく
**boost** *v* 高める
**boost** *n* 後援、景気づけ
**boot** *n* ブーツ、長靴
**booth** *n* ブース
**booty** *n* 略奪品、女体
**booze** *n* 酒
**border** *n* 国境
**border on** *v* 国境を接する
**borderline** *adj* 国境線上の
**bore** *v* 退屈させる
**bored** *adj* 退屈した
**boredom** *n* 退屈、ものぐさ
**boring** *adj* つまらない
**born** *adj* 生まれつきの
**borough** *n* 区

borrow v 借りる

bosom n 胸、おっぱい

boss n 上司

boss around v 威張り散らす

bossy adj ボスのような

botany n 植物学

botch v しくじる

both adj 両方の

bother v 気にする

bothersome adj 厄介な

bottle n 瓶

bottle v 瓶に詰める

bottleneck n 瓶首

bottom n 底

bottomless adj 底なしの

bough n 大枝

boulder n 巨石

boulevard n 大通り

bounce v 跳ねる

bounce n 跳ね返り

bound adj 縛られた

bound for adj ～行きの

boundary n 境界

boundless adj 無限の

bounty n 恵みのもの

bourgeois adj 有産階級の人

bow n 船首

bow v おじぎをする

bow out v 退出する

bowels n 便通

bowl n どんぶり

box n 箱

box office n チケット売り場

boxer n ボクサー

boxing n ボクシング

boy n 男の子

boycott v ボイコット

boyfriend n 彼氏、男友達

boyhood n 少年時代

bra n ブラジャー

brace for v ～に備える

bracelet n ブレスレット

bracket n 角括弧

brag v 自慢する

braid n ひも

brain n 脳

brainwash v 洗脳する

brake n ブレーキ

branch n 枝、支店

branch office n 支所、支部

branch out v 枝を出す

brand n 商標

brand-new adj 新品の

brandy n ブランデー

brat adj やんちゃの

brave adj 勇敢な人

bravely adv 勇敢に

bravery n 勇気

brawl n 乱闘

breach n 違反、破棄

bread n パン

breadth n 幅、大きさ

break n 中断、休み

break iv 壊れる、砕ける

**B**

**break away** v ～を取り壊す

**break down** v 壊す

**break free** v 逃げ出す

**break in** v 押し入る

**break off** v 折れて取れる

**break open** v こじ開ける

**break out** v 勃発する

**break up** v 壊れる、別れる

**breakdown** n 故障

**breakfast** n 朝食

**breakthrough** n 突破口

**breast** n 胸部

**breath** n 息、呼吸

**breathe** v 息をする

**breathing** n 呼吸

**breed** iv 子を産む

**breed** n 品種、種類

**breeze** n そよ風

**brethren** n 同胞、会員

**brevity** n 短さ

**brew** v 醸造

**brewery** n 醸造所

**bribe** v わいろを贈る

**bribe** n わいろ

**bribery** n 収賄

**brick** n れんが

**bricklayer** n れんが職人

**bridal** adj 花嫁の

**bride** n 花嫁

**bridegroom** n 花婿

**bridesmaid** n 花嫁介添人

**bridge** n 橋

**bridle** n くつわ

**brief** adj 短時間の

**brief** v 短くまとめる

**briefcase** n 書類かばん

**briefing** n 状況説明

**briefly** adv 簡潔に

**briefs** n ショーツ

**brigade** n 組織

**bright** adj 輝く、まぶしい

**brighten** v 輝かせる

**brightness** n 明るさ

**brilliant** adj 見事な

**brim** n 縁、へり

**bring** iv ～を届ける

**bring back** v 戻す

**bring down** v 下げる

**bring up** v 育成する

**brink** n 水際

**brisk** adj 活発な

**Britain** n 英国

**British** adj 英国人

**brittle** adj もろい

**broad** adj 広範囲の

**broadcast** v 放送する

**broadcast** n 放送、番組

**broadcaster** n 放送局

**broaden** v 広がる

**broadly** adv 概して、広く

**broadminded** adj 寛大な

**brochure** n 冊子

**broil** v 網焼きにする

**broiler** n 若鶏

B

broke *adj* 無一文の
broken *adj* 壊れた
bronchitis *n* 気管支炎
bronze *n* 青銅
broom *n* ほうき
broth *n* 培養液
brothel *n* 売春宿
brother *n* 兄弟
brotherhood *n* 兄弟愛
brother-in-law *n* 義理の兄弟
brotherly *adj* 兄弟の
brow *n* まゆ、額
brown *adj* 茶色の
browse *v* 閲覧する
browser *n* 雑学家
bruise *n* 傷、あざ
bruise *v* あざができる
brunch *n* ブランチ
brunette *adj* こげ茶色の
brush *n* ブラシ
brush *v* ブラシをかける
brush aside *v* 無視する
brush up *v* 身なりを整える
brusque *adj* 素っ気ない
brutal *adj* 残忍な
brutality *n* 残忍性
brutalize *v* 残忍にする
brute *adj* 野蛮な
bubble *n* 泡、シャボン玉
bubble gum *n* バブルガム
buck *n* ドル、金
bucket *n* バケツ

buckle *n* 留め金
buckle up *v* 留める
bud *n* つぼみ
buddy *n* 仲間、相棒
budge *v* 少し動く
budget *n* 予算
buffalo *n* バッファロー
bug *n* 虫
bug *v* ずらかる
build *iv* 建てる、築く
builder *n* 建築者
building *n* 建物
buildup *n* 積み重ね
built-in *adj* 内蔵式の
bulb *n* 電球
bulge *n* 出っ張り
bulk *n* かさ、体積
bulky *adj* かさばった
bull *n* 雄牛
bull fight *n* 闘牛
bull fighter *n* 闘牛士
bulldoze *v* 強引に進む
bullet *n* 弾丸
bulletin *n* 掲示、広報
bully *adj* 素晴らしい
bulwark *n* 防塁、防御
bum *n* 路上生活者
bump *n* 衝突、段差
bump into *v* ～と衝突する
bumper *n* 大豊作
bumpy *adj* 混雑した
bun *n* ロールパン

**B**

bunch _n_ 房、束
bundle _n_ 束状、一括
bundle _v_ 束にする、包む
bunk bed _n_ 二段ベッド
bunker _n_ 大きな箱
buoy _n_ ブイ、浮標
burden _n_ 荷物、重荷
burden _v_ 荷を負わす
burdensome _adj_ 厄介な
bureau _n_ 事務局、案内所
bureaucracy _n_ 官僚機構の
bureaucrat _n_ 役人
burger _n_ ハンバーガー
burglar _n_ 泥棒
burglarize _v_ 泥棒に入る
burglary _n_ 住居侵入窃盗
burial _n_ 埋葬
burly _adj_ がっしりした
burn _iv_ 燃える
burn _n_ 日焼け
burp _v_ げっぷをする
burp _n_ げっぷをする
burrow _n_ 巣穴、隠れ穴
burst _iv_ 破裂する
burst into _v_ 突然〜しだす
bury _v_ 埋める
bus _n_ バス
bus _v_ バスで行く
bush _n_ 低木の茂み
busily _adv_ 忙しく
business _n_ 業種、業界
businessman _n_ 実業家

bust _n_ 胸像、半身像
bustling _adj_ 騒がしい
busy _adj_ 忙しい
but _c_ しかし
butcher _n_ 肉屋
butchery _n_ どじ、へま
butler _n_ 執事
butt _n_ 切れ端、尻
butter _n_ バター
butterfly _n_ チョウ
button _n_ ボタン
buttonhole _n_ ボタン穴
buy _iv_ 買う
buy off _v_ 買収する
buyer _n_ 買い手
buzz _n_ 電話の音
buzz _v_ ざわつく
buzzard _n_ ハゲタカ
buzzer _n_ 汽笛
by _pre_ 〜によって
bye _e_ さようなら
bypass _n_ 迂回路
bypass _v_ 側路をつける
by-product _n_ 副産物
bystander _n_ 見物人

# C

cab *n* タクシー
cabbage *n* キャベツ
cabin *n* 船室
cabinet *n* キャビネット、閣僚
cable *n* 太綱
cafeteria *n* 食堂
caffeine *n* カフェイン
cage *n* 鳥かご
cake *n* ケーキ
calamity *n* 災難、不幸
calculate *v* 計算する
calculation *n* 計算
calculator *n* 計算機
calendar *n* 暦
calf *n* 子牛
caliber *n* 銃の口径
calibrate *v* 測定する
call *n* 叫び、呼び出し
call *v* 電話をする
call off *v* 取りやめる
call on *v* 〜を訪問する
call out *v* 呼び出す
calling *n* 叫び声、召集
callous *adj* 無神経な
calm *adj* 静かな
calm *n* 静けさ、平穏
calm down *v* 落ち着く
calorie *n* カロリー
calumny *n* 中傷すること

camel *n* ラクダ
camera *n* カメラ
camouflage *v* 隠し立てをする
camouflage *n* 偽装
camp *n* 野営地
camp *v* 野営する
campaign *v* 運動を起こす
can *iv* 〜ができる
can *v* 〜を缶詰にする
can *n* 缶、缶詰
can opener *n* 缶切り
canal *n* 運河、用水路
canary *n* カナリア
cancel *v* キャンセルする
cancellation *n* 取り消し
cancer *n* 癌
cancerous *adj* 癌の
candid *adj* 率直な
candidacy *n* 立候補
candidate *n* 立候補者
candle *n* ロウソク
candlestick *n* ロウソク立て
candor *n* 率直さ
candy *n* キャンデー
cane *n* 杖
canister *n* 小型の缶
canned *adj* 缶詰にした
cannibal *n* 人食い人種
cannon *n* 大砲
canoe *n* カヌー
canonize *v* 聖人と認める
cantaloupe *n* カンタロープ

C

**C**

canteen *n* 学生食堂
canvas *n* 画布
canyon *n* 峡谷
cap *n* 野球帽
capability *n* 能力、才能
capable *adj* 能力がある
capacity *n* 最大容積
cape *n* 岬
capital *n* 首都
capital letter *n* 大文字
capitalism *n* 資本主義
capitalize *v* 資本化する
capitulate *v* 降伏する
capsize *v* 転覆する
capsule *n* カプセル
captain *n* 船長、機長
captivate *v* 魅了する
captive *n* 捕虜、人質
capture *v* 捕らえる
capture *n* 捕獲
car *n* 自動車
carat *n* カラット
caravan *n* キャラバン
carburetor *n* 気化器
carcass *n* 動物の死体
card *n* はがき
cardboard *n* ボール紙
cardiac *adj* 心臓の
cardiac arrest *n* 心臓停止
cardiology *n* 心臓学
care *n* 心配、配慮
care *v* 心配する

care about *v* 気にかける
care for *v* ～を大事に思う
career *n* 職業、職歴
carefree *adj* 心配のない
careful *adj* 注意深い
careless *adj* 不注意な
carelessness *n* 不注意な
caress *n* 愛撫、抱擁
caress *v* 愛撫する
caretaker *n* 世話人
cargo *n* 貨物
caricature *n* 風刺画
caring *adj* 気遣う
carnage *n* 大虐殺
carnal *adj* 現世の
carnation *n* カーネーション
carol *n* 聖歌
carpenter *n* 大工
carpentry *n* 大工仕事
carpet *n* じゅうたん
carriage *n* 馬車、構え
carrot *n* にんじん
carry *v* 運ぶ
carry on *v* 続ける
carry out *v* 実行する
cart *n* カーと、荷馬車
cart *v* カートで運ぶ
cartoon *n* 漫画
cartridge *n* 替え刃
carve *v* 彫る
cascade *n* 小さな滝
case *n* 事例、状況

C

cash _n_ 現金
cashier _n_ 現金出納係
casino _n_ カジノ
casket _n_ 宝庫
casserole _n_ 鍋料理
cassock _n_ 司祭平服
cast _iv_ 投げる
castaway _n_ 漂流者
caste _n_ 社会階級
castle _n_ 城
casual _adj_ 平常どおりの
casualty _n_ 犠牲者、惨事
cat _n_ 猫
cataclysm _n_ 大変動
catacomb _n_ 地価墓地
catalog _n_ 目録
catalog _v_ ～の目録を作る
cataract _n_ 大雨、豪雨
catastrophe _n_ 大惨事
catch _iv_ 捕まえる
catch up _v_ ～に追いつく
catching _adj_ 伝染性の
catchword _n_ 標語
catechism _n_ 公教要理
category _n_ カテゴリー
cater to _v_ ～を満たす
caterpillar _n_ 毛虫
cathedral _n_ 大聖堂
catholic _adj_ 多様な
Catholicism _n_ カトリック教義
cattle _n_ 蓄牛
cauliflower _n_ カリフラワー

cause _n_ 原因、要因
cause _v_ ～の原因になる
caution _n_ 注意、用心
cautious _adj_ 用心深い
cavalry _n_ 騎兵隊
cave _n_ 洞くつ
cave in _v_ 崩れ落ちる
cavern _n_ 大洞窟
cavity _n_ 虫歯
cease _v_ 終わる、やむ
cease-fire _n_ 休戦、停戦
ceiling _n_ 天井
celebrate _v_ 祝う
celebration _n_ 祝典、称賛
celebrity _n_ 有名人、著名人
celery _n_ セロリ
celestial _adj_ 天の、神聖な
celibacy _n_ 独身の
celibate _adj_ 禁欲主義の
cellar _n_ 地下貯蔵室
cellphone _n_ 携帯電話
cement _n_ セメント
cemetery _n_ 墓地
censorship _n_ 検閲
censure _v_ 非難する
census _n_ 人口調査
cent _n_ 硬貨
centenary _n_ 100周年
center _n_ 中心
center _v_ 集中する
centimeter _n_ センチメートル
central _adj_ 中心の

**C**

centralize *v* 中心に集める
century *n* 1世紀
ceramic *n* セラミック
cereal *n* 穀草類
cerebral *adj* 脳の
ceremony *n* 儀式、式典
certain *adj* 確信して
certainty *n* 確信
certificate *n* 証明書
certify *v* 保証する
chagrin *n* 充電
chain *n* 鎖
chain *v* ～を鎖でつなぐ
chainsaw *n* チェーンソー
chair *n* いす
chair *v* 議長を務める
chairman *n* 議長、委員長
chalet *n* シャレー
chalice *n* 杯
chalk *n* 白墨
chalkboard *n* 黒板
challenge *v* 挑戦する
challenge *n* 挑戦する
challenging *adj* 挑戦的な
chamber *n* 審議会、議場
champ *n* チャンプ
champion *n* 優勝者、勝者
champion *v* 擁護する
chance *n* 機会
chancellor *n* 総長、書記
chandelier *n* シャンデリア
change *v* 変わる

change *n* 変化、移行
channel *n* 通路、水路
chant *n* 詠唱、聖歌
chaos *n* 無秩序、混乱
chaotic *adj* 大混乱の
chapel *n* 礼拝堂
chaplain *n* 宗教儀式係
chapter *n* 章、見出し
char *v* 焦げる
character *n* 性格、個性
characteristic *adj* 独特の
charade *n* シャレード
charbroil *adj* 炭焼きの
charcoal *n* 炭、木炭
charge *v* 請求する
charge *n* 使用料、告訴
charisma *n* カリスマ
charismatic *adj* カリスマ的な
charitable *adj* 慈悲深い
charity *n* 慈善、施し
charm *v* 魅力的である
charm *n* 魅力、魔力
charming *adj* 魅力的な
chart *n* 図表、グラフ
charter *n* 貸切り、設立許可
charter *v* 特許を与える
chase *n* 追跡
chase *v* 追う
chase away *v* 追い払う
chasm *n* 深い裂け目
chaste *adj* 慎み深い
chastise *v* 罰する

chastisement n せっかん

chastity n 清純

chat v 雑談する

chauffeur n 携帯こんろ

cheap adj 安い

cheat v だます

cheater n 欺く人

check n 点検、押さえ具

check v 照合する

check up n 調べあげる

checkbook n 小切手帳

cheek n ほお

cheekbone n ほお骨

cheeky adj 生意気な

cheer v 喝采、声援

cheer up v 元気づく

cheerful adj 陽気な

cheers n 乾杯

cheese n チーズ

chef n 調理師

chemical adj 化学の

chemist n 薬剤師

chemistry n 相性、化学

cherish v 〜を大事にする

cherry n サクランボ

chess n チェス

chest n 胸、収納箱

chestnut n クリ

chew v 熟考する

chick n ひよこ

chicken n ニワトリ

chicken out v おじけづく

chicken pox n 水疱瘡

chide v 〜をたしなめる

chief n 長、長官

chiefly adv 主として

child n 子供

childhood n 子供時代

childish adj 子供らしい

childless adj 子供のない

children n 子供たち

chill n 冷え、寒さ

chill out v 落ち着く

chilly adj 肌寒い

chimney n 煙突

chimpanzee n チンパンジー

chin n 顎

chip n 切れ端、小片

chisel n のみ、彫刻等

chocolate n チョコレート

choice n 選ぶこと

choir n 聖歌隊

choke v 息が詰まる

cholera n コレラ

cholesterol n コレステロール

choose iv 〜を選ぶ

chop v 霧刻む

chop n たたき切り

chopper n 肉切り包丁

chore n 雑用

chorus n コーラス

christen v 洗礼を施す

christening n 洗礼式

christian adj キリスト教の

**Christianity** n キリスト教

**Christmas** n クリスマス

**chronic** adj 慢性の

**chronicle** n 年代記、歴史

**chronology** n 年代順配列

**chubby** adj まるまる太った

**chuckle** v クスクス笑う

**chunk** n 大きい塊

**church** n 教会

**chute** n シュート

**cider** n リンゴジュース

**cigar** n 葉巻、シガー

**cigarette** n たばこ

**cinder** n 燃え殻、灰

**cinema** n 映画、シネマ

**cinnamon** n ニッケイ

**circle** n 円、円周

**circle** v 回る、旋回する

**circuit** n 回路、迂回

**circular** adj 円の、丸い

**circulate** v グルグル回る

**circulation** n 循環

**circumcise** v 割札を施す

**circumcision** n 割礼

**circumstance** n 状況、事情

**circumstancial** adj 状況の

**circus** n サーカス

**cistern** n 貯水池

**citizen** n 市民

**citizenship** n 市民権

**city** n 都市、市

**city hall** n 市役所

**civic** adj 市民の

**civil** adj 市民から成る

**civilization** n 文明

**civilize** v 文明化する

**claim** v 主張する

**claim** n 要求、主張

**clam** n ハマグリ

**clamor** v 言う

**clamp** n 締め具

**clan** n 一族

**clandestine** adj 内密の

**clap** v 拍手する

**clarification** n 明確化、釈明

**clarify** v 明確にする

**clarinet** n クラリネット

**clarity** n 透明度、明瞭

**clash** v 衝突する

**clash** n 衝突

**class** n 授業、科目

**classic** adj 古典的な

**classify** v 〜を分類する

**classmate** n 同級生

**classroom** n 教室

**classy** adj 上品な

**clause** n 節、箇条

**claw** n 昆虫のつめ

**claw** v 〜を裂く

**clay** n 粘土、土

**clean** adj きれいな

**clean** v 掃除する

**cleaner** n 掃除機、掃除人

**cleanliness** n 潔癖、清潔

cleanse *v* ～を洗浄する

cleanser *n* 洗剤

clear *adj* 透明な

clear *v* きれいになる

clearance *n* 撤去、片付け

clear-cut *adj* はっきりした

clearly *adv* はっきりと

clearness *n* 透明、明るさ

cleft *n* 裂け目

clemency *n* 慈悲

clench *v* ギュッと締まる

clergy *n* 聖職者

clergyman *n* 男性の聖職者

clerical *adj* 事務員の

clerk *n* 事務員

clever *adj* 利口な、賢い

click *v* カチッと音がする

client *n* 来談者、依頼人

clientele *n* 常連

cliff *n* がけ

climate *n* 気候、風土

climatic *adj* 気候上の

climax *n* 最高点、絶頂

climb *v* 上昇する、登る

climbing *n* 登山

clinch *v* 固定する

cling *iv* くっつく

clinic *n* 診療所

clip *v* 切り抜く

clipping *n* 切り抜き

cloak *n* クローク、覆い

clock *n* 掛け時計

clog *v* 詰まる

cloister *n* 修道院生活

clone *v* クローン化する

cloning *n* クローニング

close *v* 閉まる

close *adj* 近い、親しい

close to *pre* 寸前で

closed *adj* 閉店した

closely *adv* 綿密に

closet *n* 物置、押入れ

closure *n* 閉鎖、封鎖

clot *n* 塊

cloth *n* 布、生地

clothe *v* ～に衣服を着せる

clothes *n* 衣服

clothing *n* 衣料品

cloud *n* 雲

cloudless *adj* 晴れ渡った

cloudy *adj* 曇った

clown *n* 道化師

club *n* クラブ、同好会

club *v* ～を打つ

clue *n* 手がかり

clumsiness *n* 不器用

clumsy *adj* 不器用な

cluster *n* 房、群れ

cluster *v* 房になる

clutch *n* クラッチ

coach *v* 指導する

coach *n* 指導者、コーチ

coaching *n* 指導

coagulate *v* 凝固する

C

**C**

coagulation *n* 凝固物
coal *n* 石炭
coalition *n* 連携、連合
coarse *adj* 粗い、粗悪な
coast *n* 海岸
coastal *adj* 海岸の
coastline *n* 海外線
coat *n* コート、上着
coax *v* 説得する
cob *n* 小馬
cobblestone *n* 小さな丸石
cobweb *n* クモの巣
cocaine *n* コカイン
cock *n* 栓
cockpit *n* 操縦席
cockroach *n* ごきぶり
cocktail *n* カクテル
cocky *adj* うぬぼれた
cocoa *n* ココア
coconut *n* ココナツ
cod *n* タラ
code *n* 条例、符号
codify *v* 成文化する
coefficient *n* 共同作用
coerce *v* 強制する
coercion *n* 強制力
coexist *v* 共存する
coffee *n* コーヒー
coffin *n* 棺
cohabit *v* 共生する
coherent *adj* 理路整然と
cohesion *n* 結合

coin *n* 硬貨
coincide *v* 同時に起こる
coincidence *n* 偶然の一致
coincidental *adj* 偶然に起きる
cold *adj* 寒い
coldness *n* 冷たさ、寒さ
colic *n* コリック
collaborate *v* 共同する
collaboration *n* 協力
collaborator *n* 協力者
collapse *v* 崩壊する
collapse *n* 崩壊、倒壊
collar *n* 襟、カラー
collarbone *n* 鎖骨
collateral *adj* 相並んだ
colleague *n* 同僚
collect *v* 集める
collection *n* 収集
collector *n* 収集家
college *n* 大学
collide *v* 衝突する
collision *n* 衝突、激突
cologne *n* オーデコロン
colon *n* コロン
colonel *n* 大佐
colonial *adj* 植民地の
colonization *n* 植民地化
colonize *v* 植民地にする
colony *n* 植民地
color *n* 色
color *v* 変色する
colorful *adj* 色とりどりの

C

colossal *adj* 壮大な
colt *n* 雄の子馬
column *n* 欄、支柱
coma *n* 昏睡、コマ
comb *n* くし
comb *v* うねる
combat *n* 戦闘、闘い
combat *v* 戦う、闘う
combatant *n* 戦闘員
combination *n* 組み合わせ
combine *v* 一体化
combustible *n* 可燃の
combustion *n* 燃焼、酸化
come *iv* 来る
come about *v* 起こる
come across *v* 出くわす
come apart *v* 壊れる
come back *v* 戻ってくる
come down *v* 下がる
come forward *v* 前に進み出る
come from *v* 〜から来る
come in *v* 中に入る
come out *v* 出てくる
come up *v* 上がる
comeback *n* 受け答え
comedian *n* コメディアン
comedy *n* コメディー
comet *n* 彗星
comfort *n* 快適さ
comfortable *adj* 快適な
comforter *n* 慰める人
comical *adj* おかしな

coming *n* 到来
coming *adj* 来るべき
comma *n* 句読点のコンマ
command *v* 指令、命令
commander *n* 指揮官
commandment *n* 命令、掟
commemorate *v* 記念する
commence *v* 開始する
commend *v* 褒める
commendation *n* 推薦、称賛
comment *v* 論評する
comment *n* 論評
commerce *n* 商業、貿易
commercial *adj* 商業の
commission *n* 委託料、手数料
commit *v* 誓約する
commitment *n* 確約
committed *adj* 献身的な
committee *n* 委員会
common *adj* 共通の
commotion *n* 大興奮、騒ぎ
communicate *v* 交信する
communication *n* 交信、連絡
communion *n* 共有、親交
communism *n* 共産主義
communist *adj* 共産主義の
community *n* 地域社会
commute *v* 通勤する
compact *adj* 小型の
compact *v* 圧縮する
companion *n* 仲間、同伴者
companionship *n* 交友

**C**

company *n* 会社、友人
comparable *adj* 匹敵する
comparative *adj* 比較の
compare *v* 比較する
comparison *n* 比較
compartment *n* 区画
compass *n* コンパス
compassion *n* 同情
compassionate *adj* 同情的な
compatibility *n* 互換性
compatible *adj* 相性が良い
compatriot *n* 同国人
compel *v* 強いる
compelling *adj* 強制的な
compendium *n* 概要、一覧
compensate *v* 償う、補う
compensation *n* 埋め合わせ
compete *v* 競争する
competence *n* 能力、力量
competent *adj* 有能な
competition *n* 競争、争い
competitive *adj* 競争の
competitor *n* 競争相手
compile *v* 蓄積する
complain *v* 不満
complaint *n* 不平、不満
complement *n* 補足、補充
complete *adj* 完結した
complete *v* 完了する
completely *adv* 全面的に
completion *n* 完成、完了
complex *adj* 複合体

complexion *n* 顔色、様子
complexity *n* 複雑さ
compliance *n* 順守、準拠
compliant *adj* 従順な
complicate *v* 複雑にする
complication *n* 複雑、混乱
complicity *n* 共謀
compliment *n* 褒め言葉
complimentary *adj* お世辞を言う
comply *v* 従う、応じる
component *n* 成分、要素
compose *v* 構成する、成る
composed *adj* 落ち着いた
composer *n* 作曲家
composition *n* 組み立て
compost *n* たい肥
composure *n* 落ち着き
compound *n* 合成物
compound *v* 折り合う
comprehend *v* よく理解する
comprehensive *adj* 理解力のある
compress *v* 圧迫する
compression *n* 圧縮
comprise *v* 包む
compromise *n* 妥協、譲歩
compromise *v* 妥協する
compulsion *n* 衝動強迫
compulsive *adj* 駆り立てられた
compulsory *adj* 強制させた
compute *v* 計算する
computer *n* コンピューター
comrade *n* 同僚、同志

con man *n* 詐欺師

conceal *v* 隠す

concede *v* 譲歩する

conceited *adj* うぬぼれた

conceive *v* 思いつく

concentrate *v* 集中させる

concentration *n* 集中させる

concentric *adj* 集中的な

concept *n* 概念、観念

conception *n* 受胎、構想

concern *v* 関係する

concern *n* 関心事、心配

concerning *pre* 〜に関して

concert *n* 音楽会

concession *n* 許容、利権

conciliate *v* 調停する

conciliatory *adj* 和解の

conciousness *n* 意識、正気

concise *adj* 簡潔な

conclude *v* 結論を出す

conclusion *n* 結論、決定

conclusive *adj* 決定的な

concoct *v* 調合する

concoction *n* 混合飲料

concrete *n* 凝固物

concrete *adj* コンクリートの

concur *v* 同意する

concurrent *adj* 同時に起きた

concussion *n* 激しい振動

condemn *v* 責める

condemnation *n* 激しい非難

condensation *n* 凝縮

condense *v* 凝結する

condescend *v* 見下す態度をとる

condiment *n* 香辛料、薬味

condition *n* 状態、状況

conditional *adj* 条件付きの

conditioner *n* 調整剤

condo *n* マンション

condolences *n* お悔やみ

condone *v* 大目に見る

conducive *adj* 貢献する

conduct *n* 行為、品行

conduct *v* 導く、案内する

conductor *n* 指揮者

cone *n* 錐体、コーン

confer *v* 話し合う

conference *n* 会議、協議

confess *v* 認める

confession *n* 白状、自認

confessional *n* ざんげ室

confessor *n* 告白者

confidant *n* 親友、懐刀

confide *v* 信任する

confidence *n* 信任、自信

confident *adj* 自信のある

confidential *adj* 極秘の

confine *v* 制限する

confinement *n* 監禁

confirm *v* 確認する

confirmation *n* 確認、立証

confiscate *v* 差し押さえる

confiscation *n* 没収、押収

conflict *n* 葛藤、争い

C

C

conflict v 矛盾する
conflicting adj 相反する
conform v 一致する
conformist adj 遵法者
conformity n 服従、適合
confound v 悪化させる
confront v 直面する
confrontation n 対立
confuse v 混同する
confusing adj 紛らわしい
confusion n 混同、戸惑い
congenial adj 心地がよい
congested adj 密集した
congestion n 密集、混雑
congratulate v 祝う
congratulations n 祝辞
congregate v 集まる
congregation n 集まり
congress n 会議、総会
conjecture n 憶測
conjugal adj 婚姻の
conjugate v 活用する
conjunction n 結合、接続詞
conjure up v 〜を素早く出す
connect v 接続する
connection n 乗り継ぎ
connive v 共謀する
connote v 暗示する
conquer v 征服する
conqueror n 征服者
conquest n 征服
conscience n 道義心

conscious adj 意識のある
conscript n 徴集兵
consecrate v 聖職に任命する
consecration n 神聖化
consecutive adj 連続した
consensus n 意見の一致
consent v 承諾する
consent n 一致、承諾
consequence n 結果、結論
conservation n 保存、保全
conservative adj 保守的な人
conserve v 節約する
conserve n 果物のジャム
consider v よく考える
considerable adj 相当な
considerate adj 理解のある
consideration n 考慮、配慮
consignment n 引き渡すこと
consist v 〜から成る
consistency n 一貫性
consistent adj 一致した
consolation n 慰め、安らぎ
console v 〜を慰める
consolidate v 固まる
consonant n 子音
conspicuous adj 見やすい
conspiracy n 陰謀、謀略
conspirator n 共謀者
conspire v 共謀する
constancy n 不変性
constant adj 普遍
constellation n 星座

C

consternation *n* 仰天
constipate *v* 便秘させる
constipated *adj* 停滞した
constipation *n* 便秘
constitute *v* ～を構成する
constitution *n* 憲法、規約
constrain *v* 拘束する
constraint *n* 制約、制限
construct *v* 建築する
construction *n* 建造、建築
constructive *adj* 建設的な
consul *n* 領事
consulate *n* 領事館
consult *v* 相談する
consultation *n* 相談
consume *v* 費やす
consumer *n* 消費者
consumption *n* 消費、消耗
contact *v* 接触する
contact *n* 接触、連絡
contagious *adj* 接触伝染性の
contain *v* 収容できる
container *n* 入れ物
contaminate *v* 汚染する
contamination *n* 汚れ
contemplate *v* 沈思する
contemporary *adj* 現代の
contempt *n* 軽蔑、侮辱
contend *v* 競う
contender *n* 競争者
content *adj* 満足している
content *v* 満足させる

contentious *adj* 議論を起こす
contents *n* 目次
contest *n* 競技会
contestant *n* 競技者
context *n* 文脈、背景
continent *n* 大陸
continental *adj* 大陸の
contingency *n* 偶然性
contingent *adj* 偶然の
continuation *n* 継続
continue *v* 続く
continuity *n* 連続性
continuous *adj* 連続的な
contour *n* 輪郭、外形
contraband *n* 密輸
contract *v* 縮小する
contract *n* 契約、協定
contraction *n* 収縮、縮小
contradict *v* 矛盾する
contradiction *n* 矛盾する
contrary *adj* 正反対の
contrast *v* 対照をなす
contrast *n* 対照
contribute *v* 貢献する
contribution *n* 貢献、寄与
contributor *n* 貢献者
contrition *n* 悔い改め
control *n* 支配、制御
control *v* 支配する
controversial *adj* 議論の
controversy *n* 論争、討論
convalescent *adj* 回復期の

**convene** v 召集される

**convenience** n 便利

**convenient** adj 便利な

**convent** n 修道院

**convention** n 慣習、しきたり

**conventional** adj 慣習の

**converge** v 一点に集まる

**conversation** n 会話

**converse** v 会話をする

**conversely** adv 反対に、逆に

**conversion** n 変換

**convert** v 変わる

**convert** n 転向者

**convey** v 搬送する

**convict** v 有罪を宣告する

**conviction** n 信念、確信

**convince** v 確信させる

**convincing** adj 説得力のある

**convoluted** adj 渦巻き形の

**convoy** n 護送

**convulse** v 激しく揺する

**convulsion** n けいれん

**cook** v 料理をする

**cook** n 料理人

**cookie** n クッキー

**cooking** n 料理

**cool** adj 冷淡な

**cool** v 冷ます

**cool down** v 冷める

**cooling** adj 冷却する

**coolness** n 涼しさ

**cooperate** v 協力する

**cooperation** n 協力、提携

**cooperative** adj 助け合う

**coordinate** v 連携する

**coordination** n 連携

**coordinator** n 調整する人

**cop** n 警察官

**cope** v うまく対処する

**copier** n コピー機

**copper** n 銅

**copy** v コピーする

**copy** n コピー、写し

**copyright** n 著作権

**cord** n コード、ひも

**cordial** adj 誠心誠意の

**cordless** adj コードなしの

**cordon** n 非常線

**cordon off** v 非常線を張る

**core** n 芯、中心

**cork** n コルク栓

**corn** n トウモロコシ

**corner** n 角、窮地

**cornerstone** n 土台

**cornet** n コルネット

**corollary** n 推論

**coronary** adj 冠状動脈の

**coronation** n 戴冠式

**corporal** adj 肉体の

**corporal** n 伍長

**corporation** n 法人、会社

**corpse** n 死体、死骸

**corpulent** adj 肥満した

**corpuscle** n 小体

C

correct v 訂正する、正す
correct adj 正しい
correction n 訂正、修正
correspond v 相当する
correspondent n 通信員
corresponding adj 対応する
corridor n 廊下
corroborate v 裏付ける
corrode v 腐食する
corrupt v 堕落する
corrupt adj 買収された
corruption n 汚職、買収
cosmetic n 化粧品
cosmic adj 宇宙の
cosmonaut n 宇宙飛行士
cost iv 費用がかかる
cost n 費用、経費
costly adj 値段の高い
costume n 衣装
cottage n 小別荘
cotton n 綿
couch n 長いす
cough n 咳
cough v 咳をする
council n 地方議会
counsel v 助言する
counsel n 助言
counselor n 助言者
count v 数を数える
count n 数を数えること
countdown n 秒読み
countenance n 顔つき

counter n 計算器
counter v 対抗する
counteract v 妨げる
counterfeit v 偽物
counterfeit adj 偽造の
counterpart n 相手方
countess n 伯爵夫人
countless adj 無数の
country n 国
countryman n 田舎の住人
countryside n 田舎
county n 群
coup n 政変
couple n 二者一組
coupon n 割引購入券
courage n 勇気
courageous adj 勇気のある
courier n 宅配便業者
course n 道、方向
court n 裁判、裁判所
court v 付き合う
courteous adj 礼儀正しい
courtesy n 礼儀、作法
courthouse n 郡庁舎
courtship n 求婚、求愛
courtyard n 中庭
cousin n いとこ
cove n 入り江
covenant n 盟約、協定
cover n 覆い、カバー
cover v 覆う
cover up v 隠す

**C**

**coverage** n 報道、範囲
**covert** adj 秘密の
**coverup** n 羽織る服
**covet** v 切望する
**cow** n 乳牛
**coward** n 臆病者
**cowardice** n 臆病
**cowardly** adv 勇気のない
**cowboy** n 牛飼い
**cozy** adj 楽な
**crab** n カニ
**crack** n 割れ目、ひび
**crack** v 割れる
**cradle** n 揺りかご
**craft** n 船、飛行機
**craftsman** n 職人
**cram** v 詰め込む
**cramp** n 生理痛
**cramped** adj 窮屈な
**crane** n ツル
**crank** n 変人
**cranky** adj 不機嫌な
**crap** n 糞、たわごと
**crappy** adj くだらない
**crash** n 衝突、墜落
**crash** v 衝突する
**crass** adj 鈍い、粗野な
**crater** n 噴火口
**crave** v 切望する
**craving** n 切望、熱望
**crawl** v 徐行
**crayon** n クレヨン

**craziness** n 狂気
**crazy** adj 変わり者
**creak** v きしむ
**creak** n きしみ
**cream** n 乳脂
**creamy** adj クリーム状の
**crease** n 折り目
**crease** v しわになる
**create** v 創造する
**creation** n 創造
**creative** adj 創造的な
**creativity** n 創造性
**creator** n 創造者
**creature** n 生き物
**credibility** n 信頼性
**credible** adj 信じられる
**credit** n 信用、評判
**creditor** n 債権者
**creed** n 信念、信条
**creek** n 小川
**creep** v 忍び寄り
**creepy** adj 気味悪い
**cremate** v 火葬する
**crematorium** n 火葬場
**crest** n とさか、頂上
**crevice** n 裂け目
**crew** n 乗組員、クルー
**crib** n 幼児用寝台
**cricket** n クリケット
**crime** n 犯罪
**criminal** adj 犯罪者
**cripple** adj 肢体不自由な

C

| | |
|---|---|
| cripple <sub>v</sub> 不自由にする | crown <sub>v</sub> 冠をかぶせる |
| crisis <sub>n</sub> 危機 | crucial <sub>adj</sub> 重大な |
| crispy <sub>adj</sub> 二日酔いの | crucifix <sub>n</sub> 十字架 |
| criss-cross <sub>v</sub> 十字遺伝 | crucifixion <sub>n</sub> はりつけ |
| criterion <sub>n</sub> 標準、尺度 | crucify <sub>v</sub> 張り付けにする |
| critical <sub>adj</sub> 批判的な | crude <sub>adj</sub> 粗雑な |
| criticism <sub>n</sub> 批評、批判 | cruel <sub>adj</sub> 残酷な |
| criticize <sub>v</sub> 非難する | cruelty <sub>n</sub> 残酷さ |
| critique <sub>n</sub> 評論 | cruise <sub>v</sub> 船旅をする |
| crockery <sub>n</sub> 瀬戸物 | crumb <sub>n</sub> パンの身 |
| crocodile <sub>n</sub> クロコダイル | crumble <sub>v</sub> 粉々に崩れる |
| crony <sub>n</sub> 取り巻き連中 | crunchy <sub>adj</sub> 歯応えの良い |
| crook <sub>n</sub> 曲がったもの | crusade <sub>n</sub> 十字軍、聖戦 |
| crooked <sub>adj</sub> 湾曲した | crusader <sub>n</sub> 十字軍兵士 |
| crop <sub>n</sub> 作物、農作物 | crush <sub>v</sub> 押しつぶすこと |
| cross <sub>n</sub> 十字形 | crushing <sub>adj</sub> 圧倒的な |
| cross <sub>adj</sub> 交差している | crust <sub>n</sub> パンの耳 |
| cross <sub>v</sub> 横断する | crusty <sub>adj</sub> 堅い皮のある |
| cross out <sub>v</sub> 削除する | crutch <sub>n</sub> 松葉杖 |
| crossfire <sub>n</sub> 十字砲火 | cry <sub>n</sub> 泣き声 |
| crossing <sub>n</sub> 交差点 | cry <sub>v</sub> 泣く、叫ぶ |
| crossroads <sub>n</sub> クロスロード | cry out <sub>v</sub> 泣き叫ぶ |
| crosswalk <sub>n</sub> 横断歩道 | crying <sub>n</sub> 叫び、号泣 |
| crossword <sub>n</sub> クロスワード | crystal <sub>n</sub> 結晶 |
| crouch <sub>v</sub> うずくまる | cub <sub>n</sub> 幼獣、新米 |
| crow <sub>n</sub> カラス | cube <sub>n</sub> 立方体 |
| crow <sub>v</sub> 鳴く | cubic <sub>adj</sub> 立方体の |
| crowbar <sub>n</sub> バール | cubicle <sub>n</sub> 小個室 |
| crowd <sub>n</sub> 群衆、観衆 | cucumber <sub>n</sub> きゅうり |
| crowd <sub>v</sub> 押し寄せる | cuddle <sub>v</sub> 抱き締める |
| crowded <sub>adj</sub> 混雑した | cuff <sub>n</sub> そで口、手錠 |
| crown <sub>n</sub> 王冠、王位 | cuisine <sub>n</sub> 料理 |

C

**culminate** *v* 頂点に達する

**culpability** *n* 有責性

**culprit** *n* 容疑者、罪人

**cult** *n* 狂信的教団

**cultivate** *v* 耕す、栽培する

**cultivation** *n* 耕作、栽培

**cultural** *adj* 文化の、教養の

**culture** *n* 文化、教養

**cumbersome** *adj* 面倒な

**cunning** *adj* 悪賢い

**cup** *n* コップ、茶碗

**cupboard** *n* 食器棚

**curable** *adj* 治癒できる

**curator** *n* 館長、園長

**curb** *v* 縁石をつける

**curb** *n* 歩道の縁石

**curdle** *v* 凝固する

**cure** *v* 治療する、癒す

**cure** *n* 治療、療養

**curfew** *n* 門限

**curiosity** *n* 好奇心

**curious** *adj* 好奇心をそそる

**curl** *v* 巻き毛にする

**curl** *n* 巻き毛、カール

**curly** *adj* 巻いている

**currency** *n* 通貨

**current** *adj* 現在の

**currently** *adv* 現在は

**curse** *v* 呪い、呪文

**curtail** *v* 縮小する

**curtain** *n* カーテン、幕

**curve** *n* 曲線

**curve** *v* 曲線を描く

**cushion** *n* 座布団

**cushion** *v* 和らげる

**cuss** *v* のろう

**custard** *n* カスタード

**custodian** *n* 管理人

**custody** *n* 保管、管理

**custom** *n* 慣習

**customary** *adj* 習慣的な

**customer** *n* 客、顧客

**customs** *n* 関税、税関

**cut** *n* 切ること

**cut** *iv* 切る、削除する

**cut back** *v* 短くする

**cut down** *v* 切り下げる

**cut off** *v* 切り取る

**cut out** *v* 切り抜く

**cute** *adj* かわいい

**cutlery** *n* 刃物類

**cutter** *n* カッター

**cyanide** *n* シアン化物

**cycle** *n* 周期、循環

**cyclist** *n* サイクリスト

**cyclone** *n* 低気圧

**cylinder** *n* 円筒

**cynic** *adj* 皮肉な

**cynicism** *n* 皮肉な言葉

**cypress** *n* 糸杉

**cyst** *n* 嚢胞

**czar** *n* 皇帝

# D

dad *n* おやじ

dagger *n* 短剣、短刀

daily *adv* 毎日の

dairy farm *n* 酪農場

daisy *n* デイジー

dam *n* ダム

damage *n* 損害、被害

damage *v* 破損する

damaging *adj* 損害を与える

damn *v* ののしる

damnation *n* 破滅

damp *adj* 湿気のある

dampen *v* 湿らせる

dance *n* ダンス

dance *v* ダンスする

dancing *n* 踊り、舞踊

dandruff *n* ふけ

danger *n* 危険

dangerous *adj* 危険な

dare *v* 挑戦する

dare *n* 挑戦、大胆

daring *adj* 大胆不敵な

dark *adj* 暗い

darken *v* 暗くなる

darkness *n* 暗さ

darling *adj* 最愛の

darn *v* 〜をのろう

dart *n* ダーツ

dash *v* 突進

dashing *adj* 威勢のいい

data *n* テータ、資料

database *n* データベース

date *n* 日付、年月日

date *v* 日付を付ける

daughter *n* 娘

daughter-in-law *n* 息子の妻

daunt *v* ひるませる

daunting *adj* おびえさせる

dawn *n* 夜明け

day *n* 日、日中

daydream *v* 空想にふける

daze *v* 目をくらませる

dazed *adj* ぼんやりする

dazzle *v* 輝くもの

dazzling *adj* 輝かしい

de luxe *adj* 特別室

deacon *n* 助祭

dead *adj* 死んでいる

dead end *n* 行き止まり

deaden *v* 死滅する

deadline *n* 締め切り

deadlock *adj* 行き詰まりの

deadly *adj* 致死の

deaf *adj* 聴覚障害のある

deafness *n* 難聴

deal *iv* 扱う、配る

deal *n* 取引、取り決め

dealer *n* 販売業者

dealings *n* 取引材料

dean *n* 学部長

dear *adj* 親愛な

**dearly** *adv* 非常に
**death** *n* 死
**death toll** *n* 死亡者数
**death trap** *n* 死の落とし穴
**deathbed** *n* 死の床、臨終
**debase** *v* 品位を落とす
**debatable** *adj* 論争可能な
**debate** *v* 討論する
**debate** *n* 討論
**debit** *n* 負債、借金
**debrief** *v* 報告を受ける
**debris** *n* 破片
**debt** *n* 債務
**debtor** *n* 債務者
**debunk** *v* 誤りを暴く
**debut** *n* 初舞台
**decade** *n* １０年間
**decadence** *n* 退廃
**decapitate** *v* 首を切る
**decay** *v* 腐る、衰える
**decay** *n* 腐食、衰退
**deceased** *adj* 死去した
**deceit** *n* だますこと
**deceitful** *adj* うそつきの
**deceive** *v* うそをつく
**December** *n* １２月
**decency** *n* 礼儀、良識
**decent** *adj* 礼儀正しい
**deception** *n* だまし、うそ
**deceptive** *adj* 見掛け倒しの
**decide** *v* 決定する
**deciding** *adj* 決定的な

**decimal** *adj* 小数の
**decimate** *v* 多くを破壊する
**decipher** *v* 読み解く
**decision** *n* 決定、決意
**decisive** *adj* 決断力のある
**deck** *n* デッキ
**declaration** *n* 公表、宣言
**declare** *v* 宣言する
**declension** *n* 語形変化
**decline** *v* 下降する
**decline** *n* 下降、下落
**decompose** *v* 分解する
**décor** *n* 装飾物
**decorate** *v* 飾る
**decorative** *adj* 装飾的な
**decorum** *n* 礼儀正しさ
**decrease** *v* 減少する
**decrease** *n* 減少
**decree** *n* 法令、布告
**decree** *v* 法令を定める
**decrepit** *adj* 老衰した
**dedicate** *v* 献身する
**dedication** *n* 献身、専念
**deduce** *v* 推定する
**deduct** *v* 控除する
**deductible** *adj* 控除できる
**deduction** *n* 差し引き
**deed** *n* 行為、偉業
**deem** *v* 考える、見なす
**deep** *adj* 深い
**deepen** *v* 深まる
**deer** *n* シカ

deface <sub>v</sub> 外観を損なう

defame <sub>v</sub> 中傷する

defeat <sub>v</sub> 負かす、倒す

defeat <sub>n</sub> 敗北、負け

defect <sub>n</sub> 欠点、欠陥

defect <sub>v</sub> 離脱する

defection <sub>n</sub> 亡命、離脱

defective <sub>adj</sub> 欠点のある

defend <sub>v</sub> 守る、防衛する

defendant <sub>n</sub> 被告人

defender <sub>n</sub> 擁護者

defense <sub>n</sub> 防衛、防御

defenseless <sub>adj</sub> 無防備な人々

defer <sub>v</sub> 引き延ばす

defiance <sub>n</sub> 反逆

defiant <sub>adj</sub> 反抗的な

deficiency <sub>n</sub> 欠乏、決如

deficient <sub>adj</sub> 欠けた

deficit <sub>n</sub> 赤字額

defile <sub>v</sub> 冒とくする

define <sub>v</sub> 定義する

definite <sub>adj</sub> 確かな

definition <sub>n</sub> 定義する

definitive <sub>adj</sub> 最も確実な

deflate <sub>v</sub> 空気が抜ける

deform <sub>v</sub> 変形する

deformity <sub>n</sub> 奇形

defraud <sub>v</sub> 詐欺行為をする

defray <sub>v</sub> 費用を負担する

defrost <sub>v</sub> 霜取り装置

deft <sub>adj</sub> 器用な

defuse <sub>v</sub> 取り除く

defy <sub>v</sub> 逆らう

degenerate <sub>v</sub> 退化する

degenerate <sub>adj</sub> 悪化した

degeneration <sub>n</sub> 悪化、退化

degradation <sub>n</sub> 不名誉

degrade <sub>v</sub> 低下する

degrading <sub>adj</sub> 下品な

degree <sub>n</sub> 度合い

dehydrate <sub>v</sub> 脱水する

deign <sub>v</sub> くれる、賜る

deity <sub>n</sub> 女神

dejected <sub>adj</sub> 落胆した

delay <sub>v</sub> 遅れる

delay <sub>n</sub> 遅延

delegate <sub>v</sub> 委託する

delegate <sub>n</sub> 代表

delegation <sub>n</sub> 代表団

delete <sub>v</sub> 削除する

deliberate <sub>v</sub> 熟考する

deliberate <sub>adj</sub> 熟考した

delicacy <sub>n</sub> 繊細さ

delicate <sub>adj</sub> 繊細な

delicious <sub>adj</sub> おいしい

delight <sub>n</sub> 楽しみ

delight <sub>v</sub> 楽しむ

delightful <sub>adj</sub> 愉快な

delinquency <sub>n</sub> 非行

delinquent <sub>adj</sub> 怠慢な

deliver <sub>v</sub> 配達する

delivery <sub>n</sub> 配達、分娩

delude <sub>v</sub> 信じ込ませる

deluge <sub>n</sub> 大雨、大洪水

delusion *n* 思いこみ
demand *v* 要求する
demand *n* 要求する
demanding *adj* きつい
demean *v* 身を落とす
demeaning *adj* 屈辱的な
demeanor *n* 振る舞い
demented *adj* 発狂した
demise *n* 逝去、終焉
democracy *n* 民主主義
democratic *adj* 民主主義の
demolition *n* 取り壊し
demon *n* 悪霊
demonstrate *v* 実演する
demonstrative *adj* 例証的な
demoralize *v* 士気をくじく
demote *v* 降格させる
den *n* ねぐら
denial *n* 拒否
denigrate *v* 中傷する
Denmak *n* デンマーク
denominator *n* 分母
denote *v* 表示をする
denounce *v* 責める
dense *adj* 濃密な
density *n* 密度
dent *v* へこむ
dent *n* くぼみ
dental *adj* 歯の
dentist *n* 歯医者
dentures *n* 総入れ歯
deny *v* 否定する

deodorant *n* 脱臭剤
depart *v* 出発する
department *n* 局、部
departure *n* 出発、発車
depend *v* 次第である
dependable *adj* 頼もしい
dependence *n* 依存
dependent *adj* 依存している人
depict *v* 描く
deplete *v* 激減させる
deplorable *adj* 悲しむべき
deplore *v* 嘆き悲しむ
deploy *v* 配置につく
deployment *n* 配置、配備
deport *v* 本国送還する
deportation *n* 国外追放
depose *v* 供述する
deposit *n* 預け入れ
depot *n* バス車庫
deprave *adj* 邪魔な
depravity *n* 墜落、邪悪
depreciate *v* 価値が下がる
depreciation *n* 減価償却
depress *v* 押し下げる
depressing *adj* 憂鬱な
depression *n* 恐慌
deprivation *n* はく奪
deprive *v* 奪う
deprived *adj* 貧しい
depth *n* 深さ
derail *v* 脱線する
derailment *n* 脱線する

deranged _adj_ 乱れた
derelict _adj_ 放置された
deride _v_ あざ笑う
derivative _adj_ 派生的な
derive _v_ 引き出す
derogatory _adj_ 軽蔑的な
descend _v_ 降下する
descendant _n_ 子孫
descent _n_ 降下
describe _v_ 描写する
description _n_ 記述、描写
descriptive _adj_ 記述的な
desecrate _v_ 神聖を汚す
desert _n_ 砂漠
desert _v_ 脱走する
deserted _adj_ 見捨てられた
deserter _n_ 見捨てる人
deserve _v_ 値する
deserving _adj_ 資格のある
design _n_ 設計する
designate _v_ 指名する
desirable _adj_ 望ましい
desire _n_ 欲望
desire _v_ 望む、欲する
desist _v_ やめる
desk _n_ 机
desolate _adj_ 荒れ果てた
desolation _n_ 荒らすこと
despair _n_ 絶望
desperate _adj_ 絶望的な
despicable _adj_ 卑劣な
despise _v_ 軽蔑する

despondent _adj_ 落胆した
despot _n_ 専制君主
despotic _adj_ 独裁的な
dessert _n_ デザート
destination _n_ 目的地
destiny _n_ 運命
destitute _adj_ 極貧の
destroy _v_ 破壊する
destroyer _n_ 破壊者
destruction _n_ 破壊
destructive _adj_ 破壊的な
detach _v_ 分離する
detail _n_ 詳細
detail _v_ 詳しく述べる
detain _v_ 拘留する
detect _v_ 見つける
detective _n_ 探偵
detector _n_ 探知機
detention _n_ 監禁
deter _v_ 阻む
detergent _n_ 洗剤
deteriorate _v_ 悪化する
deterioration _n_ 悪化
determination _n_ 決心
determine _v_ 決心する
deterrence _n_ 阻止すること
detest _v_ 嫌悪する
detestable _adj_ 大嫌いな
detonate _v_ 爆発する
detonation _n_ 爆発
detonator _n_ 起爆剤
detour _n_ 回り道

detriment *n* 損害
detrimental *adj* 有害な
devalue *v* 価値が下がる
devastate *v* 壊滅させる
devastating *adj* 破壊的な
devastation *n* 荒廃
develop *v* 発展する
development *n* 発展
deviation *n* 脱線
device *n* 機器、装置
devil *n* 悪魔
devious *adj* 率直でない
devise *v* 発明する
devoid *adj* 欠いている
devote *v* ささげる
devotion *n* 献身的愛情
devour *v* むさぼり食う
devout *adj* 敬けんな
dew *n* 霜、しずく
diabetes *n* 糖尿病
diabetic *adj* 糖尿病の
diabolical *adj* 魔性の
diagnose *v* 診断する
diagnosis *n* 診断
diagonal *adj* 斜め線の
diagram *n* 略図、図表
dial *n* 文字盤
dial *v* ダイヤルを回す
dialect *n* 方言
dialogue *n* 会話、対話
diameter *n* 直径
diamond *n* ダイヤモンド

diaper *n* おむつ
diarrhea *n* 下痢
diary *n* 日記
dice *n* サイコロ
dictate *v* 指図する
dictator *n* 独裁者
dictatorial *adj* 独裁的な
dictatorship *n* 専制君主の
dictionary *n* 辞書
die *v* 死ぬ
die out *v* 絶滅する
diet *n* 食習慣
differ *v* 異なる
difference *n* 違い
different *adj* 違う
difficult *adj* 難しい
difficulty *n* 難しさ
diffuse *v* 普及した
dig *iv* 掘る
digest *v* 消化する
digestion *n* 消化
digestive *adj* 消化の
digit *n* 数字のけた
dignify *v* 威厳をつける
dignitary *n* 高位の人
dignity *n* 威厳
digress *v* 本筋をそれる
dilapidated *adj* 荒廃した
dilemma *n* ジレンマ
diligence *n* 勤勉、骨折り
diligent *adj* 勤勉な
dilute *v* 希薄な

dim *adj* 薄暗い

dim *v* 薄暗くなる

dime *n* １０セント硬貨

dimension *n* 寸法、面積

diminish *v* 縮小する

dine *v* 食事をする

diner *n* 食事をする人

dining room *n* 食堂

dinner *n* 夕食

dinosaur *n* 恐竜

diocese *n* 教区

diphthong *n* 二重母音

diploma *n* 卒業証書

diplomacy *n* 外交関係

diplomat *n* 外交官

diplomatic *adj* 外交の

dire *adj* 悲惨な

direct *adj* 直接の

direct *v* 案内する

direction *n* 方向

director *n* 指導者

directory *n* 住所氏名録

dirt *n* よごれ

dirty *adj* 汚い

disability *n* 無力

disabled *adj* 身体障害のある

disadvantage *n* 不利

disagree *v* 同意しない

disagreeable *adj* 嫌な

disagreement *n* 不一致

disappear *v* 消える

disappearance *n* 失そう

disappoint *v* 失望させる

disappointing *adj* つまらない

disappointment *n* 失望

disapproval *n* 不同意

disapprove *v* 不可とする

disarm *v* 武装解除する

disarmament *n* 軍備縮小

disaster *n* 災害、惨事

disastrous *adj* 破滅的な

disband *v* 解散する

disbelief *n* 疑念、不信

disburse *v* 支払う

discard *v* 放棄する

discern *v* 識別する

discharge *v* 排出する

discharge *n* 放出、解雇

disciple *n* 弟子

discipline *n* 規律

disclaim *v* 否定する

disclose *v* 公開する

discomfort *n* 不快

disconnect *v* 断つ

discontent *adj* 不機嫌な

discontinue *v* 終わる

discord *n* 不和、不一致

discordant *adj* 調和しない

discount *n* 割引

discount *v* ～割引する

discourage *v* がっかりさせる

discouragement *n* 落胆

discouraging *adj* 落胆させる

discourtesy *n* 無礼、不作法

D

**discover** v 発見する

**discovery** n 発見

**discredit** v 信用を落とす

**discreet** adj 配慮した

**discrepancy** n 相違

**discretion** n 分別、思慮

**discriminate** v 差別する

**discrimination** n 差別

**discuss** v 議論する

**discussion** n 議論

**disdain** n 軽蔑

**disease** n 病気

**disembark** v 下船する

**disenchanted** adj 幻滅した

**disentangle** v もつれを解く

**disfigure** v 外観を損なう

**disgrace** n 不名誉

**disgrace** v 面目を失わせる

**disgraceful** adj 不名誉な

**disgruntled** adj 不満な

**disguise** v 変装させる

**disguise** n 変装、偽装

**disgust** n 嫌悪感

**disgusting** adj むかつくような

**dish** n 皿

**dishearten** v 落胆させる

**dishonest** adj 不正直な

**dishonesty** n 不正直

**dishonor** n 不名誉

**dishonorable** adj 恥ずべき

**dishwasher** n 食器洗い機

**disillusion** n 覚醒

**disinfect** v 消毒する

**disinfectant** v 殺菌用の

**disinherit** v 相続権を奪う

**disintegrate** v 分解する

**disintegration** n 分解

**disinterested** adj 私欲のない

**disk** n 円盤

**dislike** v 嫌う

**dislike** n 嫌気

**dislocate** v 位置を変える

**dislodge** v 除去する

**disloyal** adj 不実の

**disloyalty** n 不忠

**dismal** adj 憂うつな

**dismantle** v 取り壊す

**dismay** n 落胆

**dismiss** v 解散する

**dismissal** n 解雇、免職

**dismount** v 降りる

**disobedience** n 不服従

**disobedient** adj 反抗的な

**disobey** v 背く

**disorder** n 無秩序、混乱

**disoriented** adj 狼狽して

**disown** v 勘当する

**disparity** n 格差

**dispatch** v 派遣する

**dispel** v 追い払う

**dispensation** n 分配、制度

**dispense** v 免ずる

**dispersal** n 分散、散布

**disperse** v 分散する

displace _v_ 動かす

display _n_ 表示、露呈

display _v_ 表示する

displease _v_ 不愉快にする

displeasing _adj_ 不愉快な

displeasure _n_ 不満

disposable _adj_ 使い捨ての

disposal _n_ 処分、廃棄

dispose _v_ 処置する

disprove _v_ 反証する

dispute _n_ 論争、紛争

dispute _v_ 議論する

disqualify _v_ 不適格と見なす

disregard _v_ 無視する

disrepair _n_ 破損、荒廃

disrespect _n_ 軽視

disrespectful _adj_ 失礼な

disrupt _v_ 中断させる

disruption _n_ 分裂、崩壊

dissatisfied _adj_ 不満な

disseminate _v_ 広まる

dissent _v_ 異議を唱える

dissident _adj_ 異議のある

dissimilar _adj_ 似ていない

dissipate _v_ 散る

dissolute _adj_ ふしだらな

dissolution _n_ 分解、解体

dissolve _v_ 分解する

dissonant _adj_ 耳障りな

dissuade _v_ やめさせる

distance _n_ 距離

distant _adj_ 距離がある

distaste _n_ 嫌うこと

distasteful _adj_ 嫌な、まずい

distill _v_ 蒸留する

distinct _adj_ はっきりと違う

distinction _n_ 区別、識別

distinctive _adj_ 典型的な

distinguish _v_ 見分ける

distort _v_ 曲げる

distortion _n_ ゆがめること

distract _v_ 気を散らす

distraction _n_ 気を散らすこと

distraught _adj_ 取り乱した

distress _n_ 苦悩、悲嘆

distress _v_ 苦悩している

distressing _adj_ みじめな

distribute _v_ 分配する

distribution _n_ 分配、配布

district _n_ 地区、地域

distrust _n_ 不信、疑惑

distrust _v_ 信用しない

distrustful _adj_ 疑いを抱く

disturb _v_ 妨げる

disturbance _n_ 妨害、騒動

disturbing _adj_ 動揺させる

disunity _n_ 不統一

disuse _n_ 使用停止

ditch _n_ 溝、どぶ

dive _v_ 飛び込む

diver _n_ ダイバー

diverse _adj_ 多様性のある

diversify _v_ 多様化する

diversion _n_ 排水路

**diversity** *n* 多様性

**divert** *v* 迂回する

**divide** *v* 分割する

**dividend** *n* 配当、分け前

**divine** *adj* 神聖な

**diving** *n* 飛び込み

**divinity** *n* 神性、神

**divisible** *adj* 分けられる

**division** *n* 区分、課

**divorce** *n* 離婚

**divorce** *v* 離婚する

**divorcee** *n* 離婚者

**divulge** *v* 漏らす

**dizziness** *n* 目まい

**dizzy** *adj* 目が回る

**do** *iv* する

**docile** *adj* 従順な

**docility** *n* おとなしさ

**dock** *n* 波止場

**doctor** *n* 医者

**doctrine** *n* 教義、原理

**document** *n* 書類、文書

**documentation** *n* 文書化

**dodge** *v* 避ける

**dog** *n* 犬

**dogmatic** *adj* 教義上の

**dole out** *v* 人に与える

**doll** *n* 人形

**dollar** *n* ドル

**dolphin** *n* イルカ

**dome** *n* 半球体

**domestic** *adj* 国産品

**domesticate** *v* 飼いならす

**dominate** *v* 優位に立つ

**domination** *n* 支配、優勢

**domineering** *adj* 支配的な

**dominion** *n* 支配力、領土

**donate** *v* 寄付する

**donation** *n* 寄付金

**donkey** *n* ロバ

**donor** *n* 寄贈者

**doom** *n* 運命、悲運

**doomed** *adj* 絶望的な

**door** *n* ドア、扉

**doorbell** *n* 戸口の呼び鈴

**doorstep** *n* 玄関前の階段

**doorway** *n* 戸口

**dope** *n* ドープ塗料

**dope** *v* 麻薬を常用する

**dormitory** *n* 寮

**dosage** *n* 用量、調剤

**dossier** *n* 関係書類

**dot** *n* 点、小数点

**double** *adj* 2倍の

**double** *v* 倍になる

**double-cross** *v* 欺く

**doubt** *n* 疑い、疑念

**doubt** *v* 疑う

**doubtful** *adj* 疑わしい

**dough** *n* パン生地

**dove** *n* ハト

**down** *adv* 下にある

**down payment** *n* 頭金

**downcast** *adj* うつむいた**

**downfall** _n_ 失墜、失脚
**downhill** _adv_ 下り坂の
**downpour** _n_ 土砂降り
**downsize** _v_ 小型化する
**downstairs** _adv_ 階下に
**down-to-earth** _adj_ 地道な
**downtown** _n_ 繁華街
**downtrodden** _adj_ 抑圧された
**downturn** _n_ 下降、低迷
**dowry** _n_ 持参金
**doze** _n_ まどろみ
**doze** _v_ まどろむ
**dozen** _n_ 12個
**draft** _n_ 下書き、草案
**draft** _v_ 下図を描く
**draftsman** _n_ 製図技師
**drag** _v_ 妨げ、障害
**dragon** _n_ 竜、ドラゴン
**drain** _v_ 下水管
**drainage** _n_ 排水
**dramatic** _adj_ 劇的な
**dramatize** _v_ 脚色する
**drape** _n_ カーテン
**drastic** _adj_ 激烈な
**draw** _n_ 呼び物
**draw** _iv_ 描く、〜を引く
**drawback** _n_ 障害、不利
**drawer** _n_ 引き出し
**drawing** _n_ 描画
**dread** _v_ 恐れる
**dreaded** _adj_ 非常に恐ろしい
**dreadful** _adj_ 恐ろしい

**dream** _iv_ 夢を見る
**dream** _n_ 夢
**dress** _n_ 衣服、ドレス
**dress** _v_ 衣服を着る
**dresser** _n_ 着付け係
**dressing** _n_ 着付け、身支度
**dried** _adj_ 乾いた
**drift** _v_ 漂流する
**drift apart** _v_ 離れていく
**drifter** _n_ 漂流者
**drill** _v_ 穴を開ける
**drill** _n_ ドリル、演習
**drink** _iv_ 飲む
**drink** _n_ 飲み物
**drinkable** _adj_ 飲んでも安全な
**drinker** _n_ 酒飲み
**drip** _v_ 滴る
**drip** _n_ 点滴
**drive** _n_ 運転
**drive** _iv_ 運転する
**drive at** _v_ 意図する
**drive away** _v_ 車で走り去る
**driver** _n_ 運転手
**driveway** _n_ 私道
**drizzle** _v_ 霧雨が降る
**drizzle** _n_ 霧雨
**drop** _n_ 滴
**drop** _v_ 落ちる
**drop in** _v_ 立ち寄る
**drop off** _v_ 〜から落ちる
**drop out** _v_ 脱落する
**drought** _n_ 日照り

D

**drown** v おぼれる
**drowsy** adj 眠い
**drug** n 麻薬、薬物
**drug** v 薬物中毒である
**drugstore** n 薬局
**drum** n 太鼓、ドラム
**drunk** adj 酔っ払った
**drunkenness** n 酒気
**dry** v 乾く
**dry** adj 乾いた
**dryer** n 乾燥機
**dual** adj 二重の
**dubious** adj 疑わしく思う
**duchess** n 公爵夫人
**duck** n アヒル、鴨
**duck** v かがむ、かわす
**duct** n 導管
**due** adj ～する予定である
**duel** n 決闘
**dues** n 会費、組合費
**duke** n 公爵
**dull** adj 鈍い、だるい
**duly** adv 正式に、十分に
**dumb** adj 間抜けな
**dummy** n 模型、ダミー
**dummy** adj 模造の
**dump** v 投げ捨てる
**dump** n ごみ捨て場
**dung** n 糞、こやし
**dungeon** n 地下牢
**dupe** v だます
**duplicate** v 複製、写し

**duplication** n 重複
**durable** adj 耐久性のある
**duration** n 持続期間
**during** pre ～の間に
**dusk** n 夕暮れ
**dust** n ほこり、ちり
**Dutch** adj オランダ
**duty** n 義務、職務
**dwarf** n 小人
**dwell** v 住む、存在する
**dwelling** n 住居
**dwindle** v 縮まる
**dye** v 染める
**dye** n 染料
**dying** adj 死にかけている
**dynamic** adj 力強い
**dynamite** n ダイナマイト
**dynasty** n 王朝

**E**

**each** adj それぞれの
**each other** adj お互いに
**eager** adj 切望している
**eagerness** n 熱望
**eagle** n ワシ
**ear** n 耳
**earache** n 耳痛

eardrum *n* 鼓膜

early *adv* 早く

earmark *v* 耳標を付ける

earn *v* 得る、稼ぐ

earnestly *adv* まじめに

earnings *n* 収益、所得

earphones *n* イヤホン

earring *n* イヤリング

earth *n* 地球

earthquake *n* 地震

earwax *n* 耳垢

ease *v* 緩む

ease *n* 容易さ

easily *adv* 簡単に

east *n* 東

eastbound *adj* 東回りの

Easter *n* 東風

eastern *adj* 東の、東洋の

easterner *n* 東部地方の人

eastward *adv* 東方へ

easy *adj* 簡単な

eat *iv* 食べる

eat away *v* 侵食する

eavesdrop *v* 雨垂れ

ebb *v* 引き潮

eccentric *adj* 変わった

echo *n* エコー、反響

eclipse *n* 日食、月食

ecology *n* 生態学

economical *adj* 経済的な

economize *v* 倹約する

economy *n* 経済、節約

ecstasy *n* 有頂天

edge *n* 端、へり

edgy *adj* 縁のするどい

edible *adj* 食べられる

edifice *n* 大建造物

edit *v* 編集、社説

edition *n* 版

educate *v* 教育する

educational *adj* 教育的な

eerie *adj* 不気味な

effect *n* 効果

effective *adj* 効果的な

effectiveness *n* 有効性

efficiency *n* 能率、効率

efficient *adj* 能率的な

effigy *n* 肖像、彫像

effort *n* 努力

egg *n* 卵

egg white *n* 卵白

egoism *n* 利己主義

egoist *n* 利己主義者

eight *adj* 8、8個

eighteen *adj* 18個

eighth *adj* 8分の1

eighty *adj* 80個の

either *adj* どちらか一方の

either *adv* 〜も〜しない

eject *v* 脱出する

elapse *v* 経過する

elastic *adj* 弾力性のある

elated *adj* 得意の

elbow *n* ひじ

**elder** *n* 年長者
**elderly** *adj* 年配の
**elect** *v* 選挙する
**election** *n* 選挙
**electric** *adj* 電気の
**electrician** *n* 電気技師
**electricity** *n* 電気、電力
**electrify** *v* 電気を流す
**electrocute** *v* 感電死する
**electronic** *adj* 電子の
**elegance** *n* 優雅、気品
**elegant** *adj* 優雅な
**element** *n* 成分、要素
**elementary** *adj* 初歩的な
**elephant** *n* 象
**elevate** *v* 持ち上げる
**elevation** *n* 高度、標高
**elevator** *n* エレベーター
**eleven** *adj* １１個の
**eleventh** *adj* 第１１
**eligible** *adj* 資格のある
**eliminate** *v* 削除する
**elm** *n* ニレの木
**eloquence** *n* 雄弁
**else** *adv* 別の方法で
**elsewhere** *adv* ほかの場所に
**elude** *v* 回避する
**emaciated** *adj* やせ衰えた
**emanate** *v* 放射する
**emancipate** *v* 解放する
**embalm** *v* 香気を満たす
**embark** *v* 乗船する

**embarrass** *v* 当惑させる
**embassy** *n* 大使館
**embellish** *v* 装飾する
**embers** *n* 残り火
**embezzle** *v* 横領する
**embitter** *v* 苦くさせる
**emblem** *n* 紋章、象徴
**embody** *v* 具体化する
**emboss** *v* 浮き彫りにする
**embrace** *v* 抱きしめる
**embrace** *n* 抱擁、包囲
**embroider** *v* 刺しゅうをする
**embroidery** *n* 刺しゅう
**embroil** *v* 巻き込む
**embryo** *n* 胎児、胚
**emerald** *n* エメラルド
**emerge** *v* 現れる
**emergency** *n* 緊急事態
**emigrant** *n* 移民
**emigrate** *v* 移住する
**emission** *n* 放出、排出
**emit** *v* 放つ
**emotion** *n* 感情
**emotional** *adj* 感情的な
**emperor** *n* 皇帝、天皇
**emphasis** *n* 強調
**emphasize** *v* 強調する
**empire** *n* 帝国
**employ** *v* 雇う
**employee** *n* 従業員
**employer** *n* 雇用者
**employment** *n* 雇用**

empress *n* 皇后
emptiness *n* 空虚
empty *adj* 空の
empty *v* 空になる
enable *v* 有効にする
enchant *v* 魅了する
enchanting *adj* 魅惑的な
encircle *v* 取り巻く
enclave *n* 居留地
enclose *v* 同封する
enclosure *n* 囲い、包囲
encompass *v* 包囲する
encounter *v* 出合う
encounter *n* 遭遇、出会い
encourage *v* 勇気づける
encroach *v* 侵入する
encyclopedia *n* 百科事典
end *n* 終わり、終局
end *v* 終わる
end up *v* 〜で終わる
endanger *v* 危うくする
endeavor *v* 努力する
endeavor *n* 努力、試み
ending *n* 結末、末期
endless *adj* 終わりのない
endorse *v* 裏書きする
endorsement *n* 裏書、保証
endure *v* 耐える
enemy *n* 敵、敵国
energetic *adj* 活発な
energy *n* 活力、精力
enforce *v* 実行する

engage *v* 約束する
engaged *adj* 予約済みの
engagement *n* 約束、婚約
engine *n* エンジン
engineer *n* 技術者
England *n* イギリス
English *adj* イギリスの
engrave *v* 刻む
engraving *n* 彫刻、版画
engrossed *adj* 没頭した
engulf *v* 巻き込む
enhance *v* さらによくする
enjoy *v* 楽しむ
enjoyable *adj* 楽しめる
enjoyment *n* 喜び、楽しみ
enlarge *v* 大きくなる
enlargement *n* 拡大
enlighten *v* 啓発する
enlist *v* 入隊する
enormous *adj* 莫大な
enough *adv* 十分な、足りる
enrage *v* 激怒させる
enrich *v* 充実させる
enroll *v* 名前を登録する
enrollment *n* 登録
ensure *v* 確かにする
entail *v* 伴う、課す
entangle *v* もつれさせる
enter *v* 入る
enterprise *n* 企業、事業
entertain *v* 楽しませる
entertaining *adj* 愉快な

E

entertainment _n_ 楽しみ、娯楽
enthrall _v_ 夢中にさせる
enthuse _v_ 熱中する
enthusiasm _n_ 熱心
entice _v_ 誘惑する
enticement _n_ 誘惑
enticing _adj_ 誘惑的な
entire _adj_ 全体の
entirely _adv_ 全く
entrance _n_ 入り口、玄関
entreat _v_ 懇願する
entree _n_ 前菜、入場権
entrenched _adj_ 慢性の
entrepreneur _n_ 起業家
entrust _v_ 委ねる
entry _n_ 参加
enumerate _v_ 列挙する
envelop _v_ くるむ、包む
envelope _n_ 封筒
envious _adj_ うらやましい
environment _n_ 環境
envisage _v_ 心に描く
envoy _n_ 使節
envy _n_ うらやましさ
envy _v_ うらやましがる
epidemic _n_ 流行、まん延
epilepsy _n_ てんかん
episode _n_ 挿話
epistle _n_ 書簡
epitaph _n_ 墓碑名
epitomize _v_ 典型となる
epoch _n_ 時代、時期

equal _adj_ 同等の
equality _n_ 平等
equate _v_ 一致する
equation _n_ 方程式
equator _n_ 赤道
equilibrium _n_ 均衡
equip _v_ 備える
equipment _n_ 備品、道具
equivalent _adj_ 相当する
era _n_ 時代、年代
eradicate _v_ 全滅させる
erase _v_ 消す
eraser _n_ 消しゴム
erect _v_ 直立する
erect _adj_ 直立した
err _v_ 過ちを犯す
errand _n_ 使い、用事
erroneous _adj_ 間違った
error _n_ 誤り、間違い
erupt _v_ 噴出する
eruption _n_ 噴火
escalator _n_ エスカレーター
escapade _n_ 脱線
escape _v_ 逃亡する
escort _n_ 付添人
esophagus _n_ 食道
especially _adv_ 特に
espionage _n_ スパイ
essay _n_ 小論、エッセー
essence _n_ 本質
essential _adj_ 本質的要素
establish _v_ 定着する

estate *n* 私有地、地所

esteem *v* 尊重する

estimate *v* 見積もる

estimation *n* 見積もり

estranged *adj* 疎遠になった

estuary *n* 河口、入り江

eternity *n* 永遠

ethical *adj* 倫理学の

ethics *n* 倫理学

etiquette *n* 礼儀

euphoria *n* 幸福感

Europe *n* ヨーロッパ

European *adj* ヨーロッパ人

evacuate *v* 避難する

evade *v* 回避する

evaluate *v* 評価する

evaporate *v* 蒸発する

evasion *n* 逃れること

evasive *adj* 回避的な

eve *n* 前日、前夜

even *adj* 均等の、等しい

even if *c* たとえ〜でも

even more *c* さらに

evening *n* 夜

event *n* 出来事

eventuality *n* 偶然性

eventually *adv* 最終的に

ever *adv* 今までに

everlasting *adj* 永遠の

every *adj* あらゆる

everybody *pro* 誰でも

everyday *adj* 毎日の

everyone *pro* あらゆる人

everything *pro* すべてのもの

evict *v* 立ち退かせる

evidence *n* 証拠、証言

evil *n* 悪、不運

evil *adj* 悪い、邪悪な

evoke *v* 喚起する

evolution *n* 進化

evolve *v* 進化する

exact *adj* 正確な

exaggerate *v* 誇張する

exalt *v* 高める

examination *n* 試験、検査

examine *v* 観察する

example *n* 例

exasperate *v* 憤慨させる

excavate *v* 掘る

exceed *v* 超える

exceedingly *adv* 非常に

excel *v* ほかに勝る

excellence *n* 優秀、卓越

excellent *adj* 優秀な

except *pre* 除いて

exception *n* 例外、除外

exceptional *adj* 例外的な

excerpt *n* 抜粋、引用

excess *n* 過度、過剰

excessive *adj* 過度の

exchange *v* 交換する

excite *v* 興奮させる

excitement *n* 興奮

exciting *adj* 刺激的な

E

**exclaim** v 叫ぶ

**exclude** v 排除する

**excruciating** adj 極度に痛い

**excursion** n 遠足、小旅行

**excuse** v 脇道にそれる

**excuse** n 言い訳、弁解

**execute** v 実行する

**executive** n 幹部、高官

**exemplary** adj 称賛すべき

**exemplify** v 実証する

**exempt** adj 免除する

**exemption** n 免除

**exercise** n 運動、実行

**exercise** v 運動する

**exert** v 発揮する

**exertion** n 激しい活動

**exhaust** v 排気

**exhaustion** n 極度の疲労

**exhibit** v 展示する

**exhibition** n 展示会

**exhilarating** adj 陽気にさせる

**exhort** v 強く勧める

**exile** v 追放する

**exile** n 追放

**exist** v 存在する

**existence** n 存在

**exit** n 出口、退場

**exodus** n 集団脱出

**exonerate** v 容疑を晴らす

**exorbitant** adj 途方もない

**exorcist** n エクソシスト

**exotic** adj 異国風の

**expand** v 拡大する

**expansion** n 拡大

**expect** v 予期する

**expectancy** n 見込み、予想

**expectation** n 期待、予想

**expediency** n 便宜、好都合

**expedient** adj 得策の

**expedition** n 探検、急速

**expel** v 除名する

**expenditure** n 出費、支出

**expense** n 費用、経費

**expensive** adj 高価な

**experience** n 経験

**experiment** n 実験

**expert** adj 熟達した

**expiate** v 償う

**expiation** n 罪滅ぼし

**expiration** n 期限切れ

**expire** v 満了する

**explain** v 説明する

**explicit** adj 明白な

**explode** v 爆発する

**exploit** v 不当に使う

**exploit** n 手柄、功績

**exploitation** n 開発、開拓

**explore** v 調査する

**explorer** n 探検者

**explosion** n 爆発音

**explosive** adj 爆発性の

**export** v 輸出する

**expose** v 露出する

**exposed** adj 露出した

**express** *adj* 特別の
**expression** *n* 表現、表情
**expressly** *adv* はっきりと
**expropriate** *v* 取り上げる
**expulsion** *n* 追放、除名
**exquisite** *adj* 優れた
**extend** *v* 伸びる
**extension** *n* 拡張、伸張
**extent** *n* 広さ、範囲
**extenuating** *adj* 情状酌量すべき
**exterior** *adj* 外側
**exterminate** *v* 絶滅させる
**external** *adj* 外側の
**extinct** *adj* 死に絶えた
**extinguish** *v* 火を消す
**extort** *v* 強要する
**extortion** *n* ゆすり、強要
**extra** *adv* 余分な
**extract** *v* 引き抜く
**extradite** *v* 送還する
**extradition** *n* 送還
**extraneous** *adj* 外来の
**extravagance** *n* 浪費
**extravagant** *adj* ぜいたくな
**extreme** *adj* 極端な
**extremist** *adj* 過激主義的な
**extremities** *n* 極度、先端
**extricate** *v* 解放する
**extroverted** *adj* 外交的な
**exude** *v* にじみ出る
**exult** *v* 歓喜する
**eye** *n* 目

**eyebrow** *n* 眉毛
**eye-catching** *adj* 目立つ
**eyeglasses** *n* メガネ
**eyelash** *n* まつげ
**eyelid** *n* まぶた
**eyesight** *n* 視力
**eyewitness** *n* 目撃者

E
F

**fable** *n* 寓話
**fabric** *n* 織物、布
**fabricate** *v* 組み立てる
**fabulous** *adj* 驚くべき
**face** *n* 顔
**face up to** *v* 〜に立ち向かう
**facet** *n* 面、様相
**facilitate** *v* 容易にする
**facing** *pre* 前向きの
**fact** *n* 事実
**factor** *n* 要因、因数
**factory** *n* 工場、製造所
**factual** *adj* 実際の
**faculty** *n* 教授陣、能力
**fad** *n* 一時的流行
**fade** *v* 弱まる、あせる
**faded** *adj* 消えかかった
**fail** *v* 失敗する

**F**

failure *n* 失敗、不成功

faint *v* 気絶する

faint *n* 気絶、失神

faint *adj* かすかな

fair *n* 美女

fair *adj* 快晴の

fairness *n* 公平

fairy *n* 妖精

faith *n* 信頼、信仰

faithful *adj* 信頼できる

fake *v* 偽物

fake *adj* 偽の

fall *n* 落下

fall *iv* 落ちる、降る

fall back *v* 後退する

fall behind *v* 後れをとる

fall down *v* 転ぶ

fall through *v* 失敗に終わる

fallacy *n* 間違った考え

fallout *n* 放射性降下物

falsehood *n* うそ

falsify *v* 偽る

falter *v* ためらう

fame *n* 名声

familiar *adj* おなじみの

family *n* 家族

famine *n* 飢饉、飢え

famous *adj* 有名な

fan *n* 扇風機

fanatic *adj* 熱狂的な

fancy *adj* 派手な

fang *n* 牙、歯根

fantastic *adj* 素晴らしい

fantasy *n* 空想

far *adv* 遠い、遠くへの

faraway *adj* 遠方の

farce *n* 茶番

fare *n* 運賃、料金

farewell *n* 別れ

farm *n* 農場、農園

farmer *n* 農場経営者

farming *n* 農場、飼育

farmyard *n* 農家の庭

farther *adv* さらに遠い

fascinate *v* 魅惑する

fashion *n* 流行

fashionable *adj* 流行の

fast *adj* 速い

fasten *v* 留める、締める

fat *n* 脂肪

fat *adj* でぶの

fatal *adj* 致命的な

fate *n* 運命

fateful *adj* 運命を決する

father *n* 父親

fatherhood *n* 父権

father-in-law *n* 義理の父

fatherly *adj* 父親らしい

fathom out *v* ～を理解する

fatigue *n* 疲れ、疲労

fatten *v* 太らせる

fatty *adj* でぶ

faucet *n* 蛇口

fault *n* 責任、過ち

faulty *adj* 欠点のある

favor *n* 親切、好意

favorable *adj* 有利な

favorite *adj* お気に入りの

fear *n* 恐れ、懸念

fearful *adj* 恐ろしい

feasible *adj* 可能な

feast *n* 祝宴

feat *n* 手柄、功績

feather *n* 羽

feature *n* 特徴、顔立ち

February *n* 2月

federal *adj* 連邦政府の

fee *n* 手数料、料金

feeble *adj* か弱い

feed *iv* 食べ物を与える

feedback *n* 反響、反応

feel *iv* 感じ

feeling *n* 感覚、感触

feelings *n* 感情、思い

feet *n* 足

feign *v* 〜を装う

fellow *n* 仲間、同輩

fellowship *n* 仲間同士

felon *n* 重罪犯人

felony *n* 重罪

female *n* 女性

feminine *adj* 女性らしい

fence *n* フェンス

fencing *n* フェンシング

fend *v* 生活する

fend off *v* 受け流す

fender *n* 泥よけ

ferment *v* 発酵する

ferment *n* 発酵、酵素

ferocious *adj* 凶暴な

ferocity *n* 凶暴性

ferry *n* フェリー

fertile *adj* 肥えた

fertility *n* 肥沃、多産

fertilize *v* 肥やす

fervent *adj* 熱心な

fester *v* 化膿する

festive *adj* 祝祭の

festivity *n* 祭典、祝祭

fetid *adj* 悪臭のする

fetus *n* 胎児

feud *n* 確執

fever *n* 熱

feverish *adj* 熱がある

few *adj* 少数の

fewer *adj* より少ない

fiancé *n* 男性の婚約者

fiber *n* 繊維

fickle *adj* 変わりやすい

fiction *n* 創作

fictitious *adj* 架空の

fidelity *n* 厳守、忠誠

field *n* 野原、競技場

fierce *adj* 荒々しい

fiery *adj* 火のような

fifteen *adj* 15、15個

fifth *adj* 第5、5分の1

fifty *adj* 50、50個

F

**fifty-fifty** *adv* 五分五分の
**fig** *n* イチジク
**fight** *iv* 戦う、競う
**fight** *n* 戦い、格闘
**fighter** *n* 戦士
**figure** *n* 形、外観
**figure out** *v* 見つけ出す
**file** *v* 申請する
**file** *n* 書類、ファイル
**fill** *v* 満ちる
**filling** *n* 中身、注入
**film** *n* フィルム、映画
**filter** *n* ろ過器
**filter** *v* ろ過される
**filth** *n* ごみ、悪党
**filthy** *adj* 汚れた
**fin** *n* ヒレ
**final** *adj* 最後のもの
**finalize** *v* 終わらせる
**finance** *v* 助成する
**financial** *adj* 金銭上の
**find** *iv* 捜す
**find out** *v* 調査する
**fine** *n* 微粒子、罰金
**fine** *v* 罰金を科す
**fine** *adv* 細かい、晴れた
**fine** *adj* すてきな
**finger** *n* 指
**fingernail** *n* 指のつめ
**fingerprint** *n* 指紋
**fingertip** *n* 指先
**finish** *v* 終わる

**Finland** *n* フィンランド
**Finnish** *adj* フィンランド人
**fire** *v* 火を付ける
**fire** *n* 火
**firearm** *n* 銃器
**firecracker** *n* 爆竹
**firefighter** *n* 消防士
**fireman** *n* 機関士
**fireplace** *n* 暖炉
**firewood** *n* 薪
**fireworks** *n* 花火
**firm** *adj* 堅い、頑丈な
**firm** *n* 事務所、会社
**firmness** *n* 堅さ
**first** *adj* 一番目の
**fish** *n* 魚
**fisherman** *n* 漁師
**fishy** *adj* 魚のような
**fist** *n* 握りこぶし
**fit** *n* ひきつけ
**fit** *v* 適する
**fitness** *n* 健康
**fitting** *adj* 似合いの
**five** *adj* 5の、5個の
**fix** *v* 修理する
**fjord** *n* フィヨルド
**flag** *n* 旗
**flagpole** *n* 旗棒
**flamboyant** *adj* 華々しい
**flame** *n* 炎
**flammable** *adj* 燃えやすい
**flank** *n* 横腹、わき腹

flare *n* 発煙筒
flare-up *v* 激発する
flash *n* 瞬間
flashlight *n* 懐中電灯
flashy *adj* 派手な
flat *n* 平面
flat *adj* 平らな
flatten *v* 平らになる
flatter *v* お世辞を言う
flattery *n* お世辞
flaunt *v* 見せびらかす
flavor *n* 香味料
flaw *n* 欠陥、不備
flawless *adj* 欠点のない
flea *n* ノミ
flee *iv* 逃げる
fleece *n* ヒツジの毛
fleet *n* 海軍、艦隊
fleeting *adj* つかの間
flesh *n* 肉
flex *v* 収縮する
flexible *adj* 柔軟性のある
flicker *v* 揺らめく炎
flier *n* チラシ、飛行士
flight *n* 飛行
flimsy *adj* 薄っぺらな
flip *v* 反転する
flirt *v* 浮気をする
float *v* 浮かぶ
flock *n* 群れ
flog *v* はためく
flood *v* はんらんする

floodgate *n* 水門
flooding *n* はんらん
floodlight *n* 投光照明
floor *n* 床
flop *n* 大失敗
floss *n* 綿毛
flour *n* 小麦粉
flourish *v* 繁栄する
flow *v* 流れる
flow *n* 流れ
flower *n* 花火
flowerpot *n* 植木鉢
flu *n* インフルエンザ
fluctuate *v* 変動する
fluently *adv* 流暢に
fluid *n* 流動体
flunk *v* 落第する
flush *v* 赤らみ、赤面
flute *n* フルート
flutter *v* 揺れる
fly *iv* 飛ぶ
fly *n* 飛ぶこと、飛行
foam *n* 泡、あぶく
focus *n* 焦点、的
focus on *v* 焦点を合わせる
foe *n* 敵、反対者
fog *n* 霧、濃霧
foggy *adj* 霧のかかった
foil *v* アルミ箔
fold *v* 折る
folder *n* フォルダー
folks *n* 親しい人

F

**folksy** *adj* 庶民的な
**follow** *v* 〜について行く
**follower** *n* 信棒者
**folly** *n* 愚かなこと
**fond** *adj* 好きな
**fondle** *v* なで回す
**fondness** *n* 好み
**food** *n* 食物
**foodstuff** *n* 食材
**fool** *v* ふざける
**fool** *adj* 愚かなこと
**foolproof** *adj* 誰にでもできる
**foot** *n* 足
**football** *n* フットボール
**footnote** *n* 脚注
**footprint** *n* 足跡
**footstep** *n* 足音
**footwear** *n* 履き物
**for** *pre* 〜のために
**forbid** *iv* 禁じる
**force** *n* 力、強さ
**force** *v* 強いる
**forceful** *adj* 力強い
**forcibly** *adv* 強制的に
**forecast** *iv* 予見する
**forefront** *n* 最前部
**foreground** *n* 最前面
**forehead** *n* 額、前面
**foreign** *adj* 外国の
**foreigner** *n* 外国人
**foreman** *n* 監督、主任
**foremost** *adj* 第一の

**foresee** *iv* 予感する
**foreshadow** *v* 前兆となる
**foresight** *n* 先見の明
**forest** *n* 森林
**foretaste** *n* 前触れ
**foretell** *v* 予言する
**forever** *adv* 永遠に
**forewarn** *v* 予測する
**foreword** *n* 前書き
**forfeit** *v* 喪失する
**forge** *v* 立案する
**forgery** *n* 偽造
**forget** *v* 忘れる
**forgivable** *adj* 許せる
**forgive** *v* 許す
**forgiveness** *n* 許し、容赦
**fork** *n* フォーク
**form** *n* 外形、構造
**formal** *adj* 型にはまった
**formality** *n* 形式的、儀礼
**formalize** *v* 儀式を張る
**formally** *adv* 正式に
**format** *n* 型、構成
**formation** *n* 形成、成立
**former** *adj* 前者
**formerly** *adv* 元は、昔は
**formidable** *adj* 恐怖心
**formula** *n* 公式
**forsake** *iv* 見捨てる
**fort** *n* とりで
**forthcoming** *adj* 来たるべき
**forthright** *adj* 真っすぐの

fortify *v* 補強する

fortitude *n* 不屈の精神

fortress *n* 要塞

fortunate *adj* 幸福な

fortune *n* 富、財産

forty *adj* 40個の

forward *adv* 前方への

fossil *n* 化石

foster *v* 育てる

foul *adj* くさい

foundation *n* 土台、礎

founder *n* 創始者

foundry *n* 鋳物工場

fountain *n* 噴水

four *adj* 4、4個の

fourteen *adj* 14個の

fourth *adj* 第4番目

fox *n* キツネ

foxy *adj* ずるい

fraction *n* ごく少量

fracture *n* 骨折、割れ目

fragile *adj* 壊れやすい

fragment *n* 破片

fragrance *n* 香り、香料

fragrant *adj* 良い香りの

frail *adj* 虚弱な

frailty *n* 弱点

frame *n* 骨組み

frame *v* 骨組みを作る

framework *n* 骨組み

France *n* フランス

franchise *n* 特権

frank *adj* 率直な

frankly *adv* 率直に

frankness *n* 率直さ

frantic *adj* 取り乱した

fraternal *adj* 兄弟のような

fraud *n* 詐欺

fraudulent *adj* 詐欺的な

freckle *n* そばかす

freckled *adj* そばかすのある

free *v* 自由にする

free *adj* 自由に

freedom *n* 自由

freeway *n* 高速道路

freeze *iv* 氷結、凍結

freezer *n* 冷凍庫

freezing *adj* 凍えるような

freight *n* 積荷

French *adj* フランス人

frenetic *adj* 熱狂した

frenzied *adj* ひどく興奮した

frenzy *n* 熱狂

frequency *n* 頻発、頻度

frequent *adj* たびたび起こる

frequent *v* しばしば起こる

fresh *adj* 新鮮な

freshen *v* 新しくする

freshness *n* 新鮮味

friar *n* 修道士

friction *n* 摩擦

Friday *n* 金曜日

fried *adj* 揚げ物の

friend *n* 友達

**friendship** n 友情
**fries** n フリゼ
**frigate** n 小型快速船
**fright** n 恐怖
**frighten** v 怖がらせる
**frightening** adj 恐ろしい
**frigid** adj ひどく寒い
**fringe** n へり、縁
**frivolous** adj つまらない
**frog** n カエル
**from** pre ～から
**front** n 正面
**front** adj 正面の
**frontage** n 間口
**frontier** n 国境
**frost** n 霜
**frostbite** n 凍傷
**frosty** adj 霜の降りた
**frown** v 顔をしかめる
**frozen** adj 冷凍の
**frugal** adj 質素な
**frugality** n 倹約、質素
**fruit** n 果物
**fruitful** adj 実り多い
**frustrate** v イライラさせる
**frustration** n 欲求不満
**fry** v 油で揚げる
**frying pan** n フライパン
**fuel** n 燃料
**fuel** v 燃料を供給する
**fugitive** n 逃亡者
**fulfill** v 満足させる

**fulfillment** n 満足感、成就
**full** adj いっぱいの
**fully** adv 十分に
**fumes** n 噴煙
**fumigate** v いぶす
**fun** n 楽しみ
**function** n 機能、働き
**fund** n 蓄え、資金
**fund** v 資金を出す
**fundamental** adj 基本となる
**funds** n 預金
**funeral** n 葬式
**fungus** n 菌類
**funny** adj 変な
**fur** n 毛皮
**furious** adj 激怒した
**furiously** adv 荒れ狂って
**furnace** n かまど
**furnish** v 備える
**furnishings** n 服飾品
**furniture** n 家具
**furor** n 騒動
**furrow** n 溝、わだち
**furry** adj 毛皮製の
**further** adv もっと遠い
**furthermore** adv その上に
**fury** n 激怒、憤慨
**fuse** n ヒューズ
**fusion** n 溶解
**fuss** n 大騒ぎ
**fussy** adj 気難しい
**futile** adj 無益な

futility *n* 無益
future *n* 将来
fuzzy *adj* 綿毛状の

# G

gadget *n* 装置、道具
gag *n* 冗談、猿ぐつわ
gag *v* 口止めをする
gage *v* 計測器
gain *v* 利益を得る
gain *n* 利益
gal *n* ガル
galaxy *n* 星雲
gale *n* 強風、疾風
gall bladder *n* 胆嚢
gallant *adj* 礼儀正しい
gallery *n* 画廊
gallon *n* ガロン
gallop *v* ギャロップ
gallows *n* 絞首台
galvanize *v* 電気をかける
gamble *v* 賭ける
game *n* 遊び
gang *n* 非行集団
gangrene *n* 壊疽
gangster *n* 暴力団員
gap *n* 格差、すき間

garage *n* 車庫
garbage *n* 生ゴミ
garden *n* 庭
gardener *n* 植木屋
gargle *v* うがい
garland *n* 花飾り
garlic *n* ニンニク
garment *n* 衣類
garnish *v* 飾る
garnish *n* 装飾
garrison *n* 駐屯地
garrulous *adj* おしゃべりな
garter *n* 靴下留め
gas *n* ガス
gash *n* 溝
gasoline *n* ガソリン
gasp *v* 息が止まる
gastric *adj* 胃の
gate *n* 入り口、門
gather *v* 寄り集まる
gathering *n* 集まり
gauge *v* 計る、測る
gauze *n* ガーゼ
gaze *v* じっと見る
gear *n* ギア、歯車
gem *n* 宝石、珠玉
gender *n* 性別
gene *n* 遺伝子
general *n* 概要、将官
generalize *v* 一般化する
generate *v* 〜を生む
generation *n* 同世代の人々

F
G

generator *n* 発電機

generic *adj* 属の

generosity *n* 寛容、寛大

genetic *adj* 遺伝の

genial *adj* 朗らかな

genius *n* 天才

genocide *n* 大虐殺

genteel *adj* 上品ぶった

gentle *adj* 優しい

gentleman *n* 紳士

gentleness *n* 優しさ

genuflect *v* ひざまずく

genuine *adj* 本物の

geography *n* 地理学

geology *n* 地質学

geometry *n* 幾何学

germ *n* 細菌、病原菌

German *adj* ドイツ人

Germany *n* ドイツ

germinate *v* 生まれる

gerund *n* 動名詞

gestation *n* 立案

gesture *n* 手まね

get *iv* 着く、至る

get along *v* やっていく

get away *v* 免れる

get back *v* 下がる、帰る

get down *v* 下げる

get down to *v* 取り掛かる

get in *v* 中に入る

get off *v* 降りる、離す

get out *v* 外で出る

get over *v* 乗り越える

get together *v* 一緒になる

get up *v* 起き上がる

geyser *n* 間欠泉

ghastly *adj* 不気味な

ghost *n* 幽霊

giant *n* 巨人

gift *n* 贈り物

gifted *adj* 才能のある

gigantic *adj* 膨大な

giggle *v* クスクス笑い

gimmick *n* 策略

ginger *n* 生姜

gingerly *adv* 極めて慎重に

giraffe *n* キリン

girl *n* 少女、女の子

girlfriend *n* 女友達

give *iv* 与える、渡す

give away *v* 寄贈する

give back *v* 返す

give in *v* 屈する

give out *v* 配る、発する

give up *v* あきらめる

glacier *n* 氷河

glad *adj* 満足して

gladiator *n* 剣闘士

glamorous *adj* 魅惑的な

glance *v* ちらりと

glance *n* ひと目

gland *n* 体の腺

glare *n* ギラギラする光

glass *n* ガラス

glasses n メガネ
glassware n ガラス製品
gleam n かすかな光
gleam v 光る、輝く
glide v 滑る、滑空する
glimmer n チラチラする光
glimpse n チラッと見ること
glimpse v ちらりと見る
glitter v 輝き、きらめき
globe n 地球、球体
globule n 小球
gloom n 闇
gloomy adj 憂うつな
glorify v 栄光をたたえる
glorious adj 名誉となる
glory n 栄光
gloss n 光沢、つや
glossary n 用語集
glossy adj 光沢のある
glove n 手袋、グローブ
glow v 白熱する
glucose n ブドウ糖
glue n のり
glue v 接着剤でつける
glut n 満腹
glutton n 大食家
gnaw. v ガリガリかじる
go iv 行く
go ahead v 先へ進む
go away v 立ち去る
go back v 後退する
go down v 下に行く

go in v 入る
go on v 進み続ける
go out v 外へ出る
go over v 調べる
go through v 通り抜ける
go under v 沈む
go up v 上がる
goad v 突き棒で突く
goal n 目標、ゴール
goalkeeper n ゴールキーパー
goat n ヤギ
gobble v ガツガツ食べる
God n 神
goddess n 女神
godless adj 神を認めない
goggles n 飛行メガネ
gold n 金
golden adj 金の
good adj よいこと
good-looking adj 格好いい
goodness n 良好
goods n 物品
goodwill n 親善
goof v へま
goof n へま
goose n ガン
gorge n 山あ、峡谷
gorgeous adj 華麗な
gorilla n ゴリラ
gory adj 血だらけの
gospel n 福音、教義
gossip v うわさをする

**G**

gossip *n* うわさ

gout *n* 痛風

govern *v* 支配する

government *n* 政府、政治

governor *n* 知事

gown *n* ガウン

grab *v* つかみ取る

grace *n* 優雅、品のよさ

graceful *adj* 優雅な

gracious *adj* 上品な

grade *n* 等級、評価

gradual *adj* 漸進的な

graduate *v* 卒業する

graduation *n* 卒業

graft *v* 移植する

graft *n* 移植

grain *n* 粒子、穀類

gram *n* グラム

grammar *n* 文法

grand *adj* 雄大な

grandchild *n* 孫

granddad *n* おじいさん

grandfather *n* 祖父

grandmother *n* 祖母

grandparents *n* 祖父母

grandson *n* 孫息子

grandstand *n* 特別観覧席

granite *n* 花こう岩

granny *n* おばあさん

grant *v* 承諾する

grant *n* 授与されたもの

grape *n* ブドウ

grapevine *n* ブドウのつる

graphic *adj* 図形の

grasp *n* 把握

grasp *v* 握る、つかむ

grass *n* 芝生、草

grassroots *adj* 草の根の

grateful *adj* 感謝する

gratify *v* 満足させる

gratifying *adj* 愉快な

gratitude *n* 感謝

gratuity *n* 心付け

grave *adj* 厳粛な

grave *n* 墓

gravel *n* 砂利

gravely *adv* 重大に

gravestone *n* 墓石

graveyard *n* 墓地

gravitate *v* 引き付けられる

gravity *n* 重力

gravy *n* グレイビー

gray *adj* 灰色

grayish *adj* 灰色がかった

graze *v* 草を食う

graze *n* 擦れる

grease *v* 潤滑油を塗る

grease *n* グリース

greasy *adj* 脂っぽい

great *adj* 偉大な

greatness *n* 偉大さ

Greece *n* ギリシャ

greed *n* 強欲

greedy *adj* 欲張りの

Greek *adj* ギリシャ人
green *adj* 緑の
green bean *n* 未焙煎
greenhouse *n* 温室
greet *v* あいさつする
greetings *n* 拝啓、祝電
gregarious *adj* 社交的な
grenade *n* 手榴弾
grief *n* 嘆き、悲嘆
grievance *n* 不平のもと
grieve *v* 悲しませる
grill *v* 直火で焼
grill *n* 焼き網、鉄板
grim *adj* 気味の悪い
grimace *n* しかめっ面
grime *n* あか、すす
grind *iv* ひくこと
grip *v* とらえる
grip *n* 握力、握り
gripe *n* 不平、不満
grisly *adj* 不気味な
groan *v* うめく、うなる
groan *n* うめき声
groceries *n* 食料雑貨類
groin *n* 股間
groom *n* 花婿、馬手
groove *n* 溝
gross *adj* 全体の
grossly *adv* 大幅に
grotesque *adj* 奇怪な
grotto *n* 洞くつ
grouch *v* ぼやく

grouchy *adj* 機嫌の悪い
ground *n* 地面
ground floor *n* 1階
groundless *adj* 根拠のない
groundwork *n* 基礎工事
group *n* 集団
grow *iv* 成長する
grow up *v* 大人になる
growl *v* うなる
grown-up *n* 大人
growth *n* 成長、発育
grudge *n* 悪意、恨み
grudgingly *adv* 嫌々ながら
gruesome *adj* 身の毛もよだつ
grumble *v* 不平を言う
grumpy *adj* 気難しい人
guarantee *v* 保証する
guarantee *n* 保証、担保
guarantor *n* 保証人
guard *n* 守衛
guardian *n* 保護者、後見人
guerrilla *n* ゲリラ兵
guess *v* 推測する
guess *n* 推測
guest *n* 客
guidance *n* 助言
guide *v* 導く、案内する
guide *n* 案内人
guidebook *n* 案内書
guidelines *n* 指針
guild *n* 同業組合
guile *n* 悪巧み

G

guillotine *n* ギロチン

guilt *n* 犯罪、あやまち

guilty *adj* 有罪の

guise *n* 見せかけ

guitar *n* ギター

gulf *n* 湾

gull *n* カモメ

gullible *adj* だまされやすい

gulp *v* グッと飲み込む

gulp *n* がぶ飲み

gulp down *v* がぶがぶ飲む

gum *n* ゴム

gun *n* 鉄砲

gun down *v* 撃ち落とす

gunfire *n* 発砲

gunman *n* 殺し屋

gunpowder *n* 火薬

gunshot *n* 砲撃

gust *n* 突風

gusto *n* 好み、嗜好

gusty *adj* 突風の吹く

gut *n* 腹、腸

guts *n* 元気

gutter *n* 排水路

guy *n* やつ、男

guzzle *v* 大酒を飲む

gymnasium *n* 体育館

gynecology *n* 婦人科の

gypsy *n* 放浪者

habit *n* 習慣、癖

habitable *adj* 住むのに適した

habitual *adj* 習慣の

hack *v* たたき切る

haggle *v* 言い争う

hail *n* 呼びかけ

hail *v* 歓迎する

hair *n* 髪の毛

hairbrush *n* ヘアブラシ

haircut *n* 散髪

hairdo *n* 髪形

hairdresser *n* ヘアドレッサー

hairpiece *n* ヘアピース

hairy *adj* 毛深い

half *n* 半分

half *adj* 半分の

hall *n* ホール、会館

hallucinate *v* 幻覚を起こす

hallway *n* 廊下

halt *v* 停止する

halve *v* 半分になる

ham *n* ハム

hamburger *n* ハンバーガー

hamlet *n* 村、部落

hammer *n* 金づち

hammock *n* ハンモック

hand *n* 手

hand down *v* 残す、伝える

hand in *v* 提出する

hand out _v_ 配る、分配する

hand over _v_ 手渡す

handbag _n_ ハンドバック

handbook _n_ 手引き書

handcuff _v_ 手錠をかける

handcuffs _n_ 手錠

handful _n_ 少量、一握り

handgun _n_ 拳銃

handkerchief _n_ ハンカチ

handle _v_ 処理する

handle _n_ 取っ手

handmade _adj_ 手作りの

handout _n_ 資料

handrail _n_ 手すり

handshake _n_ 握手

handsome _adj_ ハンサムな

handwritting _n_ 手書き

handy _adj_ 便利な

hang _iv_ 掛かる

hang around _v_ ぶらつく

hang on _v_ しがみつく

hang up _v_ 電話を切る

hanger _n_ ハンガー

hangup _n_ 悩み

happen _v_ 発生する

happening _n_ 出来事

happiness _n_ 幸福

happy _adj_ 幸福な

harass _v_ 困らせる

harassment _n_ 悩ますこと

harbor _n_ 港湾

hard _adj_ 難しい

harden _v_ 固まる

hardly _adv_ ほとんど〜ない

hardness _n_ 堅いこと

hardship _n_ 困難、苦痛

hardware _n_ ハードウエア

hardwood _n_ 硬材

hardy _adj_ 頑丈な

hare _n_ 野うさぎ

harm _v_ 害する

harm _n_ 害

harmful _adj_ 有害な

harmless _adj_ 無害の

harmonize _v_ 調和する

harmony _n_ 調和

harp _n_ ハープ

harpoon _n_ 銛

harrowing _adj_ 悲惨な

harsh _adj_ 厳しい

harshly _adv_ 厳しく

harshness _n_ 厳しさ

harvest _n_ 収穫

harvest _v_ 収穫する

hashish _n_ 大麻、ハシシ

hassle _v_ 口論する

hassle _n_ 口論

haste _n_ 急ぐこと

hasten _v_ 急ぐ

hastily _adv_ 急いで

hasty _adj_ 急ぎの

hat _n_ 帽子

hatchet _n_ 手おの

hate _v_ 憎む

H

**hateful** _adj_ 憎らしい

**hatred** _n_ 憎悪

**haughty** _adj_ 横柄な

**haul** _v_ 引っ張る

**haunt** _v_ 出没する

**have** _iv_ 持っている

**haven** _n_ 安息の地

**havoc** _n_ 大破壊

**hawk** _n_ タカ

**hay** _n_ 干し草

**haystack** _n_ 干し草の山

**hazard** _n_ 偶然、運

**hazardous** _adj_ 有害な

**haze** _n_ もや、かすみ

**hazy** _adj_ 霞の

**he** _pro_ 彼、その人

**head** _n_ 頭

**head for** _v_ 向かう

**headache** _n_ 頭痛

**heading** _n_ 表題、見出し

**head-on** _adv_ 真正面から

**headphones** _n_ ヘッドホン

**headquarters** _n_ 本部

**headway** _n_ 進歩、前進

**heal** _v_ 癒える、治る

**healer** _n_ 治療者

**health** _n_ 健康

**healthy** _adj_ 健康な

**heap** _n_ 山、塊

**heap** _v_ 積み上げる

**hear** _iv_ 聞く

**hearing** _n_ 尋問、公聴会

**hearsay** _n_ うわさ

**hearse** _n_ 霊柩車

**heart** _n_ 胸、心臓

**heartbeat** _n_ 鼓動、心拍

**heartburn** _n_ 胸焼け

**hearten** _v_ 元気づく

**heartfelt** _adj_ 心からの

**hearth** _n_ 暖炉、いろり

**heartless** _adj_ 無情な

**hearty** _adj_ 心のこもった

**heat** _v_ 熱くなる

**heat** _n_ 熱、暑さ

**heater** _n_ 暖房機

**heathen** _n_ 異教徒

**heating** _n_ 暖房、加熱

**heatstroke** _n_ 熱射病

**heatwave** _n_ 熱波

**heaven** _n_ 天国

**heavenly** _adj_ 天国のように

**heaviness** _n_ 重さ

**heavy** _adj_ 重い

**heckle** _v_ 質問攻めにする

**hectic** _adj_ てんてこ舞いの

**heed** _v_ 気をつける

**heel** _n_ かかと

**height** _n_ 高さ、身長

**heighten** _v_ 高まる

**heinous** _adj_ 悪質な

**heir** _n_ 相続人

**heiress** _n_ 女相続人

**heist** _n_ 強奪、強盗

**helicopter** _n_ ヘリコプター

hell *n* 地獄
hello *e* こんにちは
helm *n* かじ、指揮
helmet *n* ヘルメット
help *v* 助ける
help *n* 助け、援助
helper *n* 助手、ヘルパー
helpful *adj* 役に立つ
helpless *adj* 無力な
hem *n* へり、縁
hemisphere *n* 半球体
hemorrhage *n* 出血、損失
hen *n* めんどり
hence *adv* それ故に
henchman *n* 忠実な部下
her *adj* 彼女を
herald *v* 先触れをする
herald *n* 王の使者
herb *n* 薬草、ハーブ
here *adv* ここで
hereafter *adv* これから先
hereby *adv* これによって
hereditary *adj* 遺伝性の
heresy *n* 異説
heretic *adj* 異端者
heritage *n* 遺産、地位
hermetic *adj* 密封した
hermit *n* 隠者
hernia *n* ヘルニア
hero *n* 英雄
heroic *adj* 勇敢な
heroin *n* ヘロイン

heroism *n* 英雄的行為
hers *pro* 彼女のもの
herself *pro* 彼女自身
hesitant *adj* ためらって
hesitate *v* ためらう
hesitation *n* ためらい
heyday *n* 全盛期
hiccup *n* しゃっくり
hidden *adj* 隠された
hide *iv* 隠す
hideaway *n* 隠れ家
hideous *adj* おぞましい
hierarchy *n* 階層
high *adj* 高い
highlight *n* 見所
highly *adv* 高度に
Highness *n* 高いこと
highway *n* 主要道路
hijack *v* 乗っ取る
hijack *n* 乗っ取り
hijacker *n* 乗っ取り犯
hike *v* 引き上げる
hike *n* 引き上げ
hilarious *adj* とても愉快な
hill *n* 丘
hillside *n* 丘の中腹
hilltop *n* 丘の頂上
hilly *adj* 小高い
hilt *n* 柄
hinder *v* 妨げになる
hindrance *n* 立体障害
hindsight *n* 後知恵

H

hinge *v* ヒンジで動く

hinge *n* ヒンジ、要所

hint *n* 暗示、手がかり

hint *v* 暗示する

hip *n* 腰

hire *v* 雇う

his *adj* 彼の

his *pro* 彼のもの

Hispanic *adj* ヒスパニック

hiss *v* シューという音

historian *n* 歴史学者

history *n* 歴史

hit *n* 打撃、大当たり

hit *iv* たたく

hit back *v* 殴り返す

hitch *n* 結び目

hitchhike *n* ヒッチハイク

hitherto *adv* 今まで

hive *n* ミツバチの巣

hoard *v* 貯蔵する

hoarse *adj* しわがれ声の

hoax *n* 悪ふざけ

hobby *n* 趣味

hog *n* ブタ

hoist *v* 巻き上げる

hoist *n* 巻き上げ

hold *iv* 持続する

hold back *v* はばかる

hold on to *v* 持ち続ける

hold out *v* 伸ばす

hold up *v* 持こたえる

holdup *n* 強盗

hole *n* 穴

holiday *n* 休日

holiness *n* 神聖、高潔

Holland *n* オランダ

hollow *adj* 空洞、すき間

holocaust *n* 大虐殺

holy *adj* 神聖な

homage *n* 敬意

home *n* 家、家庭

homeland *n* 母国、祖国

homeless *adj* 孤児の

homely *adj* 家庭的な

homemade *adj* 手作りの

hometown *n* 故郷

homework *n* 宿題

homicide *n* 殺人罪

homily *n* 説教

honest *adj* 正直な

honesty *n* 正直、誠実

honey *n* はちみつ

honeymoon *n* 新婚旅行

honk *v* 警笛の音

honor *n* 光栄、名誉

hood *n* ずきん

hoodlum *n* チンピラ

hoof *n* 蹄、足

hook *n* フック

hooligan *n* ならず者

hop *v* 跳躍

hope *n* 希望

hopeful *adj* 希望に満ちた

hopefully *adv* 願わくは

hopeless _adj_ 絶望的な

horizon _n_ 水平線

horizontal _adj_ 水平の

hormone _n_ ホルモン

horn _n_ 角、ホルン

horrendous _adj_ 恐ろしい

horrible _adj_ 最悪な

horrify _v_ ゾッとさせる

horror _n_ 恐怖

horse _n_ 馬

hose _n_ ホース

hospital _n_ 病院

hospitality _n_ 手厚いもてなし

hospitalize _v_ 入院させる

host _n_ 主人、司会者

hostage _n_ 人質

hostess _n_ 女主人

hostile _adj_ 敵意を持った

hostility _n_ 敵意、対立

hot _adj_ 暑い、熱い

hotel _n_ 旅館

hound _n_ 猟犬

hour _n_ 一時間

hourly _adv_ 時間ごとの

house _n_ 住宅、家

household _n_ 家族、一家

housekeeper _n_ 家政婦

housewife _n_ 主婦

housework _n_ 家事

hover _v_ 空中に舞う

how _adv_ どのようにして

however _c_ どんなふうにでも

howl _v_ 遠ぼえする

howl _n_ 遠ぼえ

hub _n_ ハブ、拠点

huddle _v_ 群がる

hug _v_ 抱きしめる

hug _n_ 抱擁

huge _adj_ 巨大な

hull _n_ 船体

human _adj_ 人間の

human being _n_ 人間

humanities _n_ 人文科学

humankind _n_ 人類

humble _adj_ 謙虚な

humbly _adv_ 謙虚に

humid _adj_ 湿った

humidity _n_ 湿気

humiliate _v_ 屈辱を与える

humility _n_ 謙虚

humor _n_ 面白さ

humorous _adj_ ユーモアのある

hump _n_ こぶ

hunch _n_ 予感

hunchback _n_ せむし

hunched _adj_ 円背

hundred _adj_ 100個の

hundredth _adj_ 100分の1

hunger _n_ 飢え

hungry _adj_ 空腹の

hunt _v_ 狩る

hunter _n_ 狩人

hunting _n_ 狩猟

hurdle _n_ 障害物

H

**hurl** *v* 強く投げる
**hurricane** *n* ハリケーン
**hurriedly** *adv* 大騒ぎで
**hurry** *v* 急ぐ
**hurry up** *v* 急がせる
**hurt** *iv* 痛む
**hurt** *adj* けがをした
**hurtful** *adj* 傷つける
**husband** *n* 夫
**hush** *n* 静けさ、静寂
**hush up** *v* 口外しない
**husky** *adj* かすれた
**hustle** *n* 押し合い
**hut** *n* 山小屋
**hydraulic** *adj* 水力の
**hydrogen** *n* 水素
**hyena** *n* ハイエナ
**hygiene** *n* 衛生状態
**hymn** *n* 賛美歌
**hyphen** *n* ハイフン
**hypnosis** *n* 催眠術
**hypnotize** *v* 催眠する
**hypocrisy** *n* 偽善
**hypocrite** *adj* 偽善者
**hypothesis** *n* 仮説
**hysteria** *n* 興奮状態
**hysterical** *adj* 狂乱の

**I** *pro* 私は
**ice** *n* 氷
**ice cream** *n* アイスクリーム
**ice cube** *n* 角氷
**iceberg** *n* 氷山
**icebox** *n* 冷凍室
**icon** *n* 像、肖像
**icy** *adj* 氷の
**idea** *n* 考え
**ideal** *adj* 理想的な
**identical** *adj* 全く同じ
**identify** *v* 識別する
**identity** *n* 正体、身元
**ideology** *n* 価値体系
**idiom** *n* 熟語
**idiot** *n* 間抜け
**idiotic** *adj* 知的障害のある
**idle** *adj* 怠惰な
**idol** *n* 偶像
**idolatry** *n* 偶像崇拝
**if** *c* もし〜なら
**ignite** *v* 火がつく
**ignorance** *n* 無知
**ignorant** *adj* 無知な
**ignore** *v* 無視する
**ill** *adj* 病気で、不幸な
**illegal** *adj* 違法の
**illegible** *adj* 判読できない
**illegitimate** *adj* 私生の**

illicit *adj* 不法な

illness *n* 病気

illogical *adj* 非理論的な

illuminate *v* 明るくする

illusion *n* 錯覚

illustrate *v* 説明する

illustration *n* 挿絵

illustrious *adj* 著名な

image *n* 画像

imagination *n* 想像

imagine *v* 想像する

imbalance *n* 不釣合い

imitate *v* 装う、まねる

imitation *n* 模倣、偽造品

immaculate *adj* 無傷の

immature *adj* 未完成の

immaturity *n* 未熟

immediately *adv* すぐに

immense *adj* 非常に大きな

immensity *n* 無限

immerse *v* つける、浸す

immersion *n* 浸すこと

immigrant *n* 移民、移住者

immigrate *v* 移住する

immigration *n* 移住、入植

imminent *adj* 切迫した

immobile *adj* 動かない.

immobilize *v* 静止させる

immoral *adj* 不道徳な

immorality *n* 不道徳

immortal *adj* 死なない

immortality *n* 不死

immune *adj* 免疫の

immunity *n* 免疫

immunize *v* 免疫を与える

immutable *adj* 不変の

impact *n* 影響

impact *v* 影響を与える

impair *v* 損傷

impartial *adj* 偏らない

impatience *n* 短気、焦り

impatient *adj* イライラした

impeccable *adj* 罪のない

impediment *n* 障害

impending *adj* 差し迫った

imperfection *n* 不完全

imperial *adj* 皇族

imperialism *n* 帝国主義

impersonal *adj* 非人格的な

impertinent *adj* 無礼な

impetuous *adj* 性急な

implant *v* 埋め込み

implement *v* 用具、備品

implicate *v* 巻き込む

implication *n* 含み、暗示

implicit *adj* 暗黙の

implore *v* 懇願する

imply *v* ほのめかす

impolite *adj* 失礼な

import *v* 輸入する

importance *n* 重要性

importation *n* 輸入品

impose *v* だます

imposing *adj* 印象的な

imposition *n* 強制

impossibility *n* 不可能

impossible *adj* 不可能なこと

impotent *adj* 無力な

impound *v* 拘置する

impoverished *adj* 貧困に陥った

impractical *adj* 実用的でない

imprecise *adj* 不明確な

impress *v* 押印、捺印

impressive *adj* 感動的な

imprison *v* 監禁する

improbable *adj* ありそうもない

impromptu *adv* 即興で

improper *adj* 不適切な

improve *v* 上達する

improvement *n* 改良

improvise *v* 即興でやる

impulse *n* 衝動

impulsive *adj* 衝動的な

in *pre* 中で

in depth *adv* 徹底的に

inability *n* 無能、不能

inaccurate *adj* 不正確な

inadequate *adj* 不十分な

inadmissible *adj* 許容できない

inappropriate *adj* 不適切な

inasmuch as *c* できるだけ～

inaugurate *v* 任命する

inauguration *n* 就任式

incalculable *adj* 数えきれない

incapable *adj* 能力がない

incapacitate *v* 能力を奪う

incarcerate *v* 投獄された

incense *n* 香、香料

incentive *n* 動機、誘因

inception *n* 始まり、発端

incessant *adj* 絶え間のない

inch *n* インチ

incident *n* 事件、出来事

incidentally *adv* 偶然に

incision *n* 切開

incite *v* 奮い立たせる

incitement *n* 刺激、動機

inclination *n* 傾斜

incline *v* 傾ける

include *v* 含める

inclusive *adv* 包括的な

incoherent *adj* 一貫しない

income *n* 所得

incoming *adj* 入ってくる

incompatible *adj* 相性が悪い

incompetence *n* 無能力

incompetent *adj* 無能な

incomplete *adj* 不完全な

inconsistent *adj* 矛盾した

inconvenient *adj* 不便な

incorporate *v* 組み込む

incorrect *adj* 間違いの

incorrigible *adj* 矯正できない

increase *v* 増える

increase *n* 増加

increasing *adj* 増えている

incredible *adj* 信じられない

increment *n* 増加量

incriminate _v_ 告発する

incur _v_ 招く、受ける

incurable _adj_ 不治の

indecency _n_ 下品

indecision _n_ 優柔不断

indecisive _adj_ 優柔不断な

indeed _adv_ 実に

indefinite _adj_ 不明確な

indemnify _v_ 償う

indemnity _n_ 保障、免責

independence _n_ 独立

index _n_ 索引、見出し

indicate _v_ 指示する

indication _n_ 指示

indict _v_ 起訴する

indifference _n_ 無関心

indifferent _adj_ 無関心な

indigent _adj_ 貧しい

indigestion _n_ 消化不良

indiscreet _adj_ 無分別な

indiscretion _n_ 無分別

indispensable _adj_ 必須の

indisposed _adj_ 気が向かない

indivisible _adj_ 分割できない

indoctrinate _v_ 吹き込む

indoor _adv_ 室内の

induce _v_ 誘発する

indulge _v_ 従事する

indulgent _adj_ 寛大な

industrious _adj_ 勤勉な

industry _n_ 産業

ineffective _adj_ 効果のない

inefficient _adj_ 能率的でない

inept _adj_ 能力に欠ける

inequality _n_ 不等

inevitable _adj_ 避けられない

inexcusable _adj_ 許せない

inexpensive _adj_ 安い

inexperienced _adj_ 経験不足の

inexplicable _adj_ 説明し難い

infamous _adj_ 悪名高い

infancy _n_ 幼年期

infant _n_ 幼児期

infantry _n_ 歩兵

infect _v_ 感染させる

infection _n_ 感染

infectious _adj_ 伝染性の

infer _v_ 推論する

inferior _adj_ 劣った人

infertile _adj_ 生殖力のない

infested _adj_ 感染症の

infidelity _n_ 不貞

infiltrate _v_ 浸透する

infiltration _n_ 侵入、浸透

infinite _adj_ 無限のもの

infirmary _n_ 診療所

inflammation _n_ 点火、炎症

inflate _v_ 膨らむ

inflation _n_ 膨張

inflict _v_ 課する

influence _n_ 影響、作用

influential _adj_ 影響力の大きい

influx _n_ 流入

inform _v_ 告げる

**informal** *adj* 非公式の

**informality** *n* 非公式

**informant** *n* 通知者

**information** *n* 情報

**informer** *n* 密告者

**infraction** *n* 違反

**infuriate** *v* 激高させる

**infusion** *n* 注入

**ingenuity** *n* 発明の才

**ingest** *v* 取り込む

**ingot** *n* インゴット

**ingrained** *adj* 深く染みこんだ

**ingratitude** *n* 恩知らず

**ingredient** *n* 材料、原料

**inhabit** *v* 存在する

**inhabitable** *adj* 居住可能な

**inhabitant** *n* 居住者

**inhale** *v* 吸い込むこと

**inherit** *v* 相続する

**inheritance** *n* 継承

**inhibit** *v* 抑制する

**inhuman** *adj* 非人間的な

**initial** *adj* 頭文字

**initially** *adv* 初めには

**initials** *n* イニシャル

**initiate** *v* 始める

**initiative** *n* 主導権

**inject** *v* 〜を入れる

**injection** *n* 注射、注入

**injure** *v* 傷つける

**injurious** *adj* 有害な

**injury** *n* けが、負傷

**injustice** *n* 不公平

**ink** *n* インク

**inkling** *n* ほのめかし

**inlaid** *adj* はめ込まれた

**inland** *adv* 内陸に

**inland** *adj* 内陸の

**in-laws** *n* 義理の両親

**inmate** *n* 囚人、受刑者

**inn** *n* 宿屋

**innate** *adj* 生来の

**inner** *adj* 内部の

**innocence** *n* 無罪、潔白

**innocent** *adj* 純潔な

**innovation** *n* 革新

**innuendo** *n* 当て付け

**innumerable** *adj* 無数の

**input** *n* 入力、提供

**inquest** *n* 検討、査問

**inquire** *v* 尋ねる

**inquiry** *n* 質問

**inquisition** *n* 審理、探求

**insane** *adj* 正気でない

**insanity** *n* 精神異常

**insatiable** *adj* 強欲な

**inscription** *n* 題辞、記入

**insect** *n* 昆虫

**insecurity** *n* 不安定

**insensitive** *adj* 鈍感な

**insert** *v* 挿入する

**insertion** *n* 差込、挿入

**inside** *adj* 内部、内側

**inside** *pre* 〜の内部に**

**inside out** *adv* 裏返しに

**insignificant** *adj* 重要でない

**insincere** *adj* 不誠実な

**insincerity** *n* 不誠実さ

**insinuate** *v* ほのめかす

**insinuation** *n* 当てこすり

**insipid** *adj* 風味のない

**insist** *v* 強く主張する

**insistence** *n* 強い主張

**insolent** *adj* 横柄な

**insoluble** *adj* 溶けない

**insomnia** *n* 不眠

**inspect** *v* 点検する

**inspection** *n* 検査

**inspector** *n* 検査官

**inspiration** *n* 刺激

**inspire** *v* 奮起させる

**instability** *n* 不安定

**install** *v* 導入する

**installation** *n* 導入

**installment** *n* 分割払い

**instance** *n* 場合、事実

**instant** *n* 瞬間

**instantly** *adv* 即座に

**instead** *adv* 代わりに

**instigate** *v* 引き起こす

**instil** *v* 注入する

**instinct** *n* 本能、直感

**institute** *v* 協会、機関

**institution** *n* 施設、団体

**instruct** *v* 指示する

**instructor** *n* 指導者

**insufficient** *adj* 不十分な

**insulate** *v* 防護する

**insulation** *n* 絶縁

**insult** *v* 侮辱する

**insult** *n* 侮辱

**insurance** *n* 保険

**insure** *v* 保険に入る

**insurrection** *n* 反乱、暴動

**intact** *adj* 無傷の

**intake** *n* 吸入量

**integrate** *v* 統合する

**integration** *n* 統合

**integrity** *n* 誠実、完全性

**intelligent** *adj* 知性のある

**intend** *v* 意図する

**intense** *adj* 極度の

**intensify** *v* 強まる

**intensity** *n* 強烈さ、強さ

**intensive** *adj* 激しい、強い

**intention** *n* 意図、意思

**intercede** *v* 仲裁する

**intercept** *v* 妨害、防止

**intercession** *n* 仲裁

**interchange** *v* 置き換える

**interchange** *n* 交換、交流

**interest** *n* 興味、関心

**interested** *adj* 関心のある

**interesting** *adj* 興味深い

**interfere** *v* 邪魔をする

**interference** *n* 干渉、妨害

**interior** *adj* 内部の

**interlude** *n* 合間、幕あい**

intermediary *n* 仲裁者
intern *v* 抑留する
interpret *v* 通訳する
interpretation *n* 解釈、通訳
interpreter *n* 通訳者
interrogate *v* せんさくする
interrupt *v* 中断する
interruption *n* 妨害、中断
intersect *v* 交差する
intertwine *v* 結び付く
interval *n* 間隔
intervene *v* 干渉する
intervention *n* 介入
interview *n* 面接、会談
intestine *n* 腸
intimacy *n* 親密
intimate *adj* 親密な
intimidate *v* 脅かす
intolerable *adj* 耐えられない
intolerance *n* 不寛容
intoxicated *adj* 中毒になった
intravenous *adj* 静脈の
intrepid *adj* 勇敢な
intricate *adj* 込み入った
intrigue *n* 陰謀
intriguing *adj* 興味のある
intrinsic *adj* 固有の
introduce *v* 紹介する
introduction *n* 紹介
introvert *adj* 内向的な
intrude *v* 進入する
intruder *n* 侵入者

intrusion *n* 侵入
intuition *n* 直感、直覚
inundate *v* 充満させる
invade *v* 侵攻する
invader *n* 侵略国
invalid *n* 無効な
invalidate *v* 取り消す
invaluable *adj* 計り知れない
invasion *n* 侵略、侵入
invent *v* 発明する
invention *n* 発明品
inventory *n* 一覧表、在庫
invest *v* 投資する
investigate *v* 調査する
investigation *n* 調査
investment *n* 投資、出資
investor *n* 投資家
invincible *adj* 無敵の
invitation *n* 招待
invite *v* 招待する
invoice *n* 納品書
invoke *v* 引き起こす
involve *v* 含む、伴う
involved *v* 巻き込まれた
involvement *n* 関与
inward *adj* 奥地の
inwards *adv* 引き取り
iodine *n* ヨウ素
irate *adj* 激怒した
iron *n* 鉄、強固さ
ironic *adj* 皮肉な
irony *n* 皮肉

irrational *adj* 不合理な
irrefutable *adj* 反論できない
irregular *adj* 不定期な
irrelevant *adj* 無関係の
irreparable *adj* 修理不可能な
irresistible *adj* 抵抗できない
irreversible *adj* 逆にできない
irrigate *v* 水をまく
irrigation *n* かんがい
irritate *v* いら立たせる
irritating *adj* イライラさせる
Islamic *adj* イスラムの
island *n* 島
isle *n* 小島
isolate *v* 分離させる
isolation *n* 孤立、分離
issue *n* 問題、論点
Italian *adj* イタリア人
Italy *n* イタリア
itch *v* かゆい
itchiness *n* かゆさ
item *n* 事項
itemize *v* 項目別にする
itinerary *n* 旅程
ivory *n* 象牙

# J

jackal *n* ジャッカル
jacket *n* ジャケット
jackpot *n* 特賞
jaguar *n* ジャガー
jail *n* 刑務所
jail *v* 投獄する
jailer *n* 看守
jam *n* ジャム
janitor *n* 用務員
January *n* 一月
Japan *n* 日本
Japanese *adj* 日本人
jar *n* ジャー、かめ
jasmine *n* ジャスミン
jaw *n* 顎
jealous *adj* 嫉妬して
jealousy *n* ねたみ、嫉妬
jeans *n* ジーンズ
jeopardize *v* 危うくする
jerk *n* ばか、とんま
jersey *n* ジャージ
Jew *n* ユダヤ人
jewel *n* 宝石
jeweler *n* 宝石商
jewelry store *n* 宝石店
Jewish *adj* ユダヤ人
jigsaw *n* ジグゾー
job *n* 仕事
jobless *adj* 失業者

I

**join** *v* 加わる

**joint** *n* 結合

**jointly** *adv* 合同で

**joke** *n* 冗談

**joke** *v* 冗談を言う

**jokingly** *adv* 冗談っぽく

**jolly** *adj* 陽気な

**jolt** *v* ガタガタ揺らす

**jolt** *n* 衝撃

**journal** *n* 機関紙

**journalist** *n* ジャーナリスト

**journey** *n* 旅

**jovial** *adj* 陽気な

**joy** *n* 喜び

**joyful** *adj* うれしい

**joyfully** *adv* うれしそうに

**jubilant** *adj* 喜びに満ちた

**Judaism** *n* ユダヤ教

**judge** *n* 裁判官、判事

**judgment** *n* 判断

**judicious** *adj* 思慮深い

**jug** *n* 水入れ、つぼ

**juggler** *n* 手品師

**juice** *n* ジュース

**juicy** *adj* みずみずしい

**July** *n* 七月

**jump** *v* 飛ぶ

**jump** *n* ジャンプ

**jumpy** *adj* 飛んだり

**junction** *n* ジャンクション

**June** *n* 六月

**jungle** *n* 密林

**junior** *adj* 年下の人

**junk** *n* くず

**jury** *n* 陪審

**just** *adj* ちょうど

**justice** *n* 正義

**justify** *v* 弁明する

**justly** *adv* 正しく

**juvenile** *n* 年少者

**juvenile** *adj* 年少者の

**kangaroo** *n* カンガルー

**karate** *n* 空手

**keep** *iv* ～し続ける

**keep on** *v* 続行する

**keep up** *v* 持続する

**keg** *n* 小さいたる

**kennel** *n* 犬小屋

**kettle** *n* やかん

**key** *n* 鍵

**key ring** *n* キーホルダー

**keyboard** *n* 鍵版

**kick** *v* 蹴る

**kickback** *n* 反動、反発

**kickoff** *n* 開始の

**kid** *n* 子供

**kidnap** *v* 誘拐する

kidnapper *n* 誘拐犯
kidnapping *n* 誘拐
kidney *n* 腎臓
kidney bean *n* インゲン豆
kill *v* 殺す
killer *n* 殺人者
killing *n* 殺すこと
kilogram *n* キログラム
kilometer *n* キロメートル
kilowatt *n* キロワット
kind *adj* 親切な
kindle *v* 火をつける
kindly *adv* 親切に
kindness *n* 親切、思いやり
king *n* 王
kingdom *n* 王国
kinship *n* 親族関係
kiosk *n* 売店
kiss *v* キスをする
kiss *n* キス
kitchen *n* 台所、キッチン
kite *n* たこ
kitten *n* 子猫
knee *n* ひざ
kneecap *n* ひざのお皿
kneel *iv* ひざまずくこと
knife *n* ナイフ
knight *n* 騎士
knit *v* ニット、編み物
knob *n* ノブ、取っ手
knock *n* ノック、不運
knock *v* ノックする、たたく

knot *n* 結び目
know *iv* 知る
know-how *n* ノウハウ
knowingly *adv* 知っていて
knowledge *n* 知識

# L

lab *n* 研究室
label *n* 名札
labor *n* 仕事、労務
laborer *n* 作業員
labyrinth *n* 迷路
lace *n* レース、ひも
lack *v* 足りない
lack *n* 不足
lad *n* 少年、若者
ladder *n* はしご
laden *adj* 運んでいる
lady *n* 女性
ladylike *adj* しとやかな
lagoon *n* 小さな沼
lake *n* 湖
lamb *n* 子羊
lame *adj* 正常に歩けない
lament *v* 悲しむ
lament *n* 悲嘆
lamp *n* ランプ、灯火

**K**
**L**

**lamppost** *n* 街灯柱
**lampshade** *n* ランプのかさ
**land** *n* 陸地
**land** *v* 上陸する
**landfill** *n* 埋め立て
**landing** *n* 上陸
**landlady** *n* 女主人
**landlocked** *adj* 内陸の
**landlord** *n* 家主
**landscape** *n* 風景、景色
**lane** *n* 車線、小道
**language** *n* 言語、言葉
**languish** *v* 衰える
**lap** *n* ひざ
**lapse** *n* ささいな過ち
**lapse** *v* 陥る
**larceny** *n* 窃盗
**lard** *n* ラード
**large** *adj* 大きい、広い
**larynx** *n* 咽頭
**laser** *n* レーザー
**lash** *n* むち
**lash** *v* むち打つ
**lash out** *v* 蹴飛ばす
**last** *v* 続く、存続する
**last** *adj* 終わりの
**last name** *n* 姓、名字
**last night** *adv* 昨夜、最後の夜
**lasting** *adj* 長続きする
**lastly** *adv* 最後に
**latch** *n* 掛け金
**late** *adv* 遅い、遅刻の

**lately** *adv* 最近、この頃
**later** *adv* 後で
**later** *adj* 遅れた
**lateral** *adj* 横の、水平な
**latest** *adj* 最近の、最新の
**lather** *n* せっけんの泡
**latitude** *n* 緯度
**latter** *adj* 後者の、あとの
**laugh** *v* 笑う
**laugh** *n* 笑うこと
**laughable** *adj* ばかばかしい
**laughter** *n* 笑い声
**launch** *n* 打ち上げ、発射
**launch** *v* 発射する
**laundry** *n* 洗濯
**lavatory** *n* 洗面所
**lavish** *adj* ぜいたくな
**lavish** *v* 浪費する
**law** *n* 法律、法規
**law-abiding** *adj* 遵法の
**lawful** *adj* 法の認めた
**lawmaker** *n* 立法者
**lawn** *n* 芝生
**lawsuit** *n* 訴訟
**lawyer** *n* 弁護士
**lax** *adj* 緩い
**laxative** *adj* 下剤の
**lay** *n* 形状
**lay** *iv* 横たわる
**lay off** *v* 一時解雇する
**layer** *n* 皮、層
**layman** *n* 素人

layout *n* 配置、レイアウト

laziness *n* 怠惰

lazy *adj* 怠惰な

lead *iv* 導く、案内する

lead *n* 先導、リード

leaded *adj* 有鉛の

leader *n* 指導者、リーダー

leadership *n* 指導力

leading *adj* 優れた

leaf *n* 葉

leaflet *n* ちらし、小冊子

league *n* 同盟、連盟

leak *v* 漏れる

leak *n* 漏れ口

leakage *n* 漏れ

lean *adj* 赤身の

lean *iv* 傾く、頼る

lean back *v* 後ろにもたれる

lean on *v* 寄りかかる

leaning *n* 傾向

leap *iv* 飛び跳ねる

leap *n* 跳躍、ジャンプ

leap year *n* うるう年

learn *iv* 学ぶ、知る

learned *adj* 学問的な

learner *n* 学習者

learning *n* 学問、学識

lease *v* 賃貸する

lease *n* 賃貸

leash *n* 綱、鎖

least *adj* 最も少ない

leather *n* 革

leave *iv* 去る、退く

leave out *v* 除外する

lectern *n* 聖書朗読台

lecture *n* 講義

ledger *n* 台帳

leech *n* ヒル

leftovers *n* 残り物

leg *n* 脚

legacy *n* 相続財産

legal *adj* 法律上の

legality *n* 合法性

legalize *v* 合法化する

legend *n* 伝説

legible *adj* 判読可能な

legion *n* 軍団

legislate *v* 法律を制定する

legislation *n* 法律制定

legislature *n* 議会、立法府

legitimate *adj* 合法の

leisure *n* 余暇、娯楽

lemon *n* レモン

lemonade *n* レモネード

lend *iv* 〜に貸す

length *n* 長さ

lengthen *v* 延びる

lengthy *adj* 非常に長い

leniency *n* 寛大さ

lenient *adj* 大目に見た

lense *n* レンズ

Lent *n* 四旬節

lentil *n* レンティル

leopard *n* ヒョウ

L

leper *n* ハンセン病患者

leprosy *n* ハンセン病

less *adj* より少ない

lessee *n* 貸借人

lessen *v* 減少する

lesser *adj* より小さい

lesson *n* 授業

lessor *n* 賃貸人

let *iv* 貸し出す

let down *v* 失望させる

let go *v* 解雇される

let in *v* 巻き込む

let out *v* 外に出す

lethal *adj* 致命的な

letter *n* 手紙

lettuce *n* レタス

leukemia *n* 白血病

level *v* 水平にする

level *n* 高さ、地位

lever *n* レバー、てこ

leverage *n* 力、行動力

levy *v* 課す

lewd *adj* わいせつな

liability *n* 負債、債務

liable *adj* 責任がある

liaison *n* 連絡、通信

liar *adj* うそつき

libel *n* 名誉棄損

liberate *v* 自由にする

liberation *n* 釈放、解放

liberty *n* 権利、自由

librarian *n* 図書館員

library *n* 図書館

lice *n* シラミ

licence *n* ライセンス

license *v* 許可する

lick *v* なめる

lid *n* ふた

lie *iv* 横たわる

lie *v* うそをつく

lie *n* うそ

lieu *n* 〜の代わりに

lieutenant *n* 警部補

life *n* 人生、生涯

lifeguard *n* 救助員

lifeless *adj* 生命を持たない

lifestyle *n* 生き方

lifetime *adj* 一生の

lift *v* 持ち上がる

lift off *v* 打ち上げられる

lift-off *n* 離昇

ligament *n* 靭帯

light *iv* 火がつく

light *adj* 明るい

light *n* 光、明かり

lighter *n* 点灯器

lighthouse *n* 灯台

lighting *n* 照明

lightly *adv* 明るく

lightning *n* 稲妻

lightweight *n* ライト級

likable *adj* 好ましい

like *pre* 例えば、何か

like *v* 気にいる

L

likelihood _n_ ありそうな状態

likely _adv_ ありそうな

likeness _n_ 似てること

likewise _adv_ 同じく

liking _n_ 好くこと

limb _n_ 肢、手足

lime _n_ ライム

limestone _n_ 石灰岩

limit _n_ 制限

limit _v_ 制限する

limitation _n_ 限定、制限

limp _v_ 足を引きずる

limp _n_ 足を引きずること

linchpin _n_ 輪止め

line _n_ 線、直線

line up _v_ 列に加わる

linen _n_ リンネル

linger _v_ 長居する

lingerie _n_ ランジェリー

lingering _adj_ 延々と長く続く

lining _n_ 裏張りすること

link _v_ 結びつける物

link _n_ つながる

lion _n_ ライオン

lioness _n_ 雌のライオン

lip _n_ 唇

liqueur _n_ リキュール

liquid _n_ 液体

liquidate _v_ 清算

liquidation _n_ 整理、清算

liquor _n_ 酒

list _v_ 載せる

list _n_ 一覧表

listen _v_ 聴く、聞く

listener _n_ 聞き手

litany _n_ 長談義

liter _n_ リットル

literal _adj_ 誤字

literally _adv_ 文字通りに

literate _adj_ 読み書きできる人

literature _n_ 文学

litigate _v_ 訴訟を起こす

litigation _n_ 訴訟、告訴

litre _n_ リッター

litter _n_ 散乱したもの

little _adj_ 少しの、小さい

little bit _n_ わずかの

little by little _adv_ 少しずつ

liturgy _n_ 礼拝

live _adj_ 本物の

live _v_ 生活する、住む

live off _v_ 生計を立てる

live up _v_ ～に沿う

livelihood _n_ 生計、暮らし

lively _adj_ 元気いっぱいの

liver _n_ 肝臓

livestock _n_ 家畜

livid _adj_ 鉛色の

living room _n_ リビングルーム

lizard _n_ トカゲ

load _v_ 荷積みする

load _n_ 荷、多数

loaded _adj_ 荷物を積んだ

loaf _n_ ひと塊

L

**loan** v 貸し付ける

**loan** n 貸付金

**loathe** v 〜をひどく嫌う

**loathing** n 憎しみ

**lobby** n ロビー

**lobby** v 働きかける

**lobster** n ロブスター

**local** adj 地元の

**localize** v 局部集中する

**locate** v 落ち着く

**located** adj 位置して

**location** n 場所、位置

**lock** v ロックする

**lock** n ロック、錠

**lock up** v 閉じ込める

**locker room** n ロッカールーム

**locksmith** n 鍵屋

**locust** n バッタ、イナゴ

**lodge** v ロッジ、山荘

**lodging** n 住まい、宿屋

**lofty** adj 非常に高い

**log** n 丸太

**log** v 記録をとる

**log in** v ログインする

**log off** v ログオフする

**logic** n 論理

**logical** adj 論理上の

**loin** n 腰部

**loiter** v ブラブラする

**loneliness** n 孤独、寂しさ

**lonely** adv 寂しい

**loner** n 孤独が好きな人

**lonesome** adj 心細い

**long** adj 長い

**long for** v 待ちこがれる

**longing** n 切望

**longitude** n 経度

**long-standing** adj 長年の

**long-term** adj 長期の

**look** n 見ること

**look** v 見る、目を向ける

**look after** v 世話をする

**look at** v 〜を見る

**look down** v 見下ろす

**look for** v 〜を探す

**look forward** v 楽しみに待つ

**look into** v のぞき込む

**look out** v 外を見る

**look over** v 一読する

**look through** v 目を通す

**looking glass** n 鏡

**looks** n 外見

**loom** n はた、織機

**loom** v 〜を織る

**loophole** n 輪、環状のもの

**loose** v 放つ、離れる

**loose** adj ゆるい

**loosen** v 緩む、ほぐれる

**loot** v 略奪する

**loot** n 略奪品

**lord** n 封建領主

**lordship** n 閣下、支配

**lose** iv 負ける

**loser** n 敗者

loss *n* 失うこと
lot *adv* たくさん、大いに
lotion *n* 化粧水
lots *adj* 非常にたくさんの
lottery *n* くじ引き
loud *adj* 大きい
loudly *adv* 大声で
loudspeaker *n* 拡声器
lounge *n* 休憩室
louse *n* シラミ
lousy *adj* シラミのたかった
lovable *adj* 愛らしい
love *v* 愛する
love *n* 愛
lovely *adj* 愛らしい
lover *n* 恋人
loving *adj* 愛情を抱いた
low *adj* 低いもの
lower *adj* より低い
lowkey *adj* 控えめな
lowly *adj* 低い、卑しい
loyal *adj* 忠誠な
loyalty *n* 忠義、誠実
lubricate *v* 円滑にする
lubrication *n* 注油、潤滑
lucid *adj* 明快な
luck *n* 幸運
lucky *adj* 運のいい
lucrative *adj* もうかる
ludicrous *adj* こっけいな
luggage *n* 手荷物
lukewarm *adj* 生ぬるい

lull *n* 一時的な静止
lumber *n* 製材
luminous *adj* 明るい
lump *n* 塊、こぶ
lump sum *n* 一括払い額
lump together *v* 一括する
lunacy *n* 狂気
lunatic *adj* 狂人
lunch *n* 昼食
lung *n* 肺
lure *v* おとり、わな
lurk *v* 待ち伏せする
lush *adj* 緑の茂った
lust *v* 切望する
lust *n* 渇望、熱望
lustful *adj* どん欲な
luxurious *adj* 豪華な
luxury *n* 豪華さ
lynch *v* 私刑によって殺す
lynx *n* 大山猫
lyrics *n* 歌詞

**L**

# M

machine *n* 機械
machine gun *n* 機関銃
mad *adj* 怒り
madam *n* ご婦人
madden *v* 激怒する
madly *adv* 激しく
madman *n* 気違い
madness *n* 狂気
magazine *n* 雑誌
magic *n* 手品
magical *adj* 魔術の
magician *n* 手品師
magistrate *n* 治安判事
magnet *n* 磁石
magnetic *adj* 磁気の
magnetism *n* 磁性、磁気
magnificent *adj* 堂々たる
magnify *v* 拡大する
maid *n* メイド
mail *v* 郵送する
mail *n* 郵便
mailbox *n* 郵便箱
mailman *n* 郵便配達人
maim *v* 重傷を負わせる
main *adj* 主要な
mainland *n* 本土、大陸
mainly *adv* 主に
maintain *v* 持続する
maintenance *n* 持続

majestic *adj* 威厳のある
majesty *n* 王族、尊厳
major *n* 少佐、専攻科目
major *adj* 専攻の
major in *v* 専攻する
majority *n* 大多数の
make *n* 製造
make *iv* 急いで進む
make up *v* 作りあげる
make up for *v* 補う
maker *n* 製造業者
makeup *n* 化粧品
malaria *n* マラリア
male *n* 男
malevolent *adj* 悪意のある
malfunction *n* 機能不全
malice *n* 悪意
malign *v* 有害な
malignancy *n* 悪性
malignant *adj* 悪性の
malnutrition *n* 栄養失調の
malpractice *v* ミス、過誤
mammal *n* 哺乳動物
mammoth *n* マンモス
man *n* 人間、人
manageable *adj* 管理できる
management *n* 経営
manager *n* 支配人
mandate *n* 委任
mandatory *adj* 命令の
maneuver *n* 作戦行動
manger *n* 飼い葉おけ

mangle v 押しつぶす

manhandle v 乱暴に押す

manhunt n 犯人の追跡

maniac adj 凶暴な人

manifest v 積荷目録

manipulate v 操作する

mankind n 人類、人間

manliness n 男らしさ

manly adj 男らしい

manner n 行儀、態度

mannerism n マンネリ

manners n 風俗習慣

manpower n 人員、人材

mansion n 大邸宅

manslaughter n 故殺

manual n 取扱説明書

manual adj 手作業の

manufacture v 作る

manure n 肥料、肥やし

manuscript n 原稿

many adj 多数の

map n 地図

marble n 大理石

march v 行進する

march n 行進、進行

March n 3月

mare n 雌ロバ

margin n 余白

marginal adj 境界の

marinate v マリネにする

marine adj 海の

marital adj 結婚生活の

mark n 印、記号

mark v 跡を残す

mark down v 値下げをする

marker n 目印

market n 市場

marksman n 射手

marmalade n マーマレード

marriage n 結婚

married adj 結婚した

marrow n 骨髄

marry v 嫁、結婚する

Mars n 火星

marshal n 元帥、司令官

martyr n 殉教者

martyrdom n 殉死、殉教

marvel n 驚くべきこと

marvelous adj 驚くべき

masculine adj 男っぽい

mask n 仮面

masochism n マゾヒズム

mason n 石工

masquerade v 仮装する

mass n 集団、大量

massacre n 大虐殺

massage n マッサージ

massive adj ても大きな

mast n マスト

master n 親方

master v 修得する

mastermind n 立案者

mastermind v 陰で操る

masterpiece n 名作

**M**

mastery *n* 熟達、精通
mat *n* マット、ござ
match *n* マッチ、試合
match *v* 対抗する
mate *n* 仲間、友達
material *n* 物質、資料
materialism *n* 唯物論
maternal *adj* 母の、母性の
maternity *n* 母であること
math *n* 数学、計算
matriculate *v* 大学合格者
matrimony *n* 夫婦関係
matter *n* 事柄、問題
mattress *n* マットレス
mature *adj* 塾した
maturity *n* 成熟度
maul *v* 斧で割る
maxim *n* 格言
maximum *adj* 最大の
May *n* 5月
may *iv* ～かもしれない
may-be *adv* もしかして
mayhem *n* 傷害、暴力
mayor *n* 町長、市長
maze *n* 迷路、当惑
meadow *n* 牧草地
meager *adj* 貧しく
meal *n* 食事
mean *iv* ～を意味する
mean *adj* 劣った
meaning *n* 意味
meaningful *adj* 意味のある

meaningless *adj* 意味のない
meanness *n* 卑しさ
means *n* 手段、方法
meantime *adv* その間に
meanwhile *adv* それまでの間
measles *n* はしか
measure *v* 測る
measurement *n* 長さ、寸法
meat *n* 肉類
meatball *n* ミートボール
mechanic *n* 機械工
mechanism *n* 構造、装置
mechanize *v* 機械化する
medal *n* メダル
medallion *n* 大メダル
meddle *v* 余計な世話を焼く
mediate *v* 調停する
mediator *n* 仲介者
medication *n* 医薬
medicinal *adj* 薬効のある
medicine *n* 薬、医薬
medieval *adj* 中世の
mediocre *adj* 二流の
mediocrity *n* 平凡、月並み
meditate *v* めい想する
meditation *n* めい想
medium *adj* 中間の
meek *adj* 柔和な
meekness *n* 湿順、柔和
meet *iv* 会う
meeting *n* 出会い、会議
melancholy *n* 憂うつ

M

mellow *adj* 熟して甘い

mellow *v* 熟す

melodic *adj* 旋律の

melody *n* 旋律

melon *n* メロン

melt *v* 溶ける

member *n* 一員、会員

membership *n* 会員の地位

membrane *n* 細胞膜、膜

memento *n* 形見、遺品

memo *n* メモ、連絡メモ

memoirs *n* 記録、手記

memorable *adj* 覚えやすい

memorize *v* ～を覚える

memory *n* 記憶力

menace *n* 脅威

mend *v* 改める

meningitis *n* 髄膜炎

menopause *n* 更年期

menstruation *n* 月経

mental *adj* 心の

mentality *n* 知能、知力

mentally *adv* 精神的に

mention *v* 述べる

mention *n* 言及

menu *n* 献立表

merchandise *n* 商品

merchant *n* 商人

merciful *adj* 慈悲深い

merciless *adj* 無慈悲な

mercury *n* 水銀、水星

mercy *n* 慈悲、情け

merely *adv* ただ単に

merge *v* 合併する

merger *n* 合併

merit *n* 長所

merit *v* ～に値する

mermaid *n* 人魚

merry *adj* 陽気な

mesh *n* メッシュ

mess *n* 混乱

mess around *v* 騒ぐ

mess up *v* 散らかす

message *n* 伝言

messenger *n* 電報通達人

Messiah *n* メシア

messy *adj* 乱雑な

metal *n* 金属

metallic *adj* 金属製の

metaphor *n* 隠喩、暗喩

meteor *n* 流星

meter *n* メートル

method *n* 方法、方式

methodical *adj* 整然とした

meticulous *adj* 極めて注意深い

metric *adj* 測定基準

metropolis *n* 主要都市

Mexican *adj* メキシコ人

microbe *n* 微生物

microphone *n* マイクロホン

microscope *n* 顕微鏡

microwave *n* マイクロ波

midair *n* 空中の

midday *n* 真ん中

**M**

middle *n* 中央
middleman *n* 仲介者
midget *n* 小人
midnight *n* 真夜中
midsummer *n* 真夏
midwife *n* 助産師
mighty *adj* 強力な
migraine *n* 片頭痛
migrant *n* 移住者
migrate *v* 移住する
mild *adj* 温和な
mildew *n* うどん粉菌
mile *n* マイル
mileage *n* マイル距離
milestone *n* 道しるべ
militant *adj* 戦闘的な
milk *n* 牛乳
milky *adj* 牛乳のような
mill *n* 工場
millennium *n* 千年間
milligram *n* ミリグラム
millimeter *n* ミリミータ
million *n* 100万
millionaire *adj* 百万長者
mime *v* パントマイム
mince *v* 細かに切る
mincemeat *n* ひき肉
mind *v* 嫌がる
mind *n* 心情
mindful *adj* 心に留める
mindless *adj* 愚かな
mine *n* 鉱山

mine *v* 採掘する
mine *pro* 私のもの
minefield *n* 地震原
miner *n* 鉱山労働者
mineral *n* 鉱物
mingle *v* 混ぜる
miniature *n* 縮小図
minimize *v* 最小限にする
minimum *n* 最小限
miniskirt *n* ミニスカート
minister *n* 大臣、聖職者
minister *v* 助ける
ministry *n* 省庁
minor *adj* 未成年者
minority *n* 少数派
mint *n* ミント、ハッカ
mint *v* ～を鋳造する
minus *adj* 差し引いて
minute *n* 分
miracle *n* 奇跡
miraculous *adj* 奇跡の
mirage *n* 蜃気楼、幻覚
mirror *n* 鏡
misbehave *v* 不品行をする
miscalculate *v* 計算を誤る
miscarriage *n* 流産、失敗
miscarry *v* 流産する
mischief *n* いたずら、損
mischievous *adj* いたずら好きな
misconduct *n* 不品行
misconstrue *v* 誤解する
misdemeanor *n* 軽罪

M

miser *n* けち

miserable *adj* 惨めな

misery *n* 惨めさ、悲惨

misfit *adj* ぴったりしない

misfortune *n* 不運、逆境

misgivings *n* 疑惑、懸念

misguided *adj* 誤り導かれた

misinterpret *v* 誤って解釈する

misjudge *v* 誤った判断をする

mislead *v* 欺く

misleading *adj* 惑わせる

mismanage *v* ～の処置を誤る

misplace *v* 置き違える

misprint *n* ミスプリント

miss *v* 的をはずす

miss *n* ミス、失敗

missile *n* ミサイル

missing *adj* 行方不明の

mission *n* 派遣団

missionary *n* 伝道者、布教者

mist *n* 霧、かすみ

mistake *iv* 誤る、間違える

mistake *n* 誤り、過ち

mistaken *adj* 間違った

mister *n* ～さん、氏

mistreat *v* 虐待する

mistreatment *n* 虐待

mistress *n* 女主人

mistrust *n* 不信

mistrust *v* 不審に思う

misty *adj* 霞の

misunderstand *v* 誤解する

misuse *n* 悪用

mitigate *v* 和らぐ

mix *v* 混合、構成

mixed-up *adj* 混乱した

mixer *n* 混合器

mixture *n* 混合物

mix-up *n* 混乱、取り違え

moan *v* うめく

moan *n* うめき声

mob *v* 群がる

mob *n* 群衆、暴徒

mobile *adj* 動きやすい

mobilize *v* 動員する

mobster *n* 暴力団員

mock *v* 嘲り笑う

mockery *n* 冷笑的な行為

mode *n* 様式

model *n* 模型

moderate *adj* 穏健な人

moderation *n* 節度、適度

modern *adj* 近代的な

modernize *v* 現代的になる

modest *adj* 謙虚な

modesty *n* つつましさ

modify *v* 修正する

module *n* モジュール

moisten *v* 湿らす

moisture *n* 水分

molar *n* 臼歯

mold *v* 型を作る

mold *n* 金型

moldy *adj* かびた

**M**

M

mole *n* モグラ
molecule *n* 分子
molest *v* 気にする
mom *n* ママ
moment *n* 瞬間
momentarily *adv* 一瞬に
momentous *adj* 重大な
monarch *n* 絶対君主
monarchy *n* 君主制
monastery *n* 修道院
monastic *adj* 修道院の
Monday *n* 月曜日
money *n* お金
money order *n* 郵便為替
monitor *v* モニター
monk *n* 修道士
monkey *n* 猿
monogamy *n* 一夫一婦制
monologue *n* 独白
monopolize *v* 〜を独占する
monopoly *n* 独占
monotonous *adj* 単調な
monotony *n* 単調さ
monster *n* 怪物
monstrous *adj* 奇怪な
month *n* 月
monthly *adv* 月1回の
monument *n* 記念建造物
monumental *adj* 記念碑の
mood *n* 気分、雰囲気
moody *adj* 気分屋の
moon *n* 月

moor *v* 荒れ地の
mop *v* モップ
moral *adj* 道徳上の
moral *n* 教訓
morality *n* 道徳性
more *adj* もっと
moreover *adv* さらに
morning *n* 朝、夜明け
moron *adj* 能なし
morphine *n* モルヒネ
morsel *n* 一口分
mortal *adj* 死すべき
mortality *n* 死亡、死亡数
mortar *n* モルタル
mortgage *n* 抵当、担保
mortification *n* くやしさ
mortify *v* 禁欲する
mortuary *n* 遺体安置所
mosaic *n* モザイク
mosque *n* モスク
mosquito *n* 蚊
moss *n* こけ
most *adj* 最も、一番
mostly *adv* 大部分は
motel *n* モーテル
moth *n* 蛾
mother *n* 母
motherhood *n* 母性
mother-in-law *n* 姑、義母
motion *n* 動き
motionless *adj* 動かない
motivate *v* 動かす

motive *n* 動機
motor *n* モーター
motorcycle *n* オートバイ
motto *n* モットー、標語
mouldy *adj* かびの生えた
mount *n* 上がること
mount *v* 上がる、高まる
mountain *n* 山
mountainous *adj* 山の多い
mourn *v* 嘆く
mourning *n* 哀悼
mouse *n* ネズミ
mouth *n* 口
move *n* 動き、移動
move *v* 移動する、動く
move back *v* 後ろへ動かす
move forward *v* 前へ進む
move out *v* 引っ越す
move up *v* 上昇する
movement *n* 動作
movie *n* 映画
mow *v* 置き場
much *adv* 多量
mucus *n* 粘液
mud *n* 泥
muddle *n* 乱雑
muddy *adj* 泥のついた
muffle *v* 音を消すもの
muffler *n* 襟巻き
mug *v* マグ
mugging *n* 路上強盗
mule *n* 頑固なやつ

multiple *adj* 多角的な
multiplication *n* 増加、乗法
multiply *v* 〜を増す
multitude *n* 多数、群衆
mumble *v* つぶやき
mummy *n* ミイラ
mumps *n* おたふく風邪
munitions *n* 軍需品
murder *n* 殺人
murderer *n* 殺人者
murky *adj* 真っ暗な
murmur *v* ブツブツ言う
murmur *n* ざわめき
muscle *n* 筋肉
museum *n* 博物館
mushroom *n* キノコ
music *n* 音楽
musician *n* 音楽家
Muslim *adj* イスラム教の
must *iv* 〜すべきである
mustache *n* 口ひげ
mustard *n* カラシ
muster *v* 集まる
mutate *v* 変化する
mute *adj* 口の利けない人
mutilate *v* 切断する
mutiny *n* 反抗、暴動
mutually *adv* 相互に
muzzle *v* 口止めする
muzzle *n* 鼻口部
my *adj* 私の
myopic *adj* 近視の

**M**

myself *pro* 私自身の
mysterious *adj* 神秘の
mystery *n* 不思議さ
mystic *adj* 秘密の
mystify *v* 〜を煙にまく
myth *n* 神話、伝説

# N

nag *v* 口うるさく言う
nagging *adj* 口やかましい
nail *n* つめ
naive *adj* 純真な
naked *adj* 裸の
name *n* 名前
namely *adv* すなわち
nanny *n* 乳母
nap *n* 昼寝
napkin *n* ナプキン
narcotic *n* 睡眠薬
narrate *v* 物語る
narrow *adj* 限られた
narrowly *adv* 辛うじて
nasty *adj* 不快な
nation *n* 国家
national *adj* 国家の
nationality *n* 国籍
nationalize *v* 〜を国営化する

native *adj* 生まれた
natural *adj* 普通の
naturally *adv* 当然、自然に
nature *n* 自然、天然
naughty *adj* 悪い
nausea *n* 吐き気
nave *n* 会衆席
navel *n* へそ
navigate *v* 航海する
navigation *n* 航海、飛行
navy *n* 海軍
navy blue *adj* 濃紺
near *pre* 〜の近くに
nearby *adj* すぐ近くの
nearly *adv* ほとんど
nearsighted *adj* 近眼の
neat *adj* 整頓された
neatly *adv* きちんと
necessary *adj* 必要な
necessitate *v* 〜を必要とする
necessity *n* 必要
neck *n* 首
necklace *n* ネックレス
necktie *n* ネクタイ
need *v* 必要がある
need *n* 必要性
needle *n* 縫い針
needless *adj* 不必要な
needy *adj* 貧窮の
negative *adj* 否定の
neglect *v* 無視する
neglect *n* 無視、決如

negligence *n* 怠慢、手抜き

negligent *adj* 怠慢な

negotiate *v* 交渉する

negotiation *n* 交渉、協議

neighbor *n* 隣人

neighborhood *n* 近所

neither *adj* どちらの〜もない

neither *adv* 〜もまた〜ない

nephew *n* 甥

nerve *n* 神経、筋

nervous *adj* 緊張する

nest *n* 巣

net *n* 網、ネット

Netherlands *n* オランダ

network *n* 網目

neurotic *adj* ノイローゼの

neutral *adj* 中立の

neutralize *v* 中立化する

never *adv* 決して〜ない

new *adj* 新しい

newborn *n* 新生児

newcomer *n* 初心者

newly *adv* 新たに

newlywed *adj* 新婚者

news *n* 知らせ

newscast *n* ニュース放送

newsletter *n* 会報

newspaper *n* 新聞

newsstand *n* 売店

next *adj* 次の

next door *adj* お隣の

nibble *v* かじる

nice *adj* 良い

nicely *adv* うまく

nickel *n* ニッケル

nickname *n* あだ名

nicotine *n* ニコチン

niece *n* 姪

night *n* 夜、晩

nightfall *n* 夕暮れ

nightgown *n* ねまき

nightingale *n* ナイチンゲール

nightmare *n* 悪夢

nine *adj* 9、9個の

nineteen *adj* 19、19個の

ninety *adj* 90、90個の

ninth *adj* 9分の1

nip *n* はさみ

nip *v* つねる、かむ

nipple *n* 乳首

nitrogen *n* チッソ

no one *pro* 一人も〜ない

nobility *n* 貴族階級

noble *adj* 高貴の

nobleman *adj* 貴族

nobody *pro* 誰も〜ない

nocturnal *adj* 夜行性の

nod *v* うなずき

noise *n* 雑音

noisily *adv* 騒々しく

noisy *adj* 騒々しい

nominate *v* 任命する

none *pre* 誰も〜ない

nonetheless *c* とはいえ

**N**

nonsense *n* くだらなさ

nonsmoker *n* 非喫煙者

nonstop *adv* 直行で

noon *n* 正午

noose *n* 締めなわ

nor *c* そしてまた～ない

norm *n* 標準

normal *adj* 正常な

normalize *v* 標準化する

normally *adv* 正常に

north *n* 北

northeast *n* 北東

northern *adj* 北方の

northerner *adj* 北部地方の人

Norway *n* ノルウエー

Norwegian *adj* ノルウエー人

nose *n* 鼻

nosedive *v* 暴落する

nostalgia *n* 懐旧、郷愁

nostril *n* 鼻孔、小鼻

nosy *adj* おせっかいな

not *adv* ～でない

notable *adj* 著名な

notably *adv* 有名な

notary *n* 公証人

note *n* メモ、覚書

note *v* 書き留める

notebook *n* ノート

noteworthy *adj* 注目すべき

nothing *n* 無、無価値なもの

notice *v* ～に気が付く

notice *n* 通知

noticeable *adj* 顕著な

notification *n* 告示

notify *v* ～に知らせる

notion *n* 概念、観念

notorious *adj* 悪名高い

noun *n* 名詞

nourish *v* 養う

nourishment *n* 食物

novel *n* 小説

novelist *n* 小説家

novelty *n* 珍しいもの

November *n* １１月

novice *n* 未熟者

now *adv* 今、現在

nowadays *adv* 最近

nowhere *adv* どこに～ない

noxious *adj* 有毒な

nozzle *n* ノズル

nuance *n* 陰影

nuclear *adj* 原子力の

nude *adj* 裸の

nudism *n* 裸体主義

nudist *n* ヌーディスト

nudity *n* 裸

nuisance *n* 迷惑

null *adj* 無価値の

nullify *v* 取り消す

numb *adj* 無感覚な

number *n* 数字

numbness *n* 無感覚

numerous *adj* 多数の

nun *n* 修道女

nurse _n_ 看護士
nurse _v_ 看護する
nursery _n_ 保育園
nurture _v_ 養育
nut _n_ 木の実
nutrition _n_ 栄養分
nutritious _adj_ 栄養のある
nut-shell _n_ くるみ
nutty _adj_ 風変わりな

oak _n_ オーク材
oar _n_ オール
oasis _n_ 安らぎの場所
oath _n_ 誓い、誓約
oatmeal _n_ オートミール
obedience _n_ 服従、忠実
obedient _adj_ 従順な
obese _adj_ 肥満体の
obey _v_ 〜に従う
object _v_ 反対する
object _n_ 目的、対象
objection _n_ 異議
objective _n_ 目標、方針
obligate _v_ 義務付ける
obligation _n_ 義務、義理
obligatory _adj_ 義務的な

oblige _v_ 好意を示す
obliged _adj_ 感謝する
oblique _adj_ 傾いた、斜めの
obliterate _v_ 消し去る
oblivion _n_ 忘却、恩赦
oblivious _adj_ 忘れっぽい
oblong _adj_ 短形の
obnoxious _adj_ 反抗的な
obscene _adj_ 卑猥な
obscenity _n_ わいせつなもの
obscure _adj_ 目立たない
obscurity _n_ 暗がり
observation _n_ 観察
observatory _n_ 観測所
observe _v_ 見学する
obsess _v_ 頭に取り付く
obsession _n_ 執念
obsolete _adj_ 時代遅れの
obstacle _n_ 障害、妨害
obstinacy _n_ 頑固さ
obstinate _adj_ 頑固な
obstruct _v_ 〜を妨害する
obstruction _n_ 邪魔、妨害物
obtain _v_ 手に入れる
obvious _adj_ 明らかな
obviously _adv_ 明らかに
occasion _n_ 好機、出来事
occasionally _adv_ 時たま
occult _adj_ オカルト現象
occupant _n_ 占有者
occupation _n_ 職業
occupy _v_ 占領する

occur *v* 発生する

ocean *n* 大洋、海

October *n* １０月

octopus *n* タコ

ocurrence *n* 発生

odd *adj* 奇妙な

oddity *n* 異常なもの

odds *n* 勝ち目

odious *adj* 醜悪な

odometer *n* 走行距離計

odor *n* 臭気、香り

odyssey *n* 長い冒険

of *pre* 〜の

off *adv* 休みの

offend *v* 攻撃する

offense *n* 侮辱

offensive *adj* 侮辱的な

offer *v* 申し出る

offer *n* 申し出

offering *n* もし出ること

office *n* 事務所

officer *n* 役人、将校

official *adj* 公式の

officiate *v* 職務を果たす

offset *v* 相殺する

offspring *n* 子孫、所産

often *adv* しばしば

oil *n* 油、石油

ointment *n* 軟膏

okay *adv* わかりました

old *adj* 古い、年とった

old age *n* 高齢の

old-fashioned *adj* 昔風の

olive *n* オリーブ

olympics *n* オリンピック

omelette *n* オムレツ

omen *n* 前兆、予感

ominous *adj* 不吉な

omission *n* 省力、怠慢

omit *v* 除く、省略する

on *pre* 〜に接して

once *adv* 1回、一度

once *c* 〜するとすぐに

one *adj* 1の、1個の

oneself *pre* 自分自身

ongoing *adj* 継続している

onion *n* タマネギ

onlooker *n* 見物人

only *adv* ただ〜だけ

onset *n* 開始、着手

onslaught *n* 猛攻、襲来

onwards *adv* 前方へ

opaque *adj* 不透明なもの

open *v* 開く

open *adj* 開かれた

open up *v* 広げる

opening *n* 始め、序盤

open-minded *adj* 心の広い

openness *n* 開放性、率直

opera *n* 歌劇、オペラ

operate *v* 作動する

operation *n* 働き、操作

opinion *n* 意見

opinionated *adj* 気難しい

opium *n* アヘン

opponent *n* 対戦相手

opportune *adj* 適切な

opportunity *n* 機会

oppose *v* 反対する

opposite *adj* 反対側の

opposite *adv* 反対側に

opposite *n* 反対

opposition *n* 敵対

oppress *v* 虐げる

oppression *n* 抑圧する

opt for *v* 決定する

optical *adj* 視覚の

optician *n* 光学技術者

optimism *n* 楽観主義

optimistic *adj* 楽観的な

option *n* 選択肢

optional *adj* 任意の

opulence *n* 富裕

or *c* ～か、または

oracle *n* 神のお告げ

orally *adv* 口頭で

orange *n* オレンジ

orangutan *n* オラウータン

orbit *n* 軌道

orchard *n* 果樹園

orchestra *n* オーケストラ

ordain *v* 任命する

ordeal *n* 難儀

order *n* 注文する

ordinarily *adv* 通常

ordinary *adj* 普通の

ordination *n* 叙階式

ore *n* 原鉱

organ *n* オルガン、臓器

organism *n* 有機体

organist *n* オルガン奏者

organization *n* 組織

organize *v* 編成する

orient *n* 東洋

oriental *adj* 東洋の

orientation *n* 適応

oriented *adj* 指向性の

origin *n* 源、起源

original *adj* 元の、原本

originally *adv* 本来は

originate *v* 由来する

ornament *n* 装飾品、飾り

ornamental *adj* 装飾用の

orphan *n* 孤児の

orphanage *n* 自動養護施設

orthodox *adj* 正統な

ostentatious *adj* けばけばしい

ostrich *n* ダチョウ

other *adj* ほかの

otherwise *adv* さもなければ

otter *n* カワウソ

ought to *iv* ～すべきである

ounce *n* オンス

our *adj* 私たちの

ours *pro* 私たちのもの

ourselves *pro* われわれ自身の

oust *v* 追い払う

out *adv* 外に出て

O

outbreak *n* 突発、発生
outburst *n* 爆発、噴出
outcast *adj* 追放された
outcome *n* 結果、結末
outcry *n* 絶叫、悲鳴
outdated *adj* 時代遅れの
outdo *v* 〜をしのぐ
outdoor *adv* 戸外の
outdoors *adv* 屋外で
outer *adj* 圏外
outfit *n* 洋服、服装一式
outgoing *adj* 社交的な
outgrow *v* 〜より大きくなる
outing *n* 外出、散歩
outlast *v* 〜より長く生きる
outlaw *v* 時効にする
outlet *n* 直販店
outline *n* 輪郭、概略
outline *v* 概説する
outlive *v* 克服する
outlook *n* 見解、展望
outmoded *adj* 流行遅れの
outnumber *v* 数を上回る
outpatient *n* 外来患者
outpouring *n* ほとばしり
output *n* 産出、制作
outrage *n* 激怒、暴動
outrageous *adj* 非道な
outright *adj* 完全な
outrun *v* 〜を追い越す
outset *n* 着手、手始め
outshine *v* より光る、輝く

outside *adv* 外側の
outsider *n* 部外者
outskirts *n* 郊外、町はずれ
outspoken *adj* 率直な
outstanding *adj* ずば抜けた
outward *adj* 国外への
outweigh *v* 〜より重い
oval *adj* 卵形の
ovary *n* 卵巣
ovation *n* 大喝采
oven *n* オーブン
over *pre* 〜の向こう側に
overall *adv* 全体に、概して
overbearing *adj* 横柄な
overboard *adv* 船外に
overcast *adj* 陰うつな
overcharge *v* 上塗りする
overcoat *n* 上塗り
overcome *v* 克服する
overcrowded *adj* 超満員の
overdo *v* やり過ぎる
overdone *adj* 過度の
overdose *n* 薬剤の過剰摂取
overdue *adj* 期限の切れた
overestimate *v* 買いかぶる
overflow *v* あふれる
overhaul *v* 整備する
overlap *v* 重なり合う
overlook *v* 見落とす
overnight *adv* 一晩中
overpower *v* 征服する
overrate *v* 過大評価する

| | |
|---|---|
| **override** *v* ～を乗り越える |  **P** |
| **overrule** *v* 却下する | |
| **overrun** *v* 行き過ぎる | |
| **overseas** *adv* 海外の | **pace** *v* 歩調をとって歩く |
| **oversee** *v* 監視する | **pace** *n* 歩調、速度 |
| **overshadow** *v* ～を暗くする | **pacify** *v* 静める |
| **oversight** *n* 見過ごし | **pack** *v* 荷造りする |
| **overstate** *v* 大げさに言う | **package** *n* 荷物 |
| **overstep** *v* ～の限度を超す | **pact** *n* 契約、条約 |
| **overtake** *v* 追い越す | **pad** *v* 当てもの、パッド |
| **overthrow** *v* 転覆する | **padding** *n* 詰め物 |
| **overthrow** *n* 打倒、転覆 | **paddle** *v* こぐ、たたく |
| **overtime** *adv* 時間外の | **padlock** *n* 南京錠 |
| **overturn** *v* 転覆する | **pagan** *adj* 異教の |
| **overview** *n* 概観、概説 | **page** *n* ページ |
| **overweight** *adj* 超過の | **pail** *n* 手桶 |
| **overwhelm** *v* 圧倒する | **pain** *n* 痛み |
| **owe** *v* 義務を負っている | **painful** *adj* 痛い |
| **owing to** *adv* ～のおかげで | **painkiller** *n* 鎮痛薬 |
| **owl** *n* フクロウ | **painless** *adj* 痛みのない |
| **own** *v* 所有する | **paint** *v* ペンキで塗る |
| **own** *adj* 自己の | **paint** *n* ペンキ |
| **owner** *n* 所有者 | **paintbrush** *n* 絵筆 |
| **ownership** *n* 所有権 | **painter** *n* 画家 |
| **ox** *n* 雄牛 | **painting** *n* 絵画 |
| **oxen** *n* 雄牛の複数形 | **pair** *n* 一組 |
| **oxygen** *n* 酸素 | **pajamas** *n* パジャマ |
| **oyster** *n* カキ | **pal** *n* 仲間、友人 |
| | **palace** *n* 宮殿、公邸 |
| | **palate** *n* 口蓋、味覚 |
| | **pale** *adj* 青ざめた |
| | **paleness** *n* 蒼白 |

O
P

palm *n* 手のひら

palpable *adj* 容易に分かる

paltry *adj* つまらない

pamper *v* 人を甘やかす

pamphlet *n* 小冊子

pan *n* 鍋、フライパン

pancreas *n* 膵臓

pander *v* 迎合する

pang *n* 悲痛、激痛

panic *n* 恐怖

panorama *n* 全景

panther *n* ヒョウ

pantry *n* 食料庫

pants *n* ズボン

papacy *n* ローマ教皇の職

paper *n* 紙、新聞

paperclip *n* 紙クリップ

paperwork *n* 事務処理

parable *n* 寓話、比喩

parade *n* パレード

paradise *n* 天国、楽園

paradox *n* 逆説

paragraph *n* 段落

parakeet *n* インコ

parallel *n* 平行線

paralysis *n* 麻痺、停滞

paralyze *v* 麻痺させる

parameters *n* パラメーター

paramount *adj* 最高の、至上の

paranoid *adj* 偏執症の

parasite *n* 寄生虫

paratrooper *n* 落下傘降下兵

parcel *n* 小包

parcel post *n* 小包郵便

parched *adj* 乾燥した

parchment *n* 羊皮紙

pardon *v* 許す、放免する

pardon *n* 寛容、許し

parenthesis *n* 丸括弧

parents *n* 両親

parish *n* 小教区

parishioner *n* 教区民

parity *n* 同額、同等

park *v* 駐車する

park *n* 公園、駐車

parking *n* 駐車場

parliament *n* 国会、議会

parochial *adj* 教区の

parrot *n* オウム

part *v* 割れる

part *n* 一部、部分

partial *adj* 部分的な

partially *adv* 不十分な

participate *v* 参加する

participation *n* 参加

participle *n* 分詞

particle *n* 粒子、微量

particular *adj* 特定の

particularly *adv* 特に

parting *n* 別れ、分離

partisan *n* 味方、同志

partition *n* 分配、区分

partly *adv* 一部分は

partner *n* 共同出資者

P

partnership *n* 結びつき
partridge *n* 猟鳥
party *n* パーティー
pass *n* 道、通路
pass *v* 通る、過ぎる
pass around *v* 順に回す
pass away *v* 過ぎ去る
pass out *v* 出て行く
passage *n* 通路、廊下
passenger *n* 乗客、旅客
passer-by *n* 通行人
passion *n* 情熱、激情
passionate *adj* 情熱的な
passive *adj* 受け身の
passport *n* 旅券、パスポート
password *n* 暗証番号
past *adj* 過去の
paste *v* のりをつける
paste *n* のり
pasteurize *v* 殺菌された
pastime *n* 気晴らし
pastor *n* 牧師、羊使い
pastoral *adj* 田園の
pastry *n* ねり菓子
pasture *n* 牧草地
pat *n* 軽くたたくこと
patch *v* 当て布を当てる
patch *n* 布片
patent *n* 特許権
patent *adj* 特許の
paternity *n* 父系
path *n* 小道

pathetic *adj* 痛ましい
patience *n* 忍耐、我慢
patient *adj* 病人、患者
patio *n* パティオ、中庭
patriarch *n* 家長
patrimony *n* 世襲財産
patriot *n* 愛国者
patriotic *adj* 愛国的な
patrol *n* 巡回、パトロール
patron *n* 後援者
patronage *n* 後援、支援
pattern *n* 傾向、模様
pavement *n* 舗装道路
pavilion *n* 展示館
paw *n* 足、手
pawn *v* 質に入れる
pawnbroker *n* 質屋
pay *n* 支払い
pay *iv* 支払う
pay back *v* 返済する
pay off *v* 払い終える
payable *adj* 支払可能な
paycheck *n* 給与
payee *n* 受取人
payment *n* 支払い、納付
payroll *n* 給料
payslip *n* 給料明細
pea *n* エンドウ豆
peace *n* 平和
peaceful *adj* 平和な
peach *n* 桃
peacock *n* クジャク

P

peak *n* 先端、単調

peanut *n* 落花生

pear *n* 西洋ナシ

pearl *n* 真珠

peasant *n* 農夫

pebble *n* 小石

peculiar *adj* 特有な

pedagogy *n* 教育学

pedal *n* ペダル

pedantic *adj* 学者ぶった

pedestrian *n* 歩行者

peel *v* 皮をむく

peel *n* 皮

peep *v* のぞき見する

peer *n* 同業者

pelican *n* ペリカン

pellet *n* 小粒

pen *n* ペン

penalize *v* 罰する

penalty *n* 刑罰、罰金

penance *n* 自己処罰

penchant *n* 強い好み

pencil *n* 鉛筆

pendant *n* ペンダント

pending *adj* 保留中の

pendulum *n* 振り子

penetrate *v* 貫く

penguin *n* ペンギン

penicillin *n* ペニシリン

peninsula *n* 半島

penitent *n* 後悔している人

penniless *adj* 無一文の

penny *n* ペニー

pension *n* 年金、恩給

pentagon *n* 5角形

pent-up *adj* 閉じ込められた

people *n* 人々、世間

pepper *n* コショウ

per *pre* 〜につき

perceive *v* 把握する

percent *adv* パーセント

percentage *n* 割合

perception *n* 知覚、見識

perennial *adj* 永続する

perfect *adj* 完璧な

perfection *n* 完全、完成

perforate *v* 〜に穴を開ける

perforation *n* 目打ち

perform *v* 演じる

performance *n* 業績、性能

perfume *n* 香水、香料

perhaps *adv* たぶん

peril *n* 危険

perilous *adj* 危険な

perimeter *n* 周囲の

period *n* 終止符、期間

perish *v* 滅びる、死ぬ

perishable *adj* 傷みやすい

perjury *n* 偽り、偽証

permanent *adj* 永続的な

permeate *v* 浸透する

permission *n* 許可、承認

permit *v* 許可する

pernicious *adj* 有害な

perpetrate v 実行する
persecute v ～を迫害する
persevere v 辛抱する
persist v 主張する
persistence n こだわり、貫徹
persistent adj 持続性の
person n 人、人物
personal adj 個人的な
personality n 性格、人柄
personify v 人格化する
personnel n 人員、人事の
perspective n 展望、視野
perspiration n 発汗
perspire v ～を汗に出す
persuade v 説得する
persuasion n 説得、信念
persuasive adj 説得力のある
pertain v 付属する
pertinent adj 関連のある
perturb v 動揺させる
perverse adj 邪悪な
pervert adj ～を悪用する
pessimism n 悲観主義者
pessimistic adj 悲観的な
pest n 疫病、ペスト
pester v ～を苦しめる
pesticide n 殺虫剤、農薬
petal n 花弁
petite adj 小柄な
petition n 請願書
petrified adj 石化した
petroleum n 石油

pettiness n けち
petty adj わずかな
pew n 会衆席
phantom n 幽霊、幻像
pharmacist n 薬剤師
pharmacy n 薬局
phase n 段階、局面
pheasant n キジ
phenomenon n 現象、事象
philosopher n 哲学者
philosophy n 哲学、人生観
phobia n 恐怖症
phone n 電話
phone v 電話をする
phoney adj 偽の
phosphorus n リン
photo n フォト、写真
photocopy n 写真複写
photograph v 写真
photographer n 写真家
photography n 写真撮影
phrase n 言い回し、語句
physically adj 物理的に
physician n 医師
physics n 物理学
pianist n ピアニスト
piano n ピアノ
pick v 選ぶ、摘み取る
pick up v 拾い上げる
pickpocket n すり
pickup n 収集
picture n 絵、像

P

picture v ～を描写する
picturesque adj 絵のような
pie n パイ
piece n 一片
piecemeal adv 少しずつ
pier n 追悼、桟橋
pierce v ピアス
piercing n ピアスをすること
piety n 信心深さ
pig n ブタ
pigeon n ハト
piggy bank n 貯金箱
pile v 積み重なる
pile n 積み重ね
pile up v 積み重ねる
pilfer v ～をくすねる
pilgrim n 巡礼者
pilgrimage n 巡礼
pill n 錠剤、ピル
pillage v 略奪する
pillar n 柱
pillow n 枕
pillowcase n 枕カバー
pilot n パイロット
pimple n 吹き出物
pin n ピン
pincers n やっとこ
pinch v つまむ
pinch n つまむこと
pine n マツの木
pineapple n パイナップル
pink adj 桃色

pinpoint v 特定する
pint n パイント
pioneer n 開拓者
pious adj 宗教的な
pipe n 管、導管
pipeline n 輸送管路
piracy n 海賊行為
pirate n 海賊、略奪者
pistol n ピストル、銃
pit n 穴、くぼみ
pitch-black adj 漆黒の
pitchfork n くま手
pitfall n 落とし穴
pitiful adj 気の毒な
pity n 同情、哀れみ
placard n はり紙
placate v なだめる
place n 場所
placid adj 穏やかな
plague n 疫病、ペスト
plain n 質素な
plain adj 平原、平野
plainly adv 質素に
plaintiff n 原告、起訴人
plan v 計画する
plan n 計画
plane n 飛行機、平面
planet n 惑星
plant v 植える
plant n 植物
plaster n 石こう
plastic n プラスチック

plate *n* お皿
plateau *n* 高原
platform *n* 基盤
platinum *n* 白金
platoon *n* 集団
plausible *adj* もっともらしい
play *v* 遊ぶ、演奏する
play *n* 劇、演劇
player *n* 選手、演奏者
playful *adj* 遊び戯れる
playground *n* 遊び場
plea *n* 口実、言い訳
plead *v* 嘆願する
pleasant *adj* 愉快な
please *v* 喜ばせる
pleasing *adj* 楽しい
pleasure *n* 楽しみ
pleat *n* ひだ
pledge *v* 誓約する
pledge *n* 誓約
plentiful *adj* 豊富な
plenty *n* たくさんの
pliable *adj* 曲げやすい
pliers *n* プライヤー
plot *v* たくらむ
plot *n* 策略、陰謀
plow *v* すきで耕す
ploy *n* 策略
pluck *v* 引っ張る
plug *v* 栓をする
plug *n* 栓、プラグ
plum *n* プラム

plumber *n* 配管工
plumbing *n* 配管工事
plummet *v* 急落する
plump *adj* 肉つきの良い
plunder *v* こっそり盗む
plunge *v* 飛び込む
plunge *n* 飛び込み
plural *n* 複数形
plus *adv* 陽性の
plush *adj* フラシ天の
plutonium *n* プルトニウム
pneumonia *n* 肺炎
pocket *n* 財布
poem *n* 詩
poet *n* 詩人
poetry *n* 詩的作品
poignant *adj* 心を打つ
point *n* 点、得点
point *v* 指す、示す
pointed *adj* 鋭い
pointless *adj* 先のない
poise *n* 平衡
poison *v* 毒する
poison *n* 毒
poisoning *n* 中毒
poisonous *adj* 有毒な
Poland *n* ポーランド
polar *adj* 極の、極地の
pole *n* 棒、ポール
police *n* 警察
policeman *n* 警察官
policy *n* 政策

P

polish *n* 磨くこと

polish *v* 磨く

polite *adj* 丁寧な

politeness *n* 丁寧

politician *n* 政治家

politics *n* 政治

poll *n* 投票

pollen *n* 花粉

pollute *v* 汚染する

pollution *n* 汚染

polygamist *adj* 一夫多妻者

polygamy *n* 複婚

pomegranate *n* ザクロ

pomposity *n* 華やかさ

pond *n* 池

ponder *v* じっくり考える

pontiff *n* 教皇

pool *n* プール

pool *v* たまりを作る

poor *n* 貧民

poorly *adv* 貧しく

popcorn *n* ポップコーン

Pope *n* ローマ法王

poppy *n* ケシ、ポピー

popular *adj* 人気のある

popularize *v* 大衆化する

populate *v* 居住させる

population *n* 人口

porcelain *n* 磁器

porch *n* ポーチ

porcupine *n* ヤマアラシ

pore *n* 詳細を調べる

pork *n* 豚肉

porous *adj* 穴だらけの

port *n* 港

portable *adj* 携帯用の

portent *n* 前兆

porter *n* 運搬人

portion *n* 部分

portrait *n* 肖像画

portray *v* 描く

Portugal *n* ポルトガル

Portuguese *adj* ポルトガル人

pose *v* 気取る

posh *adj* こぎれいな

position *n* 位置、場所

positive *adj* 積極的な

possess *v* 所有する

possession *n* 所有、所持

possibility *n* 可能性

possible *adj* 可能性

post *n* 柱、くい

post office *n* 郵便局

postage *n* 郵便料金

postcard *n* はがき

poster *n* ポスター

posterity *n* 後世、子孫

postman *n* 郵便配達人

postmark *n* 消印

postpone *v* 延期する

postponement *n* 延期

pot *n* 鉢、つぼ

potato *n* ポテト

potent *adj* 勢力のある

potential *adj* 可能な
pothole *n* 深い穴
poultry *n* 飼っている鳥類
pound *v* 激しく打つ
pound *n* ポンド
pour *v* 注ぐ
poverty *n* 貧乏
powder *n* 粉、粉末
power *n* 力、勢力
powerful *adj* 強力な
powerless *adj* 無能な
practical *adj* 実用的な
practice *v* 練習、演習
practise *v* 練習する
practising *adj* 開業の
pragmatist *adj* 実用主義哲学者
prairie *n* 草原地帯
praise *v* 称賛する
praise *n* 称賛
praiseworthy *adj* 感心な
prank *n* 悪ふざけ
prawn *n* クルマエビ
pray *v* 祈る
prayer *n* 祈り、祈る人
preach *v* 説教する
preacher *n* 説教師
preaching *n* 説教
preamble *n* 序文
precarious *adj* 不安定な
precaution *n* 用心、警戒
precede *v* 先立つ
precedent *n* 前例、先例

preceding *adj* 〜に先行する
precept *n* 教訓
precious *adj* 高価な
precipice *n* 絶壁
precipitate *v* 沈殿物
precise *adj* 正確な
precision *n* 正確さ
precocious *adj* 早熟な
precursor *n* 先駆者
predecessor *n* 前任者
predicament *n* 窮地、苦境
predict *v* 予測する
prediction *n* 予言、予測
predilection *n* 偏愛
predisposed *adj* 傾向がある
predominate *v* 優勢である
preempt *v* 先取りする
preface *n* 前置き、序論
prefer *v* 〜を好む
preference *n* 優先、好み
prefix *n* 接頭辞
pregnancy *n* 妊娠
pregnant *adj* 妊娠した
prehistoric *adj* 先史時代の
prejudice *n* 偏見
preliminary *adj* 準備の、予備の
prelude *n* 前奏曲、前兆
premature *adj* 早過ぎる
premeditate *v* 前もって計画する
premeditation *n* 予謀
premier *adj* 第1位の
premise *n* 前提、家庭

P

**premises** *n* 建物勘定
**premonition** *n* 予感、兆候
**preoccupation** *n* 没頭
**preoccupy** *v* ～を夢中にする
**preparation** *n* 用意、準備
**prepare** *v* 準備する
**preposition** *n* 前置詞
**prerequisite** *n* 必要条件
**prerogative** *n* 特権、特典
**prescribe** *v* 指示する
**prescription** *n* 規定、指示
**presence** *n* 存在すること
**present** *adj* 存在している
**present** *v* ～を贈る
**presentation** *n* 発表、提示
**preserve** *v* ～を保つ
**preside** *v* 主宰する
**presidency** *n* 社長
**president** *n* 大統領
**press** *n* 押すこと
**press** *v* 切迫する
**pressing** *adj* 緊急の
**pressure** *v* 圧力をかける
**pressure** *n* 圧力
**prestige** *n* 名声、威信
**presume** *v* 推理する
**presumption** *n* 推定
**presupposition** *n* 前提
**pretend** *v* ～のふりをする
**pretense** *n* 偽ること
**pretension** *n* 見せかけ
**pretty** *adj* かわいい

**prevail** *v* 普及する
**prevalent** *adj* 流行した
**prevent** *v* 防ぐ、阻む
**prevention** *n* 防止、予防
**preventive** *adj* 予防の
**preview** *n* 下見、予告編
**previous** *adj* 以前の
**previously** *adv* 前に
**prey** *n* 餌食にする
**price** *n* 値段、価格
**pricey** *adj* 高価な
**prick** *v* ～を刺す
**pride** *n* 誇り、自尊心
**priest** *n* 司祭、神父
**priestess** *n* 女性の祭司
**priesthood** *n* 司祭職
**primacy** *n* 最重要
**primarily** *adv* 最初に
**prime** *adj* 最も重要な
**primitive** *adj* 原始の
**prince** *n* 王子、プリンス
**princess** *n* 王妃、皇女
**principal** *adj* 主な、重要な
**principle** *n* 原則、主義
**print** *v* 印刷する
**print** *n* 印刷
**printer** *n* プリンター
**printing** *n* 印刷字
**prior** *adj* 先立って
**priority** *n* 優先事項
**prism** *n* プリズム
**prison** *n* 刑務所

prisoner *n* 囚人、捕虜
privacy *n* 私生活
private *adj* 個人用の
privilege *n* 特権、特典
prize *n* 賞金、景品
probability *n* 可能性
probable *adj* あり得る
probe *v* 探る、探査する
probing *n* 厳密な調査
problem *n* 問題、課題
problematic *adj* 問題のある
procedure *n* 手順
proceed *v* 進展する
proceedings *n* 手続き
proceeds *n* 収益
process *v* 処理する
process *n* 過程、経過
procession *n* 行進、前進
proclaim *v* 宣告する
proclamation *n* 宣言、声明
procrastinate *v* 先延ばしにする
procreate *v* 子孫をもうける
procure *v* 入手する、得る
prod *v* 突く、刺激する
prodigious *adj* 驚異的な
prodigy *n* 神童、奇才
produce *v* 生産する
produce *n* 生産物
product *n* 製品、産物
production *n* 生産、製造
productive *adj* 生産的な
profane *adj* 俗悪な

profess *v* はっきりと言う
profession *n* 専門的職業
professional *adj* 専門の
professor *n* 大学教授
proficiency *n* 上達、熟練
proficient *adj* 堪能な
profile *n* 横顔、外形
profit *v* 利益を得る
profit *n* 利益、得
profitable *adj* 有益な
profound *adj* 意味深い
program *n* 予定表
programmer *n* プログラマー
progress *v* 進む、向上する
progress *n* 前進、進展
progressive *adj* 進歩的な
prohibit *v* 禁止する
prohibition *n* 禁止
project *v* 投影する
project *n* 事業計画
projectile *n* 発射体
prologue *n* 序詞
prolong *v* 延長する
promenade *n* 散歩道
prominent *adj* 著名な
promiscuous *adj* 乱れた
promise *n* 約束
promote *v* 推進する
promotion *n* 推進
prompt *adj* 迅速な
prone *adj* 〜しがちな
pronoun *n* 代名詞

**P**

pronounce v 音読する

proof n 証拠

propaganda n 宣伝

propagate v 繁殖する

propel v 精進させる

propensity n 性癖

proper adj 適した

properly adv 相応に

property n 所有物

prophecy n お告げ

prophet n 預言者

proportion n 割合

proposal n 提案

propose v 提案する

proposition n 提案

prose n 散文体

prosecute v 起訴する

prosecutor n 検事

prospect n 見込み

prosper v 成功させ

prosperity n 繁栄

prosperous adj 繁栄している

prostate n 前立腺

prostrate adj ひれ伏した

protect v 保護する

protection n 保護

protein n タンパク質

protest v 抗議する

protest n 抗議

protocol n 儀典、手順

prototype n 原型、試作品

protract v 長引かせる

protracted adj 長引く

protrude v ～から突き出る

proud adj 誇る

proudly adv 誇らしげに

prove v 証明する

proven adj 証明された

proverb n ことわざ

provide v 提供する

providence n 神意、摂理

providing that c ～を条件として

province n 州、地方

provision n 規定、条件

provisional adj 暫定の

provocation n 挑発

provoke v 挑発する

prow n 船首

proximity n 接近、近似

proxy n 代用物

prudence n 慎重さ

prudent adj 分別がある

prune v 刈り取る

prune n スモモ

prurient adj 好色な

pseudonym n 偽名、ペンネーム

psychiatrist n 精神科医

psychiatry n 精神科

psychic adj 精神の、心霊の

psychology n 心理学

psychopath n 狂人

puberty n 思春期

public adj 公衆の、国の

publication n 出版物

**publicity** n 評判、公表

**publicly** adv 人前で

**publish** v 出版する

**publisher** n 出版社

**pudding** n プディング菓子

**puerile** adj 幼稚な

**puff** n ひと吹き

**puffed** adj 膨らんだ

**pull** v 引っ張る

**pull ahead** v 前に出る

**pull down** v 引きおろす

**pull out** v 引き抜く

**pulley** n 滑車装置

**pulp** n パルプ

**pulpit** n 説教壇

**pulsate** v 鼓動する

**pulse** n 脈

**pulverize** v 粉々になる

**pump** v くみ上げる

**pump** n ポンプ

**pumpkin** n かぼちゃ

**punch** v 穴を開ける

**punch** n 穴開け器、一撃

**punctual** adj 定時の

**puncture** n 穴を開けること

**punish** v 罰する

**punishable** adj 罰すべき

**punishment** n 罰すること

**pupil** n 児童、生徒

**puppet** n 指人形

**puppy** n 子犬

**purchase** v 購入する

**purchase** n 購入

**pure** adj 純粋な

**puree** n ピューレ

**purgatory** n 苦行

**purge** n 浄化

**purge** v 清める

**purification** n 精製

**purify** v 浄化する

**purity** n 清らかさ

**purple** adj 紫色の

**purpose** n 目的

**purposely** adv わざと

**purse** n 財布

**pursue** v 追跡する

**pursuit** n 追いかけ

**pus** n 膿

**push** v 押す

**pushy** adj 押しの強い

**put** iv 置く

**put aside** v 脇へ置く

**put away** v 片付ける

**put off** v 〜逃れる

**put out** v 追い出す

**put up** v 掲示する

**put up with** v 我慢する

**putrid** adj 腐敗した

**puzzle** n 難問

**puzzling** adj 不可解な

**pyramid** n ピラミッド

**python** n ニシキヘビ

P

# Q

quagmire *n* ぬかるみ

quail *n* ウズラ

quake *v* 震える

qualify *v* 資格を得る

quality *n* 質、品質

qualm *n* 不安

quandery *n* 困惑

quantity *n* 量

quarrel *v* 口論する

quarrel *n* 口論

quarrelsome *adj* 短気な

quarry *n* 採石場

quarter *n* 4回

quarterly *adj* 年4回の

quarters *n* 四半期、宿舎

quash *v* 鎮圧する

queen *n* 女王

queer *adj* 変質の

quell *v* ～を鎮める

quench *v* 急冷する

quest *n* 追求

question *v* 質問する

question *n* 質問

questionable *adj* 疑わしい

questionnaire *n* アンケート

queue *n* 列

quick *adj* 速い

quicken *v* 速くなる

quickly *adv* 速く

quicksand *n* 流砂

quiet *adj* 静けさ

quietness *n* 静寂

quilt *n* キルト

quit *iv* やめる

quite *adv* すっかり

quiver *v* 震え、振動

quiz *v* 小テストをする

quotation *n* 引用文

quote *v* 引用する

quotient *n* 指数

# R

rabbi *n* 指導者

rabbit *n* ウサギ

rabies *n* 狂犬病

raccoon *n* アライグマ

race *v* 競争する

race *n* レース、競争

racism *n* 人種差別

racist *adj* 人種差別主義者

racket *n* ラケット

racketeering *n* ゆすり、たかり

radar *n* レーダー

radiation *n* 放射、放射線

radiator *n* 放熱器

radical *adj* 急進主義者

Q
R

radio *n* 無線機

radish *n* 大根

radius *n* 半径

raffle *n* ラッフル

raft *n* いかだ

rag *n* ぼろ、ぼろ切れ

rage *n* 激怒

ragged *adj* ボロボロの

raid *n* 襲撃

raid *v* 襲撃する

raider *n* 侵略者

rail *n* レール、横木

railroad *n* 鉄道路線

rain *n* 雨

rain *v* 雨が降る

rainbow *n* 虹

raincoat *n* レインコート

rainfall *n* 降雨

rainy *adj* 雨模様の

raise *n* 値上げ、昇給

raise *v* 起こす、立てる

raisin *n* 干しぶどう

rake *n* くま手、レーキ

rally *n* 会合、反発

ram *n* 雄羊

ram *v* 激突する

ramification *n* 分岐

ramp *n* 斜面

rampage *v* 暴れ回る

rampant *adj* まん延した

ranch *n* 大牧場、農場

rancor *n* 憎しみ、悪意

randomly *adv* 無作為に

range *n* 域、範囲

rank *n* 階級、地位

rank *v* 地位を占める

ransack *v* くまなく捜す

ransom *v* ～を受け渡す

ransom *n* 身代金

rape *v* 強姦する

rape *n* 強姦

rapid *adj* 迅速な

rapist *n* 強姦犯

rapport *n* 親密さ

rare *adj* まれな、珍しい

rarely *adv* めったに～しない

rascal *n* 悪党

rash *v* 軽はずみな

rash *n* 発疹、頻発

rat *n* ネズミ

rate *n* 比率、歩合

ratification *n* 批准、承認

ratify *v* 批准する

ratio *n* 割合、率

ration *v* 割り当てる

ration *n* 配給量

rational *adj* 理性的な

rationalize *v* 合理化する

rattle *v* ガタガタ走る

ravage *v* 破壊する

ravage *n* 破壊

raven *n* 略奪品

ravine *n* 峡谷

raw *adj* 生の

**R**

ray *n* 光線
raze *v* ～を破壊する
razor *n* カミソリ
reach *v* 達する、伸びる
reach *n* 伸ばすこと
react *v* 反応する
reaction *n* 反応
read *iv* 読む
reader *n* 読者
readiness *n* 迅速、すばやさ
reading *n* 解釈
ready *adj* 用意できている
real *adj* 現実の
realism *n* 現実主義
reality *n* 現実
realize *v* ～に気が付く
really *adv* 実際には
realm *n* 領域、分野
realty *n* 不動産
reap *v* 収穫する
reappear *v* 再び現れる
rear *v* 育てる
rear *n* 後方
rear *adj* 後方の、背面の
reason *v* 結論づける
reason *n* 理由、原因
reasonable *adj* 道理にかなった
reasoning *n* 推論、論拠
reassure *v* 再確認する
rebate *n* 払い戻し
rebel *v* 反抗する
rebel *n* 反逆者

rebellion *n* 反乱、反抗
rebirth *n* 再生
rebound *v* 跳ね返る
rebuff *v* はねつける
rebuff *n* 拒絶、妨げ
rebuild *v* 再建する
rebuke *v* 叱責する
rebuke *n* 叱責
rebut *v* 反論する
recall *v* 思い出す
recant *v* 撤回する
recapture *v* 奪い返す
recede *v* 退く
receipt *n* 領収書
receive *v* 受け取る
recent *adj* 最近の
reception *n* 受付、受理
receptionist *n* 受付係
receptive *adj* 受け入れる
recess *n* 休息時間
recession *n* 景気後退
recharge *v* 再充電する
recipe *n* 料理法、レシピ
reciprocal *adj* 相互の
recital *n* 独奏会
recite *v* 朗読する
reckless *adj* 無鉄砲な
reckon *v* 計算する
reckon on *v* ～を当てにする
reclaim *v* 抗議する
recline *v* もたれる
recluse *n* 世捨て人

R

recognition *n* 見覚え

recognize *v* ～だと分かる

recollect *v* 思い出す

recollection *n* 記憶、回想

recommend *v* 薦める

recompense *v* 償う

recompense *n* 償い

reconcile *v* 仲直りをする

reconsider *v* 再考する

reconstruct *v* ～を再建する

record *v* 記録する

record *n* レコード、記録

recorder *n* 録音装置

recording *n* 記載、録音

recount *n* 再集計

recoup *v* 取り戻す

recourse *v* 頼る

recourse *n* 償還

recover *v* 回復する

recovery *n* 回復

recreate *v* 気晴らしをする

recreation *n* 気晴らし

recruit *v* 採用する

recruit *n* 新入社員

recruitment *n* 採用

rectangle *n* 長方形

rectangular *adj* 長方形の

rectify *v* 正す

rector *n* 教区教師

rectum *n* 直腸

recuperate *v* 健康を取り戻す

recur *v* 再発する

recurrence *n* 再発

recycle *v* 再利用

red *adj* 赤い

red tape *n* お役所仕事

redden *v* 赤くなる

redeem *v* 買い戻す

redemption *n* 贖い

red-hot *adj* 赤熱の

redo *v* ～をやり直す

redouble *v* 倍加する

redress *v* 是正する

reduce *v* 減る

redundant *adj* 重複する

reed *n* アシ

reef *n* 暗礁

reel *n* リールダンス

reelect *v* ～を再選する

reenactment *n* 再現

reentry *n* 再入場

refer to *v* ～を参照する

referee *n* 審判員

reference *n* 参照

referendum *n* 国民投票

refill *v* ～を補充する

refinance *v* 財政を立て直す

refine *v* 精製する

refinery *n* 精製所

reflect *v* ～を反射する

reflection *n* 反射

reflexive *adj* 再帰の

reform *v* 改善する

reform *n* 改善

R

refrain _v_ 控える

refresh _v_ 活気づける

refreshing _adj_ 元気づく

refreshment _n_ 元気回復

refrigerate _v_ 冷やす

refuel _v_ 燃料補給

refuge _n_ 避難

refugee _n_ 難民

refund _v_ 払い戻す

refund _n_ 返金

refurbish _v_ ～を改造する

refusal _n_ 拒絶

refuse _v_ 拒否する

refuse _n_ 廃物

refute _v_ 反論する

regain _v_ ～を取り戻す

regal _adj_ 王の

regard _v_ ～と見なす

regarding _pre_ ～に関して

regardless _adv_ 構わない

regards _n_ よろしく

regeneration _n_ 復活

regent _n_ 摂政

regime _n_ 政治形態

regiment _n_ 連隊

region _n_ 地域

regional _adj_ 地域の

register _v_ 登録する

registration _n_ 登録

regret _v_ 後悔する

regret _n_ 後悔

regrettable _adj_ 悲しむべき

regularity _n_ 規則性

regularly _adv_ 定期的に

regulate _v_ 規制する

regulation _n_ 規則

rehabilitate _v_ 更正する

rehearsal _n_ リハーサル

rehearse _v_ けいこする

reign _v_ 支配する

reign _n_ 治世

reimburse _v_ 払い戻す

rein _v_ 操る

rein _n_ 手綱

reindeer _n_ トナカイ

reinforce _v_ 補強する

reiterate _v_ 何度も言う

reject _v_ 拒絶する

rejection _n_ 拒絶

rejoice _v_ 喜ぶ

rejoin _v_ 再結合する

rejuvenate _v_ 若返らせる

relapse _n_ 再発

related _adj_ 関連した

relationship _n_ 関係

relative _adj_ 関係のある

relative _n_ 親類、身内

relax _v_ リラックスする

relax _n_ リラックス

relaxing _adj_ 落ち着いた

relay _v_ 中継する

release _v_ 解放する

relegate _v_ 追いやる

relent _v_ 和らぐ

**R**

| | |
|---|---|
| relentless *adj* 無慈悲な | remission *n* 鎮静、緩和 |
| relevant *adj* 関係のある | remit *v* 弱まる |
| reliable *adj* 信頼できる | remittance *n* 送金 |
| reliance *n* 当てにすること | remnant *n* 名残、面影 |
| relic *n* 遺物、遺跡 | remodel *v* 改築する |
| relief *n* 除去、軽減 | remorse *n* 自責の念 |
| relieve *v* 救い出す | remorseful *adj* 後悔の |
| religion *n* 宗教 | remote *adj* 遠隔の |
| religious *adj* 宗教的な | removal *n* 除去 |
| relinquish *v* 放棄する | remove *v* 除去する |
| relish *v* 風味がある | remunerate *v* 〜を報いる |
| relive *v* 生き返る | renew *v* 新しくする |
| relocate *v* 移住する | renewal *n* 更新 |
| relocation *n* 移住、移転 | renounce *v* 放棄する |
| reluctant *adj* 気乗りしない | renovate *v* 修理する |
| reluctantly *adv* 仕方なく | renovation *n* 修復 |
| rely on *v* 〜を頼りにする | renowned *adj* 名声のある |
| remain *v* 残る | rent *v* 賃借する |
| remainder *n* 残留者 | rent *n* 貸借料 |
| remaining *adj* 残りの | reorganize *v* 再編成する |
| remains *n* 残り物、遺跡 | repair *v* 修理する |
| remake *v* 作り直す | reparation *n* 償い、補償 |
| remark *v* 感想を述べる | repatriate *v* 送還する |
| remark *n* 意見、見解 | repay *v* お金を返す |
| remarkable *adj* 優れた | repayment *n* 返済 |
| remarry *v* 〜を再婚する | repeal *v* 撤回する |
| remedy *v* 治療する | repeal *n* 撤回、無効 |
| remedy *n* 治療薬 | repeat *v* 繰り返す |
| remember *v* 思い出す | repel *v* 〜を撃退する |
| remembrance *n* 記憶 | repent *v* 悔やむ |
| remind *v* 思い出す | repentance *n* 良心の呵責 |
| reminder *n* 催促状 | repetition *n* 繰り返し |

R

replace v 交換する

replacement n 交換

replay n 再生

replenish v 満たす

replete adj 充満した

replica n 模造品

replicate v 複製する

reply v 返事をする

reply n 返事、応答

report v 報告する

report n 報告、記事

reportedly adv 報道によれば

reporter n 記者

repose v 休息する

repose n 休息

represent v 象徴する

repress v 感情を押さえ込む

repression n 抑圧

reprieve n 刑執行の延期

reprint v 再版する

reprint n 再版

reprisal n 実力行使

reproach v 非難する

reproach n 非難、叱責

reproduce v ～を再生する

reproduction n 復元

reptile n は虫類

republic n 共和制

repudiate v 拒否する

repugnant adj 不快な

repulse v 撃退する

repulse n 撃退

repulsive adj 反発する

reputation n 評判、うわさ

reputedly adv 評判では

request v 依頼する

request n 依頼、要求

require v ～を必要とする

requirement n 要件

rescue v 救助する

rescue n 救助

research v 調査する

research n 調査、研究

resemblance n 類似

resemble v ～と似ている

resent v ひどく嫌がる

resentment n 怒り、敵意

reservation n 予約

reserve v 予約する

reservoir n 容器、タンク

reside v 住む、駐在する

residence n 住居、居住地

residue n 残り、かす

resign v 辞める

resignation n 辞職

resilient adj 跳ね返る

resist v 抵抗する

resistance n 抵抗、妨害

resolute adj 意思の固い

resolution n 解明、解像度

resolve v 解く、決意する

resort v 助けを借りる

resounding adj 鳴り響く

resource n 資源、要因

R

respect _v_ 尊敬する
respect _n_ 尊敬
respectful _adj_ 敬意を表する
respective _adj_ それぞれの
respiration _n_ 呼吸作用
respite _n_ 小康、小休止
respond _v_ 反応する
response _n_ 応答、返答
responsibility _n_ 義務、責任
responsible _adj_ 責任がある
responsive _adj_ 反応の良い
rest _v_ 休息する
rest _n_ 休息
rest room _n_ トイレ
restaurant _n_ レストラン
restful _adj_ 静穏な
restitution _n_ 返還
restless _adj_ そわそわする
restoration _n_ 復元
restore _v_ 復活させる
restrain _v_ 制止する
restraint _n_ 自制
restrict _v_ 制限する
result _n_ 結果
resume _v_ 再開する
resumption _n_ 取り戻すこと
resurface _v_ 再舗装する
resurrection _n_ 蘇生
resuscitate _v_ 生き返る
retain _v_ 維持する
retaliate _v_ 報復する
retaliation _n_ 仕返し、報復

retarded _adj_ 後退している
retention _n_ 保持、保有
retire _v_ リタイア、退く
retirement _n_ 退職
retract _v_ 撤回する
retreat _v_ 撤退する
retreat _n_ 避難、引退
retrieval _n_ 復旧、検索
retrieve _v_ 復旧する
retroactive _adj_ 遡及効果のある
return _v_ 戻る
return _n_ 返すこと
reunion _n_ 同窓会、再会
reveal _v_ 見せる
revealing _adj_ 打ち明ける
revel _v_ 大いに楽しむ
revelation _n_ 見せること
revenge _v_ 復讐する
revenge _n_ 復讐
revenue _n_ 歳入、収入
reverence _n_ 敬意
reversal _n_ 逆転、反転
reverse _n_ 逆、後進
reversible _adj_ 逆にできる
revert _v_ 立ち戻る
review _v_ 再検討する
review _n_ 再検討
revise _v_ 修正する
revision _n_ 修正
revive _v_ 生き返らせる
revoke _v_ 廃止する
revolt _v_ 反逆する

**R**

**revolt** n 反逆
**revolting** adj 極めて不快な
**revolve** v 旋回する
**revolver** v 回転装置
**revue** n レビュー
**revulsion** n 憎悪
**reward** v ～に報いる
**reward** n 褒賞、恩恵
**rewarding** adj 報いのある
**rheumatism** n リウマチ
**rhinoceros** n サイ
**rhyme** n 韻
**rhythm** n 調子
**rib** n 肋骨
**ribbon** n リボン
**rice** n 米
**rich** adj 金持ちの人
**rid of** iv ～を免れる
**riddle** n なぞなぞ
**ride** iv 乗る
**ridge** n 頭部
**ridicule** v あざける
**ridicule** n 冷笑
**ridiculous** adj ばかげた
**rifle** n ライフル銃
**rift** n 裂け目
**right** adv 右に
**right** adj 右の
**right** n 右、正しい
**rigid** adj 堅い、厳格な
**rigor** n 厳しさ
**rim** n 縁、へり

**ring** iv 輪になる
**ring** n 指輪、輪
**ringleader** n 闘争的指導者
**rinse** v すすぐ、ゆすぐ
**riot** v 暴動を起こす
**riot** n 暴動
**rip** v 裂ける、破れる
**rip apart** v バラバラにする
**rip off** v 盗む、はぎ取る
**ripe** adj 熟した
**ripen** v 成熟する
**ripple** n さざ波
**rise** iv 昇る
**risk** v 危険を冒す
**risk** n 危険
**risky** adj 危険な
**rite** n 儀式、習慣
**rival** n 競争相手
**rivalry** n 競争、対抗
**river** n 川
**rivet** v 固定する
**road** n 道路
**roam** v 歩きまわる
**roar** v 怒鳴る
**roar** n 怒声
**roast** v あぶる、焼く
**roast** n あぶること
**rob** v 盗む
**robber** n 強盗
**robbery** n 強盗事件
**robe** n 式服
**robust** adj 頑丈な

R

rock *n* 岩

rocket *n* ロケット

rocky *adj* 岩の多い

rod *n* 棒、竿

rodent *n* 齧歯動物

roll *v* 転がす、丸める

romance *n* 恋愛、ロマンス

roof *n* 屋根

room *n* 部屋

roomy *adj* 広々とした

rooster *n* 気取り屋

root *n* 根

rope *n* なわ

rosary *n* ロザリオ

rose *n* バラ

rosy *adj* 健康そうな

rot *v* 腐る

rot *n* 腐敗

rotate *v* 回転する

rotation *n* 回転

rotten *adj* 腐った

rough *adj* でこぼこの

round *adj* 円形の

roundup *n* 総まとめ

rouse *v* ～を目覚めさせる

rousing *adj* 奮起させる

route *n* 手段、ルート

routine *n* 決められた方法

row *v* ～を並べる

row *n* 列、行

rowdy *adj* 乱暴な

royal *adj* 王族

royalty *n* 王族、印税

rub *v* すれる

rubber *n* ゴム、あんま

rubbish *n* くず、がらくた

rubble *n* 粗石、破片

ruby *n* ルビー、紅玉

rudder *n* かじ

rude *adj* 無礼な

rudeness *n* 無礼

rudimentary *adj* 初歩の

rug *n* じゅうたん

ruin *v* 崩壊する

ruin *n* 崩壊、廃墟

rule *v* 統治する

rule *n* 規則、ルール

ruler *n* 定規、支配者

rum *n* ラム酒

rumble *v* ゴロゴロ鳴る

rumble *n* ガラガラ鳴る音

rumor *n* うわさ

run *iv* 走る

run away *v* 走り去る

run into *v* 出くわす

run out *v* 使い果たす

run over *v* 車で引く

run up *v* 急いで上る

runner *n* ランナー

runway *n* 滑走路

rupture *n* 破裂

rupture *v* 破裂させる

rural *adj* 田舎の

ruse *n* 策略

**R**

rush *v* 大急ぎの
Russia *n* ロシア
Russian *adj* ロシア人
rust *v* さびる
rust *n* さび
rustic *adj* 田舎の
rust-proof *adj* さび止めの
rusty *adj* さびた
ruthless *adj* 非情な
rye *n* らい麦

# S

sabotage *n* 妨害
sack *v* 袋に入れる
sack *n* 布の袋
sacrament *n* 秘跡
sacred *adj* 神聖な
sacrifice *n* 犠牲
sacrilege *n* 冒とく
sad *adj* 悲しむ
sadden *v* 〜を悲しませる
saddle *n* 鞍
sadist *n* サディスト
sadness *n* 悲しさ
safe *adj* 安全な
safeguard *n* 護衛
safety *n* 無事

sail *v* 航海する
sail *n* 帆、航海
sailboat *n* 帆船
sailor *n* 船乗り
saint *n* 聖人
salad *n* サラダ
salary *n* 給料
sale *n* 販売
sale slip *n* 売上伝票
salesman *n* 販売員
saliva *n* サルビア
salmon *n* サケ
saloon *n* 大広間
salt *n* 塩
salty *adj* 塩辛い
salvage *v* 救助する
salvation *n* 救出、救済
same *adj* 同じ
sample *n* 見本
sanctify *v* 神聖にする
sanction *v* 罰する
sanction *n* 制裁
sanctity *n* 高潔、神聖
sanctuary *n* 聖域、祭壇
sand *n* 砂
sandal *n* サンダル
sandpaper *n* 紙やすり
sandwich *n* サンドイッチ
sane *adj* 正気の
sanity *n* 正気
sap *n* 樹液、活力
sap *v* 樹液をとる

saphire *n* サファイア

sarcasm *n* 嫌み

sarcastic *adj* 皮肉な

sardine *n* イワシ

satanic *adj* 悪魔のような

satellite *n* 人口衛星

satire *n* 風刺

satisfaction *n* 満足感

satisfactory *adj* 満たしている

satisfy *v* 満足させる

saturate *v* 満たす

Saturday *n* 土曜日

sauce *n* ソース

saucepan *n* 片手鍋

saucer *n* 受け皿

sausage *n* ソーセージ

savage *adj* 凶暴な

savagery *n* 残忍

save *v* 救う

savings *n* 貯金

savior *n* 救助者

savor *v* 賞味する

saw *iv* のごぎりで切る

saw *n* のこぎり

say *iv* 言う

saying *n* 格言

scaffolding *n* 足場

scald *v* 消毒する

scale *v* 量る、はがす

scale *n* 目盛り、規模

scalp *n* 頭皮

scam *n* 詐欺

scan *v* 読み取る

scandal *n* 不祥事

scandalize *v* 中傷する

scapegoat *n* 見代わり

scar *n* 傷跡

scarce *adj* まれな

scarcity *n* 食糧難

scare *v* 怖がる

scare *n* 恐怖

scare away *v* ～を追い払う

scarf *n* スカーフ

scary *adj* 恐ろしい

scatter *v* 分散する

scenario *n* 筋書き

scene *n* 場面

scenery *n* 景色

scenic *adj* 風景の

scent *n* 香り

sceptic *adj* ～に疑いを抱く

schedule *n* 計画

scheme *n* 計画

schism *n* 分裂、分派

scholar *n* 学者

scholarship *n* 奨学金

school *n* 学校

science *n* 科学

scientific *adj* 科学の

scientist *n* 科学者

scissors *n* はさみ

scoff *v* あざ笑う

scold *v* しかる

scolding *n* 小言

**S**

scooter *n* スクーター
scope *n* 範囲、余地
scorch *v* 焦げる
score *n* 得点
score *v* 得点する
scorn *v* 軽蔑する
scornful *n* 軽蔑した
scorpion *n* サソリ
scoundrel *n* 悪党
scour *v* こすって磨く
scourge *n* 災難のもと
scout *n* 偵察
scramble *v* はい進む
scrap *n* くず、かけら
scrap *v* 廃棄する
scrape *v* 擦りむく
scratch *v* 引っかく
scratch *n* かすり傷
scream *v* 絶叫する
scream *n* 悲鳴
screen *n* 仕切り
screen *v* 〜を覆う
screw *v* ねじれる
screw *n* ねじ
screwdriver *n* ねじ回し
scribble *v* 殴り書きする
script *n* 脚本、台本
scroll *n* 巻物
scrub *v* ごしごし洗う
scruples *n* 気がとがめる
scrutiny *n* 精密な調査
scuffle *n* もみ合い

sculptor *n* 彫刻家
sculpture *n* 彫刻
sea *n* 海
seafood *n* 海鮮物
seagull *n* かもめ
seal *v* 封印する
seal *n* 押印、印鑑
seal off *v* 密封する
seam *n* 縫い目
seamless *adj* 縫い目のない
seamstress *n* 女性の裁縫師
search *v* 捜す
search *n* 捜査、調査
seashore *n* 海岸、浜辺
seasick *adj* 船酔いした
seaside *adj* 海辺の
season *n* 四季
seasonal *adj* 季節の
seasoning *n* 調味料
seat *n* 座席
seated *adj* 座る
secede *v* 脱退する
secluded *adj* 隔離された
seclusion *n* 隔離
second *n* 第2番目の
secondary *adj* 第2の
secrecy *n* 内密
secret *n* 秘密
secretary *n* 秘書
secretly *adv* 秘密に
sect *n* 派閥
section *n* 区分

S

sector *n* 部門、領域

secure *v* 確保する

secure *adj* 安全な

security *n* 安全性

sedate *v* 落ち着いた

sedation *n* 鎮静状態

seduce *v* 誘惑する

seduction *n* 誘惑

see *iv* 見る

seed *n* 種子、種

seedless *adj* 種なしの

seedy *adj* 種の多い

seek *iv* 捜し出す

segment *n* 部分、区分

segregate *v* 分離する

segregation *n* 人種差別

seize *v* 急に止まる

seizure *n* 差し押さえ

select *v* 選ぶ

selection *n* 選択

self-concious *adj* 自己意識する

self-esteem *n* 自尊心

self-evident *adj* 自明の

self-interest *n* 自己の利益

selfish *adj* 利己的な

selfishness *n* 身勝手さ

self-respect *n* 自尊

sell *iv* 売る

seller *n* 売り手

sellout *n* 譲渡

semblance *n* 外見

semester *n* 学期

seminary *n* 神学校

senate *n* 上院

senator *n* 上院議員

send *iv* 送る

sender *n* 発送人

senile *adj* もうろくした

senior *adj* 年上の

seniority *n* 年長、年上

sensation *n* 知覚

sense *v* ～を感じる

sense *n* 感覚

senseless *adj* 無意識の

sensible *adj* 思慮のある

sensitive *adj* 傷つきやすい

sensual *adj* 官能的な

sentence *v* 宣告する

sentence *n* 文

sentiment *n* 感傷

sentimental *adj* 感傷的な

sentry *n* 見張り

separate *v* 分ける

separate *adj* 分かれた

separation *n* 別離

September *n* 9月

sequel *n* 続編

sequence *n* 連続するもの

serenade *n* セレナーデ

serene *adj* 静かな

serenity *n* 静穏

sergeant *n* 軍曹

series *n* 連続

serious *adj* まじめな

S

seriousness *n* 深刻さ

sermon *n* 説教

serpent *n* 悪魔

serum *n* 血清

servant *n* 使用人

serve *v* 仕える

service *n* 奉仕

service *v* 補修を行う

session *n* 期間

set *n* 一組

set *iv* 設定する

set about *v* ～に取り掛かる

set off *v* 出発する

set out *v* ～し始める

set up *v* 組み立てる

setback *n* 妨げ、逆行

setting *n* 設定

settle *v* 落ち着く

settle down *v* 身を落ち着ける

settle for *v* ～で承知する

settlement *n* 合意

settler *n* 開拓者

setup *n* 準備

seven *adj* 7個の

seventeen *adj* 17個の

seventh *adj* 第7番目

seventy *adj* 70個の

sever *v* ～を切断する

several *adj* いくつかの

severance *n* 切断

severe *adj* 厳しい

severity *n* 厳しさ

sew *v* 縫い物をする

sewage *n* 汚水

sewer *n* 下水管

sewing *n* 裁縫

sex *n* 性行動

sexuality *n* 性別、性欲

shabby *adj* 使い古した

shack *n* 掘っ建て小屋

shackle *n* 束縛

shade *n* 陰

shadow *n* 影

shady *adj* 陰にする

shake *iv* 震える

shaken *adj* 動揺した

shaky *adj* 不安定な

shallow *adj* 浅い

sham *n* ごまかし

shambles *n* 大混乱

shame *v* 恥じ入らせる

shame *n* 恥

shameful *adj* 恥ずべき

shameless *adj* 恥知らずな

shape *v* 形を作る

shape *n* 形

share *v* 共有する

share *n* 共有

shareholder *n* 株主

shark *n* サメ

sharp *adj* 鋭い

sharpen *v* とがる

sharpener *n* 鉛筆削り

shatter *v* 粉々になる

shave *v* ひげをそる

she *pro* 彼女は

shear *iv* 〜を刈る

shed *iv* 落ちる

sheep *n* ヒツジ

sheets *n* シーツ

shelf *n* 棚

shell *n* 貝殻

shellfish *n* 甲殻類

shelter *v* 〜を保護する

shelter *n* 避難所

shelves *n* 棚の複数形

shepherd *n* シェパード

sherry *n* シェリー酒

shield *v* 盾となる

shield *n* 盾

shift *n* 転換

shift *v* 変わる

shine *iv* 輝く

shiny *adj* 光る

ship *n* 船

shipment *n* 船積み

shipwreck *n* 難破

shipyard *n* 造船所

shirk *v* 責任を逃れる

shirt *n* ワイシャツ

shiver *v* 震える

shiver *n* 震え

shock *n* 衝突

shocking *adj* 衝撃的な

shoddy *adj* 見せかけ

shoe *n* 靴

shoelace *n* 靴ひも

shoepolish *n* 靴みがき

shoestore *n* 靴屋

shoot *iv* 撃つ

shoot down *v* 撃ち落とす

shop *v* 買い物をする

shop *n* 小売店

shoplifting *n* 万引き

shopping *n* 買い物

shore *n* 岸

short *adj* 短い

shortage *n* 不足

shortcoming *n* 欠点

shortcut *n* 近道

shorten *v* 短くなる

shorthand *n* 速記

shortlived *adj* 寿命

shortly *adv* 間もなく

shorts *n* 短パン

shortsighted *adj* 近眼の

shot *n* 発砲

shotgun *n* 散弾銃

shoulder *n* 肩

shout *v* 叫ぶ

shout *n* 叫び声

shouting *n* 叫び

shove *v* 押す

shove *n* 強く押すこと

shovel *n* シャベル

show *iv* 見せる

show off *v* 見せびらかす

show up *v* 現れる

S

**showdown** *n* 土壇場

**shower** *n* シャワー

**shrapnel** *n* 爆弾の金属片

**shred** *v* 細かく切る

**shred** *n* 断片

**shrewd** *adj* 鋭敏な

**shriek** *v* 悲鳴を上げる

**shriek** *n* 甲高い声

**shrimp** *n* エビ

**shrine** *n* 神社

**shrink** *iv* 縮む

**shroud** *n* 覆う物

**shrouded** *adj* 覆われた

**shrub** *n* 低木

**shrug** *v* 肩をすくめる

**shudder** *n* 身震い

**shudder** *v* 身震いする

**shun** *v* 〜を避ける

**shut** *iv* 閉まる

**shut off** *v* 止める

**shut up** *v* 話をやめる

**shuttle** *v* 左右に歩く

**shy** *adj* 臆病な

**shyness** *n* 内気

**sick** *adj* 病気で

**sicken** *v* 病気になる

**sickle** *n* 鎌

**sickness** *n* 病気

**side** *n* 側面

**sideburns** *n* もみあげ

**sidestep** *v* 回避する

**sidewalk** *n* 歩道

**sideways** *adv* 横に

**siege** *n* 包囲攻撃

**siege** *v* 包囲攻撃をする

**sigh** *n* ため息

**sigh** *v* ため息をつく

**sight** *n* 視界

**sightseeing** *v* 観光をする

**sign** *v* 契約をする

**sign** *n* 標示

**signal** *n* 合図

**signature** *n* 署名

**significance** *n* 意義

**significant** *adj* 意義深い

**signify** *v* 重要である

**silence** *n* 静寂

**silence** *v* 静める

**silent** *adj* 静かな

**silhouette** *n* 影絵

**silk** *n* 絹

**silly** *adj* ばかばかしい

**silver** *n* 銀

**silverplated** *adj* 銀めっきの

**silversmith** *n* 銀細工師

**silverware** *n* 銀器

**similar** *adj* 似ている

**similarity** *n* 類似

**simmer** *v* 煮る

**simple** *adj* 簡略した

**simplicity** *n* 単純

**simplify** *v* 単純化する

**simply** *adv* 簡単に

**simulate** *v* まねる

S

simultaneous *adj* 同時に起こる

sin *v* 罪を犯す

sin *n* 罪

since *c* ～して以来

since *pre* ～以後に

since then *adv* それ以来

sincere *adj* 誠実な

sincerity *n* 誠実

sinful *adj* 罪深い

sing *iv* 歌う

singer *n* 歌手

single *n* ひとり

single *adj* ただ一つの

singlehanded *adj* 独力の

singleminded *adj* 一意専心の

singular *adj* 唯一の

sinister *adj* 邪悪な

sink *iv* 沈む

sink in *v* ～に沈む

sinner *n* 罪人

sip *v* 少しずつ飲む

sip *n* ひとりすすり

sir *n* 貴下

sirloin *n* サーロイン

sissy *adj* 意気地なしの

sister *n* 姉妹

sister-in-law *n* 義理の姉

sit *iv* 座る

site *n* 敷地、用地

sitting *n* 座ること

situated *adj* 位置している

situation *n* 状況

six *adj* 6、6個の

sixteen *adj* 16個の

sixth *adj* 第6番目の

sixty *adj* 60個の

sizable *adj* かなり大きな

size *n* 大きさ、規模

size up *v* 大きさを測る

skate *v* スケートをする

skate *n* スケート靴

skeleton *n* 骨格、骸骨

skeptic *adj* 懐疑的な

sketch *v* スケッチする

sketch *n* 略図

sketchy *adj* 未完成品

ski *v* スキーをする

skill *n* 技能、腕前

skillful *adj* 熟練した

skim *v* かすめる

skin *v* 皮をはぐ

skin *n* 皮膚、皮

skinny *adj* やせこけた

skip *v* さぼる

skip *n* 読み飛ばし

skirmish *n* 小衝突

skirt *n* スカート

skull *n* 頭がい骨

sky *n* 空

skylight *n* 天空光

skyscraper *n* 超高層ビル

slab *n* 厚切り

slack *adj* 緩い

slacken *v* 緩む

S

slacks *n* スラックス

slam *v* 急に閉まる

slander *n* 中傷

slanted *adj* 傾斜した

slap *n* 平手打ち

slap *v* はたく

slash *n* 一撃、斜線

slash *v* 大幅に削減する

slate *n* 粘板岩

slaughter *v* 虐殺する

slaughter *n* 大虐殺

slave *n* 奴隷

slavery *n* 奴隷制

slay *iv* 殺害する

sleazy *adj* 下品な

sleep *iv* 眠る

sleep *n* 睡眠

sleeve *n* たもと、袖

sleeveless *adj* 袖なしの

sleigh *n* そり

slender *adj* ほっそりした

slice *v* 薄く切る

slice *n* 薄片

slide *iv* 滑る

slightly *adv* わずかに

slim *adj* 細い

slip *v* 外れる

slip *n* 滑ること

slipper *n* 歯止め

slippery *adj* 滑りやすい

slit *iv* 細長く切る

slob *adj* めそめそする

slogan *n* 標語

slope *n* 坂、傾斜

sloppy *adj* 不注意な

slot *n* 溝、小さな穴

slow *adj* 遅い

slow down *v* 速度を落とす

slowly *adv* ゆっくりと

sluggish *adj* ゆっくりした

slum *n* スラム街

slump *v* 沈み込む

slump *n* 落ち込み

slur *v* 中傷する

sly *adj* 中傷

smack *n* 平手打ち

smack *v* 強くたたく

small *adj* 小さい

smallpox *n* 天然痘

smart *adj* 賢明な

smash *v* 打ち砕く

smear *n* 汚れ、染み

smear *v* シミが付く

smell *iv* におい

smelly *adj* 悪臭を放つ

smile *v* ほほ笑む

smile *n* 笑顔

smith *n* 鍛冶屋

smoke *v* 喫煙する

smoked *adj* 燻製の

smoker *n* 喫煙者

smoking gun *n* 決定的な証拠

smooth *v* 滑らかにする

smooth *adj* 滑らかな

S

**smoothly** *adv* 滑らかに

**smoothness** *n* 滑らかなこと

**smother** *v* 息が詰まる

**smuggler** *n* 密輸業者

**snail** *n* カタツムリ

**snake** *n* 蛇

**snapshot** *n* スナップ写真

**snare** *v* わなで捕える

**snare** *n* 輪なわ

**snatch** *v* ひったくる

**sneak** *v* コソコソする

**sneeze** *v* くしゃみをする

**sneeze** *n* くしゃみ

**sniff** *v* においを嗅ぐ

**sniper** *n* 狙撃者

**snitch** *v* 密告する

**snooze** *v* うたた寝する

**snore** *v* いびきをかく

**snore** *n* いびき

**snow** *v* 雪が降る

**snow** *n* 雪

**snowfall** *n* 降雪

**snowflake** *n* 雪片

**snub** *v* 鼻であしらう

**snub** *n* 鼻であしらうこと

**soak** *v* 浸る、つかる

**soak in** *v* 頭に入る

**soak up** *v* 吸い上げる

**soar** *v* 舞い上がる

**sob** *v* すすり泣く

**sob** *n* すすり泣き

**sober** *adj* しらふの

**so-called** *adj* いわゆる

**sociable** *adj* 社交好きな

**socialism** *n* 社会主義

**socialist** *adj* 社会主義者の

**society** *n* 社会

**sock** *n* 靴下

**sod** *n* 芝

**soda** *n* 炭酸飲料

**sofa** *n* ソファ

**soft** *adj* 柔らかい

**soften** *v* 柔らかくなる

**softly** *adv* 柔らかく

**softness** *n* 柔軟

**soggy** *adj* ジメジメする

**soil** *v* 汚す

**soil** *n* 土、土壌

**soiled** *adj* 汚れた

**solace** *n* 慰め

**solar** *adj* 太陽の

**solder** *v* 〜を固く結合する

**soldier** *n* 軍人

**sold-out** *adj* 完売の

**sole** *n* 足底

**sole** *adj* 唯一の

**solely** *adv* ただ一人で

**solemn** *adj* 厳粛な

**solicit** *v* 懇願する

**solid** *adj* 固形の

**solidarity** *n* 団結

**solitary** *adj* 孤独な

**solitude** *n* 孤独

**soluble** *adj* 溶けやすい

S

solution _n_ 解答、解決

solve _v_ 解決する

solvent _adj_ 溶かす

somber _adj_ 地味な

some _adj_ いくらか

somebody _pro_ 誰か

someday _adv_ いつか

somehow _adv_ どういうわけか

someone _pro_ ある人

something _pro_ 何か

sometimes _adv_ 時々

someway _adv_ ともかくも

somewhat _adv_ いくぶんか

son _n_ 息子

song _n_ 歌

son-in-law _n_ 義理の息子

soon _adv_ 間もなく

soothe _v_ ～をなだめる

sorcerer _n_ 魔術師

sorcery _n_ 魔法

sore _n_ 痛む所

sore _adj_ 痛い

sorrow _n_ 悲しみ

sorrowful _adj_ 悲しんでいる

sorry _adj_ すまなく思う

sort _n_ 種類、性質

sort out _v_ 整理する

soul _n_ 魂

sound _n_ 音、音声

sound _v_ 音を出す

sound out _v_ 探る

soup _n_ スープ、汁

sour _adj_ 酸っぱい

source _n_ もと、源

south _n_ 南

southbound _adv_ 南行きの

southeast _n_ 南東

southern _adj_ 南の

southerner _n_ 南部人

southwest _n_ 南西の

souvenir _n_ 土産

sovereign _adj_ 国王

sovereignty _n_ 主権

soviet _adj_ 会議の

sow _iv_ 種をまく

spa _n_ 温泉

space _n_ 空間

space out _v_ 一定のスペース

spacious _adj_ 広々とした

spade _n_ 鍬

Spain _n_ スペイン

span _v_ 及ぶ、わたる

span _n_ 期間、長さ

Spaniard _n_ スペイン人の

Spanish _adj_ スペイン人

spank _v_ 平手打ち

spanking _n_ 勢いよく動く

spare _v_ 取っておく

spare _adj_ 予備の

spare part _n_ 予備部品

sparingly _adv_ 控えめに

spark _n_ 火花、スパーク

spark off _v_ もたらす

spark plug _n_ スパークプラグ

S

sparkle _v_ きらめく

sparrow _n_ すずめ

sparse _adj_ 希薄な

spasm _n_ 発作

speak _iv_ 演説する

speaker _n_ 演説者

spear _n_ やり

spearhead _v_ 先頭に付く

special _adj_ 特別な

specialize _v_ 専門とする

specialty _n_ 特殊芸

species _n_ 種、種類

specific _adj_ 明確な

specimen _n_ 見本、例

speck _n_ 少量、しみ

spectacle _n_ 壮観

spectator _n_ 傍観者

speculate _v_ 思索する

speculation _n_ 塾考、投機

speech _n_ 演説、話法

speechless _adj_ 無言の

speed _iv_ 加速する

speed _n_ 速度

speedily _adv_ 速く

speedy _adj_ 速い

spell _iv_ 字をつづる

spell _n_ 呪文

spelling _n_ つづり

spend _iv_ 費やす

spending _n_ 出費

sperm _n_ 精液

sphere _n_ 球、球体

spice _n_ 薬味、香辛料

spicy _adj_ 香ばしい

spider _n_ クモ

spiderweb _n_ クモの巣

spill _iv_ こぼす

spill _n_ 流出

spin _iv_ 回転する

spine _n_ とげ、脊椎

spineless _adj_ 脊椎のない

spinster _n_ 未婚女性

spirit _n_ 霊、霊魂

spiritual _adj_ 霊的な

spit _iv_ 唾をはく

spite _n_ 悪意、恨み

spiteful _adj_ 悪意のある

splash _v_ しぶきでぬらす

splendid _adj_ 素晴らしい

splendor _n_ 素晴らしさ

splint _n_ つぎ板

splinter _n_ とげ、添え木

splinter _v_ 裂ける

split _n_ 割ること

split _iv_ 割れて分かれる

split up _v_ 割れる

spoil _v_ 台無しになる

spoils _n_ 利得、利権

sponge _n_ 海綿

sponsor _n_ 保証人

spontaneity _n_ 自発的であること

spontaneous _adj_ 自発的な

spooky _adj_ 幽霊のような

spool _n_ スプール

S

spoon *n* スプーン

spoonful *n* 一さじ

sporadic *adj* 散発的な

sport *n* スポーツ

sportman *n* スポーツマン

spot *v* 目立つ

spot *n* 染み

spotless *adj* 染みのない

spotlight *n* スポット、注目

spouse *n* 配偶者

sprain *v* ねんざする

spray *v* 吹きかける

spread *iv* 広がる

spring *iv* 跳ねる、はじく

spring *n* 春、泉

springboard *n* 飛び板

sprinkle *v* ～をまく

sprout *v* 発芽する

spruce up *v* こぎれいにする

spur *v* 拍車をかける

spur *n* 拍車

spy *v* ひそかに見張る

spy *n* 密偵

squalid *adj* 荒れ果てた

squander *v* 浪費する

square *adj* 四角の

square *n* 四角

squash *v* 押しつぶす

squeak *v* きしる音

squeaky *adj* きしむ

squeamish *adj* 吐き気を催す

squeeze *v* ～を絞る

squeeze in *v* 押し込める

squeeze up *v* 詰め込む

squid *n* イカ

squirrel *n* リス

stab *v* 突き刺す

stab *n* 刺し傷

stability *n* 安定

stable *adj* 安定した

stable *n* 馬小屋

stack *v* 山積みにする

stack *n* 積み重ね

staff *n* 職員、スタッフ

stage *n* 舞台

stage *v* ～を上演する

stagger *v* よろめく

staggering *adj* ずれた

stagnant *adj* よどんだ

stagnate *v* 沈滞する

stagnation *n* 沈滞、よどみ

stain *v* 汚れをつける

stain *n* 染み、汚点

stair *n* 段

staircase *n* 階段室

stairs *n* 階段

stake *n* 賭け

stake *v* ～を賭ける

stale *adj* 新鮮でない

stalemate *n* 行き詰まり

stalk *v* 忍びよる

stalk *n* 柄、茎

stall *n* 売店、露店

stall *v* 失速する

S

stammer _v_ どもる

stamp _v_ 印を押す

stamp _n_ 切手、ゴム印

stamp out _v_ 撲滅する

stampede _n_ 殺到

stand _iv_ 立つ

stand _n_ 立場

stand for _v_ 〜を支持する

stand out _v_ 突き出る

stand up _v_ 立ち上がる

standard _n_ 基準

standardize _v_ 規格化する

standing _n_ 地位

standpoint _n_ 観点、見地

standstill _adj_ 停止

staple _v_ ホチキスでとめる

staple _n_ ホチキスの針

stapler _n_ ホチキス

star _n_ 星

starch _n_ 洗濯用のり

starchy _adj_ 糊づけした

stare _v_ じろじろ見る

stark _adj_ 荒涼とした

start _v_ 出発する

start _n_ 出発

startle _v_ びっくりさせる

startled _adj_ びっくりして

starvation _n_ 飢餓

starve _v_ 餓える

state _n_ 状態、州

state _v_ 述べる

statement _n_ 声明、発言

station _n_ 駅

stationary _adj_ 動かない

stationery _n_ 文房具

statistic _n_ 統計

statue _n_ 像

status _n_ 状況

statute _n_ 法、制定法

staunch _adj_ 忠実な

stay _v_ 滞在する

stay _n_ 滞在

steady _adj_ 着実な

steak _n_ ステーキ

steal _iv_ 盗む

stealthy _adj_ 内密の

steam _n_ 蒸気

steel _n_ 鋼鉄

steep _adj_ 険しい

stem _n_ 茎、柄

stem _v_ 始まる

stench _n_ 悪臭

step _n_ 方法

step down _v_ 降りる

step out _v_ 席をはずす

step up _v_ 進歩させる

stepbrother _n_ 義兄弟

step-by-step _adv_ 段階を追った

stepdaughter _n_ 継娘

stepfather _n_ 義父

stepladder _n_ 脚立

stepmother _n_ 義母

stepsister _n_ 義姉妹

stepson _n_ 継息子

**S**

sterile *adj* 不妊の

sterilize *v* 殺菌する

stern *n* 厳格

stern *adj* 厳格な

sternly *adv* 厳格に

stew *n* シチュー

stewardess *n* スチュワーデス

stick *v* 木の枝

stick *iv* 棒で支える

stick around *v* 近くにいる

stick out *v* 突き出す

stick to *v* 〜にくっつく

sticker *n* ステッカー

sticky *adj* 粘つく

stiff *adj* 堅い

stiffen *v* 硬直する

stiffness *n* 堅いこと

stifle *v* 息苦しくなる

stifling *adj* 暑苦しい

still *adj* 静止した

still *adv* まだ

stimulant *n* 刺激物

stimulate *v* 刺激する

stimulus *n* 刺激

sting *iv* 刺す

sting *n* 針

stinging *adj* 辛らつな

stingy *adj* けちな

stink *iv* 悪臭がする

stink *n* 悪臭

stinking *adj* くさい

stipulate *v* 規定する

stir *v* かき回す

stir up *v* かき混ぜる

stitch *v* 〜を縫う

stitch *n* 縫い目

stock *v* 物を蓄える

stock *n* 在庫

stocking *n* 靴下、タイツ

stockpile *n* 備蓄、貯蔵

stockroom *n* 商品倉庫

stoic *adj* 冷静な

stomach *n* 胃、腹

stone *n* 石

stone *v* 種を取る

stool *n* 足載せ台

stop *v* 止まる

stop *n* 停止

stop by *v* 途中で立ち寄る

stop over *v* 泊まる

storage *n* 物置

store *v* 蓄える

store *n* 店、小売店

stork *n* コウノトリ

storm *n* 嵐、荒天

stormy *adj* 嵐の

story *n* 物語

stove *n* ストーブ

straight *adj* 真っすぐな

straighten out *v* 問題を取り除く

strain *v* 裏ごしする

strain *n* 緊張

strained *adj* ピンと張った

strainer *n* ざる

S

strait *n* 海峡、苦境

stranded *adj* 座礁した

strange *adj* 奇妙な

stranger *n* 見知らぬ人

strangle *v* 〜を抑える

strap *n* つり革

strategy *n* 戦略

straw *n* わら

strawberry *n* イチゴ

stray *adj* 道にそれた

stray *v* 道からそれる

stream *n* 小川

street *n* 通り、街路

streetcar *n* 路面電車

streetlight *n* 街灯

strength *n* 力、強さ

strengthen *v* 〜を強くする

stress *n* 緊張

stressful *adj* 緊張の多い

stretch *n* 引き伸ばし

stretch *v* 伸びる

stretcher *n* 担架

strict *adj* 厳しい

stride *iv* 歩幅

strife *n* 衝突

strike *n* ストライキ

strike *iv* 地震が襲う

strike back *v* 打ち返す

strike out *v* 三振する

strike up *v* 跳ね上げる

striking *adj* 印象的な

string *n* 糸

stringent *adj* 強制的な

strip *n* 細長い切れ

strip *v* 衣服を脱ぐ

stripe *n* ストライプ

striped *adj* 縞模様の

strive *iv* 努力する

stroke *n* 打つこと

stroll *v* そぞろ歩く

strong *adj* 強い

structure *n* 構造

struggle *v* もがく

struggle *n* 苦闘

stub *n* 切り株

stubborn *adj* 頑固な

student *n* 学生

study *v* 勉強する

stuff *n* 物、物事

stuff *v* 詰める

stuffing *n* 詰め物

stuffy *adj* 息苦しい

stumble *v* よろめく

stun *v* うろたえさせる

stunning *adj* 見事な

stupendous *adj* 驚くべき

stupid *adj* ばか、あほ

stupidity *n* 愚かさ

sturdy *adj* 頑健な

stutter *v* どもる

style *n* スタイル、様式

subdue *v* 鎮圧する

subdued *adj* 抑えられた

subject *v* 支配する

S

**subject** n 主題
**sublime** adj 崇高する
**submerge** v 沈める
**submissive** adj 従順な
**submit** v 提出する
**subpoena** v 召喚状を発する
**subpoena** n 召還令状
**subscribe** v 署名する
**subscription** n 会費
**subsequent** adj 続いて起こる
**subsidiary** adj 補助するもの
**subsidize** v 助成金を払う
**subsidy** n 助成金
**subsist** v 存在する
**substance** n 物質
**substandard** adj 標準以下の
**substantial** adj 十分な
**substitute** v 代わりになる
**substitute** n 代用品
**subtitle** n 副題
**subtle** adj 微妙な
**subtract** v 控除する
**subtraction** n 控除
**suburb** n 郊外
**subway** n 地下鉄
**succeed** v 成功する
**success** n 成功
**successful** adj 成功した
**successor** n 後継者
**succulent** adj 水気の多い
**succumb** v 屈服する
**such** adj そのような

**suck** v 口で吸う
**sucker** adj 吸盤
**sudden** adj 突然の
**suddenly** adv 突然
**sue** v 訴える
**suffer** v 苦しむ
**suffer from** v ～に苦しむ
**suffering** n 苦しみ
**sufficient** adj 満足な
**suffocate** v 窒息死する
**sugar** n 砂糖
**suggest** v 提案する
**suggestion** n 提案
**suggestive** adj 連想させる
**suicide** n 自殺
**suit** n スーツ
**suitable** adj 適している
**suitcase** n スーツケース
**sullen** adj 不機嫌な
**sulphur** n 硫黄
**sum** n 合計、和
**sum up** v 合計する
**summarize** v 要約する
**summary** n 要約
**summer** n 夏
**summit** n 首脳陣
**summon** v 呼び出す
**sumptuous** adj 豪華な
**sun** n 太陽の
**sunburn** n 日焼け止め
**Sunday** n 日曜日
**sundown** n 日没

S

sunglasses *n* サングラス

sunken *adj* 沈没した

sunny *adj* 日当たりの良い

sunrise *n* 日の出

sunset *n* 夕日

superb *adj* 極上の

superfluous *adj* 過度の

superior *adj* 上等の

superiority *n* 優越

superpower *n* 超大国

supersede *v* 取って代わる

superstition *n* 迷信

supervise *v* 監督する

supervision *n* 監督

supper *n* 夜食

supple *adj* 柔軟な

supplier *n* 供給者

supplies *n* 供給品

supply *v* 供給する

support *v* 支える

supporter *n* 支援者

suppose *v* 仮定する

supposing *c* もし～ならば

supposition *n* 仮定

suppress *v* 抑える

supremacy *n* 至高、優位

supreme *adj* 至上の

surcharge *n* 追加料金

sure *adj* 確かな

surely *adv* 確実に

surf *v* 波乗りする

surface *n* 表面

surge *n* 急上昇

surgeon *n* 軍医

surgical *adv* 外科の

surname *n* 姓、名字

surpass *v* ～を上回る

surplus *n* 残り、余り

surprise *v* 驚かす

surprise *n* 驚き

surrender *v* 降伏する

surrender *n* 降伏

surround *v* 囲む

surroundings *n* 環境

surveillance *n* 監視

survey *n* 調査

survival *n* 生き残り

survive *v* 生き残る

survivor *n* 遺族、生存者

suspect *v* 疑わしく思う

suspect *n* 容疑者

suspend *v* つるす、下げる

suspenders *n* サスペンダー

suspense *n* 気がかり

suspension *n* 一時的中止

suspicion *n* 疑念、容疑

suspicious *adj* 疑わしい

sustain *v* 持ちこたえる

sustenance *n* 滋養

swallow *v* 飲み込む

swamp *n* 沼地

swamped *adj* 多忙極まりない

swan *n* ハクチョウ

swap *v* ～を交換する

**S**

swap *n* 取り換え

swarm *n* 昆虫の群れ

sway *v* 揺らぐ

swear *iv* 誓う

sweat *n* 汗

sweat *v* 汗をかく

sweater *n* セーター

Sweden *n* スウエーデン

Sweedish *adj* スウエーデン人

sweep *iv* 掃く

sweet *adj* 甘い

sweeten *v* 甘くする

sweetheart *n* 愛する人

sweetness *n* 甘さ

sweets *n* 甘党

swell *iv* 膨らむ

swelling *n* 膨れ

swift *adj* 敏速な

swim *iv* 泳ぐ

swimmer *n* 泳ぐ人

swimming *n* 水泳

swindle *v* 詐欺を働く

swindle *n* 詐欺

swindler *n* 詐欺師

swing *iv* 動く

swing *n* 揺れること

Swiss *adj* スイス人

switch *v* 切り替わる

switch *n* 転換

switch off *v* スイッチを切る

switch on *v* スイッチを入れる

Switzerland *n* スイス

swivel *v* 旋回する

swollen *adj* 腫れ上がった

sword *n* 剣

swordfish *n* メカジキ

syllable *n* 音節

symbol *n* 象徴

symbolic *adj* 象徴する

symmetry *n* 対称

sympathize *v* 同情する

sympathy *n* 同情

symphony *n* 交響曲

symptom *n* 兆候

synagogue *n* 礼拝堂

synchronize *v* 同時に起こる

synod *n* 宗教会議

synonym *n* 同義語

synthesis *n* 統合、合成

syphilis *n* 梅毒

syringe *n* 注射器

syrup *n* 蜜

system *n* 系統

systematic *adj* 組織的な

S

# T

table *n* 食卓
tablecloth *n* テーブル掛け
tablespoon *n* 大さじ
tablet *n* 錠剤
tack *n* 画鋲
tackle *v* 取り組む
tact *n* 機転
tactful *adj* 機転の利く
tactical *adj* 戦術の
tactics *n* 作戦
tag *n* 札
tail *n* しっぽ
tail *v* 尾行する
tailor *n* 仕立屋
tainted *adj* 汚れた
take *iv* 捕まえる
take apart *v* 分解する
take away *v* 取り上げる
take back *v* 取り戻す
take in *v* 取り入れる
take off *v* 離陸する
take out *v* 取り出す
take over *v* 引き継ぐ
tale *n* 怪談
talent *n* 才能
talk *v* 話す
talkative *adj* おしゃべりな
tall *adj* 背の高い
tame *v* 飼いならす

tangent *n* 接線
tangible *adj* 触れる
tangle *n* もつれ
tank *n* 槽
tantamount to *adj* ～と等しい
tantrum *n* 不機嫌
tap *n* 軽く打つこと
tap into *v* ～に入り込む
tape *n* テープ
tapestry *n* タペストリー
tar *n* タール
tarantula *n* タランチュラ
tardy *adv* 遅い
target *n* 的
tariff *n* 関税
tarnish *v* 曇る
tart *n* タルト
tartar *n* 歯石
task *n* 課題
taste *v* 味がする
taste *n* 味
tasteful *adj* 趣味の良い
tasteless *adj* 味のない
tasty *adj* うまい
tavern *n* 居酒屋
tax *n* 税金
tea *n* 茶、紅茶
teach *iv* 教える
teacher *n* 先生
team *n* チーム
teapot *n* 茶瓶
tear *iv* 裂ける

T

tear *n* 涙
tearful *adj* 涙を誘う
tease *v* いじめ
technical *adj* 技術上の
technician *n* 技術者
technique *n* 技術
technology *n* 科学技術
tedious *adj* 退屈な
teenager *n* 十代の若者
teeth *n* 威力
telegram *n* 電報
telepathy *n* テレパシー
telephone *n* 電話
telescope *n* 望遠鏡
television *n* テレビ放送
tell *iv* 言う
teller *n* 語り手
telling *adj* 物語る
temper *n* 機嫌
temperature *n* 温度
tempest *n* 大嵐
temple *n* 寺院
temporary *adj* 一時の
tempt *v* 誘惑する
temptation *n* 誘惑
tempting *adj* 心をそそる
ten *adj* １０個の
tenacity *n* 固持
tenant *n* 賃借人
tendency *n* 傾向
tender *adj* 柔らかい
tenderness *n* 柔らかさ

tennis *n* テニス
tenor *n* テノール
tense *adj* 緊張した
tension *n* ピンと張ること
tent *n* テント
tentacle *n* 触手
tentative *adj* 試験的な
tenth *n* 第１０番目の
tenuous *adj* 細長い
tepid *adj* 気のない
term *n* 期間、任期
terminate *v* 終了する
terminology *n* 専門用語
termite *n* シロアリ
terms *n* 取引条件
terrace *n* バルコニー
terrain *n* 地形
terrestrial *adj* 地球の
terrible *adj* 極度の
terrific *adj* 素晴らしい
terrify *v* 脅かす
terrifying *adj* 非常に恐ろしい
territory *n* 領土
terror *n* 恐怖
terrorism *n* テロリズム
terrorist *n* テロリスト
terrorize *v* 怖がらせる
terse *adj* 簡潔な
test *v* テストを行う
test *n* 試験
testament *n* 遺書
testify *v* 証言する

testimony *n* 供述書

text *n* 文章

textbook *n* 教科書

texture *n* 生地

thank *v* 感謝する

thankful *adj* ありがたく思う

thanks *n* ありがとう

that *adj* それ

thaw *v* 解ける

thaw *n* 雪解け

theater *n* 劇場

theft *n* 窃盗

theme *n* 話題

themselves *pro* 彼ら自身

then *adv* あのとき

theologian *n* 神学者

theology *n* 神学

theory *n* 学説

therapy *n* 治療

there *adv* あそこ

therefore *adv* それ故に

thermometer *n* 温度計

these *adj* これら

thesis *n* 卒業論文

they *pro* 彼ら

thick *adj* 厚い

thicken *v* 厚くなる

thickness *n* 濃さ

thief *n* 泥棒

thigh *n* 大腿部

thin *adj* 細い部分

thing *n* 物事

think *iv* 考える

thinly *adv* 薄く

third *adj* 第3番目

thirst *v* 喉が渇く

thirsty *adj* 喉が渇いた

thirteen *adj* 13個の

thirty *adj* 30個の

this *adj* これ

thorn *n* とげ

thorny *adj* イバラの

thorough *adj* 徹底的な

those *adj* それらの

thought *n* 考え

thoughtful *adj* 思慮深い

thousand *adj* 1000個の

thread *n* 糸

threat *n* 脅迫

threaten *v* ～を脅す

three *adj* 3個の

thresh *v* 脱穀する

threshold *n* 敷居

thrifty *adj* 倹約的な

thrill *v* 興奮する

thrill *n* 身震い

thrive *v* 繁栄する

throat *n* のど

throb *n* 動悸

throb *v* 鼓動する

thrombosis *n* 血栓症

throne *n* 王座

throng *n* 群衆

through *pre* ～を通り抜けて

T

throw *iv* 投げる

throw away *v* 投げ捨てる

throw up *v* 放り投げる

thug *n* 殺し屋

thumb *n* 親指

thumbtack *n* 画鋲

thunder *n* 雷

thunderbolt *n* 雷電

thunderstorm *n* 激しい雷雨

Thursday *n* 木曜日

thus *adv* だから

thwart *v* 妨げる

thyroid *n* 甲状腺

tickle *v* くすぐる

tidal wave *n* 高波

tide *n* 潮、潮流

tidy *adj* きれい好きな

tie *v* 結べる

tie *n* つながり

tiger *n* トラ

tight *adj* 堅い

tighten *v* 堅く締まる

tile *n* タイル、瓦

till *adv* 〜まで

till *v* 耕す

tilt *v* 傾き

timber *n* 材木

time *n* 時間

time *v* 時間を計る

timeless *adj* 永久の

timely *adj* 適時の

times *n* 時期

timetable *n* 時刻表

timid *adj* 臆病な

timidity *n* 臆病

tin *n* 缶詰

tiny *adj* とても小さい

tip *n* 内報

tiptoe *n* つま先

tired *adj* 疲れた

tiredness *n* 疲労感

tireless *adj* 疲れない

tiresome *adj* うんざりする

tissue *n* 組織

title *n* 題名

to *pre* 〜する

toad *n* ヒキガエル

toast *v* 乾杯する

toast *n* 祝杯

toaster *n* トースター

tobacco *n* 喫煙

today *adv* 今日は

toddler *n* 歩き始めの子供

toe *n* 足指

toenail *n* 足指のつめ

together *adv* 一緒に

toil *v* 骨折って働く

toilet *n* 化粧室

token *n* 記念品

tolerable *adj* 耐えられる

tolerance *n* 我慢

tolerate *v* 耐える

toll *n* 運賃

toll *v* 徴収する

tomato *n* トマト

tomb *n* 墓穴

tombstone *n* 墓石

tomorrow *adv* 明日

ton *n* トン

tone *n* 調子

tongs *n* 火ばし

tongue *n* 舌

tonic *n* 炭酸水

tonight *adv* 今晩

tonsil *n* へんとう腺

too *adv* 〜もまた

tool *n* 道具

tooth *n* 歯

toothache *n* 歯痛

toothpick *n* ようじ

top *n* 頂点

topic *n* 主題

topple *v* 倒れる

torch *n* たいまつ

torment *v* 火を付ける

torment *n* 苦痛

torrent *n* 急流

torrid *adj* 熱烈な

torso *n* 胴

tortoise *n* カメ

torture *v* 拷問にかける

torture *n* 拷問

toss *v* ポイと投げる

total *adj* 全体の

totalitarian *adj* 全体主義者

totality *n* 全体

touch *n* 手触り

touch *v* 触れる

touch on *v* 関連する

touch up *v* 改良する

touching *adj* 人の心を動かす

tough *adj* 丈夫な

toughen *v* 強くなる

tour *n* ツアー

tourism *n* 観光

tourist *n* 観光客

tournament *n* 試合

tow *v* 綱引き

tow truck *n* けん引トラック

towards *pre* 〜に向かう

towel *n* タオル

tower *n* 塔

towering *adj* そびえ立つ

town *n* 町

town hall *n* 町役場

toxic *adj* 有毒な

toxin *n* 毒

toy *n* 玩具

trace *v* たどる

track *n* 跡

track *v* 路線、行路

traction *n* けん引力

tractor *n* けん引車

trade *n* 取引

trade *v* 交換する

trademark *n* 商標

trader *n* 商人

tradition *n* 伝統

**T**

**traffic** *n* 交通
**traffic** *v* 売買する
**tragedy** *n* 悲劇
**tragic** *adj* 悲劇の
**trail** *v* 追跡する
**trail** *n* 痕跡
**trailer** *n* 追跡者
**train** *n* 電車
**train** *v* 列車
**trainee** *n* 研修員
**trainer** *n* 訓練者
**training** *n* 訓練
**trait** *n* 特質
**traitor** *n* 裏切り者
**trajectory** *n* 軌道
**tram** *n* 市街電車
**trample** *v* 踏みつける
**trance** *n* 夢うつつ
**tranquility** *n* 静けさ
**transaction** *n* 取引
**transcend** *v* 超越する
**transcribe** *v* ～を書き換える
**transfer** *v* 移す、異動する
**transfer** *n* 移動、移転
**transform** *v* 変換する
**transformation** *n* 変化
**transfusion** *n* 輸血
**transient** *adj* はかない
**transit** *n* 通過
**transition** *n* 移行
**translate** *v* 翻訳する
**translator** *n* 翻訳者

**transmit** *v* 送信する
**transparent** *adj* 透明な
**transplant** *v* 移植する
**transport** *v* 運送
**trap** *n* わな
**trash** *n* くず、ごみ
**trash can** *n* ごみ箱
**traumatic** *adj* 外傷の
**traumatize** *v* 外傷を負わせる
**travel** *v* 旅する
**traveler** *n* 旅行者
**tray** *n* 受け皿
**treacherous** *adj* 不誠実な
**treachery** *n* 不信
**tread** *iv* 足音
**treason** *n* 反逆
**treasure** *n* 宝
**treasurer** *n* 出納係
**treat** *v* 待遇する
**treat** *n* もてなし
**treatment** *n* 処置
**treaty** *n* 条約
**tree** *n* 木
**tremble** *v* 身震いする
**tremendous** *adj* 強大な
**tremor** *n* 弱い地震
**trench** *n* 溝
**trend** *n* 傾向
**trendy** *adj* 流行の
**trespass** *v* 不法侵入する
**trial** *n* 裁判、試み
**triangle** *n* 三角形

T

tribe _n_ 部族

tribulation _n_ 試練

tribunal _n_ 法廷

tribute _n_ 貢ぎ物

trick _v_ かまをかける

trick _n_ いたずら

trickle _v_ したたる

tricky _adj_ 巧妙な

trigger _v_ 引き金を引く

trigger _n_ 引き金

trim _v_ 切り取る

trimester _n_ 3ヶ月間

trimmings _n_ 添え物

trip _n_ 遠足

trip _v_ 軽快に動く

triple _adj_ 3倍の数

tripod _n_ 三脚

triumph _n_ 勝利

triumphant _adj_ 勝利を収めた

trivial _adj_ ささいな

trivialize _v_ つまらなくする

trolley _n_ 台車

troop _n_ 群れ

trophy _n_ 賞品

tropic _n_ 回帰線

tropical _adj_ 熱帯の

trouble _n_ 困難

trouble _v_ わざわざ〜する

troublesome _adj_ 面倒な

trousers _n_ ズボン

trout _n_ マス

truce _n_ 停戦

truck _n_ 運搬車

trucker _n_ トラック運転手

trumpet _n_ トランペット

trunk _n_ 主要部

trust _v_ 信頼

trust _n_ 信頼する

truth _n_ 真実

truthful _adj_ 真実の

try _v_ 試す

tub _n_ たらい、おけ

tuberculosis _n_ 結核

Tuesday _n_ 火曜日

tuition _n_ 授業料

tulip _n_ チューリップ

tumble _v_ ひっくり返る

tummy _n_ おなか

tumor _n_ 腫瘍

tumult _n_ 大騒ぎ

tumultuous _adj_ 騒然とした

tuna _n_ マグロ

tune _n_ 旋律

tune _v_ 調整する

tune up _v_ 楽器を調整する

tunic _n_ チュニック

tunnel _n_ 坑道

turbine _n_ タービン

turbulence _n_ 乱気流

turf _n_ 芝、芝地

Turk _adj_ トルコの

Turkey _n_ トルコ

turmoil _n_ 騒動

turn _n_ 旋回

T

**turn** v 曲がる
**turn back** v 後戻りする
**turn down** v 下げる
**turn in** v 返却する
**turn off** v 興味を失う
**turn on** v 興奮させる
**turn over** v 転がる
**turn up** v 上に向ける
**turret** n 小塔、タレット
**turtle** n カメ
**tusk** n 牙
**tutor** n 家庭教師
**tweezers** n ピンセット
**twelfth** adj 第１２番目
**twelve** adj １２個の
**twentieth** adj 第２０番目
**twenty** adj ２０個の
**twice** adv ２回、２倍
**twilight** n 薄明
**twin** n 双子
**twinkle** v キラキラ輝く
**twist** v ねじる
**twist** n ねじれ
**twisted** adj ねじれた
**twister** n 竜巻
**two** adj ２個の
**tycoon** n 大君
**type** n 種類
**type** v 打ち込む
**typical** adj 典型的な
**tyranny** n 専制政治
**tyrant** n 暴君

**ugliness** n 醜さ
**ugly** adj 醜い
**ulcer** n 潰瘍
**ultimate** adj 最終的な
**ultimatum** n 最後通告
**ultrasound** n 超音波
**umbrella** n 傘
**umpire** n 審判
**unable** adj できない
**unanimity** n 満場一致
**unarmed** adj 非武装の
**unassuming** adj 気取らない
**unaware** adj 無意識の
**unbearable** adj 耐えられない
**unbiased** adj 不偏の
**unbroken** adj 壊れていない
**unbutton** v ボタンを外す
**uncertain** adj 不確かな
**uncle** n 叔父
**uncommon** adj 珍しい
**unconscious** adj 無意識の
**uncover** v 明らかにする
**undecided** adj 未決定の
**undeniable** adj 否定できない
**under** pre ～の下に
**undercover** adj 秘密の
**underdog** n 負け犬
**undergo** v 耐える
**underground** adj 地下の

**underlie** *v* 根底にある

**underline** *v* 強調する

**underlying** *adj* 下部の

**undermine** *v* 下を掘る

**underneath** *pre* 〜の下に

**underpass** *n* 地下道

**understand** *v* 理解する

**understandable** *adj* 理解できる

**understanding** *adj* 理解

**undertake** *v* 負う

**underwear** *n* 下着

**undo** *v* 外す

**undoubtedly** *adv* 確かに

**undress** *v* 衣服を脱ぐ

**undue** *adj* 過度の

**unearth** *v* 掘り出す

**uneasiness** *n* 不安

**uneasy** *adj* 不安な

**uneducated** *adj* 教養のない

**unemployed** *adj* 無職の

**unemployment** *n* 失業

**unending** *adj* 果てしのない

**unequal** *adj* 同等でない

**unequivocal** *adj* 無条件の

**uneven** *adj* 同じでない

**uneventful** *adj* 事件のない

**unexpected** *adj* 意外な

**unfailing** *adj* 失敗しない

**unfair** *adj* 不公平な

**unfairly** *adv* 不当に

**unfairness** *n* 不誠実な

**unfaithful** *adj* 忠実でない

**unfamiliar** *adj* よく知らない

**unfasten** *v* 外れる

**unfavorable** *adj* 好意的でない

**unfit** *adj* 不適当な

**unfold** *v* 開く

**unforeseen** *adj* 予期しない

**unfounded** *adj* 事実無根の

**unfriendly** *adj* 不親切な

**ungrateful** *adj* 満足できない

**unhappiness** *n* 不運

**unhappy** *adj* 不幸な

**unharmed** *adj* 無傷の

**unhealthy** *adj* 不健康な

**unheard-of** *adj* 前代未聞の

**unhurt** *adj* 傷ついていない

**unification** *n* 統一

**uniform** *n* 制服

**uniformity** *n* 均一

**unify** *v* 統一する

**unilateral** *adj* 一方的な

**union** *n* 労働組合

**unique** *adj* 特有の

**unit** *n* 一個、単元

**unite** *v* 結合する

**unity** *n* 単一性

**universal** *adj* 全宇宙の

**universe** *n* 宇宙、銀河

**university** *n* 大学

**unjust** *adj* 不公平な

**unjustified** *adj* 不当な

**unknown** *adj* 知られていない

**unlawful** *adj* 非合法の

U

unleaded *adj* 無鉛の

unleash *v* ～を放つ

unless *c* ～でない限り

unlike *adj* 似ていない

unlikely *adj* ありそうもない

unlimited *adj* 制限のない

unload *v* 降ろす

unlock *v* 錠が開く

unlucky *adj* 不運な

unmarried *adj* 未婚の

unmask *v* 仮面をとる

unmistakable *adj* 間違いない

unnecessary *adj* 不必要な

unnoticed *adj* 気付かれない

unofficially *adv* 非公式に

unpack *v* 荷をほどく

unpleasant *adj* 不愉快な

unplug *v* プラグを抜く

unpopular *adj* 人気がない

unprofitable *adj* 利益のない

unprotected *adj* 無防備の

unravel *v* 解ける

unreal *adj* 実在しない

unrealistic *adj* 非現実的な

unreasonable *adj* 理性を欠いた

unrelated *adj* 関係のない

unreliable *adj* 信頼できない

unrest *n* 心配、動揺

unsafe *adj* 安全でない

unselfish *adj* 利己的でない

unstable *adj* 不安定な

unsteady *adj* グラグラする

unsuccessful *adj* 不成功の

unsuitable *adj* 不適当な

untie *v* ～を解く

until *pre* ～まで

untimely *adj* 時機を失した

untrue *adj* 虚偽の

unusual *adj* 普通でない

unveil *v* 明かす

unwillingly *adv* 嫌々ながら

unwind *v* 解く

unwise *adj* 思慮がない

unwrap *v* 包装を解く

upbringing *n* 生い立ち

upcoming *adj* 来たる

update *v* 更新する

upgrade *v* 性能を高める

uphill *adv* 上り坂の

uphold *v* 掲げる

upholstery *n* 賭け布

upon *pre* ～の上に

upper *adj* 上位のもの

upright *adj* 直立の

uprising *n* 暴動

uproar *n* 騒動

uproot *v* 根絶する

upset *v* 怒らせる

upside-down *adv* 逆さまの

upstairs *adv* 階上へ

uptight *adj* 張りつめた

up-to-date *adj* 最新の

upturn *n* 好転

upwards *adv* 上昇する

U

urban *adj* 都会の
urge *n* 本能
urge *v* 駆り立てる
urgency *n* 緊急性
urgent *adj* 緊急の
urinate *v* 排尿する
urine *n* 尿、小便
urn *n* つぼ、かめ
us *pro* われわれを
usage *n* 使用法
use *v* 使う
use *n* 利用
used to *adj* よく〜したものだ
useful *adj* 役立つ
usefulness *n* 役に立つこと
useless *adj* 役に立たない
user *n* 使用者
usher *n* 門番
usual *adj* 通常の
usurp *v* 奪う
utensil *n* 用品
uterus *n* 子宮
utilize *v* 利用する
utmost *adj* 最大限の
utter *v* 全くの

vacant *adj* 空いている
vacate *v* 身を引く
vacation *n* 休暇
vaccinate *v* 予防接種をする
vaccine *n* ワクチン
vacillate *v* 揺れる
vagrant *n* 放浪者
vague *adj* ぼんやりした
vain *adj* 虚栄心の強い
vainly *adv* 無駄に
valiant *adj* 勇敢な
valid *adj* 有効な
validate *v* 有効にする
validity *n* 妥当性
valley *n* 渓谷
valuable *adj* 貴重な
value *n* 価値
valve *n* バルブ、弁
vampire *n* 吸血鬼
van *n* 先頭
vandal *n* 破壊者
vandalism *n* 野蛮行為
vandalize *v* 破壊する
vanguard *n* 前衛
vanish *v* 消す
vanity *n* 虚栄心
vanquish *v* 負かす
vaporize *v* 蒸発する
variable *adj* 変わりやすい

U
V

**varied** *adj* 変化に富む

**variety** *n* 種類

**various** *adj* さまざまな

**varnish** *v* ニスを塗る

**varnish** *n* ニス

**vary** *v* 変わる

**vase** *n* 花瓶

**vast** *adj* 膨大な

**veal** *n* 子牛の肉

**veer** *v* 転換する

**vegetable** *v* 野菜の

**vegetarian** *v* 菜食主義の

**vegetation** *n* 植物

**vehicle** *n* 車

**veil** *n* 覆い

**vein** *n* 静脈

**velocity** *n* 速さ

**velvet** *n* ベルベット

**venerate** *v* あがめる

**vengeance** *n* 報復

**venison** *n* 鹿の肉

**venom** *n* 悪意

**vent** *n* 通風孔

**ventilate** *v* 〜に風を通す

**ventilation** *n* 換気

**venture** *n* 冒険

**verb** *n* 動詞

**verbally** *adv* 言語で

**verbatim** *adv* 逐語的に

**verdict** *n* 評決

**verge** *n* 端

**verification** *n* 根拠

**verify** *v* 実証する

**versatile** *adj* 多用途の

**verse** *n* 詩の節

**versed** *adj* 熟知した

**version** *n* 版

**versus** *pre* 対、〜に対して

**vertebra** *n* 椎骨

**very** *adv* とても

**vessel** *n* 船、導管

**vest** *n* チョッキ

**vestige** *n* 名残、痕跡

**veteran** *n* 経験豊かな

**veterinarian** *n* 獣医

**veto** *v* 拒否する

**viaduct** *n* 高架橋

**vibrant** *adj* 活気のある

**vibrate** *v* 振動する

**vibration** *n* 振動

**vice** *n* 悪徳

**vicinity** *n* 近所

**vicious** *adj* 不道徳な

**victim** *n* 犠牲者

**victimize** *v* 犠牲にする

**victor** *n* 勝利者

**victorious** *adj* 勝った

**victory** *n* 勝利

**view** *n* 景色

**view** *v* 眺める

**viewpoint** *n* 見方

**vigil** *n* 徹夜の看病

**village** *n* 村

**villager** *n* 村人

V

villain *n* 悪党

vindicate *v* 無実を証明する

vindictive *adj* 報復的な

vine *n* つる、ブドウの木

vinegar *n* 酢、ビネガー

vineyard *n* ブドウ園

violate *v* 違反する

violence *n* 暴力

violent *adj* 暴力的な

violet *n* スミレ色

violin *n* バイオリン

viper *n* 毒ヘビ

virgin *n* 童貞

virginity *n* 処女性

virile *adj* 男性的な

virility *n* 力強さ

virtually *adv* 実質的には

virtue *n* 美徳

virtuous *adj* 高潔な

virulent *adj* 悪性の

virus *n* 病原体

visibility *n* 視界

visible *adj* 目に見える

vision *n* 視覚

visit *n* 訪問

visit *v* 訪れる

visitor *n* 訪問者

visual *adj* 視覚の

visualize *v* 目に見える

vital *adj* 致命的な

vitality *n* 活力

vitamin *n* ビタミン

vivacious *adj* 生き生きとした

vivid *adj* 光り輝く

vocabulary *n* 語彙

vocation *n* 天職

vogue *n* 流行

voice *n* 声

void *adj* 無効の

volatile *adj* 一触即発の

volcano *n* 火山

voltage *n* 電圧

volume *n* 量

volunteer *n* ボランティア

vomit *v* 吐く

vomit *n* 嘔吐

vote *v* 投票する

vote *n* 票

voting *n* 投票

vouch for *v* 〜を保証する

voucher *n* 領収書

vow *v* 〜を誓う

vowel *n* 母音

voyage *n* 船旅、航海

voyager *n* 航海者

vulgar *adj* 不作法な

vulgarity *n* 下品

vulnerable *adj* 弱い

vulture *n* ハゲワシ

# W

**wafer** *n* ウエハース
**wage** *n* 賃金
**wagon** *n* 荷馬車
**wail** *v* 嘆き悲しむ
**wail** *n* 泣き叫ぶ
**waist** *n* ウエスト
**wait** *v* 待つ
**waiter** *n* ウエーター
**waiting** *n* 待つこと
**waitress** *n* ウエートレス
**waive** *v* 放棄する
**wake up** *iv* 起きる
**walk** *v* 歩く
**walk** *n* 散歩
**walkout** *n* 退場
**wall** *n* 壁
**wallet** *n* 財布
**walnut** *n* クルミ
**walrus** *n* セイウチ
**waltz** *n* ワルツ
**wanderer** *n* 放浪者
**wane** *v* 衰える
**want** *v* 〜が欲しい
**war** *n* 戦争
**ward** *n* 病棟
**warden** *n* 刑務所長
**wardrobe** *n* 洋服だんす
**warehouse** *n* 倉庫
**warfare** *n* 戦争行為

**warm** *adj* 暖かい
**warm up** *v* 暖まる
**warmth** *n* 暖かさ
**warn** *v* 警告する
**warning** *n* 警告
**warp** *v* 縦糸
**warped** *adj* そった
**warrant** *v* 〜を正当化する
**warrant** *n* 保証
**warranty** *n* 保証契約
**warrior** *n* 武士
**warship** *n* 軍艦
**wart** *n* いぼ
**wary** *adj* 警戒している
**wash** *v* 洗う
**washable** *adj* 洗える
**wasp** *n* 気難しい人
**waste** *v* 浪費される
**waste** *n* 浪費
**waste basket** *n* くず入れ
**wasteful** *adj* 浪費的な
**watch** *n* 時計
**watch** *v* 観察する
**watch out** *v* 気を付ける
**watchful** *adj* 用心深い
**watchmaker** *n* 時計屋
**water** *n* 水
**water** *v* 水をやる
**water down** *v* 水で薄める
**waterfall** *n* 滝
**waterheater** *n* 給湯器
**watermelon** *n* スイカ

| | |
|---|---|
| **waterproof** _adj_ 防水加工した | **weed** _n_ 雑草 |
| **watershed** _n_ 流域 | **weed** _v_ 雑草を取る |
| **watertight** _adj_ 防水の | **week** _n_ 週 |
| **watery** _adj_ 水っぽい | **weekday** _adj_ 平日 |
| **watt** _n_ ワット | **weekend** _n_ 週末 |
| **wave** _n_ 波 | **weekly** _adv_ 毎週の |
| **waver** _v_ 揺れ | **weep** _iv_ 嘆き悲しむ |
| **wavy** _adj_ 波状の | **weigh** _v_ 重さを量る |
| **wax** _n_ ろう | **weight** _n_ 重さ |
| **way** _n_ 方向、経路 | **weird** _adj_ 不気味な |
| **way in** _n_ 入り口 | **welcome** _v_ 歓迎される |
| **way out** _n_ 出口 | **welcome** _n_ 歓迎 |
| **we** _pro_ 私たちは | **weld** _v_ 溶接する |
| **weak** _adj_ 弱い | **welder** _n_ 溶接工 |
| **weaken** _v_ 弱くなる | **welfare** _n_ 福利 |
| **weakness** _n_ 弱さ | **well** _n_ 井戸 |
| **wealth** _n_ 富、財産 | **well-to-do** _adj_ 裕福な |
| **wealthy** _adj_ 裕福な | **west** _n_ 西 |
| **weapon** _n_ 武器 | **westbound** _adv_ 西行きの |
| **wear** _n_ 衣類 | **western** _adj_ 西部の |
| **wear** _iv_ 着る、履く | **westerner** _adj_ 西洋人 |
| **wear down** _v_ すり減る | **wet** _adj_ 湿った |
| **wear out** _v_ 使い古す | **whale** _n_ くじら |
| **weary** _adj_ 疲れた | **wharf** _n_ 埠頭 |
| **weather** _n_ 天気 | **what** _adj_ 何の、どれほど |
| **weave** _iv_ 織る | **whatever** _adj_ 何の〜が〜でも |
| **web** _n_ クモの巣 | **wheat** _n_ 小麦 |
| **web site** _n_ ウエブサイト | **wheel** _n_ 車輪 |
| **wed** _iv_ 結婚する | **wheelbarrow** _n_ 手押し車 |
| **wedding** _n_ 結婚式 | **wheelchair** _n_ 車いす |
| **wedge** _n_ くさび | **when** _adv_ いつ |
| **Wednesday** _n_ 水曜日 | **whenever** _adv_ 一体いつ |

**where** *adv* どこに

**whereabouts** *n* 行方

**whereas** *c* ～である一方で

**whereupon** *c* ～するとすぐ

**wherever** *c* どこへ～しても

**whether** *c* ～かどうか

**which** *adj* どちらか

**while** *c* ～する間に

**whim** *n* 思いつき

**whine** *v* 哀れっぽい

**whip** *v* 急に動く

**whip** *n* むち、むち打ち

**whirl** *v* グルグル回る

**whirlpool** *n* 渦

**whiskers** *n* ほおひげ

**whisper** *v* ささやく

**whisper** *n* ささやき声

**whistle** *v* 口笛を吹く

**whistle** *n* 口笛

**white** *adj* 白い

**whiten** *v* 白くする

**whittle** *v* 少しずつ削る

**who** *pro* 誰

**whoever** *pro* ～するのは誰でも

**whole** *adj* 全部の

**wholehearted** *adj* 心からの

**wholesale** *n* 卸売り

**wholesome** *adj* 健全な

**whom** *pro* 誰に、誰を

**why** *adv* なぜ、どうして

**wicked** *adj* ひどく悪い

**wickedness** *n* 邪悪

**wide** *adj* 幅広い

**widely** *adv* 広く

**widen** *v* 広くなる

**widespread** *adj* 広範囲に及ぶ

**widow** *n* 未亡人

**widower** *n* 男やもめ

**width** *n* 幅、広さ

**wield** *v* 巧みに使う

**wife** *n* 妻

**wig** *n* かつら

**wiggle** *v* 小刻みに動く

**wild** *adj* 野生の

**wild boar** *n* イノシシ

**wilderness** *n* 荒野

**wildlife** *n* 野生動物

**will** *n* ～するつもりである

**willfully** *adv* 故意に

**willing** *adj* ～する気がある

**willingly** *adv* 喜んで

**willingness** *n* 意欲

**willow** *n* 柳

**wily** *adj* ずる賢い

**wimp** *adj* ひるむ

**win** *iv* 勝つ

**win back** *v* 取り返す

**wind** *n* 風、気配

**wind** *iv* 風にさらす

**wind up** *v* 巻き上げる

**winding** *adj* 巻くこと

**windmill** *n* 風車

**window** *n* 窓

**windpipe** *n* 気管

W

windshield *n* フロントガラス

windy *adj* 風の強い

wine *n* ワイン、ブドウ酒

winery *n* ワイン醸造所

wing *n* 翼

wink *n* まばたき

wink *v* まばたき

winner *n* 勝利者

winter *n* 冬、末期

wipe *v* ぬぐう

wipe out *v* ふき取る

wire *n* 電報

wireless *adj* 無線の

wisdom *n* 賢明さ

wise *adj* 賢い

wish *v* 望む

wish *n* 望み

wit *n* 機知

witch *n* 魔女

witchcraft *n* 魔法

with *pre* ～と一緒に

withdraw *v* 退く

withdrawal *n* 撤退

withdrawn *adj* 撤退した

wither *v* 枯れる

withhold *iv* 控える

within *pre* ～の中

without *pre* ～なしで

withstand *v* 耐える

witness *n* 目撃者

witty *adj* 機知のある

wizard *n* 魔術師

wobble *v* よろめき

woes *n* 災難

wolf *n* オオカミ

woman *n* 女性

womb *n* 子宮

women *n* 女性たち

wonder *v* 疑問に思う

wonder *n* 不思議なもの

wonderful *adj* 素晴らしい

wood *n* 木

wooden *adj* 木製の

wool *n* 羊毛、毛糸

woolen *adj* 羊毛の

word *n* 語

wording *n* 言い回し

work *n* 仕事

work *v* 働く

work out *v* 解決する

workable *adj* 実行できる

workbook *n* ワークブック

worker *n* 働く人

workshop *n* 研修会

world *n* 世界

worldly *adj* 世俗的な

worldwide *adj* 世界的な

worm *n* 寄生虫

worn-out *adj* 使い古した

worrisome *adj* 厄介な

worry *v* 心配する

worry *n* 心配

worse *adj* より悪い

worsen *v* 悪化する

worship *n* 崇拝
worst *adj* 最悪
worthless *adj* 価値のない
worthwhile *adj* 価値のある
worthy *adj* 〜に値する
wound *n* 外傷
wound *v* 〜を傷つける
woven *adj* 織った
wrap *v* 包む
wrap up *v* くるまる
wrapping *n* 包装紙
wrath *n* 激怒
wreath *n* 花輪
wreck *v* 難破
wreckage *n* 漂流物
wrench *n* ねじること
wrestle *v* 闘う
wrestler *n* 力士
wrestling *n* 格闘
wretched *adj* 卑劣な
wring *iv* 絞りだす
wrinkle *v* しわの寄った
wrinkle *n* しわ
wrist *n* 手首
write *iv* 手紙を書く
write down *v* 書き留める
writer *n* 作家
writhe *v* 身をよじる
writing *n* 書き方
written *adj* 書かれた
wrong *adj* 間違った

X-mas *n* クリスマス
X-ray *n* X線

yacht *n* クルーザー
yam *n* 山芋
yard *n* 中庭
yarn *n* 毛糸
yawn *n* あくび
yawn *v* あくびをする
year *n* 年
yearly *adv* 毎年の
yearn *v* 切望する
yeast *n* 酵母菌
yell *v* 怒鳴る
yellow *adj* 黄色の
yes *adv* その通り
yesterday *adv* 昨日の
yet *c* けれども
yield *v* 産出する
yield *n* 収穫高
yoke *n* 拘束
yolk *n* 卵黄
you *pro* 貴方

young *adj* 若い
youngster *n* 若者
your *adj* あなたの
yours *pro* あなたのもの
yourself *pro* あなた自身
youth *n* 青年時代
youthful *adj* 若者の

# Z

zap *v* 素早く動く
zeal *n* 熱情
zealous *adj* 熱心な
zebra *n* シマウマ
zero *n* 零度
zest *n* 熱意
zinc *n* 亜鉛
zip code *n* 郵便番号
zipper *n* チャック
zone *n* 地帯
zoo *n* 動物園
zoology *n* 動物学

# Japanese-English

**Bilingual Dictionaries, Inc.**

# Abbreviations

**a** - article
**n** - noun
**e** - exclamation
**pro** - pronoun
**adj** - adjective
**adv** - adverb
**v** - verb
**iv** - irregular verb
**pre** - preposition
**c** - conjunction

# あ

アーチ *n* arch
アーモンド *n* almond
愛 *n* love
愛国者 *n* patriot
愛国的な *adj* patriotic
あいさつする *v* greet
相性 *n* chemistry
愛情 *n* affection
相性が良い *adj* compatible
相性が悪い *adj* incompatible
愛情を抱いた *adj* loving
合図 *n* signal
アイスクリーム *n* ice cream
愛する *v* love
愛する人 *n* sweetheart
愛想のよい *adj* affable
空いている *adj* vacant
相手方 *n* counterpart
哀悼 *n* mourning
相並んだ *adj* collateral
相反する *adj* conflicting
愛撫 *n* caress
愛撫する *v* caress
合間 *n* interlude
あいまいな *adj* ambiguous
愛らしい *adj* lovely
愛らしいい *adj* adorable

会う *v* meet
亜鉛 *n* zinc
青い *adj* blue
青ざめた *adj* pale
青写真 *n* blueprint
赤い *adj* red
赤くなる *v* redden
赤字額 *n* deficit
明かす *v* unveil
赤ちゃん *n* baby
贖い *n* redemption
赤身の *adj* lean
あがめる *v* venerate
赤らみ *v* flush
上がる *v* ascend
明るい *adj* luminous
明るく *adv* lightly
明るくする *v* illuminate
上がること *n* mount
秋 *n* autumn
明らかな *adj* obvious
明らかに *adv* apparently
明らかにする *v* uncover
あきらめる *v* give up
悪 *adj* bad, evil
悪意 *n* spite, venom
悪意のある *adj* spiteful
悪質な *adj* heinous
握手 *n* handshake

| | |
|---|---|
| 悪臭 *n* stench, stink | 足 *n* foot, paw |
| 悪臭がする *v* stink, fetid | 味 *n* taste |
| 悪臭を放つ *adj* smelly | 肢 *n* limb |
| 悪性 *n* malignancy | 足跡 *n* footprint |
| 悪性の *adj* malignant | 足音 *n* footstep |
| 悪党 *n* rascal, villain | 足音 *v* tread |
| 悪徳 *n* vice | 味がする *v* taste |
| 悪名高い *adj* infamous | 足首 *n* ankle |
| あくび *n* yawn | 足底 *n* sole |
| あくびをする *v* yawn | 明日 *adv* tomorrow |
| 悪魔 *n* devil, demon | 足載せ台 *n* stool |
| 悪魔のような *adj* satanic | 味のない *adj* tasteless |
| 悪夢 *n* nightmare | 足場 *n* scaffolding |
| 悪用 *n* abuse, misuse | 足指 *n* toe |
| 悪用する *v* abuse | 足指のつめ *n* toenail |
| 握力 *n* grip | 足を引きずる *v* limp |
| 揚げ物の *adj* fried | 預け入れ *n* deposit |
| 顎 *n* jaw, chin | アスパラガス *n* asparagus |
| あごひげ *n* beard | アスピリン *n* aspirin |
| 朝 *n* morning | アスファルト *n* asphalt |
| 浅い *adj* shallow | 汗 *n* sweat |
| あざができる *v* bruise | 焦り *n* impatience |
| 嘲り笑う *v* mock | 汗をかく *v* sweat |
| あざける *v* ridicule | あそこ *adv* there |
| 欺く *v* mislead, double-cross | 遊び戯れる *adj* playful |
| 欺く人 *n* cheater | 遊び場 *n* playground |
| あざ笑う *v* deride, scoff | 遊ぶ *v* play |
| アシ *n* reed | 値する *v* deserve |
| 脚 *n* leg | 与える *v* give |

暖かい *adj* warm

暖かさ *n* warmth

暖まる *v* warm up

あだ名 *n* nickname

アダプター *n* adapter

頭 *n* head

頭金 *n* down payment

頭に取り付く *v* obsess

頭に入る *v* soak in

新しい *adj* new

新しくする *v* renew

厚い *adj* thick

暑い *adj* hot

悪化 *n* aggravation

扱う *v* deal

悪化させる *v* aggravate

悪化した *adj* degenerate

悪化する *v* deteriorate

厚切り *n* slab

厚くなる *v* thicken

熱くなる *v* heat

暑苦しい *adj* stifling

圧縮 *n* compression

圧縮する *v* compress

合っている *adj* correct

圧倒する *v* overwhelm

圧倒的な *adj* crushing

集まり *n* gathering

集まる *v* assemble

集める *v* collect

圧力 *n* pressure

圧力をかける *v* pressure

当てこすり *n* insinuation

当て付け *n* innuendo

当てにすること *n* reliance

当て布を当てる *v* patch

当てはまる *v* apply

当てもの *v* pad

跡 *n* track

後知恵 *n* hindsight

後で *pre* after

後で *adv* later

後戻りする *v* turn back

跡を残す *v* mark

穴 *n* hole, pit

穴開け器 *n* punch

アナウンサ *n* announcer

貴方 *pro* you

あなた自身 *pro* yourself

あなたの *adj* your

あなたのもの *pro* yours

穴だらけの *adj* porous

穴を開ける *v* drill

穴を開けること *n* puncture

あのとき *adv* then

アパート *n* apartment

暴れ回る *v* rampage

油 *n* oil

脂っぽい *adj* greasy

油で揚げる *v* fry

あぶる *v* roast

あぶること *n* roast

あふれる *v* overflow

アペリチフ *n* aperitif

アヘン *n* opium

アポストロフィー *n* apostrophe

甘い *adj* sweet

甘くする *v* sweeten

甘さ *n* sweetness

雨垂れ *v* eavesdrop

アマチュア *adj* amateur

甘党 *n* sweets

網目 *n* network

網焼きにする *v* broil

雨 *n* rain

雨が降る *v* rain

雨模様の *adj* rainy

アメリカ人 *adj* American

アメリカボウフウ *n* parsnip

アメリカワニ *n* alligator

危うくする *v* endanger

操る *v* rein

過ちを犯す *v* err

誤って解釈する *v* misinterpret

誤り *n* error, mistake

誤り導かれた *adj* misguided

誤りを暴く *v* debunk

誤る *v* mistake

謝る *v* apologize

荒々しい *adj* fierce

粗い *adj* coarse

アライグマ *n* raccoon

洗う *v* wash

洗える *adj* washable

嵐 *n* storm

嵐の *adj* stormy

荒らすこと *n* desolation

新たに *adv* afresh, newly

あらためて *adv* anew

改める *v* mend

アラビアの *adj* Arabic

あらゆる *adj* every

あらゆる人 *pro* everyone

現れる *v* emerge

アリ *n* ant

あり得る *adj* probable

ありがたく思う *adj* thankful

ありがとう *n* thanks

ありそうな *adv* likely

ありそうな状態 *n* likelihood

ありそうもない *adj* unlikely

歩き始めの子供 *n* toddler

歩きまわる *v* roam

歩く *v* walk

ある人 *pro* someone

アルミニウム *n* aluminum

アルミ箔 *v* foil
荒れ狂って *adv* furiously
荒れ地の *v* moor
荒れ果てた *adj* desolate
アレルギー *n* allergy
アレルギー症の *adj* allergic
泡 *n* foam
哀れっぽい *v* whine
アンギナ *n* angina
アングリアの *adj* Anglican
アンケート *n* questionnaire
暗殺 *n* assassination
暗殺者 *n* assassin
暗殺する *v* assassinate
暗示 *n* implication
暗示する *v* connote, hint
暗礁 *n* reef
暗証番号 *n* password
アンズ *n* apricot
安全性 *n* security
安全でない *adj* unsafe
安全な *adj* safe, secure
安息の地 *n* haven
アンチョビ *n* anchovy
安定 *n* stability
安定した *adj* stable
アンテナ *n* antenna
アンテロープ *n* antelope
案内係 *n* attendant

案内書 *n* guidebook
案内する *v* guide, direct
案内人 *n* guide
暗黙の *adj* implicit
アンモニア *n* ammonia

# い

胃 *n* stomach
言い争う *v* argue, haggle
言い張る *v* assert
言い回し *n* wording
言い訳 *n* excuse
委員会 *n* committee
言う *v* tell, say
家 *n* home
家のない *adj* homeless
癒える *v* heal
硫黄 *n* sulphur
イカ *n* squid
意外な *adj* unexpected
いかだ *n* raft
いかり *n* anchor
怒り *n* anger
怒り *adj* mad
遺棄 *n* abandonment
意義 *n* significance
異議 *n* objection

域 *n* range
息 *n* breath
生き生きとした *adj* vivacious
勢いよく動く *n* spanking
生き返らせる *v* revive
生き返る *v* resuscitate
生き方 *n* lifestyle
息が詰まる *v* choke
息が止まる *v* gasp
息苦しい *adj* stuffy
息苦しくなる *v* stifle
行き過ぎる *v* overrun
遺棄する *v* abandon
行き詰まり *n* stalemate
行き詰まりの *adj* deadlock
行き止まり *n* dead end
異議のある *adj* dissident
生き残り *n* survival
生き残る *v* survive
意義深い *adj* significant
生き物 *n* creature
異教徒 *n* heathen
異教の *adj* pagan
イギリス *n* England
イギリスの *adj* English
息をする *v* breathe
異議を唱える *v* dissent
行く *v* go
意気地なしの *adj* sissy

育成する *v* bring up
いくつかの *adj* several
いくぶんか *adv* somewhat
いくらか *adj* some
池 *n* pond
畏敬すべき *adj* awesome
畏敬の念 *n* awe
意見 *n* opinion, remark
威厳 *n* dignity
威厳のある *adj* majestic
意見の一致 *n* consensus
意見の相違 *n* disagreement
威厳をつける *v* dignify
移行 *n* transition
異国風の *adj* exotic
居酒屋 *n* tavern
勇ましい *adj* brave
遺産 *n* heritage
医師 *n* physician
石 *n* stone
意識 *n* conciousness
意識のある *adj* conscious
維持する *v* retain
意思の固い *adj* resolute
いじめ *v* tease
医者 *n* doctor
移住者 *n* migrant
移住する *v* relocate
遺書 *n* testament

衣装 n costume
異常性 n abnormality
異常な adj abnormal
異常なもの n oddity
移植 n graft
移植する v implant
いす n chair
イスラム教の adj Muslim
イスラムの adj Islamic
異星人 n alien
威勢のいい adj dashing
異説 n heresy
以前の adj previous
急いで adv hastily
急いで進む v make
急いで上る v run up
忙しい adj busy
忙しく adv busily
急がせる v hurry up
急ぎの adj hasty
急ぐ v hasten, hurry
遺族 n survivor
急ぐこと n haste
依存 n dependence
板 n board
痛い adj painful, sore
遺体安置所 n mortuary
偉大さ n greatness
偉大な adj great

委託する v delegate
委託料 n commission
いたずら n trick
いたずら好きな adj mischievous
痛ましい adj pathetic
痛み n ache, pain
痛みのない adj painless
傷みやすい adj perishable
痛む v hurt
痛む所 n sore
イタリア n Italy
イタリア人 adj Italian
至る v get
異端者 adj heretic
一員 n member
一月 n January
一組 n pair, set
一撃 n punch, slash
イチゴ n strawberry
一個 n unit
一さじ n spoonful
一時解雇する v lay off
一時間 n hour
一時休止する v adjourn
イチジク n fig
位置して adj located
位置している adj situated
一時的中止 n suspension
一時的な静止 n lull

一時的流行 *n* fad

一時の *adj* temporary

一族 *n* clan

一束 *n* batch

一読する *v* look over

一番目の *adj* first

一部 *n* part

一部分は *adv* partly

一覧表 *n* inventory, list

位置を変える *v* dislocate

いつ *adv* when

いつか *adv* someday

一括する *v* lump together

一括払い額 *n* lump sum

一貫しない *adj* incoherent

一貫性 *n* consistency

一瞬に *adv* momentarily

一生の *adj* lifetime

一触即発の *adj* volatile

一緒に *adv* together

いつでも *adv* whenever

一体化する *v* combine

逸脱 *n* aberration

一致 *n* consent

一致した *adj* consistent

一致する *v* conform

一定のスペース *v* space out

いっぱいの *adj* full

一般化する *v* generalize

一夫一婦制 *n* monogamy

一夫多妻者 *adj* polygamist

一片 *n* piece

一方的な *adj* unilateral

いつも *adv* always

逸話 *n* anecdote

偽る *v* falsify

偽ること *n* pretense

遺伝子 *n* gene

遺伝性の *adj* hereditary

遺伝の *adj* genetic

意図 *n* intention

糸 *n* string, thread

緯度 *n* latitude

井戸 *n* well

移動 *n* transfer

移動する *v* move

いとこ *n* cousin

糸杉 *n* cypress

意図する *v* intend

田舎 *n* countryside

田舎の *adj* rural, rustic

田舎の住人 *n* countryman

稲妻 *n* lightning

イニシャル *n* initials

委任 *n* mandate

犬 *n* dog

犬小屋 *n* kennel

胃の *adj* gastric

イノシシ *n* wild boar
祈り *n* prayer
祈る *v* pray
イバラの *adj* thorny
威張り散らす *v* boss around
威張る *adj* bossy
違反 *n* breach
違反する *v* violate
いびき *n* snore
いびきをかく *v* snore
衣服 *n* dress, clothes
衣服を着る *v* dress
衣服を脱ぐ *v* strip, undress
いぶす *v* fumigate
遺物 *n* relic
いぼ *n* wart
違法の *adj* illegal
今 *adv* now
今まで *adv* hitherto
今までに *adv* ever
意味 *n* meaning
意味のある *adj* meaningful
意味のない *adj* meaningless
意味深い *adj* profound
移民 *n* emigrant
鋳物工場 *n* foundry
嫌々ながら *adv* unwillingly
嫌がる *v* mind
医薬 *n* medication

嫌気 *n* dislike
卑しい *adj* lowly
卑しさ *n* meanness
嫌な *adj* distasteful
イヤホン *n* earphones
嫌み *n* sarcasm
イヤリング *n* earring
意欲 *n* willingness
依頼 *n* request
依頼する *v* request
イライラさせる *v* frustrate
イライラさせる *adj* irritating
イライラした *adj* impatient
いら立たせる *v* irritate
入り江 *n* cove
入り口 *n* gate
衣料品 *n* clothing
威力 *n* teeth
衣類 *n* garment
イルカ *n* dolphin
入れ物 *n* container
色 *n* color
色とりどりの *adj* colorful
岩 *n* rock
祝う *v* celebrate
イワシ *n* sardine
岩の多い *adj* rocky
いわゆる *adj* so-called
印 *n* mark

韻 *n* rhyme
陰うつな *adj* overcast
陰影 *n* nuance
インク *n* ink
インゲン豆 *n* kidney bean
インコ *n* parakeet
インゴット *n* ingot
印刷 *n* print
印刷字 *n* printing
印刷する *v* print
隠者 *n* hermit
印象的な *adj* imposing
因人 *n* prisoner
インチ *n* inch
咽頭 *n* larynx
陰謀 *n* conspiracy
隠喩 *n* metaphor
引用 *n* excerpt
引用する *v* quote
引用文 *n* quotation
飲料 *n* beverage
印を押す *v* stamp
〜以後に *pre* since
〜行きの *adj* bound for
1回 *adv* once
1階 *n* ground floor
1個の *adj* one
1世紀 *n* century

# う

飢え *n* hunger
ウエーター *n* waiter
ウエートレス *n* waitress
植木鉢 *n* flowerpot
植木屋 *n* gardener
ウエスト *n* waist
上に向ける *v* turn up
ウエハース *n* wafer
ウエブサイト *n* web site
餓える *v* starve
植える *v* plant
うがい *v* gargle
迂回路 *n* bypass
浮かぶ *v* float
浮かんで *adv* afloat
浮き彫りにする *v* emboss
受け入れる *adj* receptive
受け答え *n* comeback
受け皿 *n* saucer, tray
受付 *n* reception
受付係 *n* receptionist
受け取り人 *n* addressee
受取人 *n* payee
受け取る *v* receive
受け流す *v* fend off
受け身の *adj* passive
受ける *v* incur

う

動かす v motivate
動かない adj motionless
動き n motion, move
動きやすい adj mobile
動く v swing
ウサギ n rabbit
失う v forfeit
失うこと n loss
後ろにもたれる v lean back
後ろへ動かす v move back
後ろ向きに登る v back up
渦 n whirlpool
薄く adv thinly
薄く切る v slice
うずくまる v crouch
薄暗い adj dim
薄暗くなる v dim
薄っぺらな adj flimsy
渦巻き形の adj convoluted
ウズラ n quail
うそ n falsehood, lie
うそつき adj liar
うそつきの adj deceitful
うそをつく v deceive, lie
歌 n song
歌う v sing
疑い n doubt
疑いを抱く adj distrustful
疑う v distrust, doubt

疑わしい adl doubtful
疑わしく思う adj dubious
うたた寝する v snooze
打ち上げ n launch
打ち上げられる v lift off
打ち明ける adj revealing
撃ち落とす v gun down
打ち返す v strike back
内気 n shyness
打ち砕く v smash
打ち込む v type
宇宙 n universe
宇宙の adj cosmic
宇宙飛行士 n astronaut
有頂天 n ecstasy
撃つ v shoot
美しい adj beautiful
美しくする v beautify
美しさ n beauty
打つこと n beating
移す n relocation
訴える v sue
うっとうしい adj annoying
うっとりさせる adj enchanting
うつむいた adj downcast
腕 n arm
うどん粉菌 n mildew
うなずき v nod
うぬぼれ n egoism

うぬぼれた *adj* conceited

うねる *v* comb

乳母 *n* nanny

奪い返す *v* recapture

奪う *v* deprive

馬 *n* horse

うまい *adj* tasty

うまく *adv* nicely

うまく対処する *v* cope

馬小屋 *n* stable

生まれた *adj* native

生まれつきの *adj* born

生まれる *v* germinate

海 *n* sea

膿 *n* pus

海の *adj* marine

海辺の *adj* seaside

うめき声 *n* groan

うめく *v* groan, moan

埋め込み *v* implant

埋め立て *n* landfill

埋める *v* bury

裏返しに *adv* inside out

裏書 *n* endorsement

裏書きする *v* endorse

裏切り *n* betrayal

裏切り者 *n* traitor

裏切る *v* betray

裏口 *n* backdoor

裏ごしする *v* strain

裏付ける *v* corroborate

裏通り *n* alley

裏庭 *n* backyard

裏張りすること *n* lining

うらやましい *adj* envious

うらやましがる *v* envy

うらやましさ *n* envy

売上伝票 *n* sale slip

売り手 *n* seller

売る *v* sell

うるう年 *n* leap year

うれしい *adj* joyful

うれしそうに *adv* joyfully

うろたえさせる *v* dismay, stun

浮気をする *v* flirt

うわさ *n* hearsay

うわさをする *v* gossip

上塗り *n* overcoat

上塗りする *v* overcharge

運河 *n* canal

うんざりする *adj* tiresome

運送 *v* transport

運賃 *n* fare, toll

運転 *n* drive

運転手 *n* driver

運転する *v* drive

運動 *n* exercise

運動競技の *adj* athletic

運動する *v* exercise
運動選手 *n* athlete
運動を起こす *v* campaign
運のいい *adj* lucky
運搬車 *n* truck
運搬人 *n* bearer, porter
運命 *n* destiny, fate
運命を決する *adj* fateful

# え

絵 *n* picture
柄 *n* stalk
永遠 *n* eternity
永遠に *adv* forever
永遠の *adj* everlasting
映画 *n* film, movie
永久の *adj* timeless
影響 *n* impact
影響を与える *v* impact
影響を及ぼす *v* affect
栄光 *n* glory
英国 *n* Britain
英国人 *adj* British
詠唱 *n* chant
衛生状態 *n* hygiene
永続する *adj* perennial
永続的な *adj* permanent

鋭敏な *adj* shrewd
英雄 *n* hero
英雄的行為 *n* heroism
栄養失調の *n* malnutrition
栄養のある *adj* nutritious
栄養分 *n* nutrition
エーカー *n* acre
笑顔 *n* smile
駅 *n* station
液体 *n* liquid
疫病 *n* pest, plague
エクソシスト *n* exorcist
エコー *n* echo
餌食にする *n* prey
エスカレーター *n* escalator
壊疽 *n* gangrene
枝を出す *v* branch out
閲覧する *v* browse
絵のような *adj* picturesque
エビ *n* shrimp
絵筆 *n* paintbrush
エプロン *n* apron
エメラルド *n* emerald
選ぶ *v* select
襟 *n* collar
襟巻き *n* muffler
得る *v* acquire, earn
エレベーター *n* elevator
円 *n* circle

え
お

縁 *n* brim, rim
延々と長く続く *adj* lingering
宴会 *n* banquet
遠隔の *adj* remote
円滑にする *v* lubricate
沿岸の *adj* coastal
延期 *n* postponement
延期する *v* postpone
援軍 *n* reinforcements
円形競技場 *n* amphitheater
円形の *adj* round
円弧 *n* arc
延史 *n* bailiff
演習 *n* drill
援助 *n* aid, assistance
炎症 *n* inflammation
演じる *v* act, perform
エンジン *n* engine
円背 *adj* hunched
縁石をつける *v* curb
演説 *n* speech
演説者 *n* speaker
遠足 *n* excursion, trip
円筒 *n* cylinder
エンドウ豆 *n* pea
煙突 *n* chimney
円の *adj* circular
縁のするどい *adj* edgy
鉛筆 *n* pencil

鉛筆削り *n* sharpener
遠方の *adj* faraway
援助する *v* aid

# お

甥 *n* nephew
追いかけ *n* pursuit
追い越す *v* overtake
おいしい *adj* delicious
追い出す *v* banish
生い立ち *n* upbringing
追い払う *v* oust, dispel
追いやる *v* relegate
王 *n* king
追う *v* chase
負う *v* undertake
押印 *n* seal
王冠 *n* crown
王国 *n* kingdom
王座 *n* throne
雄牛 *n* bull, ox
王子 *n* prince
雄牛の複数形 *n* oxen
王族 *adj* royal
王族 *n* royalty
殴打 *n* blow

横断する v cross
横断歩道 n crosswalk
王朝 n dynasty
嘔吐 n vomit
応答 n response
王の adj regal
王の使者 n herald
王妃 n princess
横柄な adj haughty, insolent
応募者 n applicant
オウム n parrot
横領する v embezzle
大雨 n deluge
多い v abound
覆い n cover, veil
大急ぎの v rush
大いに楽しむ v revel
覆う v cover
覆う物 n shroud
大枝 n bough
オオカミ n wolf
大きい adj big, large
大きい塊 n chunk
大きくなる v enlarge
大きさ n size
大きさを測る v size up
大きな箱 n bunker
大君 n tycoon
オーク材 n oak

大げさに言う v exaggerate
オーケストラ n orchestra
大興奮 n commotion
大声で adv loudly
大酒を飲む v guzzle
大さじ n tablespoon
大騒ぎ n fuss, tumult
大騒ぎで adv hurriedly
大嵐 n tempest
オーデコロン n cologne
大通り n avenue
オートバイ n motorcycle
オートミール n oatmeal
大幅に adv grossly
大幅に削減する v slash
大広間 n saloon
オーブン n oven
オーブンで焼く v bake
大昔 n antiquity
大麦 n barley
大メダル n medallion
大目に見た adj lenient
大目に見る n amnesty
大目に見る v condone
大文字 n capital letter
大山猫 n lynx
おおよその adj approximate
オール n oar
覆われた adj shrouded

お

丘 *n* hill
おかしい *adj* funny
おかしな *adj* comical
お金 *n* money
お金を返す *v* repay
丘の中腹 *n* hillside
丘の頂上 *n* hilltop
オカルト現象 *adj* occult
小川 *n* creek, stream
起き上がる *v* get up
置き違える *v* misplace
掟 *n* commandment
補う *v* make up for
お気に入りの *adj* favorite
置き場 *v* mow
起きる *v* wake up
置く *v* put
屋外で *adv* outdoors
憶測 *n* conjecture
奥地の *adj* inward
臆病 *n* cowardice
臆病な *adj* timid
臆病者 *n* coward
億万長者 *n* billionaire
お悔やみ *n* condolences
贈り物 *n* gift
送る *v* send
遅れた *adj* later
遅れる *v* delay

後れをとる *v* fall behind
起こす *v* raise
厳かに *adv* gravely
怒らせる *v* upset
起こる *v* arise
怒る *v* anger
抑えられた *adj* subdued
抑える *v* suppress
お皿 *n* plate
叔父 *n* uncle
押し合い *n* hustle
おじいさん *n* granddad
押し入る *v* break in
教える *v* teach
おじぎをする *v* bow
おじけづく *v* chicken out
押し込める *v* squeeze in
押し下げる *v* depress
押しつぶす *v* mangle
押しの強い *adj* pushy
おしゃべりな *adj* talkative
押し寄せる *v* crowd
押す *v* push, shove
汚水 *n* sewage
押すこと *n* press
雄の子馬 *n* colt
雄羊 *n* ram
雄ブタ *n* boar
お世辞 *n* flattery

お世辞を言う *v* flatter

おせっかいな *adj* nosy

汚染 *n* pollution

汚染する *v* pollute

遅い *adv* late, tardy

遅い *adj* slow

おぞましい *adj* hideous

恐れ *n* fear

恐れて *adj* afraid

恐れる *v* dread

恐ろしい *adj* appalling

お互いに *adj* each other

おだて *n* flattery

おたふく風邪 *n* mumps

穏やかな *adj* placid, bland

陥る *v* lapse

落ち込み *n* slump

落ち着いた *adj* relaxing

落ち着き *n* composure

落ち着く *v* settle, locate

落ちる *v* drop, fall

お告げ *n* prophecy

織った *adj* woven

夫 *n* husband

音 *n* sound

男 *n* guy, male

男っぽい *adj* masculine

男友達 *n* boyfriend

男の子 *n* boy

男やもめ *n* widower

男らしい *adj* manly

男らしさ *n* manliness

落とし穴 *n* pitfall

訪れる *v* visit

劣った *adj* mean

劣った人 *adj* inferior

大人 *n* adult

おとなしさ *n* docility

大人になる *v* grow up

お隣の *adj* next door

おとり *v* lure

踊り *n* dancing

衰える *v* wane

驚かす *v* astonish

驚き *n* amazement

驚くべき *adj* amazing

驚くべきこと *n* marvel

音を消すもの *v* muffle

音を出す *v* sound

おなか *n* tummy

同じ *adj* same

同じく *adv* likewise

同じでない *adj* uneven

おなじみの *adj* familiar

おの *n* ax

斧で割る *v* maul

叔母 *n* aunt

おばあさん *n* granny

おか

おびえさせる *adj* daunting

脅かす *v* intimidate

覚えやすい *adj* memorable

おぼれる *v* drown

おむつ *n* diaper

オムレツ *n* omelette

重い *adj* heavy

思いあがった *adj* bigot

思いこみ *n* delusion

思い出す *v* remember

思いつき *n* whim

思いつく *v* conceive

重さ *n* heaviness

重さを量る *v* weigh

面白がせる *v* amuse

面白さ *n* humor

主な *adj* principal

主に *adv* mainly

思われる *v* appear

親方 *n* master

お役所仕事 *n* red tape

おやじ *n* dad

親指 *n* thumb

泳ぐ *v* swim

泳ぐ人 *n* swimmer

およそ *adv* about

及ぶ *v* span

オラウータン *n* orangutan

オランダ *adj* Dutch

オランダ *n* Holland

折り合う *v* compound

オリーブ *n* olive

折り目 *n* crease

織物 *n* fabric

降りる *adv* alight

降りる *v* dismount

オリンピック *n* olympics

折る *v* fold

織る *v* weave

オルガン *n* organ

オルガン奏者 *n* organist

折れて取れる *v* break off

オレンジ *n* orange

愚かさ *n* stupidity

愚かな *adj* mindless

愚かなこと *n* folly

愚かなこと *adj* fool

卸売り *n* wholesale

降ろす *v* unload

終わらせる *v* finalize

終わり *n* end

終わりの *adj* last

終わりのない *adj* endless

終わる *v* cease, finish

音楽 *n* music

音楽家 *n* musician

音楽会 *n* concert

音響の *adj* acoustic

穏健な人 *adj* moderate
温室 *n* greenhouse
恩赦 *n* oblivion
恩知らず *n* ingratitude
オンス *n* ounce
音節 *n* syllable
温泉 *n* spa
温度 *n* temperature
音読する *v* pronounce
温度計 *n* thermometer
おんどり *n* cock
女主人 *n* hostess
女相続人 *n* heiress
女友達 *n* girlfriend
温和な *adj* mild

# か

蚊 *n* mosquito
蛾 *n* moth
ガーゼ *n* gauze
カーテン *n* curtain
カートで運ぶ *v* cart
害 *n* harm
会員 *n* member
会員の地位 *n* membership
開花 *v* bloom

絵画 *n* painting
海外線 *n* coastline
海外に *adv* abroad
海外の *adv* overseas
階下に *adv* downstairs
買いかぶる *v* overestimate
貝殻 *n* shell
会館 *n* hall
海岸 *n* coast
概観 *n* overview
外観を損なう *v* deface
会議 *n* meeting
回帰線 *n* tropic
懐疑的な *adj* skeptic
会議の *adj* soviet
懐旧 *n* nostalgia
階級 *n* rank
海峡 *n* strait
開業の *adj* practising
海軍 *n* fleet, navy
外形 *n* form
会計検査 *v* audit
会計士 *n* accountant
解決する *v* solve
外見 *n* appearance
解雇 *n* dismissal
会合 *n* rally
外交官 *n* diplomat
外交関係 *n* diplomacy

おか

か

外交的な *adj* extroverted
外交の *adj* diplomatic
外国人 *n* foreigner
外国の *adj* foreign
解雇される *v* let go
解散する *v* release
開始 *n* onset
開始する *v* commence
開示する *v* disclose
概して *adv* broadly
開始の *n* kickoff
会社 *n* company, firm
解釈 *n* interpretation
会衆席 *n* nave, pew
外出 *n* outing
外傷 *n* wound
外傷の *adj* traumatic
階上へ *adv* upstairs
外傷を負わせる *v* traumatize
害する *v* harm
改正 *n* amendment
改正する *v* amend
快晴の *adj* fair
概説する *v* outline
改善 *n* reform
改善する *v* reform, amend
海鮮物 *n* seafood
階層 *n* hierarchy
介添人 *n* best man

海賊 *n* pirate
海賊行為 *n* piracy
開拓者 *n* pioneer, settler
怪談 *n* tale
階段 *n* stairs
階段室 *n* staircase
改築する *v* remodel
懐中電灯 *n* flashlight
買い手 *n* buyer
欠いている *adj* devoid
快適さ *n* comfort
快適装備 *n* amenities
快適な *adj* comfortable
回転 *n* rotation
回転する *v* rotate, spin
回転装置 *v* revolver
街灯 *n* streetlight
解答 *n* solution
街灯柱 *n* lamppost
飼いならす *v* tame
介入 *n* intervention
概念 *n* concept, notion
飼い葉おけ *n* manger
開発 *n* exploitation
会費 *n* subscription
回避 *n* avoidance
回避する *v* elude, evade
回避的な *adj* evasive
回避できる *adj* avoidable

回復 *n* recovery
回復期の *adj* convalescent
回復する *v* recover
怪物 *n* monster
会報 *n* newsletter
解放する *v* emancipate
開放性 *n* openness
解明 *n* resolution
壊滅させる *v* devastate
海綿 *n* sponge
買い戻す *v* redeem
買い物 *n* shopping
買い物をする *v* shop
潰瘍 *n* ulcer
概要 *n* compendium
外来患者 *n* outpatient
外来の *adj* extraneous
改良 *n* improvement
改良する *v* touch up
回路 *n* circuit
会話 *n* conversation
会話をする *v* converse
買う *v* buy
カウボーイ *n* cowboy
ガウン *n* gown
返す *v* give back
返すこと *n* return
替え刃 *n* cartridge
カエル *n* frog

顔 *n* face
顔色 *n* complexion
顔つき *n* countenance
香 *n* incense
香り *n* fragrance
香りの良い *adj* aromatic
顔をしかめる *v* frown
画家 *n* painter
科学 *n* science
科学技術 *n* technology
科学者 *n* scientist
化学の *adj* chemical
科学の *adj* scientific
掲げる *v* uphold
かかと *n* heel
鏡 *n* mirror
かがむ *v* duck
輝いている *adj* ablaze
輝かしい *adj* dazzling
輝かせる *v* brighten
輝き *n* brightness
輝き *v* glitter
輝く *adj* bright
輝く *v* outshine
輝くもの *v* dazzle
掛かる *v* hang
書かれた *adj* written
カキ *n* oyster
鍵 *n* key

か

書き方 _n_ writing
書き留める _v_ note
垣根 _n_ barrier
鍵版 _n_ keyboard
かき混ぜる _v_ stir up
かき回す _v_ stir
鍵屋 _n_ locksmith
限られた _adj_ narrow
限る _v_ confine
描く _v_ depict, portray
家具 _n_ furniture
架空の _adj_ fictitious
格言 _n_ maxim
格差 _n_ disparity
角材 _n_ block
隠された _adj_ hidden
確執 _n_ feud
確実さ _n_ assurance
確実に _adv_ surely
確実にする _v_ assure
学者 _n_ scholar
学者ぶった _adj_ pedantic
学習者 _n_ learner
確証をたてる _v_ authenticate
確信 _n_ certainty
革新 _n_ innovation
確信させる _v_ convince
確信して _adj_ certain
隠す _v_ conceal, hide

覚醒 _n_ awakening
学生 _n_ student
拡声器 _n_ loudspeaker
学生食堂 _n_ canteen
学説 _n_ theory
拡大 _n_ expansion
楽隊 _n_ band
拡大する _v_ expand
拡張 _n_ extension
カクテル _n_ cocktail
角度 _n_ angle
格闘 _n_ fight
獲得 _n_ attainment
確認 _n_ confirmation
確認する _v_ confirm
学部長 _n_ dean
確保する _v_ secure
学問 _n_ learning
学問的な _adj_ academic
確約 _n_ commitment
隔離 _n_ seclusion
隔離された _adj_ secluded
閣僚 _n_ cabinet
隠れ家 _n_ hideaway
賭け _n_ bet, stake
陰 _n_ shade
影 _n_ shadow
がけ _n_ cliff
影絵 _n_ silhouette

歌劇 *n* opera

過激主義的な *adj* extremist

賭け布 *n* upholstery

掛け金 *n* latch

陰で操る *v* mastermind

掛け時計 *n* clock

陰にする *adj* shady

賭ける *v* gamble, bet

かご *n* basket

囲い *n* enclosure

下降 *n* decline

河口 *n* estuary

花こう岩 *n* granite

下降する *v* decline

化合物 *n* compound

過去の *adj* past

囲む *v* surround

傘 *n* umbrella

重なり合う *v* overlap

飾る *v* decorate

火山 *n* volcano

歌詞 *n* lyrics

かじ *n* rudder

家事 *n* housework

貸切り *n* charter

賢い *adj* wise

貸し出す *v* let

貸付金 *n* loan

貸し付ける *v* loan

カジノ *n* casino

鍛冶屋 *n* blacksmith

歌手 *n* singer

果樹園 *n* orchard

頭文字 *adj* initial

かじる *v* nibble

課す *v* entail

ガス *n* gas

かすかな *adj* faint

かすかな光 *n* gleam

カスタード *n* custard

霞の *adj* misty

かすめる *v* skim

かすり傷 *n* scratch

課する *v* inflict

かすれた *adj* husky

数を上回る *v* outnumber

下図を描く *v* draft

数を数える *v* count

火星 *n* Mars

家政婦 *n* housekeeper

風が吹く *v* blow

化石 *n* fossil

仮説 *n* hypothesis

風にさらす *v* wind

風の強い *adj* windy

画像 *n* image

仮装する *v* masquerade

火葬する *v* cremate

か

火葬場 *n* crematorium
数えきれない *adj* incalculable
家族 *n* family
加速する *v* accelerate
加速するもの *n* accelerator
ガソリン *n* gasoline
型 *n* format
肩 *n* shoulder
堅い *adj* stiff, tight
課題 *n* task
堅い皮のある *adj* crusty
堅いこと *n* hardness
過大評価する *v* overrate
ガタガタ走る *v* rattle
ガタガタ揺らす *v* jolt
堅く締まる *v* tighten
堅さ *n* firmness
形 *n* figure, shape
形を作る *v* shape
片付ける *v* put away
カタツムリ *n* snail
片手鍋 *n* saucepan
型にはまった *adj* formal
塊 *n* clot, lump
塊にする *v* agglomerate
固まる *v* consolidate
形見 *n* memento
傾いた *adj* oblique
傾き *v* tilt

傾く *v* lean
傾ける *v* incline
偏らない *adj* impartial
語り手 *n* teller
肩をすくめる *v* shrug
型を作る *v* mold
価値 *n* value
価値が下がる *v* depreciate
家畜 *n* livestock
価値体系 *n* ideology
価値のある *adj* worthwhile
価値のない *adj* worthless
勝ち目 *n* odds
家長 *n* patriarch
勝つ *v* win
閣下 *n* lordship
学会 *n* academy
ガツガツ食べる *v* gobble
学期 *n* semester
活気づける *v* refresh
活気のある *adj* vibrant
楽器を調整する *v* tune up
学校 *n* school
格好いい *adj* good-looking
喝采 *v* cheer
滑車装置 *n* pulley
がっしりした *adj* burly
活性化 *n* activation
滑走路 *n* airstrip

勝った *adj* victorious
カッター *n* cutter
飼っている鳥類 *n* poultry
葛藤 *n* conflict
活動 *n* activity
活発な *adj* active
活発にさせる *v* animate
活発にする *v* activate
カップル *n* couple
合併 *n* merger
合併する *v* merge
渇望 *n* lust
活用する *v* conjugate
かつら *n* wig
活力 *n* vitality
割礼 *n* circumcision
仮定 *n* assumption
過程 *n* process
家庭教師 *n* tutor
仮定する *v* assume
家庭的な *adj* homely
過度 *n* excess
角 *n* corner, horn
角括弧 *n* bracket
角氷 *n* ice cube
過度の *adj* excessive
金型 *n* mold
悲しさ *n* sadness
悲しませる *v* grieve

悲しみ *n* sorrow
悲しむ *v* lament
悲しむ *adj* sad
悲しむべき *adj* regrettable
悲しんでいる *adj* sorrowful
かなたに *adv* beyond
金づち *n* hammer
カナリア *n* canary
かなり大きな *adj* sizable
かなりの *adj* considerable
カニ *n* crab
カヌー *n* canoe
金持ちの人 *adj* rich
可燃の *n* combustible
化膿する *v* fester
可能性 *n* possibility
可能性 *adj* possible
可能な *adj* feasible
可能にする *v* enable
彼女自身 *pro* herself
彼女のもの *pro* hers
彼女は *pro* she
彼女を *adj* her
カバン *n* bag
かびた *adj* moldy
かびの生えた *adj* mouldy
画鋲 *n* thumbtack
花瓶 *n* vase
画布 *n* canvas

か

カフェイン *n* caffeine
がぶがぶ飲む *v* gulp down
カプセル *n* capsule
カブトムシ *n* beetle
株主 *n* shareholder
下部の *adj* underlying
がぶ飲み *n* gulp
花粉 *n* pollen
壁 *n* wall
かぼちゃ *n* pumpkin
鎌 *n* sickle
かまど *n* furnace
構わない *adv* regardless
かまをかける *v* trick
我慢 *n* tolerance
我慢する *v* put up with
神 *n* God
紙 *n* paper
髪形 *n* hairdo
紙クリップ *n* paperclip
カミソリ *n* razor
かみつく *v* bite
雷 *n* thunder
神のお告げ *n* oracle
髪の毛 *n* hair
神の恵み *n* blessing
神への冒とく *n* blasphemy
紙やすり *n* sandpaper
神を認めない *adj* godless

かむこと *n* bite
カムフラージュ *n* camouflage
カメ *n* tortoise, turtle
かめ *n* jar
カメラ *n* camera
仮面 *n* mask
仮面をとる *v* unmask
鴨 *n* duck
貨物 *n* cargo
カモメ *n* gull
かもめ *n* seagull
火薬 *n* gunpowder
かゆい *v* itch
かゆさ *n* itchiness
火曜日 *n* Tuesday
か弱い *adj* feeble
ガラガラ鳴る音 *n* rumble
カラシ *n* mustard
ガラス *n* glass
ガラス製品 *n* glassware
体 *n* body
体の腺 *n* gland
カラット *n* carat
空手 *n* karate
空になる *v* empty
カリスマ *n* charisma
カリスマ的な *adj* charismatic
駆り立てる *v* urge
刈り取る *v* prune

カリフラワー *n* cauliflower
借りる *v* borrow
狩る *v* hunt
ガル *n* gal
軽く打つこと *n* tap
軽くたたくこと *n* pat
カルト *n* cult
軽はずみな *v* rash
彼 *pro* he
華麗な *adj* gorgeous
カレッジ *n* college
彼の *adj* his
彼のもの *pro* his
彼ら *pro* they
彼ら自身 *pro* themselves
枯れる *v* wither
画廊 *n* gallery
辛うじて *adv* barely
カロリー *n* calorie
ガロン *n* gallon
革 *n* leather
川 *n* river
皮 *n* peel
かわいい *adj* cute, pretty
乾いた *adj* dried, dry
カワウソ *n* otter
乾く *v* air, dry
かわす *v* dodge
変わった *adj* eccentric

代わりに *adv* instead
代わりになる *v* substitute
代わりの *adj* alternate
変わり者 *adj* crazy
変わりやすい *adj* fickle
変わる *v* alter
皮をはぐ *v* skin, peel
管 *n* pipe
缶 *n* can
ガン *n* goose
癌 *n* cancer
かんがい *n* irrigation
考え *n* idea, thought
考える *v* deem, think
感覚 *n* feeling, sense
間隔 *n* interval
カンガルー *n* kangaroo
換気 *n* ventilation
喚起する *v* evoke
歓喜する *v* exult
環境 *n* environment
缶切り *n* can opener
監禁 *n* confinement
監禁する *v* imprison
玩具 *n* toy
関係 *n* relationship
歓迎 *n* welcome
歓迎される *v* welcome
関係書類 *n* dossier

か

関係する v concern

歓迎する v hail

関係のある adj relevant

関係のない adj unrelated

完結した adj complete

間欠泉 n geyser

簡潔な adj concise, terse

簡潔に adv briefly

頑健な adj sturdy

観光 n tourism

観光客 n tourist

観光をする v sightseeing

勧告 n admonition

勧告する v admonish

頑固さ n obstinacy

看護士 n nurse

看護する v nurse

頑固な adj obstinate

頑固なやつ n mule

観察 n observation

観察する v watch

監視 n surveillance

感じ v feel

監視する v oversee

感謝 n gratitude

感謝する adj grateful

感謝する v thank

看守 n jailer

慣習 n custom

観衆席 n auditorium

慣習の adj conventional

干渉 n interference

感傷 n sentiment

感情 n emotion, feelings

勘定書 n bill

干渉する v intervene

感傷的な adj sentimental

感情的な adj emotional

冠状動脈の adj coronary

頑丈な adj hardy, robust

環状のもの n loophole

関心 n interest

関心事 n concern

感心な adj praiseworthy

関心のある adj interested

完成 n completion

関税 n customs

関節炎 n arthritis

感染 n infection

完全 n perfection

感染させる v infect

感染症の adj infested

完全性 n integrity

幹線道路 n artery

完全な adj outright

完全に adj altogether

完全に adv completely

肝臓 n liver

乾燥機 _n_ dryer
乾燥した _adj_ arid, parched
感想を述べる _v_ remark
観測所 _n_ observatory
寛大さ _n_ leniency
寛大な _adj_ broadminded
甲高い声 _n_ shriek
カンタロープ _n_ cantaloupe
簡単な _adj_ easy
簡単に _adv_ easily
館長 _n_ curator
缶詰 _n_ tin
缶詰にした _adj_ canned
貫徹 _n_ persistence
観点 _n_ standpoint
感電死する _v_ electrocute
勘当する _v_ disown
監督 _n_ supervision
監督する _v_ supervise
かんぬきをする _v_ bar
癌の _adj_ cancerous
官能的な _adj_ sensual
乾杯 _n_ cheers
乾杯する _v_ toast
完売の _adj_ sold-out
幹部 _n_ executive
完璧な _adj_ perfect
関与 _n_ involvement
寛容 _n_ generosity

管理する _v_ administer
管理できる _adj_ manageable
管理人 _n_ custodian
簡略した _adj_ simple
官僚機構の _n_ bureaucracy
完了する _v_ complete
関連した _adj_ related
関連する _v_ touch on
関連のある _adj_ pertinent
緩和 _n_ appeasement
～か _c_ or
～ができる _v_ can
～かどうか _c_ whether
～がなければ _pre_ barring
～が欲しい _v_ want
～かもしれない _v_ may
～から _pre_ from
～から落ちる _v_ drop off
～から来る _v_ come from
～から突き出る _v_ protrude
～から成る _v_ consist
冠をかぶせる _v_ crown

か

# き

木 *n* tree, wood
キーホルダー *n* key ring
黄色の *adj* yellow
消えかかった *adj* faded
消える *v* disappear
記憶 *n* recollection
記憶喪失 *n* amnesia
記憶力 *n* memory
貴下 *n* sir
飢餓 *n* starvation
機械 *n* machine
議会 *n* legislature
機会 *n* chance, opportunity
機械化する *v* mechanize
機械工 *n* mechanic
奇怪な *adj* grotesque
幾何学 *n* geometry
気がかり *n* suspense
気化器 *n* carburetor
規格化する *v* standardize
気がついて *adj* aware
気がとがめる *n* scruples
気が向かない *adj* indisposed
期間 *n* period, term
気管 *n* windpipe
機関士 *n* fireman
機関紙 *n* journal

気管支炎 *n* bronchitis
機関銃 *n* machine gun
危機 *n* crisis
機器 *n* device
聞き手 *n* listener
棄却する *v* affirm
気球 *n* balloon
企業 *n* enterprise
起業家 *n* entrepreneur
義兄弟 *n* stepbrother
飢饉 *n* famine
聴く *v* listen
聞く *v* listen, hear
奇形 *n* deformity
危険 *n* peril, danger
機嫌 *n* temper
期限切れ *n* expiration
危険な *adj* dangerous
期限の切れた *adj* overdue
機嫌の悪い *adj* grouchy
危険を冒す *v* risk
気候 *n* climate
気候上の *adj* climatic
聞こえる *adj* audible
ぎこちない *adj* clumsy
奇才 *n* prodigy
記載 *n* recording
刻む *v* engrave
岸 *n* shore

騎士 n knight
キジ n pheasant
記事 n article
生地 n texture
儀式 n ceremony, rite
儀式を張る v formalize
岸へ adv ashore
義姉妹 n stepsister
きしみ n creak
きしむ v creak
きしむ adj squeaky
記者 n reporter
記述 n description
技術者 n technician
技術上の adj technical
記述的な adj descriptive
基準 n standard
記章 n badge
偽証 n perjury
きしる音 v squeak
キス n kiss
傷 n blemish
傷跡 n scar
築く v forge
傷ついていない adj unhurt
傷つきやすい adj sensitive
傷つける adj hurtful
傷つける v injure
キスをする v kiss

犠牲 n sacrifice
犠牲者 n casualty
規制する v regulate
寄生虫 n parasite, worm
犠牲にする v victimize
奇跡 n miracle
奇跡の adj miraculous
気絶 n faint
気絶する v faint
季節の adj seasonal
偽善 n hypocrisy
偽善者 adj hypocrite
競う v contend
偽造 n forgery
寄贈者 n donor
寄贈する v give away
偽造の adj counterfeit
規則 n regulation
貴族 n aristocrat
貴族 adj nobleman
貴族階級 n nobility
規則性 n regularity
貴族政治 n aristocracy
基礎工事 n groundwork
起訴する v prosecute
基礎の adj basic
基礎のない adj baseless
北 n north
ギター n guitar

き

き

| | |
|---|---|
| 期待 *n* expectation | 軌道 *n* orbit, trajectory |
| 議題 *n* agenda | 気取らない *adj* unassuming |
| 汚い *adj* dirty | 気取り屋 *n* rooster |
| 来たる *adj* upcoming | 気取る *v* pose |
| 来たるべき *adj* forthcoming | 気にいる *v* like |
| 機知 *n* wit | 気にかける *v* care about |
| 気違い *n* madman | 気にする *v* bother |
| 機知のある *adj* witty | 絹 *n* silk |
| 議長 *n* chairman | 疑念 *n* disbelief |
| 貴重な *adj* valuable | 記念建造物 *n* monument |
| 議長を務める *v* chair | 記念する *v* commemorate |
| きちんと *adv* neatly | 記念日 *n* anniversary |
| きつい *adj* demanding | 記念碑の *adj* monumental |
| 喫煙 *n* tobacco | 記念品 *n* token |
| 喫煙者 *n* smoker | 偽の *adj* fake, phoney |
| 喫煙する *v* smoke | 機能 *n* function |
| 気遣う *v* care | 技能 *n* skill, technique |
| 気遣う *adj* caring | 昨日の *adv* yesterday |
| 気付かれない *adj* unnoticed | 機能不全 *n* malfunction |
| 着付け *n* dressing | 木の枝 *v* stick |
| 着付け係 *n* dresser | キノコ *n* mushroom |
| 切手 *n* stamp | 気の毒な *adj* pitiful |
| キツネ *n* fox | 気のない *adj* tepid |
| 規定 *n* prescription | 木の実 *n* nut |
| 規定する *v* stipulate | 気乗りしない *adj* reluctant |
| 汽笛 *n* buzzer | 牙 *n* fang, tusk |
| 機転 *n* tact | 起爆剤 *n* detonator |
| 儀典 *n* protocol | 希薄な *v* dilute |
| 機転の利く *adj* tactful | 希薄な *adj* sparse |

気晴らし n pastime
気晴らしをする v recreate
基盤 n basis
厳しい adj harsh, severe
厳しく adv harshly
厳しさ n severity, rigor
義父 n stepfather
寄付金 n donation
寄付する v donate
偽物 v counterfeit
気分 n mood
気分屋の adj moody
騎兵隊 n cavalry
義母 n stepmother
希望 n hope
希望に満ちた adj hopeful
基本となる adj fundamental
基本にかえる n basics
気ままな adj arbitrary
気味の悪い adj grim
奇妙な adj bizarre, odd
義務 n obligation
気難しい adj fussy
気難しい人 adj grumpy
気難しい人 n wasp
義務付ける v obligate
義務的な adj obligatory
義務を負っている v owe
偽名 n pseudonym

決められた方法 n routine
疑問に思う v wonder
客 n customer
逆 n reverse
脚色する v dramatize
逆説 n paradox
虐待 n mistreatment
虐待する v abuse, mistreat
脚注 n footnote
逆転 n reversal
逆にできない adj irreversible
逆にできる adj reversible
逆の adj backward
逆火をおこす v backfire
逆へ adv backwards
脚本 n script
脚立 n stepladder
却下する v overrule
逆境 n adversity
キャビネット n cabinet
キャベツ n cabbage
キャラバン n caravan
ギャロップ v gallop
キャンデー n candy
休暇 n vacation
救急車 n ambulance
窮屈な adj cramped
休憩室 n lounge
吸血鬼 n vampire

き

き

求婚 *n* courtship
臼歯 *n* molar
休日 *n* holiday
吸収する *v* absorb
吸収力のある *adj* absorbent
救出 *n* salvation
救助 *n* rescue
救助員 *n* lifeguard
急上昇 *n* surge
救助者 *n* savior
救助する *v* rescue
急進主義者 *adj* radical
急成長 *n* boom
休戦 *n* cease-fire
休息 *n* repose, rest
休息時間 *n* recess
休息する *v* repose, rest
窮地 *n* predicament
宮殿 *n* palace
給湯器 *n* waterheater
急に動く *v* whip
牛肉 *n* beef
急に閉まる *v* slam
急に止まる *v* seize
牛乳 *n* milk
牛乳のような *adj* milky
吸入量 *n* intake
吸盤 *adj* sucker
急冷する *v* quench

給与 *n* paycheck
急落する *v* plummet
きゅうり *n* cucumber
急流 *n* torrent
給料 *n* payroll
給料明細 *n* payslip
ギュッと締まる *v* clench
脅威 *n* menace
教育学 *n* pedagogy
教育する *v* educate
教育的な *adj* educational
驚異的な *adj* astounding
協会 *v* institute
境界 *n* boundary
教会 *n* church
境界の *adj* marginal
教科書 *n* textbook
狂気 *n* craziness
教義 *n* doctrine
行儀 *n* manner
競技会 *n* contest
競技者 *n* contestant
競技場 *n* arena
供給品 *n* supplies
供給者 *n* supplier
供給する *v* supply
教区 *n* diocese
教区教師 *n* rector
教区の *adj* parochial

教区民 _n_ parishioner
教訓 _n_ precept
凝結する _v_ condense
狂犬病 _n_ rabies
恐慌 _n_ depression
教皇 _n_ pontiff
峡谷 _n_ canyon, ravine
凝固する _v_ coagulate
凝固物 _n_ coagulation
共産主義 _n_ communism
共産主義の _adj_ communist
教室 _n_ classroom
業種 _n_ business
凝縮 _n_ condensation
教授陣 _n_ faculty
供述書 _n_ testimony
供述する _v_ depose
狂人 _adj_ lunatic
狂信的な _adj_ fanatic
強制 _n_ imposition
強勢 _n_ accent
強制させた _adj_ compulsory
共生する _v_ cohabit
強制する _v_ coerce
強制的な _adj_ compelling
矯正できない _adj_ incorrigible
強制的に _adv_ forcibly
強制力 _n_ coercion
業績 _n_ performance

競争 _n_ competition
胸像 _n_ bust
競争相手 _n_ rival
競争者 _n_ contender
競争する _v_ compete
競争の _adj_ competitive
共存する _v_ coexist
兄弟 _n_ brother
兄弟愛 _n_ brotherhood
強大な _adj_ tremendous
兄弟の _adj_ brotherly
兄弟のような _adj_ fraternal
協調 _n_ partnership
強調 _n_ emphasis
強調する _v_ emphasize
共通の _adj_ common
仰天 _n_ consternation
仰天させる _v_ astound
共同出資者 _n_ partner
共同する _v_ collaborate
器用な _adj_ deft
今日は _adv_ today
競売 _n_ auction
競売人 _n_ auctioneer
競売にかける _v_ auction
脅迫 _n_ blackmail
共犯（者） _n_ accomplice
恐怖 _n_ fright, horror
胸部 _n_ breast

き

き

強風 *n* gale
恐怖症 *n* phobia
恐怖心 *adj* formidable
共謀 *n* complicity
共謀者 *n* conspirator
共謀する *v* conspire
凶暴性 *n* ferocity
凶暴な *adv* berserk
凶暴な *adj* ferocious
凶暴な人 *adj* maniac
興味 *n* interest
興味のある *adj* intriguing
興味深い *adj* interesting
興味を失う *v* turn off
共有 *n* share
共有する *v* share
強要する *v* extort
教養のない *adj* uneducated
狂乱の *adj* hysterical
恐竜 *n* dinosaur
協力 *n* cooperation
協力者 *n* collaborator
協力する *v* cooperate
強力な *adj* powerful
強烈さ *n* intensity
強烈な *adj* acute
共和制 *n* republic
虚栄心 *n* vanity
虚栄心の強い *adj* vain

許可 *n* permission
許可する *v* license, permit
虚偽の *adj* untrue
局 *n* department
曲芸師 *n* acrobat
曲線 *n* curve
極端な *adj* extreme
極度 *n* extremities
極度に痛い *adj* excruciating
極度の *adj* intense
極度の疲労 *n* exhaustion
極の *adj* polar
局部集中する *v* localize
虚弱な *adj* frail
居住可能な *adj* inhabitable
居住させる *v* populate
居住者 *n* inhabitant
巨人 *n* giant
巨石 *n* boulder
拒絶 *n* refusal, rebuff
拒絶する *v* reject
巨大な *adj* gigantic
拒否 *n* denial
拒否する *v* repudiate
清める *v* purge, bless
許容 *n* allowance
許容できない *adj* inadmissible
許容できる *adj* admissible
清らかさ *n* purity

距離 *n* distance
距離がある *adj* distant
嫌う *v* dislike
嫌うこと *n* distaste
キラキラ輝く *v* twinkle
ギラギラする光 *n* glare
嫌って *adj* averse
きらめく *v* sparkle
霧 *n* mist
切り株 *n* stub
切り替わる *v* switch
霧刻む *v* chop
切り下げる *v* cut down
霧雨 *n* drizzle
霧雨が降る *v* drizzle
ギリシャ *n* Greece
ギリシャ人 *adj* Greek
キリスト教 *n* Christianity
キリスト教の *adj* christian
規律 *n* discipline
切り詰めた *adj* austere
切り取る *v* cut off, trim
切り抜き *n* clipping
切り抜く *v* cut out
義理の姉 *n* sister-in-law
霧のかかった *adj* foggy
義理の兄弟 *n* brother-in-law
義理の父 *n* father-in-law
義理の息子 *n* son-in-law

義理の両親 *n* in-laws
キリン *n* giraffe
切る *v* cut
着る *v* wear
切ること *n* cut
キルト *n* quilt
きれい好きな *adj* tidy
きれいな *adj* clean
きれいになる *v* clear
切れ端 *n* chip
記録 *n* memoirs
記録する *v* record
キログラム *n* kilogram
記録をとる *v* log
ギロチン *n* guillotine
キロメートル *n* kilometer
キロワット *n* kilowatt
議論 *n* discussion
議論する *v* discuss
議論の *adj* controversial
疑惑 *n* misgivings
極めて慎重に *adv* gingerly
極めて不快な *adj* revolting
気をつける *v* heed
気を付ける *v* watch out
金 *n* gold
銀 *n* silver
均一 *n* uniformity
近眼の *adj* shortsighted

銀器 *n* silverware
緊急事態 *n* emergency
緊急性 *n* urgency
緊急の *adj* urgent
均衡 *n* equilibrium
銀行 *n* bank
銀細工師 *n* silversmith
禁止 *n* prohibition
禁止する *v* ban, prohibit
近視の *adj* myopic
近所 *n* neighborhood
禁じる *v* forbid
金銭上の *adj* financial
金属 *n* metal
金属製の *adj* metallic
近代的な *adj* modern
緊張 *n* strain, stress
緊張した *adj* tense
緊張する *adj* nervous
緊張の多い *adj* stressful
均等の *adj* even
筋肉 *n* muscle
金の *adj* golden
緊縛 *n* bondage
金髪の *adj* blond
勤勉 *n* diligence
勤勉な *adj* diligent
銀めっきの *adj* silverplated
金床 *n* anvil

き
く

金曜日 *n* Friday
禁欲主義の *adj* celibate
禁欲する *v* mortify
禁欲的な *adj* ascetic
菌類 *n* fungus

## く

区 *n* borough
くい *n* post
悔い改め *n* contrition
空域 *n* airspace
空間 *n* space
空気 *n* air
空気が抜ける *v* deflate
空虚 *n* emptiness
空港 *n* airport
偶然 *n* accident
偶然性 *n* contingency
偶然に *adv* incidentally
偶然に起きる *adj* coincidental
偶然の *adj* accidental
偶然の一致 *n* coincidence
空想 *n* fantasy
偶像 *n* idol
偶像崇拝 *n* idolatry
空想にふける *v* daydream

寓喩 _n_ allegory

空中に舞う _v_ hover

空中の _n_ midair

空洞 _adj_ hollow

空白 _adj_ blank

空腹の _adj_ hungry

寓話 _n_ fable, parable

区画 _n_ compartment

茎 _n_ stem

苦行 _n_ purgatory

くさい _adj_ foul, stinking

腐った _adj_ rotten

草の根の _adj_ grassroots

くさび _n_ wedge

鎖 _n_ chain

腐る _v_ decay, rot

草を食う _v_ graze

くし _n_ comb

くじ引き _n_ lottery

クジャク _n_ peacock

くしゃみ _n_ sneeze

くしゃみをする _v_ sneeze

くじら _n_ whale

くず _n_ rubbish, junk

くず入れ _n_ waste basket

クスクス笑い _v_ giggle

クスクス笑う _v_ chuckle

くすぐる _v_ tickle

薬 _n_ medicine

崩れ落ちる _v_ cave in

癖 _n_ habit

具体化する _v_ embody

果物 _n_ fruit

果物のジャム _n_ conserve

くだらない _adj_ crappy

くだらなさ _n_ nonsense

下り坂の _adv_ downhill

口 _n_ mouth

口うるさく言う _v_ nag

口で吸う _v_ suck

口止めする _v_ muzzle

口止めをする _v_ gag

口の利けない人 _adj_ mute

くちばし _n_ beak

口ひげ _n_ mustache

唇 _n_ lip

口笛 _n_ whistle

口笛を吹く _v_ whistle

口やかましい _adj_ nagging

靴 _n_ shoe

苦痛 _n_ torment, agony

苦痛の _adj_ agonizing

クッキー _n_ cookie

靴下 _n_ sock, stocking

靴下留め _n_ garter

屈辱的な _adj_ demeaning

屈辱を与える _v_ humiliate

屈する _v_ give in

くっつく v cling
グッと飲み込む v gulp
靴ひも n shoelace
屈服する v succumb
靴みがき n shoepolish
靴屋 n shoestore
くつわ n bridle
くどい小言 n homily
苦闘 n struggle
苦闘する v agonize
句読点のコンマ n comma
国 n country
国の adj public
苦悩 n distress
苦悩している v distress
配る v give out
首 n neck
首を切る v behead
区分 n division, section
区別 n distinction
クマ n bear
くま手 n pitchfork
くまなく捜す v ransack
くみ上げる v pump
組み合わせ n combination
組み込む v incorporate
組み立て n composition
組み立てる v fabricate
クモ n spider

雲 n cloud
曇った adj cloudy
クモの巣 n web
曇る v tarnish
くやしさ n mortification
悔やむ v repent
鞍 n saddle
暗い adj dark
暗がり n obscurity
暗くなる v darken
グラグラする adj unsteady
暗さ n darkness
クラッチ n clutch
クラブ n club
グラフィックの adj graphic
グラム n gram
クラリネット n clarinet
クランク n crank
クリ n chestnut
クリーム状の adj creamy
繰り返し n repetition
繰り返す v repeat
クリケット n cricket
クリスマス n Christmas
来る v come
クルーザー n yacht
グルグル回る v whirl
苦しみ n suffering
苦しむ v suffer

苦しめる v afflict
来るべき adj coming
車 n vehicle
車いす n wheelchair
クルマエビ n prawn
車で走り去る v drive away
車で引く v run over
くるまる v wrap up
クルミ n walnut
くるみ n nut-shell
グレイビー n gravy
クレヨン n crayon
くれる v deign
黒い adj black
クローク n cloak
クローニング n cloning
クローン化する v clone
クロコダイル n crocodile
黒さ n blackness
クロスロード n crossroads
鍬 n spade
加える v add, affix
詳しく述べる v detail
企て n attempt
企てる v attempt
加わる v join
群 n county
軍医 n surgeon
軍艦 n warship

軍需 n armaments
群衆 n throng, mob
君主制 n monarchy
軍需品 n munitions
軍人 n soldier
燻製の adj smoked
軍曹 n sergeant
軍隊 n army
軍団 n legion
郡庁舎 n courthouse
軍備縮小 n disarmament
訓練 n training
訓練者 n trainer
９０、９０個の adj ninety
９月 n September
９、９個の adj nine
第９番目の adj ninth

# け

敬愛 n adoration
敬意 n reverence
敬意を表する adj respectful
経営 n management
警戒した v alert
警戒している adj wary
警戒態勢 n alert

**く**
**け**

軽快に動く *v* trip
計画 *n* plan, scheme
計画する *v* plan
経過する *v* elapse
景気後退 *n* recession
景気づけ *n* boost
経験 *n* experience
軽減する *v* alleviate
敬けんな *adj* devout
経験不足の *adj* inexperienced
経験豊かな *n* veteran
傾向 *n* leaning, tendency
傾向がある *adj* predisposed
迎合する *v* pander
渓谷 *n* valley
警告 *n* warning
警告する *v* warn
けいこする *v* rehearse
経済 *n* economy
軽罪 *n* misdemeanor
経済的な *adj* economical
警察 *n* police
警察官 *n* policeman
計算 *n* calculation
計算器 *n* counter
計算機 *n* calculator
計算する *v* calculate
計算を誤る *v* miscalculate
掲示 *n* bulletin

形式的 *n* formality
啓示書 *n* apocalypse
掲示する *v* put up
刑執行の延期 *n* reprieve
傾斜 *n* inclination
傾斜した *adj* slanted
芸術 *n* art
芸術家 *n* artist
芸術的な *adj* artistic
継承 *n* inheritance
形状 *n* lay
係数 *n* coefficient
形成 *n* formation
計測器 *v* gage
継続している *adj* ongoing
携帯こんろ *n* chauffeur
携帯電話 *n* cellphone
携帯用の *adj* portable
警笛の音 *v* honk
毛糸 *n* yarn
経度 *n* longitude
系統 *n* system
刑罰 *n* penalty
啓発する *v* enlighten
景品 *n* prize
警部補 *n* lieutenant
軽蔑 *n* contempt
軽蔑した *n* scornful
軽蔑する *v* despise

軽蔑的な *adj* derogatory
警報 *n* alarm
警棒 *n* baton
刑務所 *n* jail, prison
刑務所長 *n* warden
契約 *n* contract, pact
契約をする *v* sign
形容詞 *n* adjective
けいれん *n* convulsion
経路 *n* way
ケーキ *n* cake
ケーブル *n* cable
ゲーム *n* game
外科の *adv* surgical
毛皮 *n* fur
毛皮製の *adj* furry
けがをした *adj* hurt
劇 *n* play
激減させる *v* deplete
劇場 *n* theater
撃退 *n* repulse
撃退する *v* repulse
劇的な *adj* dramatic
激怒 *n* rage, wrath
激怒させる *v* enrage
激怒した *adj* furious
激怒する *v* madden
激突する *v* ram
激発する *v* flare-up

激烈な *adj* drastic
下剤の *adj* laxative
ポピー *n* poppy
消印 *n* postmark
景色 *n* scenery, view
消しゴム *n* eraser
消し去る *v* obliterate
化粧室 *n* toilet
化粧水 *n* lotion
化粧品 *n* cosmetic
消す *v* erase, vanish
下水管 *v* drain
下水管 *n* sewer
下船する *v* disembark
けち *n* pettiness
けちな *adj* stingy
血液 *n* blood
結果 *n* outcome
結核 *n* tuberculosis
結局は *adv* eventually
月経 *n* menstruation
結合 *n* conjunction
激高させる *v* infuriate
結合する *v* unite
結婚 *n* marriage
結婚式 *n* wedding
結婚した *adj* married
結婚する *v* wed
結婚生活の *adj* marital

け

**け**

| 決して〜ない _adv_ never | 下品な _adj_ degrading |
|---|---|
| 結晶 _n_ crystal | 毛深い _adj_ hairy |
| 決心 _n_ determination | 毛虫 _n_ caterpillar |
| 決心する _v_ determine | 下痢 _n_ diarrhea |
| 血清 _n_ serum | ゲリラ兵 _n_ guerrilla |
| 血栓症 _n_ thrombosis | 蹴る _v_ kick |
| 血族の _adj_ akin | けれども _c_ yet |
| 決断力のある _adj_ decisive | 険しい _adj_ steep |
| 決定 _n_ decision | 件 _n_ affair |
| 決定する _v_ decide | 剣 _n_ sword |
| 決定的な _adj_ deciding | 権威主義の _n_ authority |
| 決定的な証拠 _n_ smoking gun | 原因 _n_ cause |
| 欠点 _n_ shortcoming | けん引車 _n_ tractor |
| 欠点のある _adj_ defective | けん引トラック _n_ tow truck |
| 欠点のない _adj_ flawless | けん引力 _n_ traction |
| 欠陥 _n_ defect, flaw | 幻影 _n_ apparition |
| 決闘 _n_ duel | 検閲 _n_ censorship |
| げっぷをする _v_ burp | 嫌悪感 _n_ disgust |
| 潔癖 _n_ cleanliness | 嫌悪する _v_ detest |
| 欠乏 _n_ deficiency | 見解 _n_ outlook |
| 結末 _n_ ending | 圏外 _adj_ outer |
| 月曜日 _n_ Monday | 厳格 _n_ austerity |
| 結論 _n_ conclusion | 見学する _v_ observe |
| 結論づける _v_ reason | 厳格な _adj_ stern |
| 結論を出す _v_ conclude | 厳格に _adv_ sternly |
| 解毒剤 _n_ antidote | 幻覚を起こす _v_ hallucinate |
| 蹴飛ばす _v_ lash out | 減価償却 _n_ depreciation |
| 気配 _n_ wind | 見代わり _n_ scapegoat |
| 下品 _n_ vulgarity | 玄関前の階段 _n_ doorstep |

元気 _n_ guts
元気 _v_ cheer up
元気いっぱいの _adj_ lively
元気回復 _n_ refreshment
元気づく _adj_ refreshing
言及 _n_ mention
研究室 _n_ lab
謙虚 _n_ humility
謙虚な _adj_ humble
謙虚に _adv_ humbly
現金 _n_ cash
現金出納係 _n_ cashier
原型 _n_ prototype
権限付与 _n_ authorization
権限を与える _v_ authorize
言語 _n_ language
健康 _n_ fitness, health
原稿 _n_ manuscript
原鉱 _n_ ore
健康そうな _adj_ rosy
健康な _adj_ healthy
健康を取り戻す _v_ recuperate
原告 _n_ plaintiff
言語で _adv_ verbally
検査 _n_ inspection
現在の _adj_ current
現在は _adv_ currently
検査官 _n_ inspector
検事 _n_ prosecutor

原子 _n_ atom
検視解剖 _n_ autopsy
現実 _n_ reality
現実主義 _n_ realism
現実の _adj_ real
原始の _adj_ primitive
原子の _adj_ atomic
厳守 _n_ fidelity
拳銃 _n_ handgun
研修員 _n_ trainee
研修会 _n_ workshop
厳粛な _adj_ grave, solemn
減少 _n_ decrease
現象 _n_ phenomenon
減少する _v_ decrease
原子力の _adj_ nuclear
献身 _n_ dedication
献身的愛情 _n_ devotion
献身的な _adj_ committed
減衰する _adj_ attenuating
建設的な _adj_ constructive
現世の _adj_ carnal
健全な _adj_ wholesome
原則 _n_ principle
現代的になる _v_ modernize
現代の _adj_ contemporary
建築 _n_ architecture
建築家 _n_ architect
建築者 _n_ builder

け

けこ

顕著な *adj* noticeable
限定 *n* limitation
検討 *n* inquest
剣闘士 *n* gladiator
顕微鏡 *n* microscope
見物人 *n* bystander
憲法 *n* constitution
原本 *adj* original
厳密な調査 *n* probing
賢明さ *n* wisdom
賢明な *adj* smart
幻滅した *adj* disenchanted
倹約 *n* frugality
倹約する *v* economize
倹約的な *adj* thrifty
権利 *n* liberty
原理 *n* axiom

# こ

語 *n* word
語彙 *n* vocabulary
小石 *n* pebble
故意に *adv* willfully
子犬 *n* puppy
恋人 *n* lover
行為 *n* conduct

合意 *n* settlement
好意的でない *adj* unfavorable
高位の人 *n* dignitary
好意を示す *v* oblige
強引に進む *v* bulldoze
降雨 *n* rainfall
豪雨 *n* cataract
幸運 *n* luck
光栄 *n* honor
後援 *n* backup
公園 *n* park
後援者 *n* benefactor
効果 *n* effect
硬貨 *n* cent
降下 *n* descent
後悔 *n* regret
航海 *n* voyage
郊外 *n* suburb
口蓋 *n* palate
後悔している人 *n* penitent
口外しない *v* hush up
航海者 *n* voyager
後悔する *v* regret
航海する *v* navigate
後悔の *adj* remorseful
高架橋 *n* viaduct
光学技術者 *n* optician
降格させる *v* demote
甲殻類 *n* shellfish

豪華さ *n* luxury
降下する *v* descend
効果的な *adj* effective
高価な *adj* expensive
豪華な *adj* sumptuous
効果のない *adj* ineffective
交換 *n* interchange
強姦 *n* rape
交換する *v* exchange, interchange
強姦する *v* rape
強姦犯 *n* rapist
好機 *n* occasion
抗議 *n* protest
講義 *n* lecture
好奇心 *n* curiosity
抗議する *v* protest
高貴の *adj* noble
号泣 *n* crying
交響曲 *n* symphony
公教要理 *n* catechism
香気を満たす *v* embalm
合金 *n* alloy
航空 *n* aeroplane
航空運賃 *n* airfare
航空会社 *n* airline
航空機 *n* aircraft
航空便 *n* airmail
合計 *n* sum

合計～になる *v* amount to
後継者 *n* successor
合計する *v* sum up
攻撃 *n* attack
攻撃者 *n* assailant
攻撃する *v* assail
高潔 *n* holiness
高潔な *adj* virtuous
貢献 *n* contribution
高原 *n* plateau
公言した *adj* avowed
貢献者 *n* contributor
貢献する *adj* conducive
貢献する *v* contribute
皇后 *n* empress
考古学 *n* archaeology
交互に行う *v* alternate
口座 *n* account
硬材 *n* hardwood
耕作 *n* cultivation
耕作可能な *adj* arable
交差している *adj* cross
交差する *v* intersect
交差点 *n* crossing
鉱山 *n* mine
鉱山労働者 *n* miner
子牛 *n* calf
公式 *n* formula
公式の *adj* official

こ

口実 n plea
子牛の肉 n veal
公爵 n duke
公爵夫人 n duchess
後者の adj latter
絞首台 n gallows
控除 n subtraction
交渉 n bargaining
工場 n factory, mill
交渉する v negotiate
向上する v progress
甲状腺 n thyroid
交渉で決める v bargain
公証人 n notary
好色な adj prurient
控除する v subtract
控除できる adj deductible
交信 n communication
更新 n renewal
行進 n march
交信する v communicate
更新する v update
行進する v march
香辛料 n condiment
香水 n perfume
後世 n posterity
更正する v rehabilitate
構成する v construct
抗生物質 n antibiotic

降雪 n snowfall
光線 n ray
好戦的な adj belligerent
構造 n structure
拘束 n yoke
皇族 adj imperial
拘束する v constrain
高速道路 n freeway
拘束力のある adj binding
後退している adj retarded
後退する v back, fall back
広大な adj boundless
光沢 n gloss
光沢のある adj glossy
強奪 n heist
硬直する v stiffen
交通 n traffic
皇帝 n emperor, czar
鋼鉄 n steel
好転 n upturn
高度 n elevation
坑道 n tunnel
行動 n action
強盗 n bandit, robber
強盗事件 n robbery
行動する v act
口頭で adv orally
合同で adv jointly
行動力 n leverage

高度に *adv* highly
購入 *n* purchase
購入する *v* purchase
更年期 *n* menopause
コウノトリ *n* stork
荒廃した *adj* dilapidated
香ばしい *adj* spicy
広範囲に及ぶ *adj* widespread
広範囲の *adj* broad
公表 *n* declaration
幸福 *n* happiness
降伏 *n* surrender
幸福感 *n* euphoria
降伏する *v* surrender
幸福な *adj* fortunate
鉱物 *n* mineral
興奮 *n* excitement
興奮させる *v* excite
公文書 *n* archive
興奮状態 *n* hysteria
興奮する *v* thrill
公平 *n* fairness
後方 *n* rear
合法化する *v* legalize
合法性 *n* legality
合法の *adj* legitimate
後方の *adj* rear
酵母菌 *n* yeast
小馬 *n* cob

巧妙な *adj* tricky
香味料 *n* flavor
項目別にする *v* itemize
拷問 *n* torture
拷問にかける *v* torture
荒野 *n* wilderness
香油 *n* balm
交友 *n* companionship
強欲 *n* avarice, greed
強欲な *adj* avaricious
合理化する *v* rationalize
小売店 *n* shop
交流 *n* interchange
拘留する *v* detain
考慮 *n* consideration
荒涼とした *adj* stark
効力がある *v* avail
考慮に入れる *v* allow
高齢の *n* old age
口論 *n* altercation
口論する *v* hassle, quarrel
港湾 *n* harbor
声 *n* voice
護衛 *n* safeguard
肥えた *adj* fertile
超える *v* exceed
声を出して *adv* aloud
コート *n* coat
コード *n* cord

コードなしの *adj* cordless
コーヒー *n* coffee
氷 *n* ice
氷の *adj* icy
誤解する *v* misconstrue
戸外の *adv* outdoor
コカイン *n* cocaine
小型快速船 *n* frigate
小型化する *v* downsize
小型の *adj* compact
小型の缶 *n* canister
小型の丸いパン *n* biscuit
小柄な *adj* petite
股間 *n* groin
互換性 *n* compatibility
小刻みに動く *v* wiggle
小切手帳 *n* checkbook
ごきぶり *n* cockroach
呼吸 *n* breathing
呼吸作用 *n* respiration
こぎれいな *adj* posh
こぎれいにする *v* spruce up
こぐ *v* paddle
語句 *n* phrase
国王 *adj* sovereign
国外追放 *n* deportation
国外への *adj* outward
穀草類 *n* cereal
国産品 *adj* domestic

告示 *n* notification
極上の *adj* superb
ごく少量 *n* fraction
国籍 *n* nationality
告訴 *n* charge
告白者 *n* confessor
告発 *n* accusation
告発する *v* accuse
黒板 *n* blackboard
極秘の *adj* confidential
極貧の *adj* destitute
克服する *v* outlive
国民投票 *n* referendum
こけ *n* moss
固形の *adj* solid
語形変化 *n* declension
こげ茶色の *adj* brunette
焦げる *v* char, scorch
午後 *n* afternoon
ココア *n* cocoa
凍えるような *adj* freezing
心地がよい *adj* congenial
心地のよい *adj* cozy
ここで *adv* here
小言 *n* scolding
ココナツ *n* coconut
個々に *adv* apiece
心からの *adj* heartfelt
心付け *n* gratuity

心に描く *v* envisage
心に留める *adj* mindful
心の *adj* mental
心のこもった *adj* hearty
心の広い *adj* open-minded
試み *n* attempt
試みる *v* attempt
心を打つ *adj* poignant
心をそそる *adj* tempting
濃さ *n* thickness
故殺 *n* manslaughter
腰 *n* hip
固持 *n* tenacity
誤字 *adj* literal
こじ開ける *v* break open
ごしごし洗う *v* scrub
孤児の *n* orphan
小島 *n* isle
コショウ *n* pepper
故障 *n* breakdown
個人的な *adj* personal
個人用の *adj* private
こすって磨く *v* scour
個性 *n* character
護送 *n* convoy
コソコソする *v* sneak
古代の *adj* ancient
答え *n* answer
答える *v* answer

小高い *adj* hilly
こだわり *n* hangup
ごちそう *n* feast
伍長 *n* corporal
国家 *n* nation
国歌 *n* anthem
国会 *n* parliament
骨格 *n* skeleton
国家の *adj* national
国旗 *n* banner
国境 *n* border
国境線上の *adj* borderline
国境を接する *v* border on
こっけいな *adj* ludicrous
骨髄 *n* marrow
骨折 *n* fracture
こっそり盗む *v* plunder
小包 *n* parcel
小包郵便 *n* parcel post
小粒 *n* pellet
コップ *n* cup
固定する *v* clinch, rivet
古典的な *adj* classic
鼓動 *n* heartbeat
鼓動する *v* pulsate, throb
事柄 *n* affair, matter
孤独 *n* solitude
孤独な *adj* solitary
異なる *v* differ

こ

子供 _n_ child, kid
子供時代 _n_ childhood
子供たち _n_ children
子供のない _adj_ childless
子供らしい _adj_ childish
ことわざ _n_ proverb
粉 _n_ powder
粉々に崩れる _v_ crumble
粉々になる _v_ shatter
子猫 _n_ kitten
好ましい _adj_ likable
好み _n_ preference
コピー _n_ copy
コピー機 _n_ copier
コピーする _v_ copy
子羊 _n_ lamb
小人 _n_ dwarf, midget
こぶ _n_ hump
古風な _adj_ antiquated
五分五分の _adv_ fifty-fifty
ご婦人 _n_ madam
子分 _n_ henchman
こぼす _v_ spill
コマ _n_ coma
細かく切る _v_ shred, mince
ごまかし _n_ sham
鼓膜 _n_ eardrum
困らせる _v_ harass
込み入った _adj_ intricate

ごみ捨て場 _n_ dump
小道 _n_ path
ごみ箱 _n_ trash can
ゴム _n_ gum, rubber
小麦 _n_ wheat
小麦粉 _n_ flour
ゴムの _adj_ elastic
コメディアン _n_ comedian
コメディー _n_ comedy
肥やす _v_ fertilize
固有の _adj_ intrinsic
雇用 _n_ employment
雇用者 _n_ employer
暦 _n_ calendar
孤立 _n_ isolation
コリック _n_ colic
孤立した _adj_ lonesome
ゴリラ _n_ gorilla
コルク栓 _n_ cork
コルネット _n_ cornet
これ _adj_ this
これから先 _adv_ hereafter
これによって _adv_ hereby
コレラ _n_ cholera
これら _adj_ these
転がす _v_ roll
転がる _v_ turn over
ゴロゴロ鳴る _v_ rumble
殺し屋 _n_ thug

こ

殺す <sub>v</sub> kill
殺すこと <sub>n</sub> killing
転ぶ <sub>v</sub> fall down
コロン <sub>n</sub> colon
怖がらせる <sub>v</sub> terrorize
怖がる <sub>v</sub> scare
壊す <sub>v</sub> break down
壊れた <sub>adj</sub> broken
壊れていない <sub>adj</sub> unbroken
壊れやすい <sub>adj</sub> fragile
壊れる <sub>v</sub> break up
婚姻の <sub>adj</sub> conjugal
懇願 <sub>n</sub> appeal
懇願する <sub>v</sub> implore, beg
根拠 <sub>n</sub> verification
根拠のない <sub>adj</sub> groundless
コンクリートの <sub>adj</sub> concrete
混合 <sub>n</sub> blend, mix
混合飲料 <sub>n</sub> concoction
混合器 <sub>n</sub> mixer
混合物 <sub>n</sub> mixture
混雑した <sub>adj</sub> crowded
昏睡 <sub>n</sub> coma
痕跡 <sub>n</sub> trail
根絶する <sub>v</sub> uproot
献立表 <sub>n</sub> menu
昆虫 <sub>n</sub> insect
昆虫のつめ <sub>n</sub> claw
昆虫の群れ <sub>n</sub> swarm

根底にある <sub>v</sub> underlie
混同 <sub>n</sub> confusion
混同する <sub>v</sub> confuse
困難 <sub>n</sub> hardship
困難な <sub>adj</sub> arduous
こんにちは <sub>e</sub> hello
今晩 <sub>adv</sub> tonight
コンピューター <sub>n</sub> computer
こん棒で殴る <sub>v</sub> bludgeon
混乱 <sub>n</sub> mess
混乱した <sub>adj</sub> mixed-up
困惑 <sub>n</sub> quandery
５０、５０個の <sub>adj</sub> fifty
五角形 <sub>n</sub> pentagon
５月 <sub>n</sub> May.
５個の <sub>adj</sub> five

# さ

サーカス <sub>n</sub> circus
サーロイン <sub>n</sub> sirloin
サイ <sub>n</sub> rhinoceros
最愛の <sub>adj</sub> beloved
最悪 <sub>adj</sub> worst
最悪な <sub>adj</sub> horrible
災害 <sub>n</sub> disaster
再開する <sub>v</sub> resume
再確認する <sub>v</sub> reassure

再帰の *adj* reflexive

最近 *adv* lately

細菌 *n* germ

最近の *adj* latest, recent

採掘する *v* mine

サイクリスト *n* cyclist

再結合する *v* rejoin

再現 *n* reenactment

再建する *v* rebuild

再検討 *n* review

再検討する *v* review

在庫 *n* stock

再考する *v* reconsider

最高点 *n* climax

最高の *adj* paramount

最後通告 *n* ultimatum

最後に *adv* lastly

最後のもの *adj* final

最後の夜 *adv* last night

サイコロ *n* dice

幸先の良い *adj* auspicious

再集計 *n* recount

最終的な *adj* ultimate

再充電する *v* recharge

最重要 *n* primacy

最小限 *n* minimum

最小限にする *v* minimize

菜食主義の *v* vegetarian

最初に *adv* primarily

最新の *adj* up-to-date

再生 *n* rebirth

採石場 *n* quarry

最前部 *n* forefront

最前面 *n* foreground

催促状 *n* reminder

最大限の *adj* utmost

最大の *adj* maximum

最大容積 *n* capacity

祭壇 *n* altar

祭典 *n* festivity

災難 *n* calamity

災難のもと *n* scourge

歳入 *n* revenue

再入場 *n* reentry

罪人 *n* sinner

才能 *n* talent

才能のある *adj* gifted

再発 *n* recurrence

再発する *v* recur

再版 *n* reprint

裁判 *n* court, trial

裁判官 *n* judge

再版する *v* reprint

財布 *n* wallet, purse

再編成する *v* reorganize

裁縫 *n* sewing

細胞膜 *n* membrane

再舗装する *v* resurface

催眠術 _n_ hypnosis
催眠する _v_ hypnotize
債務 _n_ debt
債務者 _n_ creditor
材木 _n_ timber
採用 _n_ recruitment
採用する _v_ adopt, recruit
再利用 _v_ recycle
材料 _n_ ingredient
坂 _n_ slope
逆さまの _adv_ upside-down
捜し出す _v_ seek
捜す _v_ search, find
杯 _n_ chalice
魚 _n_ fish
魚のような _adj_ fishy
逆らう _v_ defy
下がる _v_ come down
下がること _n_ depression
詐欺 _n_ fraud, scam
詐欺行為をする _v_ defraud
詐欺師 _n_ swindler
先立つ _v_ precede
先立って _adj_ prior
詐欺的な _adj_ fraudulent
先取りする _v_ preempt
先のない _adj_ pointless
先触れをする _v_ herald
先へ進む _v_ go ahead

作業員 _n_ laborer
詐欺を働く _v_ swindle
咲く _v_ blossom
柵 _n_ bar
索引 _n_ index
作者 _n_ author
削除する _v_ eliminate
作戦 _n_ tactics
作戦行動 _n_ maneuver
作物 _n_ crop
サクランボ _n_ cherry
策略 _n_ gimmick, ploy
探る _v_ probe
ザクロ _n_ pomegranate
サケ _n_ salmon
酒 _n_ liquor
酒飲み _n_ drinker
叫び _n_ call, shouting
叫び声 _n_ bark, calling
叫ぶ _v_ exclaim, shout
裂け目 _n_ crevice, rift
避けられない _adj_ inevitable
避ける _v_ dodge, avoid
下げる _v_ get down
裂ける _v_ rip, tear
鎖骨 _n_ collarbone
ささいな _adj_ trivial
ささいな過ち _n_ lapse
支える _v_ support

さ

ささげる *v* dedicate
さざ波 *n* ripple
ささやき声 *n* whisper
ささやく *v* whisper
挿絵 *n* illustration
差し押さえ *n* seizure
刺し傷 *n* stab
差込 *n* insertion
指図する *v* dictate
差し迫った *adj* impending
差し引いて *adj* minus
差し引き *n* deduction
差し引く *v* deduct
座礁した *adj* stranded
刺す *v* sting
指す *v* point
サスペンダー *n* suspenders
座席 *n* seat
サソリ *n* scorpion
札 *n* tag
雑音 *n* noise
作家 *n* writer
殺害する *v* slay
錯覚 *n* illusion
雑学家 *n* browser
作曲家 *n* composer
殺菌された *v* pasteurize
殺菌する *v* sterilize
殺菌用の *v* disinfectant

冊子 *n* brochure
雑誌 *n* magazine
殺人 *n* murder
殺人罪 *n* homicide
殺人者 *n* murderer
雑草 *n* weed
雑草を取る *v* weed
雑談する *v* chat
殺虫剤 *n* pesticide
殺到 *n* stampede
雑用 *n* chore
サディスト *n* sadist
砂糖 *n* sugar
作動する *v* operate
砂漠 *n* desert
さび *n* rust
寂しい *adv* lonely
さびた *adj* rusty
さび止めの *adj* rust-proof
さびる *v* rust
サファイア *n* saphire
座布団 *n* cushion
差別 *n* discrimination
差別する *v* discriminate
さぼる *v* skip
さまざまな *adj* various
冷ます *v* cool
妨げ *n* setback
妨げになる *v* hinder

妨げる v thwart
寒い adj cold
寒さ n chill, coldness
寒々とした adj bleak
サメ n shark
冷める v cool down
さもなければ adv otherwise
査問 n inquest
左右に歩く v shuttle
作用する v affect
さようなら e bye
皿 n dish
さらされた adj exposed
さらす v expose
サラダ n salad
さらに c even more
さらに adv moreover
さらに遠い adv farther
さりげない adj casual
猿 n monkey
去る v leave
ざる n strainer
サルビア n saliva
騒がしい adj bustling
騒ぎ n commotion
騒ぐ v mess around
ざわつく v buzz
ざわめき n murmur
酸 n acid

参加 n participation
参加する v attend
三角形 n triangle
三脚 n tripod
残虐行為 n atrocity
残虐性 n bestiality
残虐な adj atrocious
産業 n industry
サングラス n sunglasses
ざんげ室 n confessional
参考文献 n bibliography
残酷さ n cruelty
残酷な adj cruel
産出 n output
産出する v yield .
参照 n reference
三振する v strike out
算数 n arithmetic
酸性 n acidity
酸素 n oxygen
サンダル n sandal
散弾銃 n shotgun
暫定の adj provisional
サンドイッチ n sandwich
賛同 n approbation
残忍 n savagery
残忍性 n brutality
残忍な adj brutal
残忍にする v brutalize

さ

散髪 *n* haircut
散発的な *adj* sporadic
賛美歌 *n* hymn
産物 *n* product
散文体 *n* prose
散財する *v* squander
散歩 *n* walk
散歩道 *n* promenade
散乱したもの *n* litter
氏 *n* mister
残留者 *n* remainder
３０、３０個の *adj* thirty
３ヶ月間 *n* trimester
３月 *n* March
３、３個の *adj* three
３倍の数 *adj* triple

# し

死 *n* death
詩 *n* poem
試合 *n* tournament
幸せな *adj* blissful
シアン化物 *n* cyanide
虐げる *v* oppress
シーツ *n* sheets
椎骨 *n* vertebra
強いる *v* compel, force

子音 *n* consonant
寺院 *n* temple
ジーンズ *n* jeans
シェパード *n* shepherd
シェリー酒 *n* sherry
支援者 *n* supporter
支援する *v* assist
塩 *n* salt
潮 *n* tide
塩辛い *adj* salty
シカ *n* deer
視界 *n* sight
死骸 *n* corpse
司会者 *n* host
市街電車 *n* tram
仕返し *n* retaliation
四角 *n* square
視覚 *n* vision
四角の *adj* square
視覚の *adj* visual
資格のある *adj* eligible
資格を得る *v* qualify
しかし *c* but
仕方なく *adv* reluctantly
四月 *n* April
鹿の肉 *n* venison
直火で焼く *v* grill
しがみつく *v* hang on
しかめっ面 *n* grimace

しかる v admonish
時間 n time
時間外の adv overtime
時間ごとの adv hourly
時間を計る v time
四季 n season
指揮 n helm
時期 n times
磁器 n porcelain
敷居 n threshold
指揮者 n conductor
敷地 n site
磁気の adj magnetic
式服 n robe
識別する v discern
子宮 n uterus, womb
事業計画 n project
死去した adj deceased
仕切り n screen
士気をくじく v demoralize
時機を失した adj untimely
資金を出す v fund
軸 n axis
しくじる v botch
ジグゾー n jigsaw
仕組み n know-how
刺激 n stimulus
刺激する v stimulate
刺激的な adj exciting

刺激物 n stimulant
試験 n examination
事件 n incident
資源 n resource
試験的な adj tentative
事件のない adj uneventful
自己意識する adj self-concious
事項 n item
至高 n supremacy
指向性の adj oriented
時効にする v outlaw
地獄 n hell
時刻表 n timetable
自己処罰 n penance
仕事 n job, work
自己の adj own
自己の利益 n self-interest
司祭 n priest
司祭職 n priesthood
自債の念 n remorse
司祭平服 n cassock
思索する v speculate
自殺 n suicide
資産 n assets
持参金 n dowry
指示 n indication
指示する v instruct
事実 n fact, instance
事実無根の adj unfounded

し

磁石 n magnet

刺しゅう n embroidery

自主的な adj autonomous

思春期 n puberty

四旬節 n Lent

支所 n branch office

自署 n autograph

辞書 n dictionary

市場 n market

事情 n circumstance

至上の adj supreme

辞職 n resignation

指針 n guidelines

詩人 n poet

地震 n earthquake

地震が襲う v strike

自信のある adj confident

地震原 n minefield

指数 n quotient

静かな adj calm, serene

しずく n dew

滴 n drop

静けさ n calm

静けさ adj quiet

死すべき adj mortal

沈み込む v slump

沈む v go under, sink

静める v pacify

沈める v submerge

自制 n abstinence

磁性 n magnetism

私生活 n privacy

歯石 n tartar

使節 n envoy

施設 n institution

慈善 n charity

自然 n nature

慈善の adj charitable

持続 n maintenance

持続期間 n duration

持続する v keep up

持続性の adj persistent

子孫 n descendant

自尊 n self-respect

自尊心 n self-esteem

子孫をもうける v procreate

舌 n tongue

死体 n corpse

時代 n epoch, era

時代遅れの adj obsolete

次第である v depend

肢体不自由な adj cripple

従う v comply

下書き n draft

下着 n underwear

親しい adj close

親しい人 n folks

したたる v trickle

し

滴る v drip
仕立屋 n tailor
下に adv below
下にある adv down
下に行く v go down
下に曲げる v bend down
下見 n preview
下を掘る v undermine
自治 n autonomy
七月 n July
質に入れる v pawn
質屋 n pawnbroker
シチュー n stew
支柱 n column
歯痛 n toothache
実演する v demonstrate
湿気 n humidity
湿気のある adj damp
失業 n unemployment
実業家 n businessman
失業者 adj jobless
しっくいを塗る v plaster
じっくり考える v ponder
実験 n experiment
実行する v enforce
実行できる adj workable
漆黒の adj pitch-black
実在しない adj unreal
実際には adv really

実際の adj actual, factual
実際は adv actually
執事 n butler
実質的には adv virtually
温順 n meekness
実証する v verify
叱責 n rebuke
叱責する v rebuke
失そう n disappearance
失速する v stall
質素な adj frugal
質素に adv plainly
失態 v goof
湿地 n bog
失墜 n downfall
嫉妬 n jealousy
嫉妬して adj jealous
じっと見る v gaze
室内の adv indoor
実に adv indeed
失敗 n failure
失敗しない adj unfailing
失敗する v fail
失敗に終わる v fall through
しっぽ n tail
失望 n disappointment
失望させる v disappoint
失明 n blindness
失明させる v blind

し

質問 *n* inquiry

質問する *v* question, ask

実用的でない *adj* impractical

実用的な *adj* practical

実力行使 *n* reprisal

失礼な *adj* impolite

詩的作品 *n* poetry

支店 *n* branch

自転車 *n* bicycle

使徒 *n* apostle

指導 *n* coaching

私道 *n* driveway

自動 *adj* automatic

指導者 *n* instructor

自動車 *n* automobile

指導する *v* coach

自動養護施設 *n* orphanage

指導力 *n* leadership

使徒の *adj* apostolic

しとやかな *adj* ladylike

死なない *adj* immortal

死にかけている *adj* dying

死に絶えた *adj* extinct

自認 *n* confession

辞任する *v* abdicate

死ぬ *v* die

死の落とし穴 *n* death trap

詩の節 *n* verse

忍びよる *v* stalk

死の床 *n* deathbed

芝 *n* sod, turf

支配 *n* control

支配する *v* govern, reign

支配的な *adj* domineering

支配人 *n* manager

支配力 *n* dominion

しばしば *adv* often

自発的な *adj* spontaneous

芝生 *n* grass, lawn

支払い *n* pay

支払可能な *adj* payable

支払う *v* disburse, pay

縛られた *adj* bound

四半期 *n* quarters

慈悲 *n* clemency

慈悲深い *adj* merciful

指標 *n* barometer

しぶきでぬらす *v* splash

至福 *n* bliss

自分自身 *pre* oneself

死別 *n* bereavement

死別した *adj* bereaved

死亡 *n* mortality

脂肪 *n* fat

死亡者数 *n* death toll

絞りだす *v* wring

資本化する *v* capitalize

資本主義 *n* capitalism

島 *n* island
姉妹 *n* sister
シマウマ *n* zebra
縞模様の *adj* striped
閉まる *v* close, shut
自慢する *v* boast, brag
染み *n* spot
シミが付く *v* smear
地道な *adj* down-to-earth
地味な *adj* somber
染みのない *adj* spotless
染みをつける *v* blot
市民 *n* citizen
市民から成る *adj* civil
市民権 *n* citizenship
事務員 *n* clerk
事務員の *adj* clerical
事務局 *n* bureau
事務所 *n* office
事務処理 *n* paperwork
指名する *v* designate
自明の *adj* self-evident
締め切り *n* deadline
締め具 *n* clamp
ジメジメする *adj* soggy
示す *v* denote
死滅する *v* deaden
湿った *adj* humid
締めなわ *n* noose

湿らす *v* moisten
湿らせる *v* dampen
占める *v* account for
地面 *n* ground
霜 *n* dew, frost
地元の *adj* local
霜取り装置 *v* defrost
霜の降りた *adj* frosty
指紋 *n* fingerprint
邪悪 *n* wickedness
邪悪な *adj* perverse
ジャージ *n* jersey
ジャガー *n* jaguar
社会 *n* society
社会階級 *n* caste
社会主義 *n* socialism
社会主義者の *adj* socialist
市役所 *n* city hall
蛇口 *n* faucet
弱点 *n* frailty
釈放 *n* liberation
釈放する *v* acquit
ジャケット *n* jacket
車庫 *n* garage
社交好きな *adj* sociable
社交的な *adj* amiable
車軸 *n* axle
射手 *n* marksman
車掌 *n* conductor

し

写真 v photograph
写真家 n photographer
写真撮影 n photography
写真複写 n photocopy
ジャスミン n jasmine
車線 n lane
社長 n presidency
ジャッカル n jackal
しゃっくり n hiccup
シャベル n shovel
邪魔 n obstruction
邪魔な adj deprave
邪魔をする v interfere
ジャム n jam
斜面 n ramp
砂利 n gravel
車輪 n wheel
シャレー n chalet
シャレード n charade
しゃれた adj fancy
シャワー n shower
ジャンクション n junction
シャンデリア n chandelier
ジャンプ n jump
斜視の adj cocky
州 n province
週 n week
銃 n pistol
自由 n freedom

醜悪な adj odious
獣医 n veterinarian
周囲の n perimeter
収益 n earnings
収穫 n harvest
収穫する v harvest
収穫高 n yield
習慣 n habit
習慣的な adj customary
習慣の adj habitual
周期 n cycle
臭気 n odor
銃器 n firearm
住居 n dwelling
宗教 n religion
従業員 n employee
宗教会議 n synod
宗教儀式係 n chaplain
宗教的な adj religious
住居侵入窃盗 n burglary
襲撃 n raid
襲撃する v assault, raid
銃剣 n bayonet
集合 n assembly
集合体 v aggregate
重婚 n bigamy
重罪 n felony
重罪犯人 n felon
十字遺伝 v criss-cross

し

十字架 n crucifix

十字軍 n crusade

十字軍兵士 n crusader

十字形 n cross

従事する v indulge

充実させる v enrich

十字砲火 n crossfire

収集 n collection

収集家 n collector

収縮 n contraction

収縮する v flex

従順な adj docile

住所 n address

重傷を負わせる v maim

住所氏名録 n directory

就寝中の adj asleep

ジュース n juice

修正 n revision

獣性 n beast

修正する v modify

重大な adj crucial

十代の若者 n teenager

住宅 n house

集団 n group

じゅうたん n carpet, rug

銃弾 n ammunition

集団脱出 n exodus

私有地 n estate

集中させる v concentrate

集中させる n concentration

集中する v converge

集中的な adj concentric

集中砲火 n barrage

充電 n chagrin

シュート n chute

修道院 n monastery

修道院生活 n cloister

修道院長 n abbot

修道院の adj monastic

修道士 n friar, monk

修道女 n nun

修得する v master

習得する v acquire

柔軟 n softness

柔軟性のある adj flexible

柔軟な adj supple

自由に adj free

自由にする v free

就任式 n inauguration

執念 n obsession

収納箱 n chest

銃の口径 n caliber

修復 n renovation

重複 n duplication

重複する adj redundant

十分な adv enough

十分な adj substantial

十分に adv fully

し

週末 *n* weekend
充満させる *v* inundate
充満した *adj* replete
重要性 *n* importance
重要である *v* signify
重要でない *adj* insignificant
襲来 *n* onslaught
修理する *v* fix, repair
修理不可能な *adj* irreparable
終了する *v* terminate
重力 *n* gravity
収賄 *n* bribery
守衛 *n* guard
樹液 *n* sap
受益者 *n* beneficiary
樹液をとる *v* sap
酒気 *n* drunkenness
授業 *n* class, lesson
授業料 *n* tuition
熟語 *n* idiom
塾考 *n* speculation
祝祭の *adj* festive
祝辞 *n* congratulations
塾した *adj* mature
熟した *adj* ripe
熟して甘い *adj* mellow
縮小図 *n* miniature
縮小する *v* contract, curtail
熟す *v* mellow

宿題 *n* homework
熟達 *n* mastery
熟達した *adj* expert
熟知した *adj* versed
祝典 *n* celebration
祝杯 *n* toast
祝福 *n* benediction
熟練した *adj* skillful
受刑者 *n* inmate
主権 *n* sovereignty
手工芸品 *n* artwork
主宰する *v* preside
種子 *n* seed
主題 *n* topic
受胎 *n* conception
受諾する *v* accept
受諾すること *n* acceptance
受諾できる *adj* acceptable
手段 *n* means
主張 *n* assertion
主張する *v* persist, allege
出血 *n* bleeding
出血する *v* bleed
出現 *n* appearance
熟考した *adj* deliberate
熟考する *v* deliberate
出資する *v* finance
出生 *n* birth
出席 *n* attendance

出席する *v* attend
出発 *n* departure
出発する *v* depart, start
出版社 *n* publisher
出版する *v* publish
出版物 *n* publication
出費 *n* expenditure
出没する *v* haunt
首都 *n* capital
主導権 *n* initiative
取得 *n* acquisition
主として *adv* chiefly
首脳陣 *n* summit
主婦 *n* housewife
趣味 *n* hobby
趣味の良い *adj* tasteful
寿命 *adj* shortlived
呪文 *n* spell
腫瘍 *n* tumor
主要道路 *n* highway
主要都市 *n* metropolis
主要な *adj* main
主要部 *n* trunk
授与されたもの *n* grant
授与する *v* award
狩猟 *n* hunting
種類 *n* variety, type
巡回 *n* patrol
潤滑 *n* lubrication

潤滑油 *n* grease
潤滑油を塗る *v* grease
瞬間 *n* moment
循環 *n* circulation
殉教者 *n* martyr
純潔な *adj* innocent
殉死 *n* martyrdom
順守 *n* compliance
純真な *adj* naive
純粋な *adj* pure
順に回す *v* pass around
順応する *v* adjust
順応できる *adj* adjustable
準備 *n* setup
準備する *v* prepare
準備の *adj* preliminary
遵法者 *adj* conformist
遵法の *adj* law-abiding
巡礼 *n* pilgrimage
巡礼者 *n* pilgrim
章 *n* chapter
滋養 *n* sustenance
上位のもの *adj* upper
上院 *n* senate
上院議員 *n* senator
消化 *n* digestion
生姜 *n* ginger
浄化 *n* purge
紹介 *n* introduction

し

傷害 _n_ mayhem

障害 _n_ obstacle, hurdle

紹介する _v_ introduce

障害物 _n_ barricade

奨学金 _n_ scholarship

消化する _v_ digest

浄化する _v_ purify

消化の _adj_ digestive

錠が開く _v_ unlock

消化不良 _n_ indigestion

償還 _n_ recourse

召喚状を発する _v_ subpoena

召還令状 _n_ subpoena

正気 _n_ sanity

蒸気 _n_ steam

定規 _n_ ruler

正気でない _adj_ insane

正気の _adj_ sane

乗客 _n_ passenger

小球 _n_ globule

商業 _n_ commerce

状況 _n_ situation, status

小教区 _n_ parish

状況説明 _n_ briefing

商業の _adj_ commercial

状況の _adj_ circumstancial

衝撃 _n_ jolt

衝撃的な _adj_ shocking

証言する _v_ attest, testify

条件付きの _adj_ conditional

証拠 _n_ evidence, proof

正午 _n_ noon

小康 _n_ respite

照合する _v_ check

小個室 _n_ cubicle

生ゴミ _n_ garbage

詳細 _n_ detail

錠剤 _n_ tablet, pill

詳細を調べる _n_ pore

小冊子 _n_ leaflet

称賛 _n_ admiration

称賛者 _n_ admirer

称賛すべき _adj_ exemplary

称賛する _v_ praise, admire

上司 _n_ boss

正直 _n_ honesty

正直な _adj_ honest

使用者 _n_ user

乗車 _v_ board

召集される _v_ convene

少女 _n_ girl

上昇 _n_ appreciation

上昇する _v_ climb

上昇する _adv_ upwards

小衝突 _n_ skirmish

精進させる _v_ propel

小数の _adj_ few

少数派 _n_ minority

小説 *n* novel
小説家 *n* novelist
乗船する *v* embark
肖像 *n* effigy
醸造 *v* brew
肖像画 *n* portrait
醸造所 *n* brewery
小体 *n* corpuscle
招待 *n* invitation
正体 *n* identity
状態 *n* condition, state
招待する *v* invite
上達 *n* proficiency
上達する *v* improve
冗談 *n* joke
冗談っぽく *adv* jokingly
冗談を言う *v* joke
省庁 *n* ministry
象徴 *n* symbol
象徴する *v* represent
象徴する *adj* symbolic
使用停止 *n* disuse
小テストをする *v* quiz
焦点 *n* focus
譲渡 *n* sellout
衝動 *n* impulse
小塔 *n* turret
衝動強迫 *n* compulsion
衝動的な *adj* impulsive

上等の *adj* superior
消毒する *v* disinfect, scald
衝突 *n* crash, collision
衝突する *v* crash, collide
商人 *n* merchant
承認 *n* approval
使用人 *n* servant
承認する *v* approve
情熱 *n* passion, ardor
情熱的な *adj* passionate
少年 *n* lad
少年時代 *n* boyhood
蒸発する *v* evaporate
消費 *n* consumption
消費者 *n* consumer
商標 *n* brand
商品 *n* merchandise
賞品 *n* award, trophy
商品倉庫 *n* stockroom
上品な *adj* gracious
丈夫な *adj* tough
小別荘 *n* cottage
使用法 *n* usage
情報 *n* information
消防士 *n* firefighter
譲歩する *v* concede
上品ぶった *adj* genteel
賞味する *v* savor
静脈 *n* vein

静脈の *adj* intravenous

照明 *n* lighting

証明された *adj* proven

証明書 *n* certificate

証明する *v* prove

正面 *n* front

正面の *adj* front

条約 *n* treaty

将来 *n* future

勝利 *n* triumph

上陸 *n* landing

上陸する *v* land

勝利者 *n* winner

省略 *n* abbreviation

省略する *v* omit

少量 *n* handful

使用料 *n* charge

勝利を収めた *adj* triumphant

条例 *n* code

常連 *n* clientele

小論 *n* essay

唱和 *n* chorus

小惑星 *n* asteroid

女王 *n* queen

ショーツ *n* briefs

叙階式 *n* ordination

除外する *v* exclude

書簡 *n* epistle

書記 *n* chancellor

除去 *n* removal

除去する *v* remove

職員 *n* staff

職業 *n* career

食材 *n* foodstuff

食事 *n* meal

触手 *n* tentacle

食習慣 *n* diet

食事をする *v* dine

食事をする人 *n* diner

食卓 *n* table

食堂 *n* cafeteria

食道 *n* esophagus

職人 *n* craftsman

私欲のない *adj* disinterested

植物 *n* plant

植物学 *n* botany

植民地 *n* colony

植民地化 *n* colonization

植民地にする *v* colonize

植民地の *adj* colonial

職務を果たす *v* officiate

食物 *n* food

食欲 *n* appetite

食料庫 *n* pantry

食料雑貨類 *n* groceries

食糧難 *n* scarcity

助言 *n* guidance

助言者 *n* adviser

助言する v advise
助言を求める n advice
徐行 v crawl
助祭 n deacon
助産師 n midwife
序詞 n prologue
所持品 n belongings
助手 n aide, helper
処女性 n virginity
初心者 n beginner
女性 n woman
助成金 n subsidy
助成金を払う v subsidize
女性たち n women
女性の祭司 n priestess
女性の裁縫師 n seamstress
女性らしい adj feminine
書籍販売人 n bookseller
書棚 n bookcase
処置 n treatment
処置する v dispose
織機 n loom
食器洗い機 n dishwasher
食器棚 n cupboard
所得 n income
序盤 n opening
処分 n disposal
序文 n preamble
初歩的な adj elementary

初歩の adj rudimentary
庶民的な adj folksy
署名 n signature
署名する v subscribe
除名する v expel
所有 n possession
女優 n actress
所有権 n ownership
所有者 n owner
所有する v own, possess
所有物 n property
処理する v process
書類 n document, file
書類かばん n briefcase
知らせ n news
知らせる v acquaint
しらふの adj sober
調べあげる n check up
調べる v examine
シラミ n lice, louse
知られていない adj unknown
退く v withdraw
資料 n data
思慮がない adj unwise
視力 n eyesight
思慮のある adj sensible
思慮深い adj thoughtful
知る v know
指令 v command

し

事例 *n* case

司令官 *n* marshal

試練 *n* tribulation

ジレンマ *n* dilemma

城 *n* castle

シロアリ *n* termite

白い *adj* white

素人 *n* layman

白くする *v* whiten

じろじろ見る *v* stare

しわ *n* wrinkle

しわがれ声の *adj* hoarse

しわになる *v* crease

しわの寄った *v* wrinkle

字をつづる *v* spell

芯 *n* core

親愛な *adj* dear

人員 *n* manpower

進化 *n* evolution

神学 *n* theology

人格化する *v* personify

神学者 *n* theologian

進化する *v* evolve

神学校 *n* seminary

審議会 *n* chamber

蜃気楼 *n* mirage

寝具類 *n* bedding

神経 *n* nerve

人口 *n* population

人口衛星 *n* satellite

侵攻する *v* invade

人口調査 *n* census

人工的な *adj* artificial

深刻さ *n* seriousness

新婚者 *adj* newlywed

新婚旅行 *n* honeymoon

診察 *n* consultation

紳士 *n* gentleman

信じ込ませる *v* delude

寝室 *n* bedroom

真実 *n* truth

真実の *adj* truthful

神社 *n* shrine

真珠 *n* pearl

人種差別 *n* racism

心情 *n* mind

侵食する *v* eat away

信じられない *adj* incredible

信じられる *adj* believable

信じる *v* believe

信じる人 *n* believer

信心深さ *n* piety

申請 *n* application

神聖 *n* holiness

人生 *n* life

神聖化 *n* consecration

新生児 *n* newborn

申請する *v* file

神聖な *adj* sacred, holy
神聖にする *v* sanctify
神聖を汚す *v* desecrate
親切 *n* kindness
親切な *adj* considerate, kind
親切に *adv* kindly
親善 *n* goodwill
新鮮でない *adj* stale
新鮮な *adj* fresh
新鮮味 *n* freshness
腎臓 *n* kidney
心臓学 *n* cardiology
心臓停止 *n* cardiac arrest
心臓の *adj* cardiac
迅速 *n* readiness
親族関係 *n* kinship
迅速な *adj* prompt
寝台 *n* berth
靭帯 *n* ligament
診断 *n* diagnosis
診断する *v* diagnose
慎重さ *n* prudence
慎重な *adj* cautious
死んでいる *adj* dead
進展する *v* proceed
振動 *v* quiver
振動 *n* vibration
浸透する *v* permeate
振動する *v* vibrate

侵入 *n* intrusion
侵入者 *n* intruder
新入社員 *n* recruit
侵入する *v* encroach
進入する *v* intrude
信任 *n* confidence
信任する *v* confide
信念 *n* belief, creed
心配 *n* worry
心配して *adj* anxious
心配する *v* worry
心配のない *adj* carefree
審判 *n* umpire
審判員 *n* referee
神秘の *adj* mysterious
信ぴょう性 *n* authenticity
新品の *adj* brand-new
人物 *n* person
新聞 *n* newspaper
人文科学 *n* humanities
進歩 *n* headway
信棒者 *n* follower
辛抱する *v* persevere
進歩させる *v* step up
進歩する *v* advance
進歩的な *adj* progressive
親密 *n* intimacy
親密さ *n* rapport
親密な *adj* intimate

し

尋問 *n* hearing

親友 *n* confidant

信用 *n* credit

信用しない *v* distrust

信用を落とす *v* discredit

信頼 *n* faith, trust

信頼する *n* trust

信頼性 *n* credibility

信頼できない *adj* unreliable

信頼できる *adj* reliable

辛らつな *adj* stinging

審理 *n* inquisition

心理学 *n* psychology

侵略 *n* invasion

侵略国 *n* invader

侵略者 *n* raider

診療所 *n* clinic

森林 *n* forest

人類 *n* mankind

親類 *n* relative

神話 *n* myth

～しがちな *adj* prone

～して以来 *c* since

～し始める *v* set out

～し続ける *v* keep

10セント硬貨 *n* dime

10億 *n* billion

10月 *n* October

10、10個の *adj* ten

10年間 *n* decade

11月 *n* November

11個の *adj* eleven

12月 *n* December

12個 *n* dozen

12個の *adj* twelve

13個の *adj* thirteen

14個の *adj* fourteen

15個の *adj* fifteen

16個の *adj* sixteen

17個の *adj* seventeen

18個の *adj* eighteen

19個の *adj* nineteen

# す

巣 *n* nest

酢 *n* vinegar

巣穴 *n* burrow

吸い上げる *v* soak up

水泳 *n* swimming

スイカ *n* watermelon

水管 *n* aqueduct

水牛 *n* buffalo

水銀 *n* mercury

吸い込むこと *v* inhale

推進 *n* promotion

推進する *v* promote

スイス *n* Switzerland

スイス人 *adj* Swiss

彗星 *n* comet

推薦 *n* praise

水素 *n* hydrogen

膵臓 *n* pancreas

推測 *n* guess

水族館 *n* aquarium

錐体 *n* cone

スイッチを入れる *v* switch on

スイッチを切る *v* switch off

推定 *n* presumption

推定する *v* deduce

出納係 *n* treasurer

水分 *n* moisture

水平線 *n* horizon

水平にする *v* level

水平の *adj* horizontal

髄膜炎 *n* meningitis

睡眠 *n* sleep

睡眠薬 *n* narcotic

水門 *n* floodgate

水曜日 *n* Wednesday

水陸両生の *adj* amphibious

推理する *v* presume

水力の *adj* hydraulic

水路標識 *n* beacon

推論 *n* reasoning

推論する *v* infer

スウエーデン *n* Sweden

数学 *n* math

崇高する *adj* sublime

数字 *n* number

数字のけた *n* digit

スーツ *n* suit

スーツケース *n* suitcase

崇拝 *n* worship

崇拝する *v* adore

スープ *n* soup

スカート *n* skirt

スカーフ *n* scarf

頭がい骨 *n* skull

スキーをする *v* ski

過ぎ去る *v* pass away

すきで耕す *v* plow

好きな *adj* fond

すきのない *adj* airtight

救い出す *v* relieve

救う *v* save

スクーター *n* scooter

好くこと *n* liking

すぐ近くの *adj* nearby

すぐに *adv* immediately

優れた *adj* remarkable

スケート靴 *n* skate

スケートをする *v* skate

スケッチ *n* drawing

スケッチする v sketch
少し動く v budge
少しずつ adv little by little
少しずつ削る v whittle
少しずつ飲む v sip
少しの adj little
少し開いて adj ajar
筋 n nerve
筋書き n scenario
素性 n antecedents
すす n grime
鈴 n bell
すすぐ v rinse
涼しい adj cool
涼しさ n coolness
進み続ける v go on
すずめ n sparrow
薦める v recommend
すすり泣き n sob
すすり泣く v sob
スタイル n style
スチュワーデス n stewardess
頭痛 n headache
すっかり adv quite
酸っぱい adj sour
ステーキ n steak
すてきな adj fine
ステッカー n sticker
すでに adv already

ストーブ n stove
ストライキ n strike
ストライプ n stripe
砂 n sand
スナップ写真 n snapshot
すなわち adv namely
スパークプラグ n spark plug
スパイ n espionage
ずば抜けた adj outstanding
素早い adj agile
素早く動く v zap
素晴らしい adj fantastic
素晴らしさ n splendor
図表 n chart
スプール n spool
スプーン n spoon
スペイン n Spain
スペイン人 adj Spanish
スペイン人の n Spaniard
全ての adj all
すべてのもの pro everything
滑りやすい adj slippery
滑る v glide, slide
滑ること n slip
スポーツ n sport
スポーツマン n sportman
スポット n spotlight
ズボン n pants, trousers
すまなく思う adj sorry

す

炭焼きの *adj* charbroil
スミレ色 *n* violet
住む *v* inhabit
スモモ *n* prune
ずらかる *v* bug
スラックス *n* slacks
スラム街 *n* slum
すり *n* pickpocket
すり減る *v* wear down
擦りむく *v* scrape
する *v* do
ずるい *adj* cunning, foxy
ずる賢い *adj* wily
鋭い *adj* pointed, sharp
ずれた *adj* staggering
すれる *v* rub
擦れる *n* graze
座る *adj* seated
座る *v* sit
座ること *n* sitting
寸前で *pre* close to
寸法 *n* dimension
〜すべきである *v* ought to
〜する *pre* to
〜するとすぐ *c* whereupon
〜するとすぐに *c* once
〜する間に *c* while
〜する気がある *adj* willing

# せ

姓 *n* surname
聖域 *n* sanctuary
セイウチ *n* walrus
星雲 *n* galaxy
精液 *n* sperm
静穏 *n* serenity
静穏な *adj* restful
聖歌 *n* carol
正確さ *n* accuracy
正確な *adj* accurate
聖歌隊 *n* choir
生活する *v* live
請願書 *n* petition
正義 *n* justice
請求書 *n* bill
請求する *v* charge
性急な *adj* impetuous
逝去 *n* demise
生気を与える *v* animate
税金 *n* tax
生計 *n* livelihood
生計を立てる *v* live off
制限 *n* constraint, limit
制限する *v* limit, restrict
制限のない *adj* unlimited
成功 *n* success
成功させ *v* prosper

すせ

成功した *adj* successful

成功する *v* succeed

性行動 *n* sex

星座 *n* constellation

制裁 *n* sanction

製材 *n* lumber

政策 *n* policy

清算 *v* liquidate

清算 *n* liquidation

生産 *n* production

生産する *v* produce

生産的な *adj* productive

生産物 *n* produce

政治 *n* politics

政治家 *n* politician

正式に *adv* formally

政治形態 *n* regime

静止させる *v* immobilize

静止した *adj* still

制止する *v* restrain

誠実 *n* sincerity

誠実な *adj* sincere

静寂 *n* quietness

成熟する *v* ripen

成熟度 *n* maturity

清純 *n* chastity

聖書 *n* bible

正常な *adj* normal

正常に *adv* normally

正常に歩けない *adj* lame

聖職者 *n* clergy

聖職者の *adj* clerical

生殖力のない *adj* infertile

聖書の *adj* biblical

聖書朗読台 *n* lectern

聖人 *n* saint

精神異常 *n* insanity

精神科 *n* psychiatry

精神科医 *n* psychiatrist

誠心誠意の *adj* cordial

精神的に *adv* mentally

聖人と認める *v* canonize

精神の *adj* psychic

製図技師 *n* draftsman

精製 *n* purification

精製所 *n* refinery

精製する *v* refine

整然とした *adj* methodical

製造 *n* make

製造業者 *n* maker

生存して *adj* alive

生態学 *n* ecology

生態構造 *n* anatomy

ぜいたくな *adj* lavish

成長 *n* growth

成長する *v* grow

生徒 *n* pupil

青銅 *n* bronze

せ

正統な *adj* orthodox
整頓された *adj* neat
青年期 *n* adolescence
青年期の人 *n* adolescent
青年時代 *n* youth
性能を高める *v* upgrade
正反対の *adj* contrary
整備する *v* overhaul
政府 *n* government
制服 *n* uniform
征服 *n* conquest
征服者 *n* conqueror
征服する *v* conquer
生物学の *adj* biological
生物学の *n* biology
西部の *adj* western
成文化する *v* codify
性癖 *n* propensity
性別 *n* gender
政変 *n* coup
精密な調査 *n* scrutiny
声明 *n* statement
生命を持たない *adj* lifeless
誓約 *n* pledge
誓約する *v* pledge
西洋人 *adj* westerner
西洋ナシ *n* pear
生来の *adj* innate
整理 *n* liquidation

整理する *v* sort out
成立 *n* formation
生理痛 *n* cramp
精力 *n* energy
精力的な *adj* energetic
勢力のある *adj* potent
整列 *n* alignment
整列する *v* align
セーター *n* sweater
世界 *n* world
世界的な *adj* worldwide
咳 *n* cough
石炭 *n* coal
脊椎のない *adj* spineless
赤道 *n* equator
責任 *n* fault
責任がある *adj* responsible
責任を逃れる *v* shirk
赤熱の *adj* red-hot
赤面 *n* blush
赤面する *v* blush
石油 *n* petroleum
咳をする *v* cough
世間 *n* people
世襲財産 *n* patrimony
是正する *v* redress
世俗的な *adj* worldly
節 *n* clause
絶縁 *n* insulation

せ

切開 *n* incision
石灰岩 *n* limestone
石化した *adj* petrified
せっかん *n* chastisement
説教 *n* sermon
絶叫 *n* outcry
説教師 *n* preacher
説教する *v* preach
絶叫する *v* scream
説教壇 *n* pulpit
積極的な *adj* positive
接近 *n* proximity
接近可能な *adj* accessible
設計する *n* design
せっけんの泡 *n* lather
石こう *n* plaster
石工 *n* mason
接合する *v* conjugate
摂政 *n* regent
接触 *n* contact
接触する *v* contact
接触伝染性の *adj* contagious
接線 *n* tangent
接続する *v* connect
絶対君主 *n* monarch
絶対的なもの *adj* absolute
切断 *n* severance
切断術 *n* amputation
切断する *v* mutilate

接着 *n* bond
接着剤でつける *v* glue
設定 *n* setting
設定する *v* set
節度 *n* moderation
窃盗 *n* theft
接頭辞 *n* prefix
説得 *n* persuasion
説得する *v* persuade
説得力のある *adj* persuasive
切迫した *adj* imminent
切迫する *v* press
絶壁 *n* precipice
切望 *n* longing
絶望 *n* despair
切望している *adj* eager
切望する *v* covet, crave
絶望的な *adj* hopeless
説明し難い *adj* inexplicable
説明する *v* explain
絶滅させる *v* exterminate
絶滅する *v* die out
節約する *v* conserve
摂理 *n* providence
設立許可 *n* charter
瀬戸物 *n* crockery
背中 *n* back
背の高い *adj* tall
背骨 *n* backbone

せ

せむし *n* hunchback
責める *v* denounce
セメント *n* cement
セラミック *n* ceramic
セレナーデ *n* serenade
セロリ *n* celery
世話人 *n* caretaker
世話をする *v* look after
線 *n* line
栓 *n* plug
繊維 *n* fiber
全宇宙の *adj* universal
前衛 *n* vanguard
旋回 *n* turn
旋回する *v* revolve
船外に *adv* overboard
戦艦 *n* battleship
選挙 *n* election
選挙する *v* elect
先駆者 *n* precursor
全景 *n* panorama
宣言 *n* proclamation
宣言する *v* declare
先見の明 *n* foresight
専攻科目 *n* major
専攻する *v* major in
専攻の *adj* major
宣告する *v* proclaim
洗剤 *n* cleanser

前菜 *n* appetizer
繊細さ *n* delicacy
繊細な *adj* delicate
せんさくする *v* interrogate
戦士 *n* fighter
先史時代の *adj* prehistoric
船室 *n* cabin
前日 *n* eve
前者 *adj* former
船首 *n* bow, prow
選手 *n* player
戦術の *adj* tactical
前進 *n* advance
漸進的な *adj* gradual
先生 *n* teacher
全盛期 *n* heyday
専制君主 *n* despot
専制君主の *n* dictatorship
占星術師 *n* astrologer
専制政治 *n* tyranny
先祖 *n* ancestor
戦争 *n* war
前奏曲 *n* prelude
戦争行為 *n* warfare
ぜんそく *n* asthma
ぜんそくの *adj* asthmatic
船体 *n* hull
全体 *n* totality
全体主義者 *adj* totalitarian

せ

全体に *adv* overall
全体の *adj* entire, total
前代未聞の *adj* unheard-of
洗濯 *n* laundry
選択 *n* choice
選択肢 *n* option
洗濯用のり *n* starch
先端 *n* apex, peak
前置詞 *n* preposition
船長 *n* captain
前兆 *n* portent, omen
前兆となる *v* foreshadow
前提 *n* presupposition
宣伝 *n* advertising
先頭 *n* van
戦闘 *n* combat
先導 *n* lead
戦闘員 *n* combatant
扇動者 *n* agitator
戦闘的な *adj* militant
先頭に付く *v* spearhead
前任者 *n* predecessor
千年間 *n* millennium
洗脳する *v* brainwash
全能の *adj* almighty
扇風機 *n* fan
全部の *adj* whole
前方に *pre* ahead
前方へ *adv* onwards

前方への *adv* forward
全滅 *n* annihilation
全滅させる *v* eradicate
洗面所 *n* lavatory
専門的職業 *n* profession
専門とする *v* specialize
専門の *adj* professional
専門用語 *n* terminology
占有者 *n* occupant
旋律 *n* melody, tune
前立腺 *n* prostate
旋律の *adj* melodic
戦略 *n* strategy
染料 *n* dye
占領する *v* occupy
洗礼 *n* baptism
前例 *n* precedent
洗礼式 *n* christening
洗礼を施す *v* baptize
栓をする *v* plug
１０００個の *adj* thousand

# そ

層 *n* layer
槽 *n* tank
象 *n* elephant
像 *n* icon, statue
草案 *n* draft
相違 *n* discrepancy
総入れ歯 *n* dentures
憎悪 *n* hatred
相応に *adv* properly
憎悪する *v* abhor
増加 *n* increase
増加する *v* augment
増加量 *n* increment
壮観 *n* spectacle
送還 *n* extradition
双眼鏡 *n* binoculars
送還する *v* repatriate
臓器 *n* organ
増強する *v* beef up
送金 *n* remittance
遭遇 *n* encounter
象牙 *n* ivory
総計の *adj* gross
草原地帯 *n* prairie
倉庫 *n* warehouse
走行距離計 *n* odometer
相互に *adv* mutually

相互の *adj* reciprocal
捜査 *n* search
相殺する *v* offset
創作 *n* fiction
操作される *v* handle
操作する *v* manipulate
葬式 *n* funeral
掃除機 *n* cleaner
創始者 *n* founder
掃除する *v* clean
操縦席 *n* cockpit
早熟な *adj* precocious
装飾 *n* garnish
装飾する *v* adorn
装飾的な *adj* decorative
装飾品 *n* ornament
装飾物 *n* décor
装飾用の *adj* ornamental
送信する *v* transmit
造船所 *n* shipyard
騒然とした *adj* tumultuous
創造 *n* creation
想像 *n* imagination
騒々しい *adj* noisy
騒々しく *adv* noisily
創造者 *n* creator
創造する *v* create
想像する *v* imagine
創造性 *n* creativity

創造的な *adj* creative
相続権を奪う *v* disinherit
相続財産 *n* legacy
相続する *v* inherit
相続人 *n* heir
壮大な *adj* colossal
相談する *v* consult
装置 *n* gadget
騒動 *n* turmoil
相当する *v* correspond
挿入する *v* insert
蒼白 *n* paleness
増幅器 *n* amplifier
増幅する *v* amplify
総まとめ *n* roundup
挿話 *n* episode
添え物 *n* trimmings
疎遠になった *adj* estranged
ソース *n* sauce
ソーセージ *n* sausage
俗悪な *adj* profane
即座に *adv* instantly
促進する *v* boost
属する *v* belong
測定基準 *adj* metric
測定する *v* calibrate
速度 *n* speed
速度を落とす *v* slow down
属の *adj* generic

束縛 *n* shackle
続編 *n* sequel
側面 *n* side
側路をつける *v* bypass
狙撃者 *n* sniper
底 *n* bottom
底知れぬ *adj* abysmal
底なしの *adj* bottomless
粗雑な *adj* crude
組織 *n* organization
組織的な *adj* systematic
阻止すること *n* deterrence
訴訟 *n* lawsuit
訴訟を起こす *v* litigate
蘇生 *n* resurrection
祖先 *n* ancestry
注ぐ *v* pour
そぞろ歩く *v* stroll
育てる *v* foster, rear
速記 *n* shorthand
卒業 *n* graduation
卒業証書 *n* diploma
卒業する *v* graduate
即興で *adv* impromptu
即興でやる *v* improvise
卒業論文 *n* thesis
素っ気ない *adj* brusque
続行する *v* keep on
そった *adj* warped

そ

率直さ *n* frankness
率直でない *adj* devious
率直な *adj* outspoken
率直に *adv* frankly
沿って *pre* along
ゾッとさせる *v* horrify
ぞっとする *v* appall
そで口 *n* cuff
袖なしの *adj* sleeveless
外側 *adj* exterior
外側の *adj* external
外側の *adv* outside
外で出る *v* get out
外に出す *v* let out
外に出て *adv* out
外へ出る *v* go out
外を見る *v* look out
備える *v* equip
その上に *adv* furthermore
その間に *adv* meantime
その後 *adv* afterwards
その通り *adv* yes
そのような *adj* such
そばかす *n* freckle
そびえ立つ *adj* towering
祖父 *n* grandfather
ソファ *n* sofa
祖父母 *n* grandparents
祖母 *n* grandmother

背く *v* disobey
染める *v* dye
そよ風 *n* breeze
空 *n* sky
そらす *v* distract, divert
空の *adj* empty
そり *n* sleigh
それ *adj* that
それ以来 *adv* since then
それぞれの *adj* each
それに加えて *pre* besides
それまでの間 *adv* meanwhile
それ故に *adv* therefore
それらの *adj* those
そわそわする *adj* restless
損 *n* mischief
損害 *n* detriment
損害を与える *adj* damaging
尊敬 *n* respect
尊敬する *v* respect
尊敬を欠く *n* disrespect
存在 *n* existence
存在している *adj* present
存在する *v* dwell, exist
存在すること *n* presence
損傷 *v* impair
尊大 *n* arrogance
尊大 *adj* arrogant
尊重する *v* esteem

そ

〜それて *adv* aside from

# た

ダーツ *n* dart
タービン *n* turbine
タール *n* tar
対 *pre* versus
第１０番目の *n* tenth
第１１番目の *adj* eleventh
第１２番目の *adj* twelfth
第１位の *adj* premier
第２０番目の *adj* twentieth
第２番目の *adj* secondary
第２番目の *n* second
第３番目の *adj* third
第４番目の *adj* fourth
第５番目の *adj* fifth
第６番目の *adj* sixth
第７番目の *adj* seventh
第８番目の *adj* eighth
体育館 *n* gymnasium
第一の *adj* foremost
大学 *n* college, university
大学教授 *n* professor
大学合格者 *v* matriculate
大喝采 *n* ovation

戴冠式 *n* coronation
大気の *adj* atmospheric
大虐殺 *n* massacre
耐久性のある *adj* durable
大嫌いな *adj* detestable
大工 *n* carpenter
待遇する *v* treat
大工仕事 *n* carpentry
退屈 *n* boredom
退屈させる *v* bore
退屈した *adj* bored
退屈な *adj* tedious
大群 *n* battalion
大建造物 *n* edifice
太鼓 *n* drum
対抗する *v* counter, match
大根 *n* radish
大混乱 *n* shambles
大混乱の *adj* chaotic
大佐 *n* colonel
滞在 *n* stay
滞在する *v* stay
大惨事 *n* catastrophe
大使 *n* ambassador
題辞 *n* inscription
胎児 *n* embryo, fetus
大使館 *n* embassy
大司教 *n* archbishop
大失敗 *n* blunder, flop

台車 *n* trolley
貸借人 *n* lessee
貸借料 *n* rent
大衆化する *v* popularize
大修道院 *n* abbey
退出する *v* bow out
対照 *n* contrast
対称 *n* symmetry
退場 *n* walkout
大丈夫で *adv* alright
対照をなす *v* contrast
退職 *n* retirement
大食家 *n* glutton
大臣 *n* minister
代数学 *n* algebra
大聖堂 *n* cathedral
体積 *n* bulk
対戦相手 *n* opponent
怠惰 *n* laziness
大腿部 *n* thigh
代替物 *n* alternative
大多数の *n* majority
怠惰な *adj* idle, lazy
大胆 *n* audacity
大胆さ *n* boldness
大胆不敵な *adj* daring
台帳 *n* ledger
大邸宅 *n* mansion
態度 *n* attitude

大洞窟 *n* cavern
大統領 *n* president
台所 *n* kitchen
台無しになる *v* spoil
ダイナマイト *n* dynamite
ダイバー *n* diver
退廃 *n* decadence
大破壊 *n* havoc
たい肥 *n* compost
代表 *n* delegate
代表団 *n* delegation
大部分は *adv* mostly
大変動 *n* cataclysm
逮捕 *n* arrest
大砲 *n* artillery
大豊作 *n* bumper
大牧場 *n* ranch
逮捕される *v* arrest
大麻 *n* hashish
たいまつ *n* torch
怠慢 *n* negligence
怠慢な *adj* negligent
題名 *n* title
代名詞 *n* pronoun
大望 *n* ambition
大望のある *adj* ambitious
ダイヤモンド *n* diamond
ダイヤルを回す *v* dial
大洋 *n* ocean

た

| | |
|---|---|
| 太陽の *adj* solar | だから *adv* hence, thus |
| 太陽の *n* sun | 滝 *n* waterfall |
| 代用品 *n* substitute | 薪 *n* firewood |
| 代用物 *n* proxy | 抱きしめる *v* embrace |
| 平らな *adj* flat | 抱き締める *v* cuddle |
| 平らになる *v* flatten | たき火 *n* bonfire |
| 大陸 *n* mainland | 妥協 *n* compromise |
| 大陸の *adj* continental | 妥協する *v* compromise |
| 大理石 *n* marble | たくさん *adv* lot |
| 代理店 *n* agency | たくさんの *n* plenty |
| 代理人 *n* agent | タクシー *n* cab |
| 大量 *n* mass | 宅配便業者 *n* courier |
| タイル *n* tile | 巧みに使う *v* wield |
| 絶え間のない *adj* incessant | たくらむ *v* plot |
| 耐えられない *adj* unbearable | 蓄え *n* fund |
| 耐えられる *adj* tolerable | 蓄える *v* store |
| 耐える *v* tolerate | 竹 *n* bamboo |
| タオル *n* towel | 打撃 *n* hit |
| 倒れる *v* topple | タコ *n* octopus |
| タカ *n* hawk | たこ *n* kite |
| 高い *adj* high | 確かな *adj* definite |
| 高いこと *n* Highness | 確かに *adv* undoubtedly |
| 多角的な *adj* multiple | 確かにする *v* ensure |
| 高さ *n* altitude, height | 多数 *n* multitude |
| 高波 *n* tidal wave | 多数の *adj* many |
| 高飛車な *adj* aloof | 助け *n* help |
| 高まる *v* heighten, exalt | 助け合う *adj* cooperative |
| 耕す *v* cultivate, till | 助ける *v* help, minister |
| 宝 *n* treasure | 助けを借りる *v* resort |

た

尋ねる <sub>v</sub> ask, inquire

ただ～だけ <sub>adv</sub> only

戦い <sub>n</sub> battle

戦う <sub>v</sub> battle, fight

闘う <sub>v</sub> wrestle

たたき切り <sub>n</sub> chop

たたき切る <sub>v</sub> hack

たたく <sub>v</sub> beat, hit

ただし <sub>pre</sub> except

正しく <sub>adv</sub> justly

正す <sub>v</sub> rectify

ただ単に <sub>adv</sub> merely

ただ一つの <sub>adj</sub> single

ただ一人で <sub>adv</sub> solely

立ち上がる <sub>v</sub> stand up

立ち去る <sub>v</sub> go away

立ち退かせる <sub>v</sub> evict

立場 <sub>n</sub> stand

立ち戻る <sub>v</sub> revert

ダチョウ <sub>n</sub> ostrich

立ち寄る <sub>v</sub> drop in

断つ <sub>v</sub> disconnect

立つ <sub>v</sub> stand

脱穀する <sub>v</sub> thresh

脱臭剤 <sub>n</sub> deodorant

脱出する <sub>v</sub> escape, eject

脱水する <sub>v</sub> dehydrate

達する <sub>v</sub> achieve

達成 <sub>n</sub> achievement

達成する <sub>v</sub> accomplish

脱線 <sub>n</sub> deviation; escapade

脱線する <sub>v</sub> derail

脱線する <sub>n</sub> derailment

脱走する <sub>v</sub> desert

脱退する <sub>v</sub> secede

手綱 <sub>n</sub> rein

竜巻 <sub>n</sub> twister

脱落する <sub>v</sub> drop out

盾 <sub>n</sub> shield

縦糸 <sub>v</sub> warp

盾となる <sub>v</sub> shield

建物 <sub>n</sub> building

建物勘定 <sub>n</sub> premises

建てる <sub>v</sub> build

打倒 <sub>n</sub> overthrow

妥当性 <sub>n</sub> validity

たとえ～でも <sub>c</sub> even if

例えば <sub>pre</sub> like

たどる <sub>v</sub> trace

棚 <sub>n</sub> shelf

棚の複数形 <sub>n</sub> shelves

種 <sub>n</sub> species

種なしの <sub>adj</sub> seedless

種の多い <sub>adj</sub> seedy

種を取る <sub>v</sub> stone

種をまく <sub>v</sub> sow

楽しい <sub>adj</sub> amusing

楽しませる <sub>v</sub> entertain

た

| | |
|---|---|
| 楽しみ *n* amusement | 試す *v* try |
| 楽しみに待つ *v* look forward | ためらい *n* hesitation |
| 楽しむ *v* enjoy | ためらう *v* hesitate |
| 楽しめる *adj* enjoyable | ためらって *adj* hesitant |
| 頼もしい *adj* dependable | たもと *n* sleeve |
| たばこ *n* cigarette | 多様化する *v* diversify |
| 束状 *n* bundle | 多様性 *n* diversity |
| 束にする *v* bundle | 多様性のある *adj* diverse |
| 旅 *n* journey | 多用途の *adj* versatile |
| 旅する *v* travel | 頼る *v* lean |
| だぶだぶの *adj* baggy | タラ *n* cod |
| たぶん *adv* perhaps | たらい *n* basin, tub |
| タペストリー *n* tapestry | タランチュラ *n* tarantula |
| 食べ物を与える *v* feed | 足りない *v* lack |
| 食べられる *adj* edible | 多量 *adv* much |
| 食べる *v* eat | たる *n* barrel |
| 玉 *n* ball | タルト *n* tart |
| 球 *n* sphere | 誰 *pro* who |
| 卵 *n* egg | 誰か *pro* somebody |
| だまし *n* deception | 誰でも *pro* anybody |
| 魂 *n* soul | 誰に *pro* whom |
| だます *v* cheat | 誰も *pro* anyone |
| だますこと *n* deceit | 誰も〜ない *pro* nobody |
| タマネギ *n* onion | 誰も〜ない *pre* none |
| たまりを作る *v* pool | 俵 *n* bale |
| 賜る *v* deign | 段 *n* stair |
| ダム *n* dam | 単一性 *n* unity |
| ため息 *n* sigh | 担架 *n* stretcher |
| ため息をつく *v* sigh | 段階 *n* phase |

た
ち

段階を追った *adv* step-by-step
弾丸 *n* bullet
嘆願する *v* beseech
短気 *n* impatience
短気な *adj* quarrelsome
短形の *adj* oblong
団結 *n* solidarity
探検 *n* expedition
短剣 *n* dagger
探検者 *n* explorer
探検する *v* explore
断言する *v* allege, claim
炭酸飲料 *n* soda
炭酸水 *n* tonic
短時間の *adj* brief
胆汁 *n* bile
短縮 *n* abbreviation
短縮する *v* abridge
単純 *n* simplicity
単純化する *v* simplify
誕生日 *n* birthday
ダンス *n* dance
ダンスする *v* dance
男性的な *adj* virile
男性の婚約者 *n* fiancé
男性の聖職者 *n* clergyman
探知機 *n* detector
単調さ *n* monotony
単調な *adj* monotonous

探偵 *n* detective
断定的な *adj* affirmative
短刀 *n* dagger
断念する *v* affirm
胆嚢 *n* gall bladder
堪能な *adj* proficient
タンパク質 *n* protein
短パン *n* shorts
断片 *n* shred
暖房 *n* heating
暖房機 *n* heater
段落 *n* paragraph
〜だと分かる *v* recognize
暖炉 *n* fireplace, hearth

# ち

治安判事 *n* magistrate
地位 *n* standing
地域 *n* region, area
地域社会 *n* community
地域の *adj* regional
小さい *adj* small
小さいたる *n* keg
小さくなる *v* diminish
小さな穴 *n* slot
小さな滝 *n* cascade

| | |
|---|---|
| 小さな沼 *n* lagoon | 地球 *n* earth, globe |
| 小さな丸石 *n* cobblestone | 地球の *adj* terrestrial |
| チーズ *n* cheese | 地区 *n* district |
| チーム *n* team | 蓄牛 *n* cattle |
| 地位を占める *v* rank | 逐語的に *adv* verbatim |
| チェーンソー *n* chainsaw | 蓄積する *v* accumulate |
| チェス *n* chess | 乳首 *n* nipple |
| 遅延 *n* delay | 地形 *n* terrain |
| 誓い *n* oath | 知事 *n* governor |
| 違い *n* difference | 知識 *n* knowledge |
| 誓う *v* swear | 致死の *adj* deadly |
| 違う *adj* different | 知人 *n* acquaintance |
| 知覚 *n* perception | 地図 *n* map |
| 近くにいる *v* stick around | 治世 *n* reign |
| 近くの *adj* adjacent | 知性のある *adj* intelligent |
| 地下室 *n* basement | 地帯 *n* zone |
| 地下貯蔵室 *n* cellar | 血だらけの *adj* gory |
| 近づく *v* approach | 乳脂 *n* cream |
| 近づくこと *n* approach | 父親 *n* father |
| 地下鉄 *n* subway | 父親らしい *adj* fatherly |
| 地下道 *n* underpass | 縮まる *v* dwindle |
| 地下の *adj* underground | 縮む *v* shrink |
| 地価墓地 *n* catacomb | チッソ *n* nitrogen |
| 近道 *n* shortcut | 窒息 *n* asphyxiation |
| 力 *n* strength, power | 窒息死する *v* suffocate |
| 力強い *adj* dynamic | 窒息する *v* asphyxiate |
| 力強さ *n* virility | 血に飢えた *adj* bloodthirsty |
| 力のある *adj* forceful | 血の *adj* bloody |
| 地下牢 *n* dungeon | 知能 *n* mentality |

ち

地の底 *n* abyss

地方議会 *n* council

致命的な *adj* fatal, lethal

茶 *n* tea

茶色の *adj* brown

着実な *adj* steady

着手 *n* outset

チャック *n* zipper

茶番 *n* farce

茶瓶 *n* teapot

チャンプ *n* champ

注意 *n* caution

注意する *v* beware

注意深い *adj* careful

中央 *n* middle

仲介者 *n* mediator

中間の *adj* medium

忠義 *n* loyalty

中継する *v* relay

仲裁 *n* intercession

仲裁者 *n* intermediary

仲裁する *v* intercede

中止 *v* abort

忠実でない *adj* unfaithful

忠実な *adj* staunch

注射 *n* injection

注射器 *n* syringe

注釈をつける *v* annotate

注釈をつける *n* annotation

駐車場 *n* parking

駐車する *v* park

中傷 *n* slander

中傷 *adj* sly

中傷する *v* defame

中傷すること *n* calumny

抽象的なもの *adj* abstract

昼食 *n* lunch

中心 *n* center

中心に集める *v* centralize

中心の *adj* central

虫垂炎 *n* appendicitis

忠誠 *n* allegiance

忠誠な *adj* loyal

中世の *adj* medieval

中断 *v* abort

中断させる *v* disrupt

中断する *v* interrupt

中毒 *n* addiction

中毒性の *adj* addictive

中毒になった *adj* intoxicated

駐屯地 *n* garrison

注入 *n* injection

注入する *v* instil

注目すべき *adj* noteworthy

注文する *n* order

中立化する *v* neutralize

中立の *adj* neutral

チューリップ *n* tulip

ち

中和する *v* counteract

治癒できる *adj* curable

チュニック *n* tunic

チョウ *n* butterfly

長 *n* chief

超越する *v* transcend

超音波 *n* ultrasound

聴覚障害のある *adj* deaf

超過の *adj* overweight

長期の *adj* long-term

兆候 *n* symptom

調合する *v* concoct

超高層ビル *n* skyscraper

彫刻 *n* sculpture

彫刻家 *n* sculptor

調査 *n* investigation

調査する *v* research

調子 *n* rhythm, tone

聴衆 *n* audience

徴収する *v* toll

徴集兵 *n* conscript

長所 *n* merit

頂上 *n* crest

朝食 *n* breakfast

調整剤 *n* conditioner

調整する *v* tune

調整する人 *n* coordinator

調節 *n* adjustment

挑戦 *n* dare

挑戦する *v* challenge, dare

挑戦する *n* challenge

挑戦的な *adj* challenging

彫像 *n* effigy

超大国 *n* superpower

町長 *n* mayor

調停 *n* arbitration

調停者 *n* arbiter

調停する *v* conciliate

頂点 *n* apex, top

頂点に達する *v* culminate

ちょうど *adj* just

挑発 *n* provocation

挑発する *v* provoke

長方形 *n* rectangle

長方形の *adj* rectangular

超満員の *adj* overcrowded

調味料 *n* seasoning

跳躍 *n* leap

調理師 *n* chef

調和 *n* accord

調和しない *adj* discordant

調和する *v* harmonize

貯金 *n* savings

貯金箱 *n* piggy bank

直接の *adj* direct

直線 *n* line

直腸 *n* rectum

直販店 *n* outlet

直面する *v* confront

直立した *adj* erect

直立する *v* erect

直立の *adj* upright

チョコレート *n* chocolate

著作権 *n* copyright

貯水池 *n* cistern

貯蔵庫 *n* bunker

貯蔵する *v* hoard

貯蔵武器 *n* arsenal

直感 *n* intuition

チョッキ *n* vest

直径 *n* diameter

直行で *adv* nonstop

著名な *adj* prominent

散らかす *v* mess up

ちらりと *v* glance

ちらりと見る *v* glimpse

地理学 *n* geography

治療 *n* cure

治療者 *n* healer

治療する *v* cure

治療薬 *n* remedy

散る *v* dissipate

鎮圧 *v* crush

鎮圧する *v* quash, subdue

賃金 *n* wage

沈思する *v* contemplate

賃借する *v* rent

賃借人 *n* tenant

鎮静 *n* remission

鎮静状態 *n* sedation

賃貸 *n* lease

沈滞 *n* stagnation

沈滞する *v* stagnate

賃貸する *v* lease

賃貸人 *n* lessor

鎮痛薬 *n* painkiller

沈殿物 *v* precipitate

チンパンジー *n* chimpanzee

陳腐さ *n* banality

沈没した *adj* sunken

# つ

ツアー *n* tour

追加 *n* addition

追加の *adj* additional

追加料金 *n* surcharge

追求 *n* quest

追跡 *n* chase

追跡者 *n* trailer

追跡する *v* pursue, trail

追悼 *n* pier

追放 *n* expulsion

追放された *adj* outcast

ち
つ

追放する _v_ exile

費やす _v_ consume

墜落 _n_ depravity

通貨 _n_ currency

通過 _n_ transit

通勤する _v_ commute

通行人 _n_ passer-by

通常 _adv_ ordinarily

通常の _adj_ usual

通信員 _n_ correspondent

通知 _n_ notice

通知者 _n_ informant

痛風 _n_ gout

通風孔 _n_ vent

通訳者 _n_ interpreter

通訳する _v_ interpret

通路 _n_ passage

杖 _n_ cane

使い捨ての _adj_ disposable

使い果たす _v_ run out

使い古した _adj_ shabby

使い古す _v_ wear out

使う _v_ use

仕える _v_ serve

つかの間 _adj_ fleeting

つかみ取る _v_ grab

疲れ _n_ fatigue

疲れた _adj_ tired, weary

疲れない _adj_ tireless

月 _n_ month, moon

月1回の _adv_ monthly

付き合う _v_ associate

つぎ板 _n_ splint

突き刺す _v_ stab

付添人 _n_ escort

突き出す _v_ stick out

突き出る _v_ stand out

突き止める _v_ ascertain

次の _adj_ next

突き棒で突く _v_ goad

継息子 _n_ stepson

継娘 _n_ stepdaughter

机 _n_ desk

償い _n_ reparation

償う _v_ compensate

作りあげる _v_ make up

作り直す _v_ remake

作る _v_ manufacture

告げる _v_ inform

つける _v_ immerse

伝える _v_ acquaint

土 _n_ soil

続いて起こる _adj_ subsequent

続く _v_ continue, last

つつくこと _n_ peck

続ける _v_ carry on

続けること _n_ continuation

慎み深い _adj_ chaste

慎む v abstain

つつましさ n modesty

包む v wrap, envelop

つづり n spelling

綱 n leash

つながり n association, tie

つながる n link

綱引き v tow

つねる v nip

翼 n wing

翼板 n blade

唾をはく v spit

つぶやき v mumble

つぼ n pot, urn

つぼみ n bud

妻 n wife

つま先 n tiptoe

つまむ v pinch

つまむこと n pinch

つまらない adj frivolous

つまらなくする v trivialize

詰まる v clog

罪 n sin

積み上げる v heap

積み重なる v pile

積み重ね n stack, pile

積み重ねる v pile up

摘み取る v pick

積荷 n freight

積荷目録 v manifest

罪のない adj impeccable

罪深い adj sinful

罪滅ぼし n expiation

罪滅ぼしをする v expiate

罪を犯す v sin

つむじ風 n cyclone

つめ n nail

詰め込む v cram

詰め物 n padding

強い adj strong

強い願望 n aspiration

強い好み n penchant

強い主張 n insistence

強く押すこと n shove

強く主張する v insist

強く勧める v exhort

強くたたく v smack

強く投げる v hurl

強くなる v toughen

強まる v intensify

貫く v penetrate

釣り合い n balance

つり革 n strap

ツル n crane

つる n vine

つるす v suspend

つ

# て

手 *n* hand
出合う *v* encounter
手厚いもてなし *n* hospitality
提案 *n* suggestion
提案する *v* suggest
低下する *v* degrade
定義する *v* define
定義する *n* definition
定期的に *adv* regularly
提供 *n* input
定期旅客機 *n* airliner
提携 *n* affiliation
提携する *v* affiliate
抵抗 *n* resistance
抵抗する *v* resist
抵抗できない *adj* irresistible
帝国 *n* empire
帝国主義 *n* imperialism
偵察 *n* scout
停止 *adj* standstill
停止 *n* stop
デイジー *n* daisy
停止する *v* halt
定時の *adj* punctual
提出する *v* submit
ディスク *n* disk
訂正 *n* correction

訂正する *v* correct
停戦 *n* truce
停滞した *adj* constipated
停電 *n* blackout
抵当 *n* mortgage
提督 *n* admiral
丁寧 *n* politeness
丁寧な *adj* courteous
低木 *n* shrub
低木の茂み *n* bush
データベース *n* database
テープ *n* tape
テーブル掛け *n* tablecloth
手桶 *n* pail
手押し車 *n* wheelbarrow
手おの *n* hatchet
手がかり *n* clue
手書き *n* handwritting
手紙 *n* letter
手紙を書く *v* write
手柄 *n* exploit, feat
敵 *n* adversary
敵意 *n* animosity
敵意を持った *adj* hostile
適応 *n* adaptation
適応する *v* accommodate
適応性のある *adj* adaptable
敵国 *n* enemy
出来事 *n* event, incident

適した *adj* proper
適している *adj* suitable
適時の *adj* timely
適する *v* fit
適正な *adj* adequate
適切な *adj* appropriate
敵対 *n* opposition
できない *adj* unable
適用できる *adj* applicable
できるだけ～ *c* inasmuch as
出口 *n* exit, way out
手首 *n* wrist
出くわす *v* come across
でこぼこの *adj* rough
デザート *n* dessert
手作業の *adj* manual
手触り *n* touch
弟子 *n* disciple
手品 *n* magic
手品師 *n* magician
手順 *n* procedure
手錠 *n* handcuffs
手錠をかける *v* handcuff
手数料 *n* fee
テストを行う *v* test
手すり *n* handrail
鉄 *n* iron
撤回 *n* repeal
撤回する *v* recant

哲学 *n* philosophy
哲学者 *n* philosopher
デッキ *n* deck
撤去 *n* clearance
手作りの *adj* homemade
撤退 *n* withdrawal
撤退した *adj* withdrawn
撤退する *v* retreat
手続き *n* proceedings
徹底的な *adj* thorough
徹底的に *adv* in depth
鉄道路線 *n* railroad
出っ張り *n* bulge
鉄砲 *n* gun
徹夜の看病 *n* vigil
出て行く *v* pass out
出てくる *v* come out
手に入れる *v* obtain
テニス *n* tennis
手荷物 *n* luggage
テノール *n* tenor
手のひら *n* palm
手配する *v* arrange
手配する *n* arrangement
手引き書 *n* handbook
デビュー *n* debut
でぶ *adj* fatty
手袋 *n* glove
でぶの *adj* fat

て

ても大きな *adj* massive

手榴弾 *n* grenade

テレパシー *n* telepathy

テレビ放送 *n* television

テロリスト *n* terrorist

テロリズム *n* terrorism

手渡す *v* hand over

点 *n* dot, point

電圧 *n* voltage

田園の *adj* pastoral

電化製品 *n* appliance

てんかん *n* epilepsy

転換 *n* switch, shift

転換する *v* veer

伝記 *n* biography

電気 *n* electricity

天気 *n* weather

電気技師 *n* electrician

電気の *adj* electric

電球 *n* bulb

電気をかける *v* galvanize

電気を流す *v* electrify

天空光 *n* skylight

典型的な *adj* typical

典型となる *v* epitomize

点検 *n* check

点検する *v* inspect

転向者 *n* convert

転向する *v* convert

天国 *n* heaven

天国のように *adj* heavenly

伝言 *n* message

天才 *n* angel

展示会 *n* exhibition

展示館 *n* pavilion

展示する *v* exhibit

電子の *adj* electronic

天使のような *adj* angelic

電車 *n* train

天井 *n* ceiling

天職 *n* vocation

伝説 *n* legend

伝染性の *adj* catching, infectious

電池 *n* battery

点滴 *n* drip

テント *n* tent

伝統 *n* tradition

点灯器 *n* lighter

伝道者 *n* missionary

天然痘 *n* smallpox

転覆する *v* overturn

展望 *n* perspective

電報 *n* telegram, wire

電報通達人 *n* messenger

デンマーク *n* Denmak

天文学 *n* astronomy

天文学者 *n* astronomer

天文学の *adj* astronomic

て

電話 *n* telephone
電話の音 *n* buzz
電話を切る *v* hang up
電話をする *v* call, phone
〜である一方で *c* whereas
〜でない *adv* not
〜でない限り *c* unless
〜ではあるが *c* although
〜で終わる *v* end up
〜で承知する *v* settle for
〜で生まれた *v* be born

# と

ドア *n* door
度合い *n* degree
ドイツ *n* Germany
ドイツ人 *adj* German
トイレ *n* rest room
塔 *n* tower
胴 *n* torso
銅 *n* copper
同意 *n* agreement
どういうわけか *adv* somehow
同意しない *v* disagree
同意する *v* agree, assent
統一 *n* unification

統一する *v* unify
動員する *v* mobilize
投影する *v* project
灯火 *n* lamp
同化 *n* assimilation
動画 *n* animation
同額 *n* parity
同化する *v* assimilate
導管 *n* duct
動機 *n* incentive
動悸 *n* throb
同義語 *n* synonym
道義心 *n* conscience
等級 *n* grade
闘牛 *n* bull fight
闘牛士 *n* bull fighter
同級生 *n* classmate
同業組合 *n* guild
同業者 *n* peer
道具 *n* gadget, tool
洞くつ *n* cave, grotto
統計 *n* statistic
道化師 *n* clown
統合 *n* integration
同好会 *n* club
投光照明 *n* floodlight
統合する *v* integrate
同行する *v* accompany
投獄された *v* incarcerate

同国人 *n* compatriot

投獄する *v* jail

動作 *n* movement

投資 *n* investment

動詞 *n* verb

同志 *n* partisan

投資家 *n* investor

投資する *v* invest

同時に起きた *adj* concurrent

同時に起こる *v* coincide

凍傷 *n* frostbite

同情 *n* compassion

同情する *v* sympathize

同情的な *adj* compassionate

同世代の人々 *n* generation

当然 *adv* naturally

同窓会 *n* reunion

灯台 *n* lighthouse

到着 *n* arrival

到着する *v* arrive

童貞 *n* virgin

堂々たる *adj* magnificent

同等でない *adj* unequal

同等と見なす *v* equate

同等の *adj* equal

道徳上の *adj* moral

道徳心がない *adj* amoral

道徳性 *n* morality

導入 *n* installation

導入する *v* install

糖尿病 *n* diabetes

糖尿病の *adj* diabetic

頭皮 *n* scalp

投票 *n* voting, poll

投票する *v* vote

頭部 *n* ridge

東風 *n* Easter

同封する *v* enclose

東部地方の人 *n* easterner

動物 *n* animal

動物園 *n* zoo

動物学 *n* zoology

動物の死体 *n* carcass

同胞 *n* brethren

逃亡者 *n* fugitive

東方へ *adv* eastward

動脈 *n* artery

透明 *n* clearness

同盟 *n* alliance

同盟国 *n* ally

動名詞 *n* gerund

同盟している *adj* allied

同盟する *v* ally

透明度 *n* clarity

透明な *adj* clear

トウモロコシ *n* corn

東洋 *n* orient

動揺させる *adj* disturbing

動揺させる *v* perturb

動揺した *adj* shaken

東洋の *adj* oriental

到来 *n* coming

同僚 *n* colleague

道路 *n* road

登録 *n* registration

登録する *v* register

討論 *n* debate

討論する *v* debate

当惑させる *v* confound

遠い *adv* far

遠くに *adv* afar

トースター *n* toaster

ドープ塗料 *n* dope

遠ぼえ *n* howl

遠ぼえする *v* howl

ドーム *n* dome

通り *n* street

通り抜ける *v* go through

通る *v* pass

都会の *adj* urban

トカゲ *n* lizard

溶かす *adj* solvent

とがる *v* sharpen

時たま *adv* occasionally

時々 *adv* sometimes

毒 *n* poison, toxin

解く *v* resolve

得意の *adj* elated

独裁者 *n* dictator

独裁的な *adj* despotic

得策の *adj* expedient

特質 *n* trait

読者 *n* reader

特殊芸 *n* specialty

特賞 *n* jackpot

独身者 *n* bachelor

独身の *n* celibacy

毒する *v* poison

独占 *n* monopoly

独奏会 *n* recital

独断的な *adj* dogmatic

戸口 *n* doorway

戸口の呼び鈴 *n* doorbell

特徴 *n* feature

特徴のある *adj* characteristic

特定する *v* pinpoint

特定の *adj* particular

得点 *n* score

得点する *v* score

独特の *adj* distinctive

特に *adv* especially

独白 *n* monologue

特別観覧席 *n* grandstand

特別室 *adj* de luxe

特別賞与 *n* bonus

特別な *adj* special

と

特別の *adj* express
毒ヘビ *n* viper
匿名 *n* anonymity
匿名の *adj* anonymous
特有な *adj* peculiar
特有の *adj* unique
独立 *n* independence
独力の *adj* singlehanded
得をする *v* benefit
とげ *n* thorn, splinter
時計 *n* watch
時計屋 *n* watchmaker
溶けない *adj* insoluble
溶けやすい *adj* soluble
遂げられる *adj* attainable
解ける *v* unravel, thaw
溶ける *v* dissolve
どこに *adv* where
どこに～ない *adv* nowhere
どこへ～しても *c* wherever
登山 *n* climbing
都市 *n* city
年 *n* year
どじ *n* butchery
年上の *adj* senior
閉じ込められた *adj* pent-up
閉じ込める *v* lock up
年下の人 *adj* junior
都市の *adj* civic

土砂降り *n* downpour
図書館 *n* library
図書館員 *n* librarian
怒声 *n* roar
土台 *n* foundation
土壇場 *n* showdown
途中で立ち寄る *v* stop by
どちらか *adj* which
どちらか一方の *adj* either
特許権 *n* patent
特許の *adj* patent
特許を与える *v* charter
ドッキングする *v* dock
特権 *n* privilege
突進 *v* dash
突然 *adv* suddenly
突然～しだす *v* burst into
突然の *adj* sudden
取っ手 *n* knob
取っておく *v* spare
取って代わる *v* supersede
突破口 *n* breakthrough
突発 *n* outbreak
突風 *n* gust
突風の吹く *adj* gusty
とても *adv* very
とても小さい *adj* tiny
とても愉快な *adj* hilarious
とどろく *v* growl

と

トナカイ *n* reindeer

隣の *adj* adjoining

怒鳴る *v* roar, yell

とにかく *pro* anyhow

どのようにして *adv* how

とはいえ *c* nonetheless

飛び板 *n* springboard

飛び込み *n* diving, plunge

飛び込む *v* plunge, dive

飛び地 *n* enclave

飛び跳ねる *v* leap

飛ぶ *v* jump

途方もない *adj* exorbitant

トマト *n* tomato

止まる *v* stop, shut off

泊まる *v* stop over

富 *n* fortune, wealth

留め金 *n* buckle

留める *v* fasten

ともかくも *adv* someway

友達 *n* friend

伴う *v* involve

どもる *v* stammer

土曜日 *n* Saturday

トラ *n* tiger

とらえる *v* grip

捕らえる *v* capture, catch

トラック運転手 *n* trucker

トランペット *n* trumpet

鳥 *n* bird

取り上げる *v* expropriate

取扱説明書 *n* manual

取り入れる *v* take in

取り換え *n* swap

取り返す *v* win back

取り掛かる *v* get down to

鳥かご *n* cage

取り決め *n* appointment

取り組む *v* tackle

取り消し *n* annulment

取り消しする *v* cancel

取り消す *v* invalidate

取り込む *v* ingest

取り壊し *n* demolition

取り出す *v* take out

とりで *n* fort

取り除く *v* defuse

取引 *n* transaction

取引材料 *n* dealings

取引条件 *n* terms

取り巻き連中 *n* crony

取り巻く *v* encircle

取り乱した *adj* distraught

取り戻す *v* recoup

取り戻すこと *n* resumption

取りやめる *v* call off

努力 *n* effort

努力する *v* endeavor

と

ドル *n* dollar, buck

トルコ *n* Turkey

トルコの *adj* Turk

奴隷 *n* slave

奴隷制 *n* slavery

どれでも *adj* any

泥 *n* mud

泥のついた *adj* muddy

泥棒 *n* burglar, thief

泥棒に入る *v* burglarize

泥よけ *n* fender

トン *n* ton

鈍感な *adj* insensitive

ドングリ *n* acorn

飛んだり *adj* jumpy

どんふうにでも *c* however

どんぶり *n* bowl

とんま *n* jerk

～と *c* and

～と一緒に *pre* with

～と見なす *v* regard

～と似ている *v* resemble

～と衝突する *v* bump into

～と等しい *adj* tantamount to

どん欲な *adj* lustful

# な

内向的な *adj* introvert

内蔵式の *adj* built-in

ナイチンゲール *n* nightingale

ナイフ *n* knife

内部 *adj* inside

内部の *adj* inner, interior

内報 *n* tip

内密 *n* secrecy

内密の *adj* clandestine

内陸に *adv* inland

内陸の *adj* inland

長い *adj* long

長いす *n* couch

長居する *v* linger

長い冒険 *n* odyssey

長靴 *n* boot

長さ *n* length

長談義 *n* litany

長続きする *adj* lasting

中で *pre* in

仲直りをする *v* reconcile

中に入る *v* come in

中庭 *n* courtyard, patio

長年の *adj* long-standing

長引かせる *v* protract

長引く *adj* protracted

仲間 *n* companion, pal

仲間同士 n fellowship
中身 n filling
眺める v view
流れ n flow
流れる v flow
泣き声 n cry
泣き叫ぶ v cry out, wail
泣く v cry
鳴く v crow
慰め n consolation
慰める人 n comforter
殴り返す v hit back
殴り書きする v scribble
殴る v beat
嘆き n grief
嘆き悲しむ v weep, wail
嘆く v mourn
投げ捨てる v dump
投げる v cast
名残 n vestige
なぜ adv why
なぜならば c because
なぞなぞ n riddle
なだめる v appease
雪崩 n avalanche
夏 n summer
捺印 v impress
なで回す v fondle
斜め線の adj diagonal

何か pro something
ナプキン n napkin
名札 n label
鍋 n pan
鍋料理 n casserole
生意気な adj cheeky
名前 n name
生ぬるい adj lukewarm
生の adj raw
鉛色の adj livid
波 n wave
涙 n tear
涙を誘う adj tearful
波乗りする v surf
滑らかな adj smooth
滑らかなこと n smoothness
滑らかに adv smoothly
滑らかにする v smooth
なめる v lick
納屋 n barn
慣らす v accustom
鳴り響く adj resounding
慣れる v acclimatize
なわ n rope
難儀 n ordeal
南京錠 n padlock
軟膏 n ointment
南西の n southwest
難聴 n deafness

な

何でも *pro* anything
南東 *n* southeast
何度も言う *v* reiterate
何の *adj* what
何の〜が〜でも *adj* whatever
難破 *v* wreck
南部人 *n* southerner
難民 *n* refugee
難問 *n* puzzle
〜なしで *pre* without
７０個の *adj* seventy
７個の *adj* seven

# に

荷 *n* load
似合いの *adj* fitting
におい *v* smell
においを嗅ぐ *v* sniff
苦い *adj* bitter
苦くさせる *v* embitter
苦々しく *adv* bitterly
苦味 *n* bitterness
握りこぶし *n* fist
握る *v* grasp
肉 *n* flesh
肉切り包丁 *n* chopper

憎しみ *n* loathing
肉体的に *adj* bodily
肉体的暴力 *n* assault
肉体の *adj* corporal
肉つきの良い *adj* plump
憎む *v* hate
肉屋 *n* butcher
憎らしい *adj* hateful
肉類 *n* meat
逃げ出す *v* break free
逃げる *v* flee
二言語使用者 *adj* bilingual
ニコチン *n* nicotine
煮こぼれる *v* boil over
西 *n* west
虹 *n* rainbow
ニシキヘビ *n* python
にじみ出る *v* exude
二重の *adj* dual
二重母音 *n* diphthong
西行きの *adv* westbound
ニス *n* varnish
ニスを塗る *v* varnish
日没 *n* sundown
日曜日 *n* Sunday
日記 *n* diary
荷造りする *v* pack
ニッケイ *n* cinnamon
ニッケル *n* nickel

なに

日光浴をする v bask
日食 n eclipse
ニット v knit
煮詰まって v boil down to
荷積みする v load
似ていない adj dissimilar
似ている adj alike, similar
似てること n likeness
荷馬車 n cart, wagon
鈍い adj blunt, dull
日本 n Japan
日本人 adj Japanese
荷物 n burden
荷物を積んだ adj loaded
入院させる v hospitalize
入学する v enroll
乳牛 n cow
入札 n bid
入札する v bid
入手する v procure
入場 n admittance
ニュース放送 n newscast
入隊する v enlist
柔和な adj meek
尿 n urine
二流の adj mediocre
煮る v simmer
ニレの木 n elm
庭 n garden

ニワトリ n chicken
荷を負わす v burden
荷をほどく v unpack
任意の adj optional
人気がない adj unpopular
人気のある adj popular
人魚 n mermaid
人形 n doll
人間 n human being
人間の adj human
認識 n awareness
妊娠 n pregnancy
にんじん n carrot
妊娠した adj pregnant
妊娠中絶 n abortion
忍耐 n patience
ニンニク n garlic
任命する v appoint
～に pre at
～にくっつく v stick to
～について pre about
～について行く v follow
～につき pre per
～になる v become
～にもかかわらず c despite
～によって pre by
～によれば pre according to
～に囲まれて pre amid
～に衣服を着せる v clothe

に

～に沿う *v* live up
～に関して *pre* concerning
～に気が付く *v* notice, realize
～に疑いを抱く *adj* sceptic
～に苦しむ *v* suffer from
～に穴を開ける *v* perforate
～に向かう *pre* towards
～に合図する *v* beckon
～に取り掛かる *v* set about
～に従う *v* obey
～に申し込む *v* apply for
～に接して *pre* on
～に先行する *adj* preceding
～に貸す *v* lend
～に値する *v* merit
～に値する *adj* worthy
～に知らせる *v* notify
～に沈む *v* sink in
～に追いつく *v* catch up
～に入り込む *v* tap into
～に備える *v* brace for
～に風を通す *v* ventilate
～に報いる *v* reward
～に目隠しをする *v* blindfold
～に立ち向かう *v* face up to
～に隣接する *v* adjoin
２０個の *adj* twenty
２回 *adv* twice
２月 *n* February

２個の *adj* two
２倍の *adj* double

# ぬ

縫い針 *n* needle
縫い目 *n* seam, stitch
縫い目のない *adj* seamless
縫い物をする *v* sew
ヌーディスト *n* nudist
ぬかるみ *n* quagmire
ぬぐう *v* wipe
盗む *v* rob, steal
布 *n* cloth
布片 *n* patch
布の袋 *n* sack
沼地 *n* swamp
塗る *v* anoint
脱ぐ *v* put off

にぬ

# ね

根 *n* root
値上げ *n* raise
願わくは *adv* hopefully
ネクタイ *n* necktie
ねぐら *n* den
猫 *n* cat
値下げをする *v* mark down
ねじ *n* screw
ねじ回し *n* screwdriver
ねじる *v* twist
ねじること *n* wrench
ねじれ *n* twist
ねじれた *adj* twisted
ねじれる *v* screw
ネズミ *n* mouse, rat
値段 *n* price
値段の高い *adj* costly
熱 *n* fever, heat
熱意 *n* zest
熱がある *adj* feverish
熱狂 *n* frenzy
熱狂した *adj* frenetic
ネックレス *n* necklace
熱射病 *n* heatstroke
熱情 *n* zeal
熱心 *n* enthusiasm
熱心な *adj* fervent

熱帯の *adj* tropical
熱中する *v* enthuse
熱波 *n* heatwave
熱望 *n* eagerness
熱望する *v* aspire
熱烈な *adj* ardent, avid
寝場所 *n* bed
粘つく *adj* sticky
値引き *n* allowance
ねまき *n* nightgown
眠い *adj* drowsy
眠る *v* sleep
ねり菓子 *n* pastry
練る *v* bind
年4回の *adj* quarterly
粘液 *n* mucus
年月日 *n* date
年金 *n* pension
ねんざする *v* sprain
年次 *adj* annual
燃焼 *n* combustion
年少者 *n* juvenile
年少者の *adj* juvenile
年代記 *n* chronicle
年代順配列 *n* chronology
粘着性のもの *adj* adhesive
年長 *n* seniority
年長者 *n* elder
粘土 *n* clay

ね

年配の *adj* elderly
粘板岩 *n* slate
燃料 *n* fuel
燃料補給 *v* refuel
燃料を供給する *v* fuel
年齢 *n* age

# の

ノアの箱舟 *n* ark
ノイローゼの *adj* neurotic
脳 *n* brain
農家の庭 *n* farmyard
農業の *adj* agricultural
農業の *n* agriculture
濃紺 *adj* navy blue
野うさぎ *n* hare
農場 *n* farm, farming
農場経営者 *n* farmer
能なし *adj* moron
脳の *adj* cerebral
納品書 *n* invoice
納付 *n* payment
農夫 *n* peasant
濃密な *adj* dense
濃霧 *n* fog
能率 *n* efficiency

能率的でない *adj* inefficient
能率的な *adj* efficient
能力 *n* ability
能力がある *adj* capable
能力がない *adj* incapable
能力に欠ける *adj* inept
能力を奪う *v* incapacitate
ノート *n* notebook
逃れること *n* evasion
のこぎり *n* saw
のこぎりで切る *v* saw
残す *v* hand down
残り *n* surplus, residue
残りの *adj* remaining
残り火 *n* embers
残り物 *n* leftovers, remains
残る *v* remain
ノズル *n* nozzle
載せる *v* list
のぞき込む *v* look into
のぞき見する *v* peep
望ましい *adj* advisable
望み *n* wish
望む *v* desire, wish
ノック *n* knock
ノックする *v* knock
乗って *adv* aboard
乗っ取り *n* hijack
乗っ取り犯 *n* hijacker

ね
の

乗っ取る _v_ hijack
のど _n_ throat
喉が渇いた _adj_ thirsty
喉が渇く _v_ thirst
ののしる _v_ damn
伸ばす _v_ hold out
伸ばすこと _n_ reach
野原 _n_ field
延びる _v_ lengthen
伸びる _v_ extend, stretch
述べる _v_ mention, state
上り坂の _adv_ uphill
昇る _v_ rise
ノミ _n_ flea
飲み込む _v_ swallow
飲み物 _n_ drink
飲む _v_ drink
のり _n_ glue, paste
乗組員 _n_ crew
乗り越える _v_ get over
乗り継ぎ _n_ connection
糊づけした _adj_ starchy
のりをつける _v_ paste
乗る _v_ ride
ノルウエー _n_ Norway
ノルウエー人 _adj_ Norwegian
呪い _v_ curse
のろう _v_ cuss
～の _pre_ of

～のおかげで _adv_ owing to
～のせいにする _v_ attribute
～のそばに _pre_ beside
～のために _pre_ because of
～のふりをする _v_ pretend
～のままで _adv_ as
～のように _c_ as
～の間に _pre_ among
～の近くに _pre_ near
～の原因になる _v_ cause
～の限度を超す _v_ overstep
～の後ろに _pre_ behind
～の向こう側に _pre_ over
～の処置を誤る _v_ mismanage
～の上に _pre_ above, upon
～の状態で _v_ be
～の真下に _pre_ beneath
～の前に _pre_ before
～の代わりに _n_ lieu
～の中 _pre_ within
～の内部に _pre_ inside
～の目録を作る _v_ catalog
～の予定を決める _v_ schedule

の

# は

歯 *n* tooth
葉 *n* leaf
場合 *n* instance
把握 *n* grasp
把握する *v* perceive
パーセント *adv* percent
パーティー *n* party
バーテンダー *n* barman
ハードウエア *n* hardware
ハープ *n* harp
バーベキュー *n* barbecue
バール *n* crowbar
灰 *n* ash
肺 *n* lung
パイ *n* pie
灰色 *adj* gray
灰色がかった *adj* grayish
ハイエナ *n* hyena
肺炎 *n* pneumonia
バイオリン *n* violin, fiddle
倍加する *v* redouble
配管工 *n* plumber
配管工事 *n* plumbing
排気 *v* exhaust
廃棄する *v* scrap
配給量 *n* ration
廃墟 *n* devastation

ハイキング *n* hike
バイク *n* bike
配偶者 *n* spouse
拝啓 *n* greetings
背景 *n* background
背後の *adv* back
灰皿 *n* ashtray
廃止する *v* revoke
歯医者 *n* dentist
敗者 *n* loser
買収 *n* corruption
買収された *adj* corrupt
買収される *v* corrupt
買収する *v* buy off
排出する *v* discharge
売春宿 *n* brothel
陪審 *n* jury
排水 *n* drainage
排水路 *n* diversion
はい進む *v* scramble
配達 *n* delivery
配達する *v* deliver
配置 *n* deployment
配置につく *v* deploy
入ってくる *adj* incoming
売店 *n* stall, kiosk
配当 *n* dividend
梅毒 *n* syphilis
パイナップル *n* pineapple

倍になる *v* double

売買する *v* traffic

廃物 *n* refuse

ハイフン *n* hyphen

敗北 *n* defeat

はい回る *adj* creepy

俳優 *n* actor

培養液 *n* broth

配慮 *n* care

配慮した *adj* discreet

入る *v* enter, go in

入ること *n* admission

入ることを許す *v* admit

配列 *n* array

パイロット *n* pilot

パイント *n* pint

はうこと *v* creep

羽織る服 *n* coverup

墓 *n* grave

ばか *adj* stupid

破壊 *n* destruction

墓石 *n* gravestone

破壊者 *n* vandal

破壊する *v* destroy

破壊的な *adj* devastating

はがき *n* card

ばかげた *adj* absurd

ばかな *adj* dumb, idiotic

はかない *adj* transient

ばかばかしい *adj* laughable

計り知れない *adj* invaluable

計る *v* gauge

測る *v* measure

量る *v* scale

吐き気 *n* nausea

吐き気を催す *adj* squeamish

履き物 *n* footwear

掃く *v* sweep

吐く *v* vomit

爆撃 *n* bombing

拍車 *n* spur

伯爵夫人 *n* countess

拍車をかける *v* spur

拍手 *n* applause

拍手する *v* applaud, clap

莫大な *adj* enormous

はく奪 *n* deprivation

爆弾 *n* bomb

爆弾の金属片 *n* shrapnel

爆竹 *n* firecracker

ハクチョウ *n* swan

バクテリア *n* bacteria

白熱する *v* glow

爆発 *n* outburst

爆発音 *n* explosion

爆発する *v* explode, blow

爆発性の *adj* explosive

爆風 *n* blast

**は**

| | |
|---|---|
| 博物館 n museum | 破産した adj bankrupt |
| 薄片 n slice | 橋 n bridge |
| 白墨 n chalk | 端 n verge, edge |
| 薄明 n twilight | 恥 n shame |
| 歯車 n gear | 恥じ入らせる v shame |
| はげ頭の adj bald | はしか n measles |
| 激しい adj intensive | はしけ n barge |
| 激しい活動 n exertion | はしご n ladder |
| 激しい苦痛 n anguish | 恥知らずな adj shameless |
| 激しい振動 n concussion | 始まり n inception |
| 激しい非難 n condemnation | 始まる v stem, begin |
| 激しい雷雨 n thunderstorm | 初め n beginning |
| 激しく adv madly | 初めには adv initially |
| 激しく打つ v pound | 馬車 n carriage |
| 激しく揺する v convulse | パジャマ n pajamas |
| ハゲタカ n buzzard | 場所 n location, position |
| バケツ n bucket | 波状の adj wavy |
| バゲット n baguette | 柱 n pillar, post |
| ハゲワシ n vulture | 走り去る v run away |
| 派遣する v dispatch | 走る v run |
| 派遣団 n mission | バス n bus |
| 箱 n box | 恥ずかしい adj ashamed |
| 歯応えの良い adj crunchy | 恥ずかしい v embarrass |
| 運ぶ v carry | 恥ずかしそうな adj shy |
| 運んでいる adj laden | バス車庫 n depot |
| バザー n bazaar | 外す v undo |
| はさみ n scissors | バスで行く v bus |
| 破産 n bankruptcy | 恥ずべき adj dishonorable, shameful |
| 破産させる v bankrupt | |

は

| | |
|---|---|
| 外れる *v* unfasten | 罰金 *n* fine |
| バスローブ *n* bathrobe | 罰金を科す *v* fine |
| 派生的な *adj* derivative | バックパック *n* backpack |
| 破損 *n* disrepair | バックログ *n* backlog |
| 破損する *v* damage | 白血病 *n* leukemia |
| 旗 *n* flag | 発見 *n* discovery |
| バター *n* butter | 発見する *v* discover |
| 裸 *n* nudity | 発酵 *n* ferment |
| 裸の *adj* nude, naked | 発酵する *v* ferment |
| はたく *v* slap | 発射 *n* launch |
| 肌寒い *adj* chilly | 発射体 *n* projectile |
| はだしの *adj* barefoot | 発射する *v* launch |
| 旗棒 *n* flagpole | 発疹 *n* rash |
| はためく *v* flog | 罰すべき *adj* punishable |
| 働き *n* operation | 罰する *v* punish |
| 働きかける *v* lobby | 罰すること *n* punishment |
| 働く *v* work | 発生 *n* occurrence |
| 働く人 *n* worker | 発生する *v* happen, occur |
| 八月 *n* August | 発送人 *n* sender |
| はちみつ *n* honey | バッタ *n* locust |
| は虫類 *n* reptile | 発展 *n* development |
| 発煙筒 *n* flare | 発電機 *n* generator |
| 発芽する *v* sprout | 発展する *v* develop |
| 発汗 *n* perspiration | バット *n* bat |
| 発揮する *v* exert | 発表 *n* presentation |
| 発狂した *adj* demented | 発砲 *n* gunfire, shot |
| はっきりと *adv* clearly | 発明する *v* devise, invent |
| はっきりと言う *v* profess | 発明の才 *n* ingenuity |
| 白金 *n* platinum | 発明品 *n* invention |

は

果てしのない *adj* unending

派手な *adj* flashy

ハト *n* dove, pigeon

波止場 *n* dock

歯止め *n* slipper

鼻 *n* nose

花飾り *n* garland

鼻口部 *n* muzzle

話し合う *v* confer

話をやめる *v* shut up

話す *v* speak, talk

放つ *v* emit

鼻であしらう *v* snub

鼻であしらうこと *n* snub

バナナ *n* banana

花蜂 *n* bee

華々しい *adj* flamboyant

花火 *n* flower

花弁 *n* petal

華やかさ *n* pomposity

花嫁 *n* bride, groom

花嫁介添人 *n* bridesmaid

花嫁の *adj* bridal

離れて *adv* apart, away

離れていく *v* drift apart

離昇 *n* lift-off

離れる *v* loose

花輪 *n* wreath

羽 *n* feather

跳ね上げる *v* strike up

跳ね返り *n* bounce

跳ね返る *v* rebound

跳ね返る *adj* resilient

はねつける *v* rebuff

跳ねる *v* bounce

歯の *adj* dental

母 *n* mother

幅 *n* breadth, width

パパ *n* dad

はばかる *v* hold back

派閥 *n* sect

母であること *n* maternity

母の *adj* maternal

幅広い *adj* wide

阻む *v* deter

ハブ *n* hub

バブルガム *n* bubble gum

破片 *n* fragment

葉巻 *n* cigar

ハマグリ *n* clam

ハム *n* ham

はめ込まれた *adj* inlaid

破滅 *n* damnation

破滅的な *adj* disastrous

場面 *n* scene

刃物類 *n* cutlery

速い *adj* fast, quick

早く *adv* early

は

速く _adv_ quickly

速くなる _v_ quicken

速さ _n_ velocity

早過ぎる _adj_ premature

腹 _n_ abdomen, belly

バラ _n_ rose

払い終える _v_ pay off

払いのける _v_ brush aside

払い戻し _n_ rebate

払い戻す _v_ refund

バラバラにする _v_ rip apart

バラバラの _adv_ asunder

パラメーター _n_ parameters

腹をたてて _adj_ angry

はり _n_ beam

針 _n_ sting

はり紙 _n_ placard

ハリケーン _n_ hurricane

はりつけ _n_ crucifixion

張り付けにする _v_ crucify

張りつめた _adj_ uptight

春 _n_ spring

バルコニー _n_ balcony

パルプ _n_ pulp

バルブ _n_ valve

腫れ上がった _adj_ swollen

パレード _n_ parade

晴れた _adv_ fine

破裂 _n_ rupture

破裂させる _v_ rupture

破裂する _v_ burst

晴れ渡った _adj_ cloudless

版 _n_ edition, version

パン _n_ bread

範囲 _n_ extent

繁栄 _n_ prosperity

繁栄している _adj_ prosperous

繁栄する _v_ flourish, thrive

版画 _n_ engraving

ハンガー _n_ hanger

繁華街 _n_ downtown

ハンカチ _n_ handkerchief

反感 _n_ aversion

パン生地 _n_ dough

反逆 _n_ defiance, revolt

反逆者 _n_ rebel

反逆する _v_ revolt

半球体 _n_ dome

反響 _n_ feedback

番組 _n_ broadcast

半径 _n_ radius

反抗 _n_ mutiny

反抗する _v_ rebel

反抗的な _adj_ defiant

犯罪 _n_ crime, guilt

犯罪者 _adj_ criminal

ハンサムな _adj_ handsome

反射 _n_ reflection

は

反証する v refute

パン職人 n baker

帆船 n sailboat

ハンセン病 n leprosy

ハンセン病患者 n leper

搬送する v convey

ハンター n hunter

反対 n opposite

反対側に adv opposite

反対側の adj opposite

反対して pre against

反対する adj adverse

反対する v oppose

反対に adv conversely

判断 n judgment

反転する v flip

半島 n peninsula

反動 n kickback

判読可能な adj legible

判読できない adj illegible

ハンドバック n handbag

パントマイム v mime

犯人の追跡 n manhunt

反応 n reaction

反応する v react

反応の良い adj responsive

パンの身 n crumb

パンの耳 n crust

ハンバーガー n hamburger

販売 n sale

販売員 n salesman

販売業者 n dealer

反発 n backlash

反発する adj repulsive

半分 n half

半分になる v halve

半分の adj half

ハンモック n hammock

パン屋 n bakery

はんらん n flooding

反乱 n insurrection

はんらんする v flood

反論できない adj irrefutable

８０、８０個の adj eighty

８、８個の adj eight

繁殖する v breed, propagate

# ひ

火 n fire

日 n day

ピアス v pierce

ピアスをすること n piercing

日当たりの良い adj sunny

ピアニスト n pianist

ピアノ n piano

| | | | |
|---|---|---|---|
| ビーチ *n* beach | | 引き潮 *v* ebb |
| ビート *n* beet | | 引き出し *n* drawer |
| ビーバー *n* beaver | | 非喫煙者 *n* nonsmoker |
| ピーマン *n* bell pepper | | 引き継ぐ *v* take over |
| ビール *n* beer | | ひきつけ *n* fit |
| 控えめな *adj* lowkey | | 引き付けられる *v* gravitate |
| 控えめに *adv* sparingly | | ひきつける *v* attract |
| 控える *v* refrain | | ひきつけるもの *n* attraction |
| 比較 *n* comparison | | 引き取り *adv* inwards |
| 比較する *v* compare | | ひき肉 *n* mincemeat |
| 比較の *adj* comparative | | 引き抜く *v* extract |
| 美学の *adj* aesthetic | | 引き伸ばし *n* stretch |
| 東 *n* east | | 引き延ばす *v* defer |
| 東の *adj* eastern | | 引き渡す *v* extradite |
| 東回りの *adj* eastbound | | 低いもの *adj* low |
| 火がつく *v* ignite | | ひくこと *v* grind |
| 光 *n* light | | 悲劇 *n* tragedy |
| 光り輝く *adj* vivid | | 悲劇の *adj* tragic |
| 光る *v* gleam | | 非結晶質の *adj* amorphous |
| 光る *adj* shiny | | ひげをそる *v* shave |
| 悲観主義者 *n* pessimism | | 非現実的な *adj* unrealistic |
| 悲観的な *adj* pessimistic | | 非行 *n* delinquency |
| 引き上げる *v* hike | | 飛行 *n* flight, fly |
| 引き起こす *v* instigate | | 鼻孔 *n* nostril |
| 引きおろす *v* pull down | | 飛行機 *n* airplane |
| ヒキガエル *n* toad | | 飛行士 *n* aviator, flier |
| 引き金 *n* trigger | | 非公式 *n* informality |
| 引き金を引く *v* trigger | | 非公式に *adv* unofficially |
| 引き下がる *v* back down | | 非公式の *adj* informal |

| | |
|---|---|
| 非行集団 _n_ gang | ひそかに見張る _v_ spy |
| 飛行場 _n_ airfield | ひだ _n_ pleat |
| 尾行する _v_ tail | 浸すこと _n_ immersion |
| 非合法の _adj_ unlawful | ビタミン _n_ vitamin |
| 飛行メガネ _n_ goggles | 浸る _v_ soak |
| 被告人 _n_ defendant | 悲嘆 _n_ lament |
| ひざ _n_ knee | 備蓄 _n_ stockpile |
| ひざのお皿 _n_ kneecap | 非嫡子 _n_ bastard |
| ひざまずく _v_ genuflect | 悲痛 _n_ pang |
| ひざまずくこと _v_ kneel | 引っかく _v_ scratch |
| 悲惨な _adj_ distressing | 引っ掛ける _v_ dupe |
| ひじ _n_ elbow | 棺 _n_ coffin |
| ひじ掛けいす _n_ armchair | ひっくり返る _v_ tumble |
| 批准 _n_ ratification | びっくりさせる _v_ startle |
| 批准する _v_ ratify | びっくりして _adj_ startled · |
| 秘書 _n_ secretary | 日付を付ける _v_ date |
| 美女 _n_ fair | 引っ越す _v_ move out |
| 非常線 _n_ cordon | ヒツジ _n_ sheep |
| 非常線を張る _v_ cordon off | ヒツジの毛 _n_ fleece |
| 非情な _adj_ ruthless | 必須の _adj_ indispensable |
| 非常に _adv_ exceedingly | ひったくる _v_ snatch |
| 非常に大きな _adj_ immense | ぴったりしない _adj_ misfit |
| 非常に恐ろしい _adj_ dreaded | ヒッチハイク _n_ hitchhike |
| 非常に長い _adj_ lengthy | 匹敵する _adj_ comparable |
| 非人格的な _adj_ impersonal | 引っ張る _v_ haul, pull |
| ヒスパニック _adj_ Hispanic | 蹄 _n_ hoof |
| 微生物 _n_ microbe | 必要 _n_ necessity |
| 秘跡 _n_ sacrament | 必要がある _v_ need |
| ヒ素 _n_ arsenic | 必要条件 _n_ prerequisite |

必要性 *n* need
必要な *adj* necessary
否定する *v* deny
否定できない *adj* undeniable
否定の *adj* negative
日照り *n* drought
ひどい *adj* awful
非道な *adj* outrageous
ひと塊 *n* loaf
ひと月おきの *adj* bimonthly
人柄 *n* personality
美徳 *n* virtue
人食い人種 *n* cannibal
ひどく嫌がる *v* resent
ひどく苦しむ *v* agonize
ひどく興奮した *adj* frenzied
ひどく寒い *adj* frigid
一口分 *n* morsel
ひどく悪い *adj* wicked
人質 *n* captive
一つの *a* a
人に与える *v* dole out
人の心を動かす *adj* touching
一晩中 *adv* overnight
ひと吹き *n* puff
人前で *adv* publicly
人見知りをする *adj* bashful
ひと目 *n* glance
ひとり *n* single

ひとすすり *n* sip
独りで *adj* alone
一人も〜ない *pro* no one
人を甘やかす *v* pamper
人を驚かせる *adj* alarming
避難 *n* refuge, retreat
非難 *n* blame, reproach
避難所 *n* shelter
避難する *v* evacuate
非難する *v* accuse, blame
皮肉 *n* irony
皮肉な *adj* ironic
皮肉な言葉 *n* cynicism
日の出 *n* sunrise
火のような *adj* fiery
火ばし *n* tongs
火花 *n* spark
批判 *v* criticize
批判的な *adj* critical
批評 *n* criticism
備品 *n* equipment
皮膚 *n* skin
非武装の *adj* unarmed
肥満した *adj* corpulent
肥満体の *adj* obese
秘密 *n* secret
秘密に *adv* secretly
秘密の *adj* undercover
微妙な *adj* subtle

| | |
|---|---|
| 悲鳴 *n* scream | 表示する *v* display |
| 悲鳴を上げる *v* shriek | 描写する *v* describe |
| 媚薬 *adj* aphrodisiac | 標準 *n* criterion |
| 百万長者 *adj* millionaire | 標準以下の *adj* substandard |
| 日焼け *n* burn | 標準化する *v* normalize |
| 日焼け止め *n* sunburn | 表題 *n* heading |
| 冷やす *v* refrigerate | 病棟 *n* ward |
| 百科事典 *n* encyclopedia | 平等 *n* equality |
| ヒューズ *n* fuse | 病人 *adj* patient |
| ピューレ *n* puree | 漂白剤 *n* bleach |
| ヒョウ *n* leopard | 漂白する *v* bleach |
| 票 *n* ballot, vote | 評判 *n* reputation |
| 費用 *n* cost, expense | 評判では *adv* reputedly |
| 病院 *n* hospital | 表明 *n* assertion |
| 評価 *n* appraisal | 表面 *n* surface |
| 氷河 *n* glacier | 秒読み *n* countdown |
| 費用がかかる *v* cost | 漂流している *adv* adrift |
| 評価する *v* evaluate | 漂流者 *n* drifter |
| 病気 *n* disease, illness | 漂流する *v* drift |
| 病気で *adj* ill, sick | 漂流物 *n* wreckage |
| 病気になる *v* sicken | 評論 *n* critique |
| 氷結 *v* freeze | 費用を負担する *v* defray |
| 評決 *n* verdict | 肥沃 *n* fertility |
| 表現 *n* expression | 日よけ *n* awning |
| 病原体 *n* virus | ひよこ *n* chick |
| 標語 *n* slogan | 開かれた *adj* open |
| 氷山 *n* iceberg | 開く *v* open, unfold |
| 標示 *n* sign | 平手打ち *n* slap, smack |
| 表示 *n* display | ピラミッド *n* pyramid |

比率 *n* rate
ビリヤード *n* billiards
肥料 *n* manure
非理論的な *adj* illogical
ヒル *n* leech
昼寝 *n* nap
ひるませる *v* daunt
ひるむ *adj* wimp
ヒレ *n* fin
卑劣な *adj* despicable
ひれ伏した *adj* prostrate
拾い上げる *v* pick up
疲労感 *n* tiredness
広がった *v* diffuse
広がる *v* spread
広く *adv* widely
広くなる *v* widen
広々とした *adj* spacious
広まる *v* disseminate
卑猥な *adj* obscene
火を消す *v* extinguish
火をつける *v* kindle
火を付ける *v* fire, torment
瓶 *n* bottle
ピン *n* pin
品位を落とす *v* debase
貧窮の *adj* needy
瓶首 *n* bottleneck
貧血 *n* anemia

貧血症の *adj* anemic
品行 *n* demeanor
貧困に陥った *adj* impoverished
ヒンジ *n* hinge
品質 *n* quality
ヒンジで動く *v* hinge
品種 *n* breed
ピンセット *n* tweezers
敏速な *adj* swift
ピンと張った *adj* strained
ピンと張ること *n* tension
瓶に詰める *v* bottle
頻発 *n* frequency
貧乏 *n* poverty
貧民 *n* poor
１００個の *adj* hundred
１００周年 *n* centenary
１００番目の *adj* hundredth
１００万 *n* million

# ふ

無愛想さ *n* bluntness
分厚い *adj* bulky
ファッション *n* fashion
不安 *n* uneasiness
不安定 *n* insecurity
不安定な *adj* precarious
不安な *adj* uneasy
不意に *adv* abruptly
フィヨルド *n* fjord
封印する *v* seal
風変わりな *adj* nutty
風景 *n* landscape
風景の *adj* scenic
封鎖 *n* blockade
封鎖する *v* blockade
風刺 *n* satire
風刺画 *n* caricature
風車 *n* windmill
ブース *n* booth
風俗習慣 *n* manners
フード *n* hood
封筒 *n* envelope
夫婦関係 *n* matrimony
風味がある *v* relish
風味のない *adj* insipid
フーリガン *n* hooligan
プール *n* pool

不運 *n* unhappiness
不運な *adj* unlucky
増えている *adj* increasing
フェリー *n* ferry
増える *v* increase
フェンシング *n* fencing
フェンス *n* fence
フォーク *n* fork
フォルダー *n* folder
深い *adj* deep
不快 *n* discomfort
深い穴 *n* pothole
深い裂け目 *n* chasm
部外者 *n* outsider
不快な *adj* nasty
不可解な *adj* puzzling
深さ *n* depth
不可知論者 *n* agnostic
不可とする *v* disapprove
不可能 *n* impossibility
不可能なこと *adj* impossible
深まる *v* deepen
不完全 *n* imperfection
不完全な *adj* deficient
不寛容 *n* intolerance
武器 *n* weapon
吹きかける *v* spray
吹き消す *v* blow out
不機嫌 *n* tantrum

不機嫌な *adj* cranky, sullen

吹き込む *v* indoctrinate

不吉な *adj* ominous

吹き出物 *n* pimple

ふき取る *v* wipe out

不気味な *adj* eerie, weird

普及する *v* prevail

不器用 *n* clumsiness

不器用な *adj* awkward

福音 *n* gospel

復元 *n* restoration

複合体 *adj* complex

複婚 *n* polygamy

複雑 *n* complication

複雑さ *n* complexity

複雑にする *v* complicate

副産物 *n* by-product

副詞 *n* adverb

復讐 *n* revenge

服従 *n* obedience

服従しない *adj* disobedient

復讐する *v* revenge

復讐をする *v* avenge

服飾品 *n* furnishings

複数形 *n* plural

複製 *v* duplicate

複製する *v* replicate

副題 *n* subtitle

不屈の精神 *n* fortitude

含む *v* contain

含める *v* include

膨らませる *v* blow up

膨らむ *v* inflate, swell

膨らんだ *adj* puffed

福利 *n* welfare

膨れ *n* swelling

膨れた *adj* bloated

膨れる *v* bloat

フクロウ *n* owl

袋に入れる *v* sack

嚢胞 *n* cyst

ふけ *n* dandruff

父系 *n* paternity

父権 *n* fatherhood

不健康な *adj* unhealthy

不幸な *adj* unhappy

不公平 *n* injustice

不公平な *adj* unfair, unjust

不合理な *adj* irrational

房 *n* cluster, bunch

負債 *n* debit, liability

不在の *adj* absent

ふざける *v* fool

房になる *v* cluster

不作法な *adj* vulgar

不死 *n* immortality

無事 *n* safety

武士 *n* warrior

ふ

不思議さ *n* mystery
不思議なもの *n* wonder
ふしだらな *adj* dissolute
不実の *adj* disloyal
不治の *adj* incurable
不自由にする *v* cripple
不十分な *adj* inadequate
負傷 *n* injury
不祥事 *n* scandal
不正直 *n* dishonesty
不正直な *adj* dishonest
腐食 *n* decay
侮辱 *n* insult, offense
腐食する *v* corrode
侮辱する *v* affront, insult
侮辱する *n* affront
侮辱的な *adj* offensive
不信 *n* mistrust
婦人科の *n* gynecology
不親切な *adj* unfriendly
不審に思う *v* mistrust
付随する *adj* corresponding
不成功の *adj* unsuccessful
不誠実さ *n* insincerity
不誠実な *adj* insincere
不正な *adj* abusive
防ぐ *v* prevent
武装解除する *v* disarm
武装した *adj* armed

武装する *v* arm
不足 *n* shortage, lack
部族 *n* tribe
付属する *v* pertain
ふた *n* lid
ブタ *n* pig, hog
舞台 *n* stage
双子 *n* twin
不確かな *adj* uncertain
再び *adv* again
再び現れる *v* reappear
豚肉 *n* pork
付着 *n* attachment
付着した *adj* attached
付着する *v* adhere
不忠 *n* disloyalty
不注意な *adj* careless
普通でない *adj* unusual
普通の *adj* natural
復活 *n* regeneration
復活させる *v* restore
二日酔いの *adj* crispy
復旧 *n* retrieval
復旧する *v* retrieve
フック *n* hook
物質 *n* material
沸騰する *v* boil
フットボール *n* football
物品 *n* goods

| | |
|---|---|
| ブツブツ言う v murmur | 船旅をする v cruise |
| 物々交換する v barter | 船積み n shipment |
| 不釣合い n imbalance | 船乗り n sailor |
| 物理学 n physics | 船酔いした adj seasick |
| 物理的に adj physically | 不妊の adj sterile |
| 不貞 n infidelity | 船 n ship, vessel |
| 不定期な adj irregular | 腐敗 n rot |
| 不適格と見なす v disqualify | 腐敗した adj putrid |
| 不適切な adj improper | 不必要な adj unnecessary |
| 不適当な adj unsuitable | 浮標 n buoy |
| ふてぶてしい adj audacious | 不品行 n misconduct |
| 不等 n inequality | 不品行をする v misbehave |
| ブドウ n grape | 不服従 n disobedience |
| 埠頭 n wharf | 部分 n portion |
| 不同意 n disapproval | 部分的な adj partial |
| 不統一 n disunity | 不平 n complaint |
| ブドウ園 n vineyard | 不平のもと n grievance |
| 不動産 n realty | 不平を言う v grumble |
| ブドウ糖 n glucose | 不変性 n constancy |
| 不道徳 n immorality | 普遍的な adj catholic |
| 不道徳な adj immoral | 不便な adj inconvenient |
| 不当な adj unjustified | 不偏の adj unbiased |
| 不当に adv unfairly | 不変の adj immutable |
| 不当に使う v exploit | 不変のもの adj constant |
| ブドウのつる n grapevine | 不法侵入する v trespass |
| 舞踏場 n ballroom | 不法な adj illicit |
| 不透明なもの adj opaque | 不満 v complain |
| 太綱 n cable | 不満 n displeasure |
| 太らせる v fatten | 不満な adj dissatisfied |

ふ

踏みつける *v* trample
不眠 *n* insomnia
不明確な *adj* imprecise
不名誉 *n* disgrace
不名誉な *adj* disgraceful
不毛の *adj* barren
部門 *n* sector
富裕 *n* opulence
不愉快な *adj* unpleasant
不愉快にする *v* displease
フライパン *n* frying pan
プライヤー *n* pliers
ブラウス *n* blouse
プラグを抜く *v* unplug
ブラシ *n* brush
フラシ天の *adj* plush
ブラジャー *n* bra
ブラシをかける *v* brush
プラスチック *n* plastic
ぶらつく *v* hang around
ブラックベリー *n* blackberry
ブラブラする *v* loiter
プラム *n* plum
フランス *n* France
フランス人 *adj* French
ブランチ *n* brunch
ブランデー *n* brandy
不利 *n* disadvantage
振り子 *n* pendulum

プリズム *n* prism
フリゼ *n* fries
武力侵略 *n* aggression
不倫 *n* adultery
プリンター *n* printer
古い *adj* old
部類 *n* category
奮い立たせる *v* incite
フルート *n* flute
震え *n* shiver
震える *v* quake, shake
故郷 *n* hometown
ブルジョワ *adj* bourgeois
プルトニウム *n* plutonium
振舞う *v* behave
無礼 *n* rudeness
無礼な *adj* impertinent
ブレーキ *n* brake
ブレスレット *n* bracelet
触れる *adj* tangible
触れる *v* touch
付録 *n* appendix
プログラマー *n* programmer
フロス *n* floss
フロントガラス *n* windshield
不和 *n* discord
糞 *n* crap, , dung
分 *n* minute
文 *n* sentence

雰囲気 n atmosphere
噴煙 n fumes
文化 n culture
分解 n disintegration
憤慨させる v exasperate
分解する v disintegrate
文学 n literature
噴火口 n crater
分割できない adj indivisible
分割払い n installment
分割返済する v amortize
文化の adj cultural
分岐 n ramification
奮起させる v inspire
奮起させる adj rousing
分散 n dispersal
分散する v disperse, scatter
分子 n molecule
分詞 n participle
噴出 n belch
噴出する v erupt, belch
文章 n text
文書化 n documentation
噴水 n fountain
分析 n analysis
分析する v analyze
分配 n distribution
分配する v distribute
分別 n discretion

分別がある adj prudent
分母 n denominator
文法 n grammar
文房具 n stationery
文脈 n context
文明 n civilization
文明化する v civilize
分離させる v isolate
分離する v segregate

# へ

ヘアドレッサー n hairdresser
ヘアピース n hairpiece
ヘアブラシ n hairbrush
米 n rice
平均 n average
平原 adj plain
平衡 n poise
併合 n annexation
平行して adv abreast
平行して pre alongside
平行線 n parallel
平衡を保つ v balance
閉鎖 n closure
平日 adj weekday
兵舎 n barracks

へ

閉店した *adj* closed
平凡 *n* mediocrity
平面 *n* flat
平和 *n* peace
平和な *adj* peaceful
ベーコン *n* bacon
ページ *n* page
へこみ *n* dent
へこむ *v* dent
へそ *n* belly button
ペダル *n* pedal
ベッド掛け *n* bedspread
ヘッドホン *n* headphones
別の方法で *adv* else
別離 *n* separation
ペニー *n* penny
ペニシリン *n* penicillin
蛇 *n* snake
ベビーシッター *n* babysitter
部屋 *n* room
へり *n* fringe
ペリカン *n* pelican
ヘリコプター *n* helicopter
減る *v* reduce
ベルギー *n* Belgium
ベルギーの *adj* Belgian
ベルト *n* belt
ヘルニア *n* hernia
ベルベット *n* velvet

ヘルメット *n* helmet
ベレー帽 *n* beret
ヘロイン *n* heroin
ペン *n* pen
偏愛 *n* predilection
変化 *n* transformation
変化する *v* mutate
変化に富む *adj* varied
変換 *n* conversion
返還 *n* restitution
変換する *v* transform
便宜 *n* expediency
ペンキ *n* paint
ペンキで塗る *v* paint
返却する *v* turn in
勉強する *v* study
返金 *n* refund
ペンギン *n* penguin
変形する *v* deform
偏見 *n* bias, prejudice
変更 *n* alteration
弁護士 *n* lawyer
返済 *n* repayment
返済する *v* pay back
返事 *n* reply
変質の *adj* queer
編集 *v* edit
偏執症の *adj* paranoid
変色する *v* color

返事をする v reply
片頭痛 n migraine
編成する v organize
変装 n disguise
変装させる v disguise
ペンダント n pendant
ベンチ n bench
便通 n bowels
変動する v fluctuate
へんとう腺 n tonsil
便秘 n constipation
弁明する v justify
便利 n convenience
便利な adj convenient

# ほ

帆 n sail
保育園 n nursery
ボイコット v boycott
ポイと投げる v toss
ボイラー n boiler
母音 n vowel
法 n statute
棒 n rod, pole
包囲攻撃 n siege
包囲攻撃をする v siege

包囲する v encompass
防衛 n defense
望遠鏡 n telescope
放火 n arson
崩壊 n collapse, ruin
妨害 n sabotage
崩壊する v collapse
妨害する v block
妨害物 n blockage
包括的な adv inclusive
放火犯 n arsonist
傍観者 n spectator
ほうき n broom
放棄 n abandonment
放棄する v renounce
防御 n defense
暴君 n tyrant
砲撃 n gunshot
方言 n dialect
冒険 n adventure
封建領主 n lord
宝庫 n casket
方向 n direction, way
膀胱 n bladder
芳香の adj balmy
報告 n report
報告する v report
報告を受ける v debrief
防護する v insulate

| | |
|---|---|
| 奉仕 *n* service | 暴動 *n* uprising, riot |
| 帽子 *n* hat | 報道によれば *adv* reportedly |
| 防止 *n* prevention | 暴動を起こす *v* riot |
| 放射 *n* radiation | 冒とく *n* sacrilege |
| 放射する *v* emanate | 冒とくする *v* blaspheme |
| 放射性降下物 *n* fallout | 放熱器 *n* radiator |
| 放出 *n* emission | 法の認めた *adj* lawful |
| 褒賞 *n* reward | 豊富 *n* abundance |
| 法人 *n* corporation | 報復 *n* vengeance |
| 防水加工した *adj* waterproof | 報復する *v* retaliate |
| 防水の *adj* watertight | 報復的な *adj* vindictive |
| 宝石 *n* gem, jewel | 豊富である *v* abound |
| 宝石商 *n* jeweler | 豊富な *adj* plentiful |
| 宝石店 *n* jewelry store | 方法 *n* step, method |
| 放送局 *n* broadcaster | 亡命 *n* defection |
| 放送される *v* air | 放免する *v* acquit |
| 包装紙 *n* wrapping | 訪問 *n* visit |
| 放送する *v* broadcast | 訪問者 *n* visitor |
| 包装を解く *v* unwrap | 抱擁 *n* embrace, hug |
| 包帯 *n* bandage | 暴落する *v* nosedive |
| 膨大な *adj* vast | 法律 *n* law |
| 包帯をする *v* bandage | 法律家 *n* attorney |
| 砲弾 *n* bombshell | 法律上の *adj* legal |
| 放置された *adj* derelict | 法律制定 *n* legislation |
| 膨張 *n* inflation | 法律を制定する *v* legislate |
| 法廷 *n* tribunal | 放り投げる *v* throw up |
| 方程式 *n* equation | 暴力 *n* violence |
| 棒で支える *v* stick | 暴力団員 *n* gangster |
| 報道 *n* coverage | 暴力的な *adj* violent |

ほ

**ほ**

| | |
|---|---|
| 防塁 *n* bulwark | 撲滅する *v* stamp out |
| 法令 *n* decree | ほぐれる *v* loosen |
| 法令を定める *v* decree | 墓穴 *n* tomb |
| 放浪者 *n* gypsy | 保険 *n* insurance |
| ほえ声 *n* bark | 保険に入る *v* insure |
| ほえる *v* bark | 保護 *n* protection |
| ほお *n* cheek | 歩行者 *n* pedestrian |
| ホース *n* hose | 母国 *n* homeland |
| ポーチ *n* porch | 保護施設 *n* asylum |
| ボート *n* boat | 保護者 *n* guardian |
| ほおひげ *n* whiskers | 保護する *v* protect |
| ほお骨 *n* cheekbone | 誇らしげに *adv* proudly |
| ポーランド *n* Poland | ほこり *n* dust |
| ボール紙 *n* cardboard | 誇り *n* pride |
| 捕獲 *n* capture | 誇る *adj* proud |
| ほかに勝る *v* excel | 星 *n* star |
| ほかの *adj* other | 保持 *n* retention |
| ほかの場所に *adv* elsewhere | 星占い *n* astrology |
| 朗らかな *adj* genial | 干し草 *n* hay |
| 保管 *n* custody | 干し草の山 *n* haystack |
| 簿記 *n* bookkeeping | 星印 *n* asterisk |
| 簿記係 *n* bookkeeper | 干しぶどう *n* raisin |
| 補強する *v* fortify | 保釈 *n* bail |
| ボクサー *n* boxer | 保釈する *v* bail out |
| 牧師 *n* pastor | 補修を行う *v* service |
| ボクシング *n* boxing | 保守的な人 *adj* conservative |
| 牧草地 *n* meadow | 保証 *n* guarantee |
| 北東 *n* northeast | 保障 *n* indemnity |
| 北部地方の人 *adj* northerner | 補償金 *n* compensation |

ほ

| | |
|---|---|
| 保証契約 *n* warranty | 掘っ建て小屋 *n* shack |
| 保証する *v* certify | 没頭 *n* preoccupation |
| 保証人 *n* guarantor | 没頭した *adj* engrossed |
| 補助するもの *adj* subsidiary | 勃発する *v* break out |
| 補助の *adj* auxiliary | ホップ *v* hop |
| ポスター *n* poster | ポップコーン *n* popcorn |
| 母性 *n* motherhood | 北方の *adj* northern |
| 細い *adj* slim | ポテト *n* potato |
| 細い部分 *adj* thin | ホテル *n* hotel |
| 舗装道路 *n* pavement | 歩道 *n* sidewalk |
| 補足 *n* complement | 歩道の縁石 *n* curb |
| 細長い *adj* tenuous | 施し物 *n* alms |
| 細長い切れ *n* strip | ほとばしり *n* outpouring |
| 細長く切る *v* slit | ほとんど *adv* almost |
| 保存 *n* conservation | ほとんど〜ない *adv* hardly |
| ボタン *n* button | 哺乳動物 *n* mammal |
| ボタン穴 *n* buttonhole | 骨 *n* bone |
| ボタンを外す *v* unbutton | 骨折って働く *v* toil |
| 墓地 *n* cemetery | 骨組み *n* framework |
| ホチキス *n* stapler | 骨組みを作る *v* frame |
| ホチキスでとめる *v* staple | 炎 *n* flame |
| ホチキスの針 *n* staple | ほのめかし *n* allusion |
| 歩調 *n* pace | ほのめかす *v* insinuate |
| 歩調をとって歩く *v* pace | 歩幅 *v* stride |
| 北極の *adj* arctic | 墓碑名 *n* epitaph |
| 発作 *n* spasm | 歩兵 *n* infantry |
| 没収 *n* confiscation | 粗石 *n* rubble |
| 没収する *v* confiscate | ほほ笑む *v* smile |
| ほっそりした *adj* slender | 褒め言葉 *n* compliment |

褒める *v* commend
ぼやく *v* grouch
ぼやけた *adj* blurred
ぼやける *v* blur
ボランティア *n* volunteer
掘り出す *v* unearth
保留中の *adj* pending
捕虜 *n* captive
掘る *v* dig
彫る *v* carve
ボルト *n* bolt
ポルトガル *n* Portugal
ボルトで留まる *v* bolt
ホルモン *n* hormone
ぼろ *n* rag
滅びる *v* perish
滅ぼす *v* annihilate
ボロボロの *adj* ragged
本 *n* book
本国送還する *v* deport
本質 *n* essence
本質的要素 *adj* essential
本筋をそれる *v* digress
本土 *n* mainland
ポンド *n* pound
本能 *n* instinct, urge
本部 *n* headquarters
ポンプ *n* pump
本物の *adj* genuine, live

本屋 *n* bookstore
翻訳者 *n* translator
翻訳する *v* translate
ぼんやりした *adj* vague
ぼんやりする *adj* dazed
本来は *adv* originally

**ほ**
**ま**

# ま

マーマレード *n* marmalade
舞い上がる *v* soar
マイクロ波 *n* microwave
マイクロホン *n* microphone
毎週の *adv* weekly
埋葬 *n* burial
巻いている *adj* curly
毎年の *adv* yearly
毎日の *adv* daily
毎日の *adj* everyday
マイル *n* mile
マイル距離 *n* mileage
前置き *n* preface
前書き *n* foreword
前に *adv* before
前に出る *v* pull ahead
前触れ *n* foretaste
前へ進む *v* advance

| | | | |
|---|---|---|---|
| 前向きの | *pre* facing | 魔術師 | *n* sorcerer |
| 前もって | *adv* beforehand | 魔術の | *adj* magical |
| 負かす | *v* defeat | 魔女 | *n* witch |
| 曲がったもの | *n* crook | 魔性の | *adj* diabolical |
| 曲がる | *v* curve, turn | 真正面から | *adv* head-on |
| 巻き上げ | *n* hoist | マス | *n* trout |
| 巻き上げる | *v* hoist | 麻酔 | *n* anesthesia |
| 巻き毛 | *n* curl | 貧しい | *adj* deprived |
| 巻き毛にする | *v* curl | 貧しく | *adj* meager |
| 巻き込まれた | *v* involved | 貧しく | *adv* poorly |
| 巻き込む | *v* embroil | マスト | *n* mast |
| 巻物 | *n* scroll | 混ぜ物をした | *v* adulterate |
| 紛らわしい | *adj* confusing | 混ぜる | *v* mingle |
| マグ | *v* mug | マゾヒズム | *n* masochism |
| 巻くこと | *adj* winding | まだ | *adv* still |
| 間口 | *n* frontage | 町 | *n* town |
| 枕 | *n* pillow | 待ち受ける | *v* await |
| 枕カバー | *n* pillowcase | 間違いない | *adj* unmistakable |
| マグロ | *n* tuna | 間違いの | *adj* incorrect |
| 負け犬 | *n* underdog | 間違った | *adj* mistaken, wrong |
| 曲げやすい | *adj* pliable | 間違った考え | *n* fallacy |
| 負ける | *v* lose | 待ちこがれる | *v* long for |
| 曲げる | *v* distort, bend | 町はずれ | *n* outskirts |
| 孫 | *n* grandchild | 待ち伏せする | *v* ambush |
| 孫息子 | *n* grandson | 町役場 | *n* town hall |
| 摩擦 | *n* friction | 待つ | *v* wait |
| 混ざる | *v* blend | 末期 | *n* winter |
| まじめな | *adj* serious | 真っ暗な | *adj* murky |
| まじめに | *adv* earnestly | まつげ | *n* eyelash |

ま

ま

待つこと *n* waiting
マッサージ *n* massage
真っすぐな *adj* straight
真っすぐの *adj* forthright
全く *adv* entirely
全く同じ *adj* identical
全くの *v* utter
マッチ *n* match
マット *n* mat
マットレス *n* mattress
マツの木 *n* pine
松葉杖 *n* crutch
的 *n* target
窓 *n* window
まどろみ *n* doze
まどろむ *v* doze
惑わせる *adj* misleading
的をはずす *v* miss
真夏 *n* midsummer
学ぶ *v* learn
免れる *v* get away
間抜け *n* idiot
まねる *v* simulate
まばたき *v* blink, wink
まばたき *n* wink
麻痺 *n* paralysis
麻痺させる *v* paralyze
まぶた *n* eyelid
魔法 *n* witchcraft

ママ *n* mom
豆 *n* bean
間もなく *adv* shortly, soon
守る *v* defend
麻薬 *n* drug
麻薬を常用する *v* dope
まゆ *n* brow
眉毛 *n* eyebrow
真夜中 *n* midnight
迷わせる *v* baffle
マラリア *n* malaria
マリネにする *v* marinate
丸括弧 *n* parenthesis
丸太 *n* log
まるまる太った *adj* chubby
まれな *adj* scarce, rare
周りに *pro* around
回り道 *n* detour
回る *v* circle
まん延した *adj* rampant
漫画 *n* cartoon
満場一致 *n* unanimity
マンション *n* condo
慢性の *adj* entrenched
満足感 *n* satisfaction
満足させる *v* satisfy
満足して *adj* glad
満足している *adj* content
満足できない *adj* ungrateful

**まみ**

満足な *adj* sufficient
満足のいく *adj* gratifying
真ん中 *n* midday
マンネリ *n* mannerism
万引き *n* shoplifting
満腹 *n* glut
マンモス *n* mammoth
満了する *v* expire
～まで *adv* till
～まで *pre* until
～も～しない *adv* either
～もまた *adv* also, too
～もまた～ない *adv* neither

# み

見いだす *v* find out
ミートボール *n* meatball
ミイラ *n* mummy
見える *v* appear
見落とす *v* overlook
見覚え *n* recognition
見下ろす *v* look down
磨く *v* polish
磨くこと *n* polish
見掛け倒しの *adj* deceptive
見方 *n* viewpoint

身勝手さ *n* selfishness
未完成の *adj* immature
未完成品 *adj* sketchy
右 *n* right
ミキサー *n* blender
右に *adv* right
右の *adj* right
水際 *n* brink
未決定の *adj* undecided
見事な *adj* stunning
見込み *n* prospect
未婚女性 *n* spinster
未婚の *adj* unmarried
ミサイル *n* missile
岬 *n* cape
短い *adj* short
短くする *v* abbreviate
短くまとめる *v* brief
短さ *n* brevity
惨めさ *n* misery
惨めな *adj* miserable
未熟 *n* immaturity
未熟者 *n* novice
見知らぬ人 *n* stranger
ミス *n* miss
ミス *v* malpractice
水 *n* water
水入れ *n* jug
湖 *n* lake

水気の多い *adj* succulent

見過ごし *n* oversight

水っぽい *adj* watery

水で薄める *v* water down

見捨てられた *adj* deserted

見捨てる *v* forsake

見捨てる人 *n* deserter

水の *adj* aquatic

水膨れ *n* blister

ミスプリント *n* misprint

水疱瘡 *n* chicken pox

みずみずしい *adj* juicy

水を浴びる *v* bathe

水をまく *v* irrigate

水をやる *v* water

店 *n* store

未成年者 *adj* minor

見せかけ *n* pretension

見せかけ *adj* shoddy

見せびらかす *v* show off

見せる *v* reveal, show

見せること *n* revelation

溝 *n* trench, ditch

見出し *n* index

満たしている *adj* satisfactory

満たす *v* saturate

乱れた *adj* deranged

道 *n* course, pass

道からそれる *v* stray

道しるべ *n* milestone

道にそれた *adj* stray

道に迷って *v* astray

導く *v* conduct, lead

満ちる *v* fill

蜜 *n* syrup

三つ編みの *n* braid

貢ぎ物 *n* tribute

見つけ出す *v* figure out

見つける *v* detect

密告者 *n* informer

密告する *v* snitch

密集 *n* congestion

密集した *adj* congested

密偵 *n* spy

密度 *n* density

ミツバチの巣 *n* hive

ミツバチの巣箱 *n* beehive

密封した *adj* hermetic

密封する *v* seal off

見積もり *n* estimation

見積もる *v* appraise

密輸 *n* contraband

密輸業者 *n* smuggler

密林 *n* jungle

見所 *n* highlight

認める *v* acknowledge

緑の *adj* green

緑の茂った *adj* lush

港 *n* port
南 *n* south
南の *adj* southern
南行きの *adv* southbound
源 *n* origin
見習い *n* apprentice
身なりを整える *v* brush up
醜い *adj* ugly
醜さ *n* ugliness
ミニスカート *n* miniskirt
身代金 *n* ransom
実り多い *adj* fruitful
未焙煎 *n* green bean
見張り *n* sentry
身ふり *n* gesture
身震い *n* shudder, thrill
身震いする *v* tremble
未亡人 *n* widow
見本 *n* sample
見守る *v* behold
耳 *n* ear
耳垢 *n* earwax
耳障りな *adj* dissonant
耳痛 *n* earache
耳標を付ける *v* earmark
脈 *n* pulse
脈拍 *n* beat
土産 *n* souvenir
ミリグラム *n* milligram

ミリミータ *n* millimeter
魅了する *v* captivate
魅力 *n* allure, appeal
魅力がある *v* appeal
魅力的である *v* charm
魅力的な *adj* appealing
魅力のある *adj* attractive
見る *v* see, look
見ること *n* look
魅惑する *v* fascinate
魅惑的な *adj* glamorous
見分ける *v* distinguish
身を落とす *v* demean
身を引く *v* vacate
身をよじる *v* writhe
民主主義 *n* democracy
民主主義の *adj* democratic
ミント *n* mint

み

# む

無 n nothing
無意識の adj unaware
無一文の adj broke
無益 n futility
無益な adj futile
無鉛の adj unleaded
無害の adj harmless
向かう v head for
昔は adv formerly
昔風の adj old-fashioned
無価値の adj null
無感覚 n numbness
無感覚な adj numb
無関係の adj irrelevant
無関心 n indifference
無関心な adj indifferent
向き合うこと n confrontation
無傷の adj intact
報いのある adj rewarding
無限 n immensity
無限の adj boundless
無限のもの adj infinite
無効な n invalid
無効にする v abolish
無効の adj void
無言の adj speechless
無罪 n innocence

無罪放免 n acquittal
無罪を言い渡す v absolve
無作為に adv randomly
むさぼり食う v devour
虫 n bug
無視 n neglect
無視する v ignore
無実を証明する v vindicate
虫歯 n cavity
無慈悲な adj merciless
矛盾した adj inconsistent
矛盾する v contradict
矛盾する n contradiction
無条件の adj unequivocal
無情な adj heartless
無職の adj unemployed
無神経な adj callous
無神論 n atheism
無心論者 n atheist
無数の adj countless
難しい adj difficult, hard
難しさ n difficulty
息子 n son
息子の妻 n daughter-in-law
結び付く v intertwine
結びつける物 v link
結び目 n hitch, knot
結べる v tie
娘 n daughter

無政府主義者 *n* anarchist
無政府状態 *n* anarchy
無線機 *n* radio
無線の *adj* wireless
無駄口をたたく *v* babble
無駄に *adv* vainly
むち *n* lash, whip
無知 *n* ignorance
むち打つ *v* lash
無秩序 *n* chaos
無知な *adj* ignorant
夢中にさせる *v* enthrall
無敵の *adj* invincible
無鉄砲な *adj* reckless
胸 *n* bosom, chest
胸焼け *n* heartburn
無能 *n* inability
無能な *adj* incompetent
無能力 *n* incompetence
無分別 *n* indiscretion
無分別な *adj* indiscreet
無分別に *adv* blindly
無防備な人々 *adj* defenseless
無防備の *adj* unprotected
村 *n* hamlet, village
群がる *v* mob
紫色の *adj* purple
村人 *n* villager
無力 *n* disability

む
め

無力な *adj* helpless
群れ *n* troop, flock

## め

目 *n* eye
姪 *n* niece
明確化 *n* clarification
明確な *adj* specific
明確にする *v* clarify
名作 *n* masterpiece
名詞 *n* noun
名手 *n* ace
迷信 *n* superstition
名人 *n* ace
名声 *n* fame, prestige
名声のある *adj* renowned
めい想 *n* meditation
めい想する *v* meditate
メイド *n* maid
明白な *adj* conspicuous
明敏な *adj* astute
盟約 *n* covenant
名誉棄損 *n* libel
名誉となる *adj* glorious
明瞭な発音 *n* articulation
命令 *n* commandment

命令の *adj* mandatory
迷路 *n* labyrinth
迷惑 *n* harassment
目打ち *n* perforation
メートル *n* meter
目隠し *n* blindfold
目が覚めて *adj* awake
目が覚める *v* awake
メカジキ *n* swordfish
メガネ *n* eyeglasses
目が回る *adj* dizzy
女神 *n* deity, goddess
メキシコ人 *adj* Mexican
恵みのもの *n* bounty
目覚まし時計 *n* alarm clock
目覚める *v* arouse
メシア *n* Messiah
目印 *n* marker
雌のライオン *n* lioness
珍しい *adj* uncommon
珍しいもの *n* novelty
雌ロバ *n* mare
めそめそする *adj* slob
目立たない *adj* obscure
目立つ *adj* eye-catching
目立つ *v* spot
メダル *n* medal
メッシュ *n* mesh
めったに～しない *adv* rarely

目に見える *adj* visible
目に見える *v* visualize
目まい *n* dizziness
メモ *n* memo, note
目盛り *n* scale
メロン *n* melon
目をくらませる *v* daze
目を通す *v* look through
面 *n* facet
免疫 *n* immunity
免疫の *adj* immune
免疫を与える *v* immunize
免除 *n* exemption
免除する *adj* exempt
免ずる *v* dispense
面接 *n* interview
面倒な *adj* troublesome
面倒なこと *n* hassle
めんどり *n* hen
面目を失わせる *v* disgrace
綿密に *adv* closely

め

# も

もうかる *adj* lucrative
申し込み *n* application
申し立て *n* allegation
申し出 *n* offer
申し出る *v* offer
もう一つ *adj* another
毛布 *n* blanket
猛吹雪 *n* blizzard
盲目の *adj* blind
もうろくした *adj* senile
燃え殻 *n* cinder
燃えさかる *v* blaze
燃えやすい *adj* flammable
燃える *v* burn
モーター *n* motor
モーテル *n* motel
もがく *v* struggle
目撃者 *n* eyewitness
目次 *n* contents
木製の *adj* wooden
木炭 *n* charcoal
目的 *n* purpose
目的地 *n* destination
目的のない *adj* aimless
目標 *n* objective
木曜日 *n* Thursday
モグラ *n* mole

目録 *n* catalog
模型 *n* model
モザイク *n* mosaic
文字 *n* alphabet
もし〜なら *c* if
もし〜ならば *c* supposing
もしかして *adv* may-be
もし出ること *n* offering
文字通りに *adv* literally
文字盤 *n* dial
モジュール *n* module
モスク *n* mosque
模造の *adj* dummy
模造品 *n* replica
もたらす *v* spark off
もたれる *v* recline
餅 *n* bait
持ち上がる *v* lift
持ち上げる *v* elevate
持ちこたえる *v* sustain
持っている *v* have
もっと *adj* more
モットー *n* motto
もっと遠い *adv* further
最も *adj* most
最も確実な *adj* definitive
最も重要な *adj* prime
最も少ない *adj* least
最も良い *adj* best

モップ v mop
もつれ n tangle
もつれさせる v entangle
もつれを解く v disentangle
もてなし n treat
もと n source
戻す v bring back
戻ってくる v come back
戻る v return
モニター v monitor
物 v stuff
物 n stuff
物置 n closet, storage
物語 n story
物語る v narrate
物語る adj telling
物ごい n beggar
物事 n thing
物を蓄える v stock
模倣 n imitation
もみ合い n scuffle
もみあげ n sideburns
桃 n peach
桃色 adj pink
もや n haze
漏らす v divulge
銛 n harpoon
盛り合わせの adj assorted
モルタル n mortar

モルヒネ n morphine
漏れ n leakage
漏れ口 n leak
漏れる v leak
もろい adj brittle
門限 n curfew
紋章 n emblem
問題 n issue, matter
問題のある adj problematic
問題を取り除く v straighten out
門番 n usher

も
や

# や

矢 n arrow
野営する v camp
野営地 n camp
やかん n kettle
ヤギ n goat
焼き網 n grill
野球 n baseball
野牛 n bison
野球帽 n cap
やくざ n hoodlum
薬剤師 n pharmacist
薬草 n herb
約束 n engagement

約束する *v* engage
役立つ *adj* useful
役に立たない *adj* useless
役に立つ *adj* helpful
役に立つこと *n* usefulness
役人 *n* bureaucrat
薬物中毒である *v* drug
薬味 *n* spice
夜行性の *adj* nocturnal
野菜の *v* vegetable
優しい *adj* gentle
優しさ *n* gentleness
養う *v* nourish
野獣の *adj* bestial
夜食 *n* supper
安い *adj* cheap
安売り *n* bargain
休みの *adv* off
安らぎの場所 *n* oasis
野生動物 *n* wildlife
野生の *adj* wild
やせ衰えた *adj* emaciated
やせ我慢をする *v* bluff
やせこけた *adj* skinny
厄介な *adj* worrisome
薬局 *n* pharmacy
薬効のある *adj* medicinal
やっていく *v* get along
雇う *v* employ, hire

宿屋 *n* inn, lodging
柳 *n* willow
家主 *n* landlord
屋根 *n* roof
屋根裏部屋 *n* attic
野蛮 *n* barbarism
野蛮行為 *n* vandalism
野蛮人 *n* barbarian
野蛮人の *adj* barbaric
野蛮な *adj* brute
山 *n* mountain
山あ *n* gorge
ヤマアラシ *n* porcupine
山芋 *n* yam
山小屋 *n* hut
山積みにする *v* stack
山の多い *adj* mountainous
闇 *n* gloom
やめさせる *v* dissuade
やめる *v* desist, quit
辞める *v* resign
やり *n* spear
やり過ぎる *v* overdo
柔らかい *adj* soft, tender
柔らかく *adv* softly
柔らかくなる *v* soften
柔らかさ *n* tenderness
和らぐ *v* mitigate
和らげる *v* cushion

やんちゃの *adj* brat
病んでいる *adj* ailing

# ゆ

唯一の *adj* singular, sole
遺言で譲る *v* bequeath
唯物論 *n* materialism
優位に立つ *v* dominate
憂うつ *n* melancholy
憂うつな *adj* dismal
憂鬱な *adj* depressing
有益な *adj* beneficial
優越 *n* superiority
有鉛の *adj* leaded
優雅 *n* elegance
誘拐 *n* kidnapping
誘拐する *v* abduct, kidnap
有害な *adj* harmful
誘拐犯 *n* kidnapper
優雅な *adj* graceful
勇敢な *adj* bold, heroic
勇敢に *adv* bravely
勇気 *n* courage
有機体 *n* organism
勇気づける *v* encourage
勇気のある *adj* courageous

勇気のない *adv* cowardly
夕暮れ *n* nightfall
有効性 *n* effectiveness
友好的な *adj* amicable
有効な *adj* valid
有効にする *v* validate
有罪の *adj* guilty
有罪を宣告する *v* convict
優秀 *n* excellence
優秀な *adj* excellent
優柔不断 *n* indecision
優柔不断な *adj* indecisive
友情 *n* friendship
優勝者 *n* champion
夕食 *n* dinner
友人になる *v* befriend
優勢 *n* ascendancy
優勢である *v* predominate
有責性 *n* culpability
優先事項 *n* priority
郵送する *v* mail
有毒な *adj* noxious, toxic
有能な *adj* competent
誘発する *v* induce
夕日 *n* sunset
郵便 *n* mail
郵便為替 *n* money order
郵便局 *n* post office
郵便配達人 *n* mailman

郵便箱 *n* mailbox

郵便番号 *n* zip code

郵便料金 *n* postage

裕福な *adj* wealthy

雄弁 *n* eloquence

有名人 *n* celebrity

有名な *adj* famous

有名な *adv* notably

有用な *n* asset

有利 *n* advantage

有利な *adj* favorable

幽霊 *n* ghost

幽霊のような *adj* spooky

誘惑 *n* temptation

誘惑する *v* seduce

誘惑的な *adj* enticing

床 *n* floor

愉快な *adj* pleasant

ゆがむ *v* buckle up

ゆがめること *n* distortion

雪 *n* snow

雪片 *n* snowflake

雪が降る *v* snow

雪解け *n* thaw

行方 *n* whereabouts

行方不明の *adj* missing

輸血 *n* transfusion

輸出する *v* export

ゆすり *n* extortion, racketeering

輸送管路 *n* pipeline

豊かさ *n* affluence

委ねる *v* entrust

ユダヤ教 *n* Judaism

ユダヤ人 *n* Jew

ユダヤ人 *adj* Jewish

ゆっくりした *adj* sluggish

ゆっくりと *adv* slowly

輸入する *v* import

輸入品 *n* importation

指 *n* finger

指先 *n* fingertip

指人形 *n* puppet

指のつめ *n* fingernail

指輪 *n* ring

夢 *n* dream

夢うつつ *n* trance

夢を見る *v* dream

由来する *v* originate

揺らぐ *v* sway

揺らめく炎 *v* flicker

揺りかご *n* cradle

ゆるい *adj* loose

緩い *adj* lax, slack

許し *n* forgiveness

許す *v* forgive

許せない *adj* inexcusable

許せる *adj* forgivable

緩む *v* ease, loosen

揺れ *v* waver
揺れる *v* vacillate
揺れること *n* swing

# よ

ヨーロッパ *n* Europe
夜明け *n* dawn
良い *adj* nice
良い香りの *adj* fragrant
よいこと *adj* good
用意 *n* preparation
養育 *v* nurture
容易さ *n* ease
用意できている *adj* ready
容易にする *v* facilitate
容易に分かる *adj* palpable
要因 *n* factor
溶解 *n* fusion
容器 *n* reservoir
容疑者 *n* culprit
陽気な *adj* cheerful
陽気にさせる *adj* exhilarating
要求 *n* claim
要求する *v* demand
要求する *n* demand
容疑を晴らす *v* exonerate

用具 *v* implement
要件 *n* requirement
擁護者 *n* defender
用語集 *n* glossary
擁護する *adv* behalf (on)
擁護する *v* champion
要塞 *n* fortress
ようじ *n* toothpick
用事 *n* errand
様式 *n* mode
幼児期 *n* infant
幼獣 *n* cub
幼児用寝台 *n* crib
用心 *n* precaution
用心深い *adj* attentive
様子 *n* aspect
用水路 *n* canal
妖精 *n* fairy
陽性の *adv* plus
溶接工 *n* welder
溶接する *v* weld
ヨウ素 *n* iodine
要素 *n* element
幼稚な *adj* puerile
幼年期 *n* infancy
羊皮紙 *n* parchment
用品 *n* utensil
腰部 *n* loin
洋服 *n* outfit

洋服だんす *n* wardrobe
用務員 *n* janitor
羊毛 *n* wool
羊毛の *adj* woolen
要約 *n* summary
要約する *v* summarize
用量 *n* dosage
ヨーロッパ人 *adj* European
よく〜する *adj* used to
余暇 *n* leisure
予感 *n* premonition
予感する *v* foresee
予期しない *adj* unforeseen
予期する *v* expect, predict
預金 *n* funds
抑圧 *n* repression
抑圧された *adj* downtrodden
抑圧する *n* oppression
よく考える *adj* unfamiliar
浴室 *n* bathroom
よく知らない *v* comprehend
抑制する *v* inhibit
浴槽 *n* bath, bathtub
欲張りの *adj* greedy
欲望 *n* desire
よく理解する *n* dirt
抑留する *v* intern
予言 *n* prediction
預言者 *n* prophet

予見する *v* forecast
予言する *v* foretell
横顔 *n* profile
横切って *pre* across
汚す *v* soil
横たわる *v* lay, lie
横に *adv* sideways
横の *adj* lateral
横腹 *n* flank
よごれ *adj* stagnant
汚れ *n* blot, smear
汚れた *adj* filthy, soiled
汚れをつける *v* stain
予算 *n* budget
世捨て人 *n* recluse
予想 *n* anticipation
予想する *v* anticipate
装う *v* imitate
欲求不満 *n* frustration
酔っ払った *adj* drunk
予定表 *n* program
よどんだ *adj* worse
予謀 *n* premeditation
余白 *n* margin
呼びかけ *n* hail
呼び出し *n* call
呼び出す *v* summon
予備の *adj* spare
予備部品 *n* spare part

呼び物 *n* draw
余分な *adv* extra
予防接種をする *v* vaccinate
予防の *adj* preventive
読み解く *v* decipher
読み飛ばし *n* skip
読み取る *v* scan
読む *v* read
嫁 *v* marry
予約 *n* reservation
予約済みの *adj* engaged
予約する *v* reserve
寄り集まる *v* gather
寄りかかる *v* lean on
より少ない *adj* lower
より低い *adj* better
より良い *n* armor
夜 *n* evening, night
よろい *n* regards
喜ばせる *v* please
喜び *n* joy
喜びに満ちた *adj* jubilant
喜ぶ *v* rejoice
喜んで *adv* willingly
よろしく *v* wobble
よろめき *v* stagger
よろめく *adj* staggery
弱い *adj* vulnerable
弱い地震 *n* tremor

弱くなる *v* weaken
弱さ *n* weakness
弱まる *v* attenuate
～より下に *pre* below
～より重い *v* outweigh
～より大きくなる *v* outgrow
～より長く生きる *v* outlast
４０、４０個の *adj* forty
４回 *n* quarter
４個の *adj* four

## ら

ラード *n* lard
ライオン *n* lion
ライセンス *n* licence
来談者 *n* lightweight
雷電 *n* client
ライト級 *n* thunderbolt
ライフル銃 *n* rifle
ライム *n* lime
らい麦 *n* rye
ラクダ *n* camel
落第する *n* flunk
落胆 *v* discouragement
落胆 *n* dismay
落胆させる *n* discouraging

落胆させる *adj* dishearten
落胆した *v* dejected
酪農場 *n* dairy farm
ラケット *n* racket
羅針盤 *n* compass
裸体主義 *n* nudism
落下 *n* fall
落下傘降下兵 *n* paratrooper
落花生 *n* peanut
楽観主義 *n* optimism
楽観的な *adj* optimistic
ラッフル *n* raffle
ラム酒 *n* rum
欄 *n* column
卵黄 *n* yolk
乱気流 *n* turbulence
卵形の *n* oval
乱雑 *adj* muddle
乱雑な *n* messy
ランジェリー *adj* lingerie
卵巣 *n* ovary
乱闘 *n* brawl
ランナー *n* runner
卵白 *n* egg white
ランプのかさ *n* lampshade
乱暴な *adj* rowdy
乱暴に押す *v* manhandle

# り

リールダンス *n* reel
リウマチ *n* rheumatism
リキュール *n* liqueur
利益 *n* profit
利益のない *adj* unprofitable
利益を得る *n* gain
理解 *n* understand
理解する *adj* understanding
理解する *v* apprehend
理解できる *v* understandable
理解力のある *adj* comprehensive
力士 *adj* wrestler
リス *n* squirrel
陸地 *n* land
利口な *n* clever
利己主義者 *adj* egoist
利己的でない *n* unselfish
利己的な *adj* selfish
離婚 *adj* divorce
離婚者 *n* divorcee
離婚する *n* divorce
リタイア *v* retire
理性的な *v* rational
理性を欠いた *adj* unreasonable
理想的な *adj* ideal
リットル *adj* litre
離脱する *n* defect

立案 v gestation

立案者 n mastermind

立候補 n candidacy

立候補者 n candidate

リッター n liter

立体障害 n hindrance

リハーサル n rehearsal

立派な n admirable

立法者 adj lawmaker

立方体 n cube

立方体の n cubic

利得 adj spoils

リビングルーム n living room

理髪師 n barber

リボン n ribbon

リラックス n relax

略図 n sketch

略奪品 n booty, loot

略奪する n loot, pillage

竜 v dragon

理由 n reason

流域 n watershed

流行 n epidemic; vogue

流行遅れの n outmoded

流行した adj prevalent

流行の adj fashionable, trendy

流砂 adj quicksand

流産 n miscarriage

流産する n miscarry

粒子 v particle

流出 n spill

流星 n meteor

流暢に n fluently

流動体 adv fluid

流入 n influx

寮 n dormitory

量 n quantity, amount

利用 n use

領域 n realm

猟犬 n hound

良好 n goodness

漁師 n fisherman

領事 n consul

領事館 n consulate

領収書 n voucher

両親 n parents

良心の呵責 n repentance

利用する n utilize

良性の v benign

利用できる adj available

領土 n territory

猟鳥 n partridge

両方の n both

両面感情の adj ambivalent

料理 adj cooking

料理人 n cook

料理法 n recipe

料理をする n cook

り

旅券 *v* passport
旅行者 *n* traveler
旅程 *n* itinerary
リン *v* phosphorus
離陸する *n* take off
理路整然と *v* coherent
りんご *adj* apple
輪郭 *n* contour
りんご酒 *n* cider
リンネル *n* linen
隣人 *n* neighbor
倫理学 ethics
倫理学の *n* ethical

# る

類似 *n* similarity
類人猿 *n* ape
ルビー *adj* ruby

# れ

レインコート *n* raincoat
例 *n* example
霊 *n* spirit
例外 *n* exception
例外的な *n* exceptional
礼儀 *adj* courtesy
礼儀正しい *n* decent, gallant
礼儀正しさ *adj* decorum
冷却する *n* cooling
霊柩車 *adj* hearse
冷笑 *n* ridicule
例証的な *n* demonstrative
冷笑的な行為 *adj* mockery
冷静な *n* stoic
冷淡 *adj* apathy
霊的な *n* spiritual
零度 *adj* zero
冷凍庫 *n* freezer
冷凍室 *n* icebox
冷凍の *n* frozen
礼拝 *adj* liturgy
礼拝堂 *n* chapel
レーザー *n* laser
レース *n* race
レーダー *n* radar
レール *n* rail
レコード *n* record

歴史 n history
歴史学者 n historian
レストラン n restaurant
レタス n lettuce
レバー n lever
列 n queue, row
列挙する n enumerate
列車 v train
列に加わる v line up
レビュー v revue
レモネード n lemonade
レモン n lemon
れんが n brick
恋愛 n romance
れんが職人 n bricklayer
レンズ n lense
連携 n coordination
連携する n coordinate
練習 n practice
練習する v practise
レンティル v lentil
連想させる n suggestive
連続 adj series
連続した n consecutive
連続するもの adj sequence
連続性 n continuity
連続的な n continuous
連隊 adj regiment
連打する n batter

連邦政府の adj federal
連盟 adj league
連絡 n liaison
レントゲン写真 n X-ray

# ろ

ろう n wax
ロウソク n candle
廊下 n corridor
老衰した n decrepit
ロウソク立て adj candlestick
ローマ教皇の職 n papacy
労働組合 n union
朗読する n recite
狼狽して v disoriented
浪費される n waste
浪費的な adj wasteful
ローマ法王 adj Pope
ロールパン n bun
ログインする n log in
ろ過器 n filter
ろ過される v filter
ログオフする n log off
ロケット v rocket
録音装置 n recorder
六月 n June

れ
ろ

ロザリオ *n* rosary
ロシア *n* Russia
ロシア人 *n* Russian
路上強盗 *n* mugging
路上生活者 *n* bum
路線 *n* track
ロック *v* lock
ロックする *n* lock
ロッジ *v* lodge
肋骨 *v* rib
ロバ *n* donkey
ロビー *n* lobby
ロブスター *n* lobster
路面電車 *v* streetcar
論説 *n* article
論争 *n* controversy
論争可能な *n* debatable
論争的な *adj* contentious
論点 *adj* issue
論評 *n* comment
論評する *n* comment
論理 *v* logic
論理上の *n* logical
６０個の *adj* sixty
６個の *adj* six
浪費 *adj* extravagance, waste
浪費する *v* extravagant, lavish

**ろ**
**わ**

# わ

ワークブック *n* workbook
輪 *n* loophole
ワイシャツ *n* shirt
わいせつな *adj* lewd
わいせつなもの *n* obscenity
わいろ *n* bribe
わいろを贈る *v* bribe
ワイン *n* wine
ワイン醸造所 *n* winery
わかりました *adv* okay
若い *adj* young
和解の *adj* conciliatory
若返らせる *v* rejuvenate
若鶏 *n* broiler
若者 *n* youngster
若者の *adj* youthful
わきへ *adv* aside
別れ *n* parting
分かれた *adj* separate
脇に *pre* beside
脇の下 *n* armpit
ワクチン *n* vaccine
脇へ置く *v* put aside
脇道にそれる *v* excuse
惑星 *n* planet
わざわざ〜する *adv* purposely
分けられる *adj* divisible

分ける *v* divide

わざと *v* trouble

ワシ *n* eagle

わずか *n* bit

わずかな *adj* petty

わずかに *adv* slightly

わずかの *n* little bit

ワット *n* watt

忘れっぽい *adj* oblivious

忘れる *v* forget

綿 *n* cotton

話題 *n* theme

私自身の *pro* myself

私生の *adj* illegitimate

私たちの *adj* our.

私たちのもの *pro* ours

私たちは *pro* we

私の *adj* my

私のもの *pro* mine

私は *pro* I

わな *n* trap

輪止め *n* linchpin

わなで捕える *v* snare

わび *n* apology

輪なわ *n* snare

輪になる *v* ring

わら *n* straw

ワルツ *n* waltz

笑い草 *n* laughing stock

笑い声 *n* laughter

笑う *v* laugh

笑うこと *n* laugh

割合 *n* proportion

割り当て *n* allotment

割り当てる *v* allocate, ration

割札を施す *v* circumcise

割引 *n* discount

割引購入券 *n* coupon

割り振る *v* allot

悪く *adv* badly

悪ふざけ *n* hoax, prank

割ること *n* split

私たち *pro* us

悪巧み *n* guile

割れて分かれる *v* split

割れ目 *n* cleft, crack

割れる *v* crack, split up

悪事 *n* evil

われわれ自身 *pro* ourselves

湾 *n* bay, gulf

湾曲した *adj* crooked

割引する *v* discount

わ

# を

〜をくすねる *v* pilfer
〜をしのぐ *v* outdo
〜をたしなめる *v* chide
〜をつつく *v* poke
〜をなだめる *v* soothe
〜をのろう *v* darn
〜をひどく嫌う *v* loathe
〜をまく *v* sprinkle
〜をやり直す *v* redo
〜を悪用する *adj* pervert
〜を暗くする *v* overshadow
〜を意味する *v* mean
〜を慰める *v* console
〜を煙にまく *v* mystify
〜を解く *v* untie
〜を改造する *v* refurbish
〜を覚える *v* memorize
〜を刈る *v* shear
〜を感じる *v* sense
〜を汗に出す *v* perspire
〜を缶詰にする *v* can
〜を強くする *v* strengthen
〜を脅かす *v* blackmail
〜を脅す *v* threaten
〜を苦しめる *v* pester
〜を撃退する *v* repel
〜を見くびる *v* belittle

〜を見る *v* look at
〜を固く結合する *v* solder
〜を交換する *v* swap
〜を好む *v* prefer
〜を構成する *v* constitute
〜を絞る *v* squeeze
〜を国営化する *v* nationalize
〜を鎖でつなぐ *v* chain
〜を再建する *v* reconstruct
〜を再婚する *v* remarry
〜を再生する *v* reproduce
〜を再選する *v* reelect
〜を参照する *v* refer to
〜を刺す *v* prick
〜を支持する *v* stand for
〜を取り壊す *v* break away
〜を取り戻す *v* regain
〜を受け渡す *v* ransom
〜を授ける *v* bestow
〜を書き換える *v* transcribe
〜を傷つける *v* wound
〜を上演する *v* stage
〜を上回る *v* surpass
〜を乗り越える *v* override
〜を条件として *c* providing that
〜を織る *v* loom
〜を正当化する *v* warrant
〜を生む *v* generate
〜を誓う *v* vow

～を切断する ᵥsever
～を洗浄する ᵥcleanse
～を選ぶ ᵥchoose
～を素早く出す ᵥconjure up
～を装う ᵥfeign
～を増す ᵥmultiply
～を贈る ᵥpresent
～を打つ ᵥclub
～を大事にする ᵥcherish
～を大事に思う ᵥcare for
～を探す ᵥlook for
～を鋳造する ᵥmint
～を鎮める ᵥquell
～を追い越す ᵥoutrun
～を追い払う ᵥscare away
～を通り抜けて ₚᵣₑthrough (thru)
～を賭ける ᵥstake
～を当てにする ᵥreckon on
～を当惑させる ᵥbewilder
～を独占する ᵥmonopolize
～を届ける ᵥbring
～を入れる ᵥinject
～を悩ませる ᵥbeset
～を破壊する ᵥraze
～を迫害する ᵥpersecute
～を反射する ᵥreflect

～を悲しませる ᵥsadden
～を避ける ᵥshun
～を必要とする ᵥrequire
～を描写する ᵥpicture
～を覆う ᵥscreen
～を分類する ᵥclassify
～を並べる ᵥrow
～を保つ ᵥpreserve
～を保護する ᵥshelter
～を保証する ᵥvouch for
～を補充する ᵥrefill
～を包囲する ᵥbesiege
～を報いる ᵥremunerate
～を放つ ᵥunleash
～を縫う ᵥstitch
～を訪問する ᵥcall on
～を妨害する ᵥobstruct
～を魔法にかける ᵥbewitch
～を満たす ᵥcater to
～を夢中にする ᵥpreoccupy
～を免れる ᵥrid of
～を目覚めさせる ᵥrouse
～を抑える ᵥstrangle
～を頼りにする ᵥrely on
～を理解する ᵥfathom out
～を裂く ᵥclaw

# Word to Word® Bilingual Dictionary Series

| Language - Item #<br>ISBN # |
| --- |

**Albanian - 500X**
ISBN - 978-0-933146-49-5

**Amharic - 820X**
ISBN - 978-0-933146-59-4

**Arabic - 650X**
ISBN - 978-0-933146-41-9

**Bengali - 700X**
ISBN - 978-0-933146-30-3

**Burmese - 705X**
ISBN - 978-0-933146-50-1

**Cambodian - 710X**
ISBN - 978-0-933146-40-2

**Chinese - 715X**
ISBN - 978-0-933146-22-8

**Czech - 520X**
ISBN - 978-0-933146-62-4

**Farsi - 660X**
ISBN - 978-0-933146-33-4

**French - 530X**
ISBN - 978-0-933146-36-5

**German - 535X**
ISBN - 978-0-933146-93-8

**Greek - 540X**
ISBN - 978-0-933146-60-0

**Gujarati - 720X**
ISBN - 978-0-933146-98-3

**Haitian-Creole - 545X**
ISBN - 978-0-933146-23-5

**Hebrew - 665X**
ISBN - 978-0-933146-58-7

**Hindi - 725X**
ISBN - 978-0-933146-31-0

**Hmong - 728X**
ISBN - 978-0-933146-31-0

**Italian - 555X**
ISBN - 978-0-933146-51-8

**Japanese - 730X**
ISBN - 978-0-933146-42-6

**Korean - 735X**
ISBN - 978-0-933146-97-6

**Lao - 740X**
ISBN - 978-0-933146-54-9

**Nepali - 755X**
ISBN - 978-0-933146-61-7

**Pashto - 760X**
ISBN - 978-0-933146-34-1

**Polish - 575X**
ISBN - 978-0-933146-64-8

**Portuguese - 580X**
ISBN - 978-0-933146-94-5

**Punjabi - 765X**
ISBN - 978-0-933146-32-7

**Romanian - 585X**
ISBN - 978-0-933146-91-4

**Russian - 590X**
ISBN - 978-0-933146-92-1

**Somali - 830X**
ISBN- 978-0-933146-52-5

**Spanish - 600X**
ISBN - 978-0-933146-99-0

**Swahili - 835X**
ISBN - 978-0-933146-55-6

**Tagalog - 770X**
ISBN - 978-0-933146-37-2

**Thai - 780X**
ISBN - 978-0-933146-35-8

**Turkish - 615X**
ISBN - 978-0-933146-95-2

**Ukrainian - 620X**
ISBN - 978-0-933146-25-9

**Urdu - 790X**
ISBN - 978-0-933146-39-6

**Vietnamese - 795X**
ISBN - 978-0-933146-96-9

All languages are two-way:
English-Language / Language-English.
More languages in planning and production.

# Order Information

To order our Word to Word® bilingual dictionaries or any other products from Bilingual Dictionaries, Inc., please contact us at (951) 296-2445 or visit us at **www.BilingualDictionaries.com**. Visit our website to download our current catalog/order form, view our products, and find information regarding Bilingual Dictionaries, Inc.

 **Bilingual Dictionaries, Inc.**

PO Box 1154 • Murrieta, CA 92564 • Tel: (951) 296-2445 • Fax: (951) 296-9911
www.BilingualDictionaries.com

## Special Dedication & Thanks

Bilingual Dicitonaries, Inc. would like to thank all the teachers from various districts accross the country for their useful input and great suggestions in creating a Word to Word® standard. We encourage all students and teachers using our bilingual learning materials to give us feedback. Please send your questions or comments via email to **support@bilingualdictionaries.**